Cancer in Women

2nd Edition

WESTERN® SCHOOLS

Revised By
Suzanne M. Mahon, RN, DNSc, AOCN, APNG
1st Edition Author
Ellen Carr, RN, MSN, AOCN

28 contact hours will be awarded upon successful completion of this course.

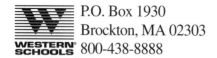

P.O. Box 1930
Brockton, MA 02303
800-438-8888

ABOUT THE SECOND EDITION AUTHOR

Suzanne M. Mahon, RN, DNSc, AOCN, APNG, is a Clinical Professor of Internal Medicine, School of Medicine and Clinical Professor of Nursing, Adult Nursing, School of Nursing at Saint Louis University in St. Louis, MO. She has worked in the area of cancer prevention and early detection for over 20 years. She provides cancer genetics education services at the Saint Louis University Cancer Center. She has published extensively on topics in cancer prevention and genetics.

> **Suzanne M. Mahon** has disclosed that she has no significant financial or other conflicts of interest pertaining to this course book.

ABOUT THE ORIGINAL AUTHOR

Ellen Carr, RN, MSN, AOCN, has been a healthcare and medical writer for more than 20 years. She specializes in assignments about clinical nursing, therapeutic and diagnostic technologies, and patient advocacy. She earned her bachelor's degree in journalism from the University of Colorado in 1976 and her master's degree in oncology nursing from the MGH Institute of Health Professions in Boston in 1988. Since 1997, she has been an advanced certified oncology nurse. Ms. Carr is currently a medical and surgical oncology case manager at the Rebecca and John Moores University of California, San Diego (UCSD) Cancer Center. Ms. Carr continues to participate in local and national Oncology Nursing Society projects.

ABOUT THE SUBJECT MATTER REVIEWER

Mary Louise Kanaskie, MS, RN-BC, AOCN, has been a nurse educator for over 25 years with experience in oncology and medical-surgical nursing. In this role, she designs, implements, and evaluates basic and advanced education programs and specialty courses related to oncology and medical-surgical nursing. Ms. Kanaskie lectures in oncology nursing core review courses on the topics of cancer pain management, the biology of cancer, and ethical decision making. In addition, she is an ONS Chemotherapy/Biotherapy Course Trainer and Genetics Course Trainer. An active member of the Oncology Nursing Society, she has served as Coordinator of the Staff Education Special Interest Group and has been a presenter at the National ONS Congress. In 2007, she was awarded the ONS Mary Nowotny Excellence in Cancer Nursing Education Award. Ms. Kanaskie is a contributing author and co-editor of the 2005 ONS Second Edition *Continuing Education Activities – A Planning Manual*.

> **Mary Louise Kanaskie** has disclosed that she has no significant financial or other conflicts of interest pertaining to this course book.

Nurse Planner: Amy Bernard, MS, BSN, RN-BC; Anne P. Manton, PhD, RN, PMHNP-BC, FAEN, FAAN

> The planners have disclosed that they have no significant financial or other conflicts of interest pertaining to this course book.

Copy Editor: Dorothy Terry

Indexer: Sylvia Coates

Western Schools' courses are designed to provide nursing professionals with the educational information they need to enhance their career development. The information provided within these course materials is the result of research and consultation with prominent nursing and medical authorities and is, to the best of our knowledge, current and accurate. However, the courses and course materials are provided with the understanding that Western Schools is not engaged in offering legal, nursing, medical, or other professional advice.

Western Schools' courses and course materials are not meant to act as a substitute for seeking out professional advice or conducting individual research. When the information provided in the courses and course materials is applied to individual circumstances, all recommendations must be considered in light of the uniqueness pertaining to each situation.

Western Schools' course materials are intended solely for *your* use and *not* for the benefit of providing advice or recommendations to third parties. Western Schools devoids itself of any responsibility for adverse consequences resulting from the failure to seek nursing, medical, or other professional advice. Western Schools further devoids itself of any responsibility for updating or revising any programs or publications presented, published, distributed, or sponsored by Western Schools unless otherwise agreed to as part of an individual purchase contract.

Products (including brand names) mentioned or pictured in Western School's courses are not endorsed by Western Schools, the American Nurses Credentialing Center (ANCC) or any state board.

ISBN: 978-1-57801-416-3

COURSE INSTRUCTIONS
IMPORTANT: Read these instructions *BEFORE* proceeding!

COMPLETING THE FINAL EXAMINATION

Enclosed with your course book you will find a FasTrax® answer sheet. Use this answer sheet to respond to all the final exam questions that appear in this course. If the course has less than 100 questions, leave any remaining answer circles on the FasTrax answer sheet blank.

Be sure to fill in circles completely using **blue or black ink.** The FasTrax grading system will not read pencil. If you make an error, you may use correction fluid (such as White Out) to correct it.

FasTrax answer sheets are preprinted with your name and address and the course title. If you are completing more than one course, be sure to record your answers on the correct corresponding answer sheet.

A PASSING SCORE

The final exam is a multiple choice exam. You must score 70% or better in order to pass this course and receive a certificate of completion. Should you fail to achieve the required score, an additional FasTrax answer sheet will be sent to you so that you may make a second attempt to pass the course. You will be allowed three chances to pass the same course without incurring additional charges. After three failed attempts, your file will be closed.

RECORDING YOUR HOURS

Use the Study Time Log provided in this course book to monitor and record the time it takes to complete this course. Upon completion, tally your total time spent and use this information to respond to the final question of the course evaluation.

COURSE EVALUATIONS

The Course Evaluation provided in this course book is a critical component of the course and must be completed and submitted with your final exam. Responses to evaluation statements should be recorded in the lower right hand corner of the FasTrax answer sheet, in the section marked "Evaluation." Evaluations provide Western Schools with vital feedback regarding courses. Your feedback is important to us; please take a few minutes to complete the evaluation.

To provide additional feedback regarding this course, Western Schools services, or to suggest new course topics, use the space provided on the Important Information form found on the back of the FasTrax instruction sheet included with your course. Return the completed form to Western Schools with your final exam.

SUBMITTING THE COMPLETED FINAL EXAM

For your convenience, Western Schools provides a number of exam grading options. Full instructions and complete grading details are listed on the FasTrax instruction sheet provided with this course. If you are mailing your answer sheet(s) to Western Schools, we recommend you make a copy as a back-up.

COURSE COMPLETION TIME FRAMES AND EXTENSIONS

You have two (2) years from the date of purchase to complete this course. If you are not able to complete the course within 2 years, a six (6) month extension may be purchased. If you have not completed the course within 30 months from the original enrollment date, your file will be closed and no certificate will be issued.

CHANGE OF ADDRESS?

In the event that your address changes prior to completing this course, please call our customer service department at 1-800-618-1670, so that we may update your file.

WESTERN SCHOOLS GUARANTEES YOUR SATISFACTION

If any continuing education course fails to meet your expectations, or if you are not satisfied for any reason, you may return the course materials for an exchange or a refund (less shipping and handling) within 30 days. Software, video, and audio courses must be returned unopened. Textbooks must not be written in or marked up in any other way.

Thank you for using Western Schools to fulfill your continuing education needs!

WESTERN SCHOOLS
P.O. Box 1930
Brockton, MA 02303
800-438-8888
www.westernschools.com

WESTERN SCHOOLS
STUDY TIME LOG

CANCER IN WOMEN

INSTRUCTIONS: Use this log sheet to document the amount of time you spend completing this course. Include the time it takes you to read the instructions, take the pretest, read the course book, take the final examination, and complete the evaluation.

	Time Spent	
Date	**Hours**	**Minutes**
_____	_____	_____
_____	_____	_____
_____	_____	_____
_____	_____	_____
_____	_____	_____
_____	_____	_____
_____	_____	_____
_____	_____	_____
_____	_____	_____
_____	_____	_____
_____	_____	_____
_____	_____	_____
_____	_____	_____
_____	_____	_____

TOTAL* [   ] [   ]

Hours   **Minutes**

* Please use this total study time to answer the final question of the course evaluation.

iv

WESTERN SCHOOLS
COURSE EVALUATION

CANCER IN WOMEN

INSTRUCTIONS: Using the scale below, please respond to the following evaluation statements. All responses should be recorded in the right-hand column of the FasTrax answer sheet, in the section marked "Evaluation." Be sure to fill in each corresponding answer circle completely using blue or black ink. Leave any remaining answer circles blank.

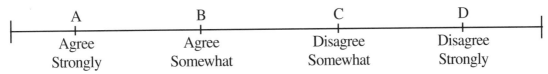

| A | B | C | D |
| Agree Strongly | Agree Somewhat | Disagree Somewhat | Disagree Strongly |

OBJECTIVES: After completing this course, I am able to

1. Describe trends associated with major cancers in women.

2. Discuss breast cancer's epidemiology, risk factors, prevention and detection strategies, and common staging schemas and treatments.

3. Discuss endometrial cancer's epidemiology, risk factors, prevention and detection strategies, common staging schemas, and treatments.

4. Discuss the epidemiology, risk factors, prevention and detection strategies, common staging schemas, and treatments for ovarian cancer.

5. Discuss cervical cancer's epidemiology, risk factors, prevention and detection strategies, common staging schemas, and treatments.

6. Discuss the epidemiology, risk factors, prevention and detection strategies, and main treatments for lung cancer in women.

7. Discuss the epidemiology, risk factors, prevention and detection strategies, and main treatments for colorectal cancer in women.

8. Discuss the epidemiology, risk factors, prevention and detection strategies, and main treatments for skin cancer in women.

9. Discuss the psychosocial concerns that may accompany a diagnosis of cancer.

10. Discuss psychologic, functioning, and fertility issues associated with sexuality in women with cancer and identify interventions to address these issues.

11. Discuss why cancer patients seek out complementary and alternative medicine (CAM) options, list some common CAMs, and identify ways to evaluate their merit and usefulness.

12. Discuss ways for the clinician and patient to evaluate and access a variety of educational resources.

COURSE CONTENT

13. The course materials were presented in a well organized and clearly written manner.

14. The course content was presented in a fair, unbiased and balanced manner.

15. The course expanded my knowledge and enhanced my skills related to the subject matter.

continued on next page

16. I intend to apply the knowledge and skills I've learned to my nursing practice. (Select the appropriate response below.)

A. Yes   B. Unsure   C. No   D. Not Applicable

ATTESTATION

17. By submitting this answer sheet, I certify that I have read the course materials and personally completed the final examination based on the material presented. Mark "A" for Agree and "B" for Disagree.

COURSE HOURS

18. Choose the response that best represents the total number of clock hours it took to complete this **28 hour** course.

A. More than 30 hours   B. 26–30 hours   C. Less than 26 hours

Note: To provide additional feedback regarding this course, Western Schools services, or to suggest new course topics, use the space provided on the Important Information form found on the back of the FasTrax instruction sheet included with your course.

CONTENTS

FIGURES AND TABLES

Chapter 4: Ovarian Cancer

Chapter 5: Cervical Cancer

Chapter 6: Lung Cancer

Chapter 7: Colorectal Cancer

Chapter 10: Sexuality: Women with Cancer

Chapter 11: Complementary and Alternative Medicine

Chapter 12: Patient Education Considerations

PRETEST

1. Begin this course by taking the pretest. Circle the answers to the questions on this page, or write the answers on a separate sheet of paper. Do not log answers to the pretest questions on the FasTrax test sheet included with the course.

2. Compare your answers to the PRETEST KEY located at the end of the Pretest. The pretest key indicates the chapter where the content of that question is discussed. Make note of the questions you missed, so that you can focus on those areas as you complete the course.

3. Complete the course by reading the chapters and completing the exam questions at the end of each chapter. Answers to these exam questions should be logged on the FasTrax test sheet included with the course.

Note: Choose the one option that BEST answers each question.

1. Absolute risk is

   ✓ a. a characteristic associated with an increased risk of developing a disease.

   b. comparison of the incidence or deaths among those with a particular risk factor compared to those without the risk factor.

   c. the amount of disease within the population that could be prevented by alteration of a risk factor.

   d. a measure of the occurrence of cancer, either incidence or mortality, in the general population.

2. Recommended strategies for the early detection of breast cancer in a woman of average risk would include

   a. mammography and magnetic resonance imaging (MRI).

   b. clinical breast exam and mammography.

   ✓ c. breast self-exam and mammography.

   d. breast self-exam, mammography, and MRI.

3. In the United States, of the gynecologic cancers, cancer of the endometrium is the

   a. fourth most common.

   ✓ b. second most common.

   c. most common.

   d. third most common.

4. A malignant condition of the endometrium is

   a. fibroid tumors.

   b. endometriosis.

   ✓ c. adenocarcinoma.

   d. endometrial hyperplasia.

5. Ovarian cancer is the fourth leading killer of women and kills more women than these two cancers combined

   a. breast and cervical.

   ✓ b. cervical and endometrial.

   c. breast and endometrial.

   d. lung and breast.

continued on next page

6. Stage II ovarian cancer is

   a. growth limited to both ovaries; no ascites.

   b. tumor of one or both ovaries with histologically confirmed implants of abdominal peritoneal surfaces, none exceeding 2 centimeters in diameter; nodes negative.

   c. growth involving one or both ovaries with pelvic extension.

   d. growth involving one or both ovaries with distant metastasis.

7. When cervical cells become abnormal, they change in

   a. size, shape, and number of cells on the surface of the cervix.

   b. size, shape, and number of cells, only in the test tube.

   c. color only.

   d. number only.

8. A Papanicolaou (Pap) test appointment should be scheduled preferably

   a. during the last half of the menstrual cycle following ovulation.

   b. during the first half of the menstrual cycle before ovulation but after completion of menses.

   c. at least 10 days after the first day of menses.

   d. at least 20 days after the last day of menses.

9. The leading cause of death in women due to malignancy is

   a. breast.

   b. colorectal.

   c. lung.

   d. skin.

10. The most common type of lung cancer is

    a. mucinous.

    b. non-small cell lung cancer.

    c. carcinoid.

    d. small cell lung cancer.

11. For women in the United States, colorectal cancer is

    a. the main cause of death.

    b. the 2nd leading cause of death.

    c. the 3rd leading cause of death.

    d. equal to breast cancer as cause of death.

12. A type of nonmelanoma skin cancer is

    a. actinic keratoses.

    b. squamous cell carcinoma.

    c. seborrheic keratoses.

    d. hemangiomas.

13. The minimum recommended sun protection factor (SPF) for sunscreen is

    a. 4.

    b. 10.

    c. 15.

    d. 20.

14. Studies about support indicate that one of the most supportive interventions a nurse can offer the patient is to

    a. ask a question.

    b. develop a plan of action.

    c. listen.

    d. document.

15. The PLISSIT model is an acronym for the levels of

    a. planning, limited information, specific suggestion, and idealism.

    b. permission, limited information, specific suggestion, and intensive therapy.

    c. prioritizing, limited ideas, some suggestions, and ideal timing.

    d. permission, levels of intervention, specific suggestions, ideas, and treatment.

16. Those being treated for cancer may wish to preserve their reproductive options. Therefore, a first step to start a plan is to

    a. immediately start tissue banking.

    b. choose to cryopreserve embryos.

    c. seek counseling about options.

    d. seek counseling about losing their ability to be parents.

17. Strategies to cope with sexual dysfunction include

    a. avoiding physical recovery, including diet and physical activities.

    b. omit your partner in discussions.

    c. avoid romance.

    d. use a water-soluble lubricant (Astroglide, K-Y jelly, Lubrin), if needed.

18. An example of a complementary and alternative therapies category is

    a. chemotherapy.

    b. biotherapy.

    c. mind-body interventions.

    d. immunotherapy.

19. Examples of manual healing methods are

    a. acupressure and massage.

    b. macrobiotic diets and transcutaneous electrical nerve stimulation.

    c. music and prayer.

    d. echinacea and evening primrose.

20. A disadvantage of an Internet support group is

    a. the inability to assess body language.

    b. it is always available for a person to seek support.

    c. the time limitation.

    d. the limited geographical reach.

PRETEST KEY

#	Answer	Reference
1.	D	Chapter 1
2.	B	Chapter 2
3.	C	Chapter 3
4.	C	Chapter 3
5.	B	Chapter 4
6.	C	Chapter 4
7.	A	Chapter 5
8.	B	Chapter 5
9.	C	Chapter 6
10.	B	Chapter 6
11.	C	Chapter 7
12.	B	Chapter 8
13.	C	Chapter 8
14.	C	Chapter 9
15.	B	Chapter 10
16.	C	Chapter 10
17.	D	Chapter 10
18.	C	Chapter 11
19.	A	Chapter 11
20.	A	Chapter 12

INTRODUCTION

Cancer is a major public health problem. An estimated 739,940 women are diagnosed annually with cancer and 270,290 women die from the disease annually. Breast, lung, colorectal, and uterine cancers alone account for approximately 59% of newly diagnosed cancers each year (American Cancer Society (ACS), 2010). One in three women in the United States is at risk for developing cancer during her lifetime (ACS, 2010). Cancer is the second leading cause of death in women (Mayo Clinic, 2009). This course will enable nurses to better understand the major cancers affecting women and the nursing care needs of the women and their families.

The experience of a woman diagnosed with cancer is distinctive. First, her cancer site may be uniquely female, including a diagnosis of ovarian, uterine, or cervical cancer. Women assume many varied roles in modern society, which leave them impacted by the experience of the diagnosis and treatment differently than men.

This fully-referenced course reviews many of the major concepts in nursing care when women are diagnosed with malignancies. The major cancers affecting women are addressed, including breast, ovarian, uterine, cervical, lung, colorectal, and skin cancers. Information about each of these cancers includes an overview of the epidemiology of the cancer, modifiable and nonmodifiable risk factors, risk assessment, prevention strategies, strengths and limitations of detection strategies, diagnosis, staging, and standard treatment modalities, including surgery, chemotherapy, biotherapy, and radiotherapy. There are also chapters that address psychosocial concerns, sexuality, alternative and complementary medicine, and health education issues.

The purpose of this course is to provide the generalist nurse caring for female patients with an overview of the major cancers that affect women. Nurses with an interest in oncology will benefit from the resources provided in the course. Case studies and commentaries following each chapter on a cancer type help to illustrate the content.

REFERENCES

American Cancer Society. (2010). *Cancer facts & figures 2010*. Atlanta, GA: Author.

Mayo Clinic. (2009). *Women's health: Preventing top 10 threats*. Retrieved September 15, 2009, from http://www.mayoclinic.com/health/womens-health/WO00014

CHAPTER 1

OVERVIEW OF CANCER IN WOMEN

CHAPTER OBJECTIVE

After completing this chapter, the reader will be able to describe trends associated with major cancers in women.

LEARNING OBJECTIVES

After studying this chapter, the reader will be able to

1. cite at least two general trends concerning cancer diagnosis, incidence, and death in women

2. specify the primary reason for a cancer risk assessment.

3. identify at least two readily available resources for information about cancer epidemiology and trends in women.

WHAT IS CANCER?

Women face both uniquely "women's cancers" and also almost all other types of cancers as well. Women diagnosed with cancer have specific and distinctive needs. These needs impact epidemiology, prevention, early detection, treatment, and long-term survival. Nurses have important roles as patient educators, advocates, and providers of direct patient care. Figure 1-1 demonstrates how many women are affected by cancer each year.

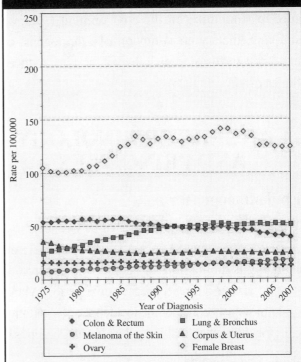

FIGURE 1-1: AGE-ADJUSTED SEER INCIDENCE RATES BY CANCER SITE ALL AGES, ALL RACES, FEMALE 1975-2007 (SEER 9)

Cancer sites include invasive cases only unless otherwise noted.

Incidence source: SEER 9 areas (San Francisco, Connecticut, Detroit, Hawaii, Iowa, New Mexico, Seattle, Utah, and Atlanta).

Rates are per 100,000 and are age-adjusted to the 2000 US Std Population (19 age groups – Census P25-1130). Regression lines are calculated using the Joinpoint Regression Program Version 3.4.3, April 2010, National Cancer Institute.

Ovary excludes borderline cases or histologies 8442, 8451, 8462, 8472, and 8473.

Note. From SEER Cancer Statistics Review, 1975-2007, by S.F. Altekruse, C.L. Kosary, M. Krapcho, N. Neyman, R. Aminou, W. Waldron, et al. (Eds), Bethesda, MD: National Cancer Institute. Retrieved from http://seer.cancer.gov/csr/1975_2007/, based on November 2009 SEER data submission, posted to the SEER web site, 2010.

Cancer develops when cells in the body begin to grow and divide in a disorderly fashion that is out of control. Normal cells grow, divide, and die. Instead of dying, malignant cells continue to grow and form new abnormal cells. Cancer cells often spread (metastasize) to other organs (often through the blood stream or lymph vessels) where they grow, invade, and replace normal tissue. All of cancer is genetic because of damage to DNA. In most cases when DNA becomes damaged, the body is able to repair it. In malignant cells, the damage cannot be repaired. People can inherit damaged DNA, which accounts for inherited cancers (about 5% of all new cases). In about 80% of cancer cases, however, DNA becomes damaged by exposure to something in the environment (such as smoking, dietary consumption of carcinogens, or exposure to ultraviolet light) (American Cancer Society [ACS], 2010b).

CANCER TERMINOLOGY AND PRINCIPLES

Epidemiologic Terms

Incidence refers to the number of new cancers in a given time period in a specific population. Mortality is the number of people who die from a specific cancer during a specific time period. Many epidemiologists consider the incidence and mortality rates together when making public health decisions.

Risk Assessment

A risk factor is a trait or characteristic that is associated with an increased likelihood of developing a disease. It is important to note, however, that having a risk factor does not mean a person will develop a disease, such as malignancy, nor does the absence of a risk factor mean one will not develop a disease or malignancy.

There are several types of risk. Absolute risk is a measure of the occurrence of cancer, either incidence (new cases) or mortality (deaths), in the gen-

eral population. Absolute risk is helpful when a patient needs to understand what the chances are for all persons in a population of developing a particular disease. For example women in the US have a one in eight chance of developing breast cancer in their lifetime (ACS, 2009b).

The term relative risk refers to a comparison of the incidence or deaths among those with a particular risk factor compared to those without the risk factor. By using relative risk factors, an individual can determine her risk factors and thus better understand her personal chances of developing a specific cancer as compared to an individual without such risk factors. If the risk of a person with no known risk factors is 1.0, one can evaluate the risk of those with risk factors in relation to this figure. This can be illustrated by considering several of the relative risk factors of breast cancer. A woman who has her first menstrual period before 12 years of age has a 1.3 relative risk of developing breast cancer when compared to a woman who has her first menstrual period after 12 years of age (ACS, 2009b). This means she is 1.3 times more likely to develop breast cancer than the woman with later menarche.

Attributable risk is the amount of disease within the population that could be prevented by alteration of a risk factor. Some risk factors that can be altered could potentially decrease the morbidity and mortality associated with malignancy in a large number of people. Smoking is a perfect example. The ACS estimates that one in five premature deaths (443,000 deaths) in the United States can be attributed to smoking (ACS, 2010a). An additional 8.6 million persons are affected by chronic disease related to smoking. Smoking accounts for 30% of all cancer deaths and 87% of lung cancer deaths. Clearly, altering this risk factor could significantly alter the morbidity and mortality associated with cancer in the future.

Basic elements of a cancer risk assessment may include a review of medical history, a history of exposures to carcinogens in daily living, and a detailed family history. Once all information is gathered, it must be interpreted to the patient in understandable terms. Often this is accomplished by using various risk calculations, such as absolute risk, relative risk, attributable risk, or specific risk models for various cancers. The primary reason for conducting a risk assessment is to select an appropriate screening plan.

Levels of Cancer Prevention

There are three levels of cancer prevention. Primary prevention refers to the prevention of disease, such as immunization against childhood diseases, avoiding tobacco products, or reducing exposure to ultraviolet rays. Secondary prevention refers to the early detection or screening for and treatment of subclinical, asymptomatic, or early disease in persons without signs or symptoms of cancer. Forms of secondary cancer prevention include the use of the Papanicolaou (Pap) smear to detect cervical cancer or mammogram to detect a nonpalpable breast cancer. Cancer screening is aimed at asymptomatic persons with the goal of finding disease when it is most easily treated. Tertiary prevention refers to the management of an illness such as cancer to prevent progression, recurrence, or other complications.

Selection of a Screening Test

The primary reason for conducting a risk assessment is to select an appropriate screening protocol. A screening protocol or recommendation defines how cancer screening tests should be used. Table 1-1 illustrates the current ACS recommendations for the early detection of cancer in asymptomatic women. This is an example of a screening protocol. Such recommendations can vary among organizations and practitioners. These recommendations are readily available for comparison at www.guidelines.gov. Recommendations are often modified for persons with many risk factors.

Staging

Staging is the process of finding out how much cancer there is in the body and where it is located. This information is used to plan treatment and to predict prognosis. Cancers with the same stage usually have similar outlooks and are often treated the same way.

For most cancers, the stage is based on three main factors, which include tumor size, lymph node invasion, and spread to distant areas of the body. Staging is based on physical exam, radiologic studies, biopsy, and other surgical techniques. The American Joint Committee on Cancer (AJCC) developed the TNM classification system as a tool for doctors to stage different types of cancer based on certain standards (Edge, Byrd, Carducci, Compton, Fritz, Greene, & Trotti, 2010). In the TNM system, each cancer is assigned a T, N, and M category. The T category describes the original (primary) tumor in metric measurements. The N category describes whether the cancer has spread into nearby lymph nodes. The M category tells whether there are distant metastases (spread of cancer to other parts of body). Once the T, N, and M have been determined, they are combined and an overall "stage" of 0, I, II, III, or IV is assigned.

Prognosis is also affected by the grade of the tumor. Tumor grade describes how different the cancer cells look when compared to normal ones. Higher grade cancers (1 on a scale of 1 to 4) usually have a poorer prognosis and sometimes need different treatments.

Treatment

Surgery is the oldest form of cancer treatment and in many cases can be curative. It also plays a key role in diagnosing cancer and staging cancer. Advances in surgical techniques have allowed surgeons to successfully operate on a growing number of patients, often with less invasive procedures. Surgery can be used to debulk (remove as much tumor as possible), palliate (treat advanced compli-

TABLE 1-1: SUMMARY OF ACS RECOMMENDATIONS FOR THE EARLY DETECTION OF CANCER IN WOMEN*

Cancer-related Checkup

For people 20 years of age and older having periodic health exams, a cancer-related checkup should include health counseling and might include exams for cancers of the thyroid, oral cavity, skin, lymph nodes, and ovaries.

Breast Cancer

- Yearly mammograms are recommended starting at 40 years of age and continue for as long as a woman is in good health.

- Clinical breast exam (CBE) every 3 years for women in their 20s and 30s and every year for women 40 and older.

- Breast self-exam (BSE) is an option for women starting in their 20s.

- Women at high risk (greater than 20% lifetime risk) should have magnetic resonance imaging and a mammogram every year.

Colorectal Cancer

Beginning at age 50, men and women at average risk for developing colorectal cancer should use one of the screening tests below:

Tests that find polyps and cancer

- flexible sigmoidoscopy every 5 years, followed by colonoscopy if positive
- colonoscopy every 10 years
- double contrast barium enema every 5 years, followed by colonoscopy if positive
- computed tomographic colonography (virtual colonoscopy) every 5 years, followed by colonoscopy if positive

Tests that mainly find cancer (All to be followed by colonoscopy if positive)

- yearly fecal occult blood test (gFOBT) every year
- yearly fecal immunochemical test (FIT) every year
- stool DNA test (sDNA), interval uncertain

Persons of moderate or high risk should consult a healthcare provider for specific recommendations that consider risk factors and age of affected relatives.

Cervical Cancer

- All women should begin cervical cancer screening about 3 years after they begin having vaginal intercourse, but no later than when they are 21 years old.

- Beginning at 30 years of age, women who have had three normal Pap test results in a row may get screened every 2 to 3 years (assumes no increase in risk factors).

- Women 70 years of age and older who have had three or more normal Pap tests in a row and no abnormal Pap test results in the last 10 years may choose to stop having cervical cancer screening (assumes no increase in risk factors).

- Women who have had a total hysterectomy (including removal of the uterus and cervix) may choose to stop having cervical cancer screening, unless the surgery was done as a treatment for cervical cancer or pre-cancer or for uterine cancer.

Endometrial Cancer

- At menopause, all women should be informed about the risks and symptoms of endometrial cancer, and strongly urged to report any unexpected bleeding or spotting.

* Screening protocol for persons of average risk from the ACS.

(ACS, 2009a; 2010a; 2010b)

cations of cancer), restore (reconstructive surgery), or prevent (prophylactic) cancer. Often, less invasive operations can be done to remove tumors while preserving as much normal tissue and function as possible.

Radiation therapy uses high-energy particles or waves, such as X-rays, gamma rays, electrons, or protons to destroy or damage cancer cells. Radiation therapy uses special equipment to deliver high doses of radiation to cancer cells, killing or damaging them so they cannot grow or spread. Radiation therapy works by breaking a strand of the DNA molecule inside the cancer cell, which prevents the cell from growing and dividing. Although some normal cells may be affected by radiation, most recover fully from the effects of the treatment.

Chemotherapy uses drugs to kill cancer cells that have metastasized or spread to parts of the body far away from the primary tumor. More than 100 "chemo" drugs are used in many combinations. A single chemotherapy drug can be used to treat cancer; however, for the most part, the drugs work better when used in certain combinations, called "combination chemotherapy." A combination of drugs with different actions can work together to kill more cancer cells as well as reduce the chance that the cancer may become resistant to any one chemotherapy drug. Chemotherapeutic agents may be administered in a number of ways, including intravenously or orally. Newer drugs are being developed, called "targeted therapies," that focus on destroying cancer cells with specific biologic characteristics.

Epidemiologic Resources

Each year the ACS publishes *Cancer Facts and Figures*. This is a helpful and quick reference nurses can use to quickly gather incidence data about estimated cancer cases. The information is presented in several different formats, including the estimated incidence and mortality rates and can be found at www.cancer.org/.

Another source of commonly cited cancer data is the Surveillance, Epidemiology and End Results Program (SEER) data. SEER data includes incidence, mortality, and survival data. Their data dates back to 1973. This information can be obtained easily at the National Cancer Institute website (http://seer.cancer.gov/).

TRENDS: WOMEN AND CANCER

Cancer is the second leading cause of death in the United States, following cardiovascular disease. It affects three of every four families. According to the American Cancer Society (ACS, 2010a) during 2010, an estimated 739,940 women in the United States will be diagnosed with cancer; 270,290 women will die from a cancer diagnosis.

Clearly, cancer is a staggering public health concern. Approximately one out of every two American men and one out of every three American women will have some type of cancer at some point during their lifetimes (ACS, 2010a). Anyone can get cancer at any age; however, about 77% of all cancers are diagnosed in people aged 55 years and older. Although cancer occurs in Americans of all racial and ethnic groups, the rate of cancer occurrence (called the incidence rate) varies from group to group.

The 5-year relative survival rate for all cancers diagnosed between 1999 and 2005 is 68%, up from 50% between 1975 and 1977 (ACS, 2010a). The survival statistics vary greatly by cancer type and stage at diagnosis. It is estimated that over 11.4 million people are living with cancer or have been cured of the disease (ACS, 2010a). The earlier a cancer is detected and the sooner treatment is initiated, the better a patient's chances are of long-term survival.

Breast cancer – although sometimes diagnosed in men – is predominantly a woman's disease. Breast cancer is the most common new cancer diagnosed in women (followed by lung cancer); however, more women die from lung cancer each year (ACS, 2010a). Breast cancer is the second leading cause of cancer deaths in women. Because of this, women are highly concerned with ways to prevent, diagnose, and treat that particular cancer diagnosis. For African American women, the interest is heightened because it is frequently diagnosed at a later stage than in Caucasian women, leading to a higher mortality rate (ACS, 2009a).

Extensive cancer research in recent years has increased what we know about cancer prevention. The risk of developing some types of cancer can be clearly reduced by changes in a person's lifestyle. The ACS (2010b) estimates that at least half of all cancers could be prevented by embracing a healthier lifestyle, or detected earlier through screening. Important reduction behaviors are quitting smoking, avoiding ultraviolet light exposure, eating healthier, exercising regularly, and maintaining an ideal body weight. In addition, we know that early detection and treatment increases the patient's chances of control or cure of the disease. Early detection is important because it frequently results in less radical treatment and improved quality of life.

SUMMARY

Nurses caring for women with cancer should be aware of the special context of care and focus for the female patient. Emotional support, information, open communication, and help with coping are key to the woman's experience. Trends continue to develop related to cancer in women. Breast and lung cancer are the major cancers in women with the highest incidence rates. Lifestyle issues contribute to cancers in women, as they do in men – the most predominant being smoking. Nurses work with women at risk for cancer to ensure they understand and engage in appropriate cancer prevention and early detection practices. Nurses provide specialized care during the staging work-up and treatment phase and provide supportive care through long-term survival from cancer and in the terminal phases of cancer.

EXAM QUESTIONS

CHAPTER 1
Questions 1-6

Note: Choose the one option that BEST answers each question.

1. A comparison of the incidence or deaths among those with a particular risk factor compared to those without the risk factor is

   a. absolute risk.
   b. relative risk.
   c. mutation risk.
   d. attributable risk.

2. A website source nurses can use to gather incidence data about estimated cancer cases is

   a. www.cancercure.com/.
   b. www.nationalcancerregistry.com/.
   c. www.cancer.org/.
   d. www.survival.com/.

3. More than 77% of new cancer cases affect people older than

   a. 55 years of age.
   b. 65 years of age.
   c. 75 years of age.
   d. 85 years of age.

4. The leading cause of death from cancer in women is

   a. breast cancer.
   b. ovarian cancer.
   c. lung cancer.
   d. colon cancer.

5. The two most common cancers in women are

   a. endometrial and breast cancer.
   b. breast and colon cancer.
   c. lung and breast cancer.
   d. lung and colon cancer.

6. What percentage of cancers could be prevented by embracing a healthier lifestyle?

   a. one-eighth
   b. one-fourth
   c. one-third
   d. one-half

REFERENCES

Altekruse, S.F., Kosary, C.L., Krapcho, M., Neyman, N., Aminou, R., Waldron, W., et al. (Eds). SEER Cancer Statistics Review, 1975-2007. Bethesda, MD: National Cancer Institute. Retrieved from http://seer.cancer.gov/csr/1975_2007/, based on November 2009 SEER data submission, posted to the SEER web site, 2010.

American Cancer Society. (2009a). *Breast cancer: Early detection.* Retrieved June 16, 2010, from http://www.cancer.org/docroot/CRI/content/CRI_2_6x_Breast_Cancer_Early_Detection.asp

American Cancer Society. (2009b). *Breast cancer facts & figures 2009-2010.* Atlanta, GA: Author. Retrieved June 16, 2010, from http://our.cancer.org/downloads/STT/F861009_final%209-08-09.pdf

American Cancer Society. (2010a). *Cancer facts & figures 2010.* Atlanta, GA: American Cancer Society.

American Cancer Society. (2010b). *Guidelines for the early detection of cancer.* Retrieved June 16, 2010, from http://www.cancer.org/docroot/ped/content/ped_2_3x_acs_cancer_detection_guidelines_36.asp

Edge, S.B., Byrd, D.R., Carducci, M., Compton, C.C., Fritz, A.G., Greene, F.L., & Trotti, A. (2010). *AJCC cancer staging manual,* 7th ed. New York: Springer.

CHAPTER 2

BREAST CANCER

CHAPTER OBJECTIVE

After completing this chapter on breast cancer, the reader will be able to discuss the disease's epidemiology, risk factors, prevention and detection strategies, and common staging schemas and treatments.

LEARNING OBJECTIVES

After studying this chapter, the reader will be able to

1. recognize the main risk factors for breast cancer.

2. identify advantages and disadvantages of screening modalities.

3. list tests commonly included in the diagnostic workup of breast cancer.

4. list components of a pathology report for breast cancers.

5. discuss the roles of various treatment modalities for breast cancer.

6. discuss options for breast restoration.

EPIDEMIOLOGY

Breast cancer is the most common cancer among women in the U.S., and a cause of significant fear for women. The statistics in Box 2-1 demonstrate the significance of breast cancer in the U.S. Currently there are about two and a half mil-

lion breast cancer survivors. The absolute lifetime risk of developing invasive breast cancer is about 1 in 8. The estimated risk of dying from breast cancer is about 1 in 35 (ACS, 2009b). ✓

BOX 2-1: BREAST CANCER FACTS

- 207,090 estimated new cases of invasive cancer annually in women
- 1,970 estimated new cases annually in men
- Most frequently diagnosed cancer in women
- 54,010 new cases of in situ breast cancer annually
- 40,230 estimated deaths annually
- 2nd leading cause of cancer death in women
- 5-year survival rate for localized cancer is 98%
- 5-year survival rate for metastatic disease is 23%
- 10 year survival rate for all stages is 82%

(ACS, 2009b; 2010b)

Although breast cancer remains a major public health problem, there is an ever increasing pool of long-term survivors and the mortality rate from breast cancer continues to fall. Much of this success can be attributed to improved cancer screening, especially the widespread use of mammography and improvements in treatment.

Table 2-1 illustrates the lifetime risk of developing breast cancer at various ages for women of average risk. Although women have a cumulative lifetime risk of 12.1% or one in eight women, the risk is spread over time (ACS, 2009). As a women ages she passes through risk. Absolute risk figures for breast cancer are best explained in terms of a woman's current age.

TABLE 2-1: LIFETIME PROBABILITY OF BEING DIAGNOSED WITH INVASIVE BREAST CANCER

from age 30 through age 39	.0.44 percent (1 in 229)
from age 40 through age 49	.1.44 percent (1 in 69)
from age 50 through age 59	.2.39 percent (1 in 42)
from age 60 through age 69	.3.40 percent (1 in 29)
lifetime	.12.08 percent (1 in 8)

(ACS, 2009b)

From 2003 to 2007, the median age at death for breast cancer was 68 years of age (Altekruse et al., 2010). Approximately 0.9% died between 20 and 34 years of age; 6.0% between 35 and 44 years of age; 15.0% between 45 and 54 years of age; 20.8% between 55 and 64 years of age; 19.7% between 65 and 74 years of age; 22.6% between 75 and 84 years of age; and 15.1% were older than 85 years of age. The age-adjusted death rate was 24.0 per 100,000 women per year. There are significant disparities in death rates in some races that may be attributed to difficulties with accessing screening or timely evaluation and treatment of breast abnormalities. The lack of health insurance is associated with more advanced stages at diagnosis. Breast cancer patients with lower incomes have lower 5-year relative survival rates than higher-income patients at every stage of diagnosis (ACS, 2009b). Racial disparities in mortality are illustrated in Table 2-2.

The most recent data of relative survival rates for women diagnosed with breast cancer are (ACS, 2009b):

- 89% at 5 years after diagnosis;
- 82% after 10 years;
- 75% after 15 years.

TABLE 2-2: BREAST CANCER DEATH RATES BY RACE

Race/Ethnicity	Rate (per 100,000 women)
All Races	24.0
White	23.4
Black	32.4
Asian/Pacific Islander	12.2
American Indian/Alaska Native	17.6
Hispanic	15.3

Note. From *SEER Cancer Statistics Review, 1975-2007*, by S.F. Altekruse, C.L. Kosary, M. Krapcho, N. Neyman, R. Aminou, W. Waldron, et al. (Eds.), Bethesda, MD: National Cancer Institute. Retrieved from http://seer.cancer.gov/csr/1975_2007/, based on November 2009 SEER data submission, posted to the SEER web site, 2010.

BREAST ANATOMY

Figure 2-1 shows the basic breast anatomy. The breasts are milk-producing, tear-shaped glands. They are supported by and attached to the front of the chest wall on either side of the breast bone, or sternum, by ligaments. They rest on the major chest muscle, the pectoralis major. The breast has no muscle tissue. A layer of fat surrounds the glands and extends throughout the breast.

The breast is stimulated by a complex interplay of hormones that cause the tissue to develop, enlarge, and produce milk. The three major hormones affecting the breast are estrogen, progesterone, and prolactin. Estrogen and progesterone in particular cause glandular tissue in the breast and the uterus to change during the menstrual cycle.

Each breast contains 15 to 20 lobes arranged in a circular fashion. The fat (subcutaneous adipose tissue) that covers the lobes gives the breast its size and shape. Each lobe is comprised of many lobules, at the end of which are tiny bulb-like glands, or sacs, where milk is produced in response to hormonal signals, especially by prolactin. Ducts connect the lobes, lobules, and glands in nursing mothers. These ducts deliver milk to openings in the nipple. The areola is the darker-pigmented area around the nipple.

FIGURE 2-1: BREAST ANATOMY

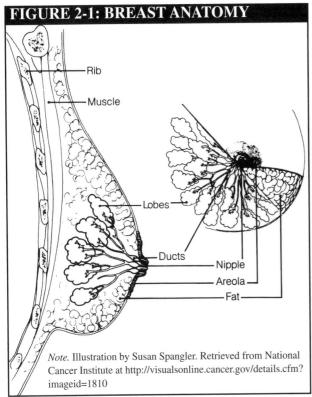

Rib

Muscle

Lobes

Ducts

Nipple

Areola

Fat

Note. Illustration by Susan Spangler. Retrieved from National Cancer Institute at http://visualsonline.cancer.gov/details.cfm? imageid=1810

A woman's breasts can change over the course of her lifetime. The breasts of younger women tend to have less fat and more glandular tissue. Whereas for women who have undergone menopause, the glandular tissue tends to disappear and is replaced with fat. One factor in this change is the lower level of estrogen that occurs with menopause (Wood, Muss, Solin, & Olopade, 2005).

RISK FACTORS

Clarity on the causes of breast cancer is elusive. Women are very worried about developing breast cancer. This stems from extensive media coverage of the topic, which is often confusing and conflicting. Most women know someone who has been affected by the diagnosis of breast cancer. Women who receive breast cancer screening and other healthcare would like to better understand what their risk for developing breast cancer is and what can specifically be done to reduce that risk and, ultimately, their worry about the disease.

Family history of breast cancer is a significant risk factor and is covered in the next section.

Age

One of the most consistently documented uncontrollable risk factors for the development of breast cancer is increasing age. Table 2-1 illustrates how at different ages, women have different statistical risks for developing breast cancer. One way to consider this risk is that if all women younger than 65 years of age are compared with women 65 years of age and older, the relative risk of breast cancer associated with increased age is 5.8 (Singletary, 2003).

Reproductive Factors

A woman's hormone levels normally change throughout her life for a variety of reasons. These hormonal fluctuations can lead to changes in the breast tissue. Hormonal changes occur during puberty, pregnancy, and menopause. Multiple studies have linked age at menarche, menopause, and first live pregnancy to breast cancer risk. Collectively, the patterns of risk associated with reproductive history suggest that prolonged exposure to ovarian hormones increases breast cancer occurrence. The number of menstrual cycles during a lifetime may have a greater risk impact than the number of cycles until the first full-term pregnancy (Chavez-MacGregor et al., 2005). Thus, women who have experienced menarche before age 12 or menopause after age 50 are considered at somewhat higher risk because of a total increased number of ovulatory cycles in a lifetime (Singletary, 2003).

Breast tissue damage or aging starts at a constant rate at menarche and continues at that rate until the time of the first pregnancy, at which point there is a decrease in the rate of tissue aging. This continues to menopause when there is an additional decrease and after menopause a more constant but decreased rate (Colditz, 2005). Thus, if the first full-term pregnancy is delayed, the proliferation due to pregnancy hormones would be acting on a more damaged or aged set of DNA and carry a greater adverse effect.

Increasing parity is associated with a long-term risk reduction in breast cancer risk, presumably because of the interruption of estrogen cycling. Breastfeeding is also associated with a decreased risk of breast cancer (Collaborative Group on Hormonal Factors in Breast Cancer, 2002).

History of Benign Breast Disease

Nonproliferative lesions (which account for more that 70% of all breast biopsies) include adenosis, fibrosis, cysts, mastitis, duct ectasia, fibroadenomas, and mild hyperplasia and confer no added risk for developing breast cancer. Pathology reports that suggest the presence of atypical hyperplasia or lobular carcinoma suggest an increased risk for developing breast cancer (Singletary, 2003).

Oral Contraceptive Use

The exact risk of breast cancer conferred by the use of oral contraceptives is controversial. The composition of oral contraceptives has changed greatly over time. There may be different risks of specific histologic types based on the type and duration of oral contraceptive used (Newcomer, Newcomb, Trentham-Dietz, Longnecker, & Greenberg, 2003). Oral contraceptives have been associated with a slightly increased risk of breast cancer in current users that gradually diminishes over time (Marchbanks et al., 2002).

Hormone Replacement Therapy

Evidence supporting an association between the use of exogenous hormones after menopause and breast cancer is more consistent than that for oral contraceptive use. The landmark Women's Health Initiative study has suggested that hormone replacement therapy may not be as safe or as effective as originally thought (Anderson et al., 2004). Combination hormone replacement therapy using an estrogen and progestin is associated with an increased risk of developing breast cancer. The exact risk is unclear because of the multiple forms available and the number of years of use vary; however, it is thought to be approximately a 24% increase overall (Anderson et al., 2004). The evidence concerning the association between estrogen only therapy and breast cancer is not clear.

Alcohol Consumption

Alcohol consumption of more than two drinks per day increases the risk of developing breast cancer. Alcohol stimulates the metabolism of carcinogens such as acetaldehyde and more global mechanisms such as decreased DNA repair efficiency, and contributes to the poor nutritional intake of protective nutrients (Singletary, 2003).

Increased Body Mass

Increased body mass may be a more important risk factor in postmenopausal women rather than in premenopausal women. Adipose tissue is an important source of extragonadal estrogens in postmenopausal women. The more tissue available, theoretically, the higher the circulating levels of these estrogens (Singletary, 2003). Obesity is associated with increased breast cancer risk, especially among postmenopausal women.

Ionizing Radiation

Exposure of the breast to ionizing radiation is associated with an increased risk of developing breast cancer, especially when the exposure occurs at a young age (Travis et al., 2003).

Protective Factors

Women who have lower body mass may exercise more, which can decrease the number of ovulatory cycles. This may offer a small amount of protection against breast cancer in women who are physically active on a regular basis (Singletary, 2003).

A low-fat diet might decrease breast cancer risk and serve as a preventative measure to decrease risk or delay the development of breast cancer. Fruit and vegetable consumption may be associated with reduced breast cancer risk, especially when it is combined with a low-fat diet. (ACS, 2010b). Micronutrient intake, especially vitamin D and vitamin E, may also play a small role in preventing the development of breast cancer (Singletary, 2003).

GENETIC RISK

Although risk factors for breast cancer are not yet clear or definitive, family history has emerged as an important risk factor for breast and ovarian cancer. After gender and age, for some women, a positive family history is the strongest known predictive risk factor for breast cancer. Estimates suggest that BRCA1/2 mutation carriers have up to an 87% lifetime risk of developing at least one breast cancer and an approximate 30% to 50% risk of developing ovarian cancer (Lynch, Snyder, Lynch, Riley, & Rubinstein, 2003). Approximately one-half of women with a BRCA1 or BRCA2 mutation develop breast cancer by 50 years of age.

Because of autosomal dominant transmission, approximately 50% of susceptible individuals inherit the predisposing genetic alteration that is associated with breast cancer. The susceptibility may be inherited through either the maternal or paternal side of the family.

Key indicators of hereditary breast cancer are shown in Table 2-3. Women with such family histories should be referred to a genetics professional for counseling and evaluation for genetic testing.

A genetics professional usually begins a hereditary assessment by constructing a family tree or pedigree as shown in Figure 2-2. A pedigree should include the ages and causes of death for three generations. Paternal and maternal sides should both be assessed and recorded, as most hereditary susceptibility genes are located on autosomes and can be passed with equal frequency from the maternal or paternal side. For those diagnosed with cancer, the type of primary cancer(s) and age(s) at diagnosis should also be recorded. In many cases, the patient may be unsure of the accuracy of the information and ideally information about cancers should be confirmed by pathology reports, medical records, and/or death certificates. Often once such records are collected, the family history appears very different and this may ultimately change recommendations regarding testing.

Ethnic background also needs to be considered when deciding if testing may be appropriate and this information may alter testing strategies. An estimated 2% of Ashkenazi Jews are estimated to carry one of three common BRCA1 and BRCA2 mutations associated with increased risk for breast, ovarian, and prostate cancers; 20% of Ashkenazi women with breast cancer before 40 years of age have one of the three common mutations (Brandt-Rauf, Raveis, Drummond, Conte, & Rothman, 2006). This is due to a phenomenon referred to as "founder effects" when a population has descended

---

TABLE 2-3: KEY INDICATORS OF BREAST/OVARIAN CANCER SYNDROME

- Personal and/or family history of breast cancer diagnosed at 50 years of age or younger
- Personal and/or family history of ovarian cancer diagnosed at any age
- Women of Ashkenazi Jewish ancestry diagnosed with breast and/or ovarian cancer at any age, regardless of family history
- Personal and/or family history of male breast cancer
- Affected first-degree relatives with a known BRCA1 or BRCA2 mutation
- Bilateral breast cancer, especially if the diagnosis was at an early age
- Breast and ovarian cancer in the same woman

The presence of one or more of these factors in an individual or family history is suggestive or hereditary breast/ovarian cancer syndrome and warrants further evaluation.

(Lynch et al., 2003; Guillem et al., 2006).

FIGURE 2-2: PEDIGREE OF HEREDITARY BREAST/OVARIAN CANCER

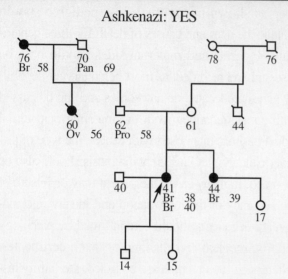

Ashkenazi: YES

Squares represent males and circles represent females. A slash represents a deceased person. Filled in circles and squares represent diagnoses confirmed with pathology reports. The family member's current age or age at death is shown as well as the age at any cancer diagnosis. The arrow represents the proband or spokesperson for the family. There are three generations showing both maternal and paternal sides. If information is known about ethnicity, it can also be included. In this family, three generations are affected. Note the early age of onset of breast cancer, bilateral breast cancer, and ovarian cancer.

from a relatively small number of people without other groups.

The commercial availability of genetic testing for the cancer susceptibility genes associated with hereditary breast/ovarian cancer syndromes has greatly changed oncology risk assessment practices. Cancer susceptibility genetic testing has the potential to identify whether a person is at increased risk for a particular cancer or cancers associated with hereditary breast/ovarian cancer syndrome. These tests, however, cannot predict when, where, or if the individual will be diagnosed with the cancer. One of the challenges in the communication of genetic risk information and genetic test results is that probabilities and uncertainties surround genetic information.

Whether a patient might benefit from predisposition genetic testing will depend upon their degree of genetic risk, whether testing is likely to address their needs, their motivation to actively engage in prevention strategies, and the availability of an appropriate cancer predisposition test. Due to the high cost of some genetic tests (approximately $3300 for full sequencing of BRCA1/2), reimbursement factors may need to be considered. Most insurers cover some or all of the cost of genetic testing in persons who meet eligibility criteria set by the insurer. There may be additional costs for counseling and education. The final testing decision, however, will depend upon the patient understanding the potential risks and benefits and whether she wants to proceed.

Deciding who is the most appropriate candidate for cancer predisposition testing requires clinical judgment due to the complexity of the issues involved. Ideally, an affected family member will be the first one to be tested. In the case of testing for BRCA1/2, a woman who has been diagnosed with breast (particularly premenopausal) or ovarian cancer will usually be the most informative for the rest of the family. Models for predicting risk of developing breast cancer or having a mutation are listed in Table 2-4. If an unaffected relative has been tested and found to carry a deleterious mutation known to be associated with increased cancer risk, then at-risk family members are likely to benefit from single site testing for the same mutation (which is significantly less expensive usually costing $375 to $400 for single site testing).

If a woman tests negative for a known mutation, she has the same risk of developing breast cancer as any woman in the general population. If the woman tests negative and she is the first woman in her family to test, the family could still have a hereditary risk for developing breast cancer, but it might be an odd mutation for which testing is

TABLE 2-4: SELECTED MODELS FOR BREAST CANCER RISK AND MUTATION RISK ASSESSMENT

Models to Predict Risk of Developing Breast Cancer

Gail Model: Estimates breast cancer risk in women without a diagnosis of cancer.

Claus Model: Estimates risk of developing breast cancer over time in ten year increments in women with a family history of breast cancer

NCI Breast Risk Tool: Estimates risk of developing breast cancer in five years and lifetime. Available at http://www.cancer.gov/bcrisktool/

Models to Predict Risk of Having a Mutation in BRCA1 and/or BRCA2

Berry Model (BRCAPRO): Estimates risk of carrying a BRCA1 or BRCA2 mutation

Couch Model: Estimates risk of carrying a BRCA1 mutation

Frank Model (Myriad Tables): Estimates risk of carrying a BRCA1 or BRCA2 mutation

Manchester Model: Estimates risk of carrying a BRCA1 or BRCA2 mutation

Pedigree Assessment Tool (PAT): Identifies women at increased risk for HBOC and to offer genetic testing

Shattuck-Eidens Model: Estimates risk of carrying a BRCA1 mutation

(Claus, Schildkraut, Thompson, & Risch, 1996; Couch et al., 1997; Decarli et al., 2006; Evans et al., 2004; Frank et al., 2002; Hoskins, Zwaagstra, & Ranz, 2006; Parmigani et al., 2007; Shattuck-Eidens et al., 1997)

not available. There is always a remote chance a woman could have a test result that shows a variant of unknown significance. In this case, the risk for developing cancer is not clear.

For women who test positive, the risk of developing breast and ovarian cancer is significant. They must make difficult decisions about how to manage the risk. One option is to screen more aggressively than in the general population, but the woman will still develop breast cancer and need some treatment. In some cases hormonal manipulation with a drug such as tamoxifen may be used. Prevention of cancer in those with a known mutation is best achieved with prophylactic mastectomy and oophorectomy (Lynch et al., 2003).

HORMONE THERAPY AS PREVENTION

Tamoxifen (Nolvodex) is a hormone frequently used to help prevent breast cancer. It blocks the action of estrogen in breast tissue, thereby preventing estrogen from stimulating the proliferation of breast cells (ACS, 2009b).

Tamoxifen has been shown to decrease the risk of developing breast cancer in women with lobular carcinoma in situ (LCIS). Women treated with tamoxifen have a reduced rate of several benign breast diseases, including atypical hyperplasia, a condition in which noncancerous cells multiply to an abnormal extent, which can develop into invasive breast cancer (Vogel et al., 2006).

Tamoxifen may cause weight gain, hot flashes, vaginal discharge or irritation, nausea, and irregular periods. Women who are still menstruating and having irregular periods may become pregnant more easily when taking tamoxifen (Vogel et al., 2006). Blood clots and cataract development are also rare but significant adverse effects. Some studies show that tamoxifen can slightly increase the risk of developing endometrial cancer.

Raloxifene

In addition to tamoxifen, another antiestrogen agent, raloxifene, is being studied as a preventive hormonal agent. Its intended advantage is to reduce the incidence of both breast and uterine cancers. The study evaluating the efficacy of tamoxifen and raloxifene in postmenopausal women is the STAR trial

(Study of Tamoxifen and Raloxifene). The goal of the trial is to follow more than 20,000 women on these preventive hormonal agents for 5 to 10 years. In an early analysis (Vogel et al., 2006) there were fewer cases of noninvasive breast cancer in the tamoxifen group (57 cases) than in the raloxifene group (80 cases). There were 36 cases of uterine cancer with tamoxifen and 23 with raloxifene. No differences were found for other invasive cancer sites, for ischemic heart disease events, or for stroke.

SCREENING

The proper use of screening and genetic testing can potentially decrease the morbidity and mortality associated with breast cancer. Screening is appropriate for asymptomatic women. Symptomatic women should be referred directly for a diagnostic evaluation, which might include an ultrasound, additional mammographic views, MRI, and biopsy. Table 2-5 lists signs and symptoms of breast cancer. The ACS recommendations for the early detection of cancer are outlined in Table 2-6.

TABLE 2-5: SIGNS AND SYMPTOMS OF BREAST CANCER

- lump or mass in the breast
- swelling in all or part of the breast
- skin irritation or dimpling
- breast pain
- nipple pain or the nipple turning inward
- redness, scaliness, or thickening of the nipple or breast skin
- a nipple discharge other than breast milk
- a lump in the underarm area

(ACS, 2009b; ACS, 2010b)

Most of the gains in reducing the mortality from breast cancer stem directly from screening efforts and an ever increasing public awareness of the importance of breast cancer screening. There are government programs that promote and fund breast cancer screening, and many private organi-

TABLE 2-6: RECOMMENDATIONS FOR THE EARLY DETECTION OF BREAST CANCER

- Yearly mammograms are recommended starting at 40 years of age and continue for as long as a woman is in good health.
- Clinical breast exam (CBE) every 3 years for women in their 20s and 30s and every year for women 40 years of age and older.
- Breast self-exam (BSE) is an option for women starting in their 20s.
- Women at high risk (greater than 20% lifetime risk) should get an MRI and a mammogram every year.

(ACS, 2010a)

zations such as Susan G. Komen for the Cure that are dedicated to promoting awareness and screening for breast cancer, especially in underserved populations.

Congress passed the *Breast and Cervical Cancer Mortality Prevention Act of 1990,* which resulted in the National Breast and Cervical Cancer Early Detection Program (NBCCEDP). The program provides low-income, uninsured, and underserved women access to breast and cervical cancer screening and diagnostic services. It is estimated that 8% to 11% of U.S. women of screening age are eligible to receive NBCCEDP services (Centers for Disease Control and Prevention [CDC], 2007). Federal guidelines establish an eligibility baseline to direct services to uninsured and underinsured women at or below 250% of federal poverty level; 18 to 64 years of age for cervical screening; 40 to 64 years of age for breast screening. Services include clinical breast examinations, mammograms, Pap tests, diagnostic testing for women whose screening outcome is abnormal, surgical consultation, and referrals to treatment. Since 1991, the NBCCEDP has served more than 3 million women, provided more than 7.2 million screening examinations, and diagnosed 30,963 breast cancers. At 65 years old women become eligible for Medicare, which provides coverage for breast cancer screening, including annual mammography.

Breast Self-Examination

Breast self-examination (BSE) has long been a means for patients to have control and an early awareness of breast changes, but its practice has recently become controversial. Figure 2-3 demonstrates a strategy for BSE as well as a clinical breast examination (CBE).

Although the ACS no longer recommends that all women perform monthly BSE, women should be informed about the potential benefits and limita-

tions associated with BSE. Research has shown that structured BSE is less important than self awareness. Women who detect their own breast cancer usually find it outside of a structured breast self-exam while bathing or getting dressed. A woman who wishes to perform periodic BSE should receive instruction from her healthcare provider and have her technique reviewed periodically. Potential benefits of BSE include the detection of tumors that develop between professional examinations or mammography and the detection of breast cancers not seen on mammography.

FIGURE 2-3: STEPS FOR BSE AND CBE

A series of 16 photos demonstrating the 16 steps of a clinical breast examination. The steps are as follows:

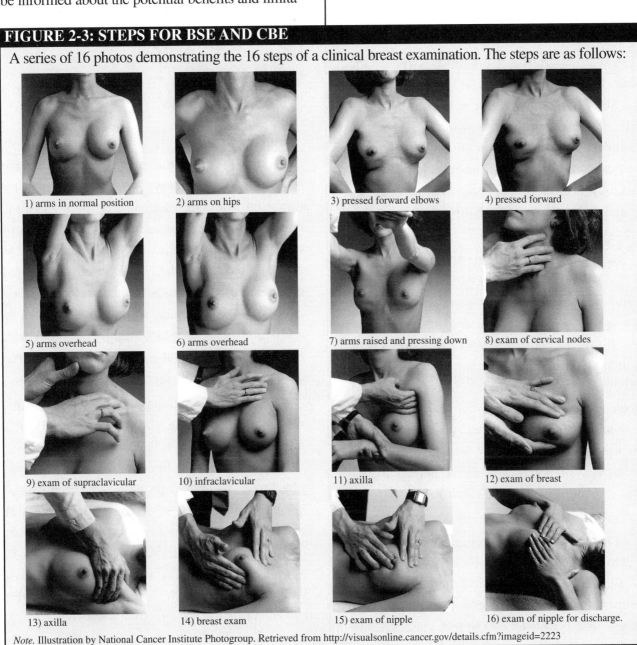

1) arms in normal position
2) arms on hips
3) pressed forward elbows
4) pressed forward
5) arms overhead
6) arms overhead
7) arms raised and pressing down
8) exam of cervical nodes
9) exam of supraclavicular
10) infraclavicular
11) axilla
12) exam of breast
13) axilla
14) breast exam
15) exam of nipple
16) exam of nipple for discharge.

Note. Illustration by National Cancer Institute Photogroup. Retrieved from http://visualsonline.cancer.gov/details.cfm?imageid=2223

Clinical Breast Examination

Clinical breast examination (CBE) is a manual breast examination performed by a trained clinician. Although recommended at regular intervals for women at risk for breast cancer, studies are limited that prove that CBE is effective in reducing incidence and mortality (United Nations Population Fund, 2002). CBE is recommended especially for women who carry the BRCA1 or BRCA2 high-risk mutation and usually at a more frequent interval. Like BSE, it can sometimes detect lesions and breast cancers not found on mammography.

Mammography

A mammogram is a low-dose X-ray of the breast. Screening mammography is widely used to look for breast disease in women who are asymptomatic. Mammograms can show masses, cysts, and small deposits of calcium in the breast. Although most calcium deposits are benign, microcalcifications may be an early sign of cancer. Most agencies recommend women routinely begin having mammograms at 40 years of age.

Mammography is the single most effective method of early detection because it can identify cancer several years before physical symptoms such as a lump develop. Mammography is a low-dose X-ray procedure that allows visualization of the internal structure of the breast. The breast is compressed to better visualize all tissue. Standard screening views include the cranio-caudal view and the medio-lateral oblique view. Typical views for a diagnostic mammogram may also include supplemental views tailored to better visualize the specific problem. Figure 2-4 shows a patient positioned for a mammogram.

Mammography will detect about 80% to 90% of breast cancers in women without symptoms (ACS, 2009b). It is somewhat more accurate in postmenopausal than in premenopausal women because their breasts tend to be less dense. Factors

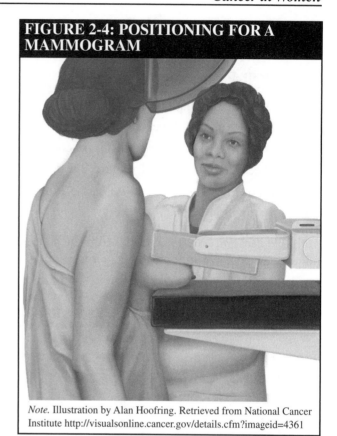

FIGURE 2-4: POSITIONING FOR A MAMMOGRAM

Note. Illustration by Alan Hoofring. Retrieved from National Cancer Institute http://visualsonline.cancer.gov/details.cfm?imageid=4361

that contribute to false negative mammogram reports include increased breast density, faster tumor growth rate, inadequate positioning of the breast, or simply failing to see the small early signs of an abnormality. Each year approximately 5% to 10% of women have their mammogram interpreted as abnormal or inconclusive until further tests are done. In most instances, additional tests, such as additional mammogram imaging studies and biopsy, lead to a final interpretation of normal breast tissue or benign changes.

There is no specific upper age at which mammography screening should be discontinued according to ACS the 2009-2010 guidelines (ACS, 2009b). The decision to stop regular mammography screening should be based on the potential benefits and risks of screening in the context of overall health status and estimated longevity of each individual woman. As long as a woman is in good health and would be a candidate for breast cancer treatment, she should continue to be screened with mammography.

The routine use of mammography is partially responsible for the reduction in mortality rates for breast cancer (ACS, 2009b). Mammography can detect breast cancers long before they would be palpable as shown in Figure 2-5. All mammogram facilities should be certified by the American College of Radiology and use dedicated mammogram machines. When a woman presents for a mammogram she should anticipate that she will be questioned about previous films, breast problems, hormone use, and breast surgery. If films have been done at another facility, a release will need to be signed for the films to be sent for comparison. The woman should be instructed to avoid using deodorant or antiperspirant, lotions, and creams on the breast area on the day of the exam because some of these contain substances that can interfere with mammogram interpretation by appearing on the X-ray film as white spots. Some women find it more convenient to wear a skirt or pants, so that they only need to remove the blouse for the exam. Ideally the mammogram should be scheduled when the breasts are not tender or swollen to help reduce discomfort; that means avoiding the week prior to the menses. Federal law mandates women receive a written summary of the findings. The woman needs to be instructed that if she does not receive a report in 7 to 10 days, she needs to contact the facility.

Conventional screening with mammography for women with a high lifetime risk of developing breast cancer is often inadequate due to increased breast density in young women, frequency of atypical imaging presentations in women younger than 40 years of age, and the rapid growth of hereditary breast cancer, resulting in a higher rate of interval cancer necessitating the need for more frequent screening. Screening recommendations differ for women with a known mutation in BRCA1 or BRCA2 or greater than 25% lifetime risk of developing breast cancer with 50% of these women developing breast cancer, before 50 years of age.

FIGURE 2-5: SMALL ABNORMALITY DETECTED ON MAMMOGRAPHY

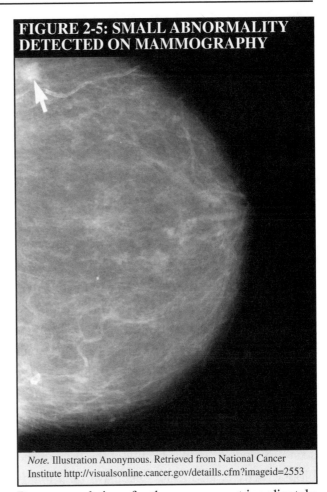

Note. Illustration Anonymous. Retrieved from National Cancer Institute http://visualsonline.cancer.gov/detaills.cfm?imageid=2553

Recommendations for these women at inordinately high risk of developing breast cancer include mammography, beginning at 25 years of age and MRI of the breasts (Saslow et al., 2007). Mutation carriers have a 65% to 85% lifetime risk of developing breast cancer, and yearly mammograms may not provide adequate screening for high-risk women. Women with a known mutation should be counseled about prophylactic mastectomy and prophylactic oophorectomy. Prophylactic mastectomy offers a 99% reduction in breast cancer risk and prophylactic oophorectomy offers a 50% reduction in breast cancer risk and a 97% reduction in ovarian cancer risk (Guillem et al., 2006). Those women with significant family history or a known BRCA mutation should undergo mammography at a younger age and should seek guidance from a healthcare provider with expertise in cancer genetics (NCCN, 2010). For those from high risk families for which a mutation cannot be identified, or for women who are unwilling or unable to undergo prophylactic surgery, there should be consideration for a breast MRI.

MRI uses magnetic fields instead of X-rays to produce very detailed, cross-sectional images of the body. It should be done on a dedicated breast MRI machine. Breast MRI exams usually use a contrast material (gadolinium DTPA) that is injected intravenously. For women at high risk for breast cancer, based on the previously outlined criteria (lifetime risk greater than 20%), a screening MRI is recommended along with a yearly mammogram. Although the MRI is more sensitive than mammograms in detecting cancers, it also has a higher false-positive rate, which results in more recalls and biopsies (ACS, 2009a). It is important that screening MRIs be done at facilities that are capable of performing an MRI-guided breast biopsy at the time of the exam if abnormalities are detected. This will prevent the need to have the scan repeated at another facility at the time of the biopsy. MRI is also more expensive than mammography. Many major insurance companies will likely pay for these screening tests if a woman is documented to be at high risk.

DIAGNOSING BREAST CANCER

When suspicious masses are found on BSE, CBE, or mammography, diagnostic strategies are considered. The diagnostic workup often includes a CBE by a surgeon, diagnostic mammogram, ultrasound and, often, a biopsy. Biopsies can be fine-needle, needle, or surgical. Additional imaging technologies used to determine a diagnosis include digital mammography, MRI, and positron emission tomography (PET). Further tests to detect the spread of cancer include X-rays, bone scans, liver scans, and lung scans.

A more specific use of ultrasound is stereotactic needle biopsy. This technique allows computers

to map the exact location of the mass using mammograms taken from two angles. A computer then guides the needle to the right spot.

Diagnostic mammograms are X-ray pictures of the breast that produce clearer, more detailed images of areas that looked abnormal on a screening mammogram. Often only a specific area in question is compressed, and magnification may be added. Doctors use them to learn more about unusual breast changes, such as a lump, pain, thickening, nipple discharge, or change in breast size or shape. They typically involve special techniques and more views than screening mammograms.

An ultrasound device uses sound waves to create an image of the breast. The waves bounce off tissues, and a computer uses the echoes to create a picture. These images often clarify if a lump or abnormality seen on mammography is solid or filled with fluid. A cyst is a fluid-filled sac and is a benign finding. A solid mass may be suggestive of a malignancy and requires further evaluation.

In addition to being utilized for screening in high-risk women, breast MRI may be used in a diagnostic evaluation to further examine a suspicious area or in a woman with a confirmed breast cancer to determine if there are other areas of malignancy.

Some abnormalities require a biopsy. Fluid or tissue is removed to determine if there is a malignancy. Some suspicious areas can be seen on a mammogram but cannot be felt during a clinical breast exam. In this case an imaging procedure is utilized to help see the area and remove tissue. Such procedures include ultrasound-guided, needle-localized, or stereotactic biopsy.

Fine-needle aspiration utilizes a thin needle to remove fluid from a breast lump. If the fluid appears to contain cells, a pathologist evaluates the cells for cancer under a microscope. If the fluid is clear, it may not need to be checked by a lab.

A core biopsy utilizes a thick needle to remove breast tissue. A pathologist checks for cancer cells. This procedure is also called a needle biopsy.

In a surgical biopsy, a surgeon removes a sample of tissue. A pathologist checks the tissue for cancer cells. During an incisional biopsy the surgeon takes a sample of a lump or abnormal area. During an excisional biopsy the surgeon removes the entire lump or area.

PATHOLOGY REPORT

Breast cancer is a heterogeneous disease with many different subtypes. Targeted therapies aim to provide optimal treatment for a specific subtype, based on the biologic characteristics of the tumor often described in the pathology report. When a woman receives a pathology report describing the breast cancer diagnosis, there are a number of factors that need to be considered and discussed. Women diagnosed with breast cancer should have an understanding of why these tests are ordered and how they impact treatment decisions. The pathology report provides insight into the prognosis for the diagnosis as well as information about features that might predict a response to a particular therapy (see Table 2-7). Together, all of this information influences treatment decisions and is a step in individualizing therapy.

The majority of primary breast cancers are adenocarcinomas which can be divided into subtypes. The two major subtypes are ductal and lobular carcinomas. Based on microscopic findings, breast carcinomas are further classified as either in situ (non-invasive) or invasive (Wood et al., 2005).

In situ breast carcinomas are defined by the presence of malignant epithelial cells within the ducts or lobules with no extension beyond the basement membrane. In situ carcinomas do not exhibit lymphvascular invasion and have not metastasized. They are considered non-invasive cancers and are further described as ductal carcinoma in situ (DCIS) or lobular carcinoma in situ (LCIS). Although DCIS is a noninvasive condition, it can progress to become invasive cancer; however, estimates of risk are variable (National Cancer Institute [NCI], 2010). The frequency of the diagnosis of DCIS has increased markedly in the U.S. since the widespread use of screening mammography. In 1998, DCIS accounted for about 18% of all newly diagnosed invasive and noninvasive breast tumors in the U.S.; in 2008 it accounted for more than 27% (NCI, 2010). Very few cases of DCIS present as a palpable mass; 80% are diagnosed by mammography alone.

The term lobular carcinoma in situ is misleading; it is really lobular neoplasia. LCIS is a marker that identifies women at an increased risk for subsequent development of invasive breast cancer. This risk remains elevated even beyond 2 decades,

TABLE 2-7: PROGNOSTIC FACTORS REPORTED ON PATHOLOGY REPORT

Tumor Size: Smaller size usually means better prognosis.

Lymph Node Involvement: Few or no nodes usually means better prognosis.

Histopathologic Grade (Scarff-Bloom-Richardson Scale): Scale that considers nuclear grade, mitotic index, and cellular differentiation (ranges from 3 to 9). A lower score is associated with better prognosis.

Estrogen Receptors and Progesterone Receptors: determine if the cancer is sensitive to estrogen or progesterone.

HER2 Status: HER2 positive tumors tend to be aggressive.

OncotypeDXTM assay (Genomic Health, Inc., Redwood, California): Useful for assessing the risk of recurrence and the potential benefit from chemotherapy in newly diagnosed stage I or II, node-negative, estrogen receptor-positive breast cancer.

(Harris et al., 2007; Hayes & Picard, 2006)

and most of the subsequent cancers are ductal rather than lobular.

Invasive or infiltrating carcinomas extend beyond the basement membrane. Extension may continue through the breast parenchyma, into lymphvascular spaces, and may metastasize into regional lymph nodes or distant sites.

After a diagnosis of cancer is made, special lab tests are conducted on the breast tissue that was removed. These tests help with evaluating the tumor and planning treatment:

- *Hormone receptor test:* This test shows whether the tissue has certain hormone receptors. Tissue with these receptors needs hormones (estrogen or progesterone) to grow. Tumors that are sensitive to estrogen and progesterone might benefit from hormonal manipulation.

- *HER2 testing:* This test shows whether the tissue has a protein called human epidermal growth factor receptor-2 (HER2) or the HER2/neu gene. Having too much protein or too many copies of the gene in the tissue may increase the chance that the breast cancer will come back after treatment. Tumors with this marker should be treated with specific drugs such as trastuzumab.

The majority of invasive breast carcinomas occur in the upper outer quadrant of the breast. Most begin as calcifications that can be detected with mammography. Invasive carcinomas are usually small and lymph nodes are usually negative. A noted density is the most common mammographic finding for invasive carcinomas. Invasive carcinomas exhibiting this pattern are usually half the size of masses found first by palpation and have nodal metastases in less than 20% of the cases (ACS, 2009b). In women not undergoing mammography, invasive carcinomas usually present as a palpable mass and positive lymph nodes can be anticipated in 50% of those cases.

TREATMENT

Staging emerges from the diagnostic workup and is based on the existence and size of a malignant tumor (T), whether malignant cells have spread to lymph nodes (L), and whether malignant cells have spread distant to the primary tumor (M = metastasis). Numbers are added to staging schemas to provide more specific information about the tumor and its behavior. For example, a Stage IIB tumor can be a tumor 2 to 5 cm (T2) or greater than 5 cm (T3) with involvement in the axillary lymph node (N1) or no involvement (N0) and no metastasis (M0). Table 2-8 highlights staging criteria for breast cancer. Standard local treatments are surgery and radiation therapy. Systemic treatments are hormone therapy, chemotherapy, and biological therapy.

Surgery

Surgery is the classic local treatment. Figure 2-6 shows various surgical procedures in the workup and treatment of breast cancer. Breast-sparing surgeries include lumpectomy and segmental (partial) mastectomy. During surgery, axillary lymph nodes are removed to determine cancer spread. Every woman must understand the ramifications of her pathology report and make a decision that is in keeping with her personal value system.

In breast-sparing surgery (lumpectomy), the surgeon removes the tumor in the breast and some tissue around it. The surgeon may also remove axillary lymph nodes and some of the lining over the chest muscles below the tumor. Lumpectomy is almost always followed by radiotherapy. The choice between breast-sparing surgery (followed by radiation therapy) and mastectomy depends on many factors:

- The size, location, and stage of the tumor

- The size of the woman's breast

- Certain features of the cancer

- How the woman feels about saving her breast

- How the woman feels about radiation therapy

TABLE 2-8: STAGING SCHEMAS

Breast cancer stage grouping

	T (Tumor)	N (Nodes)	M (Metastasis)
Stage 0	Tis	N0	M0
Stage 1A	T1	N0	M0
Stage 1B	T0	N1	M0
	T1	N1	M0
Stage IIA	T0	N1	M0
	T1	N1	M0
	T2	N0	M0
Stage IIB	T2	N1	M0
	T3	N0	M0
Stage IIIA	T0	N2	M0
	T1	N2	M0
	T2	N2	M0
	T3	N1	M0
	T3	N2	M0
Stage IIIB	T4	N0, N1, N2	M0
Stage IIIC	Any T	N3	M0
Stage IV	Any T	Any N	M1

Breast cancer survival by stage

Stage	5-year relative survival rate
0	100%
I	99%
IIA	92%
IIB	81%
IIIA	67%
IIIB	54%
IIIC	50%
IV	22%

(ACS, 2009; NCI, 2010; Edge et al., 2010)

- The woman's ability to travel to a radiation treatment center

In a total (simple) mastectomy the surgeon removes the whole breast. Some lymph nodes under the arm are usually removed (typically through a sentinel lymph node biopsy). In a modified radical mastectomy, the surgeon removes the whole breast and, often, many or all of the axillary lymph nodes

FIGURE: 2-6: SURGICAL APPROACHES TO THE MANAGEMENT OF BREAST CANCER

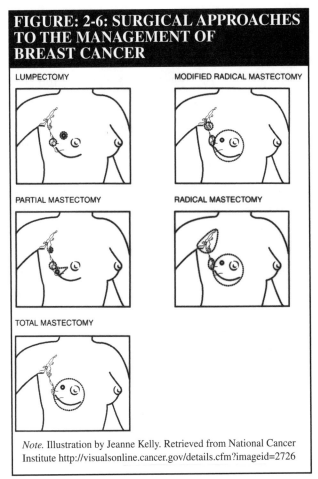

Note. Illustration by Jeanne Kelly. Retrieved from National Cancer Institute http://visualsonline.cancer.gov/details.cfm?imageid=2726

and the lining over the chest muscles. A small amount of chest muscle may also be removed to make it easier to remove the lymph nodes.

Sentinel Lymph Node Biopsy

Approximately 70% of women with early-stage breast cancer at the time of surgery will have no evidence of regional lymph node involvement. Sentinel lumph node biopsy offers a means to sample the lymph nodes with a minimally invasive procedure that may also reduce the risk of lymphedema. Sentinel lymph node biopsy may help in determining which patients can avoid axillary node dissection and the removal of 10 to 30 lymph nodes. Most patients have only one to three sentinel lymph nodes under the arm. Thus, an average of only two lymph nodes are removed in each patient with a sentinel node biopsy. This, in turn, may reduce post-operative complications.

Prior to performing a sentinel lymph node biopsy, the doctor injects a radioactive substance near the tumor. The injected contrast substance flows through the lymphatic system to the first lymph node or nodes where cancer cells are likely to have spread (the "sentinel" node or nodes). The doctor uses a scanner to locate the radioactive substance in the sentinel nodes. The surgeon can make a small incision and remove only the nodes with radioactive material (Gawlick, Mone, Hansen, Connors, & Nelson, 2008). Sentinel lymph node biopsy has been shown to significantly minimize the morbidity associated with axillary lymph node dissection, while providing accurate diagnostic and prognostic information (Gawlick et al., 2008).

Radiation Therapy

Radiation therapy can be used alone, before or after surgery, or with chemotherapy or hormone therapy. Radiation therapy uses high-energy rays to kill cancer cells. Most women receive radiation therapy after breast-sparing surgery. Some women receive radiation therapy after a mastectomy. Treatment depends on the size of the tumor and other factors. The radiation destroys breast cancer cells that may remain in the area.

In external radiation, the radiation comes from outside the body. Most women go to a hospital or clinic for treatment. Treatments are usually 5 days a week for several weeks.

There are two types of brachytherapy commonly used in breast cancer. In intracavitary brachytherapy (MammoSite) a small deflated balloon attached to a thin tube is inserted into the space left by the lumpectomy and is filled with a saline solution. The balloon and tube are left in place throughout treatment (with the end of the tube sticking out of the breast). Twice a day a source of radioactivity is placed into the middle of the balloon through the tube and then removed. This is done for 5 days as an outpatient treatment. The balloon is then deflated and removed.

In interstitial brachytherapy several small catheters are inserted into the breast around the area of the lumpectomy and are left in place for several days. Radioactive pellets are inserted into the catheters for short periods of time each day and then removed.

Side effects depend mainly on the dose and type of radiation (external or brachytherapy). It is common for the skin in the treated area to become red, dry, tender, and itchy. Many women report that the breast feels heavy and tight. Some women experience moist desquamation toward the end of therapy. Exposing this area to air as much as possible can help the skin heal.

Bras and some other types of clothing that rub the skin may cause soreness. Women are advised to wear loose-fitting cotton clothes during this time. Gentle skin care also is important. During treatment, women should not apply any deodorants, lotions, or creams on the treated area. The effects of radiation therapy on the skin goes away and the area gradually heals when treatment is completed; however, there may be a lasting change in the color of the skin. Fatigue is a major side effect of radiation therapy and women should be encouraged to obtain adequate rest.

For the treatment of some invasive breast cancer, studies over the past 10 years have shown that radiation therapy with lumpectomy is considered as effective a treatment as mastectomy and is associated with fewer complications (Nesvold, Dahl, Løkkevik, Marit Mengshoel, & Fosså, 2008). Radiation therapy with lumpectomy has been shown to improve survival when provided as an adjunct to breast-conserving surgery. For patients with more than four positive lymph nodes, studies have shown that with radiation therapy after surgery, local and regional recurrence can be reduced as much as 40% compared to surgery alone (Perun, 2004).

Hormone Therapy

Hormone therapy generally should be considered as initial treatment for a postmenopausal patient with newly diagnosed metastatic disease if the patient's tumor is estrogen receptor positive (ER+), progesterone receptor positive (PR+), or ER/PR-unknown.

A blood test can indicate if a woman can bind estrogen or progesterone to the ER or PR sites on the nuclear cell membrane of breast tumor tissue. If binding can occur, then breast tumor cells are stimulated. Hormonal therapy attempts to compete with estrogen or reduce the amount of circulating estrogen that stimulates breast tumor development and in many cases will prevent a recurrence of breast cancer.

Approximately 80% of breast tumors in postmenopausal women are ER+, but only 50% to 70% in premenopausal women indicate ER expression (Dienger, 2004). About 30% of ER+ tumors are progesterone receptor negative (PR–). Fewer than 5% of estrogen receptor negative (ER–) tumors are PR+. Women with both ER+ and PR+ status are the best candidates for hormone therapy (Dienger, 2004).

Hormone therapy is especially indicated if the woman's disease involves only bone and soft tissue and if she has not received adjuvant (following primary surgery) antiestrogen therapy (for example, tamoxifen) or has been off of antiestrogen therapy for more than 1 year (Dienger, 2004).

In addition to tamoxifen, several agents are used to block the effect of estrogen or lower estrogen levels. Table 2-9 lists some of these hormone therapies.

The side effects of hormone therapy depend largely on the specific drug or type of treatment. In general, the side effects of many of these agents are similar to some of the symptoms of menopause. The most common are hot flashes and vaginal discharge. Other side effects are irregular menstrual periods, headaches, fatigue, nausea, vomiting, vaginal dryness or itching, irritation of the skin around the vagina, and skin rash.

Monoclonal Antibodies

A rapidly growing area of research in breast oncology includes a newer class of drugs known as monoclonal antibodies. The most common of these is Herceptin which is often used in women with tumors that are HER2 positive.

Herceptin is given intravenously to women whose lab tests show that a breast tumor has too much of a specific protein known as HER2. By blocking HER2, it can slow or stop the growth of the cancer cells. It may be given alone or with chemotherapy. The first time a woman receives Herceptin, the most common

TABLE 2-9: HORMONAL TREATMENT APPROACHES IN THE MANAGEMENT OF BREAST CANCER

Class	Action	Example
Selective Estrogen-Receptor Modulators	Bind to estrogen receptors in breast cancer cells and block cancer cells	Nolvodex (tamoxifen) Evista (raloxifene) Fareston (toremifene)
Aromatase Inhibitors	Prevent production of estrogen in adrenal glands	Aromasin (exemestane) Femara (letrozole) Arimidex (anastrozole) Megace (megestrol)
Other Hormonal Therapies	Treat breast cancers that are dependent on estrogen for survival	Zoladex (goserelin acetate) Faslodex (fulvestrant)
Biologic Response Modifiers	Bind with certain proteins on breast cancer cells, preventing their growth	Herceptin (trastuzumab) Avastin (bevacizumab) Tykerb (lapatinib)

side effects are fever and chills. Some women also have pain, weakness, nausea, vomiting, diarrhea, headaches, difficulty breathing, or rashes. Side effects usually become milder after the first treatment. Herceptin also may cause cardiac toxicity, which may lead to heart failure.

Chemotherapy

Neoadjuvant (before surgery) and adjuvant (after surgery) chemotherapy protocols are offered as systemic therapies to boost the effectiveness of surgery and radiation and to treat tumors that have metastasized. Table 2-10 lists common chemotherapy agents used in the treatment of breast cancer. Most women will receive some combination of an anthracycline, alkylating agent, and a taxane for initial therapy.

Stages I, II, IIIA, and Operable IIIC

Women with Stage I, II, IIIA, and operable IIIC breast cancer usually must choose from a combination of treatments. Some may have breast-sparing surgery followed by radiation therapy to the breast. This choice is common for women with Stage I or II breast cancer. Others decide to have a mastectomy.

With either approach, women (especially those with Stage II or IIIA breast cancer) often have lymph nodes under the arm removed, usually with a sentinel lymph node biopsy. The doctor may suggest radiation therapy after mastectomy if cancer

TABLE 2-10: CHEMOTHERAPY AGENTS USED IN THE TREATMENT OF BREAST CANCER			
Class	**Action**	**Side Effects**	**Examples**
Anthracyclines	Alter DNA structure of cancer cells	• Decreased white blood cell count with increased risk of infection • Decreased platelet count with increased risk of bleeding • Loss of appetite • Darkening of nail beds and skin creases of hands • Hair loss • Nausea and vomiting • Mouth sores	Adriamycin (doxorubicin) Ellence (epirubicin)
Taxanes	Prevent cancer cells from dividing	• Decrease in white blood cells with increased risk of infection • Fever (often a warning sign of infection) • Fluid retention • Allergic reactions • Hair loss	Taxol (paclitaxel) Taxotere (docetaxel)
Alkylating Agents	Target DNA of cancer cells	• Decreased white blood cell count with increased risk of infection • Hair loss • Nausea and vomiting • Loss of appetite • Sores in mouth or on lips • Diarrhea • Ceasing of menstrual periods	Cytoxan (cyclophosphamide)

(Gullatte, 2007)

cells are found in one to three lymph nodes under the arm, or if the tumor in the breast is large. If cancer cells are found in more than three lymph nodes under the arm, the doctor usually will suggest radiation therapy after mastectomy.

Some women have chemotherapy before surgery to destroy cancer cells and shrink the tumor. Doctors use this approach when the tumor is large or difficult to remove. This is referred to as neoadjuvant therapy. Women with large Stage II or IIIA breast tumors often choose neoadjuvant therapy, usually with chemotherapy, before surgery.

After surgery, many women receive adjuvant chemotherapy, especially women with Stage II and III breast tumors. Adjuvant therapy is treatment given after the main treatment to increase the chances of a cure. Radiation treatment can kill cancer cells in and near the breast. Women may also have systemic treatment, such as chemotherapy, hormone therapy, or both. This treatment can destroy cancer cells that remain anywhere in the body and can prevent the cancer from coming back in the breast or elsewhere.

Stages IIIB and Inoperable IIIC

Women with Stage IIIB (including inflammatory breast cancer) or inoperable Stage IIIC breast cancer usually have chemotherapy. If the chemotherapy shrinks the tumor, the doctor then may suggest further treatment, such as a mastectomy, lymph node dissection and, possibly, radiation therapy.

Stage IV

In most cases, women with Stage IV breast cancer have hormone therapy, chemotherapy, or both. Some may also have biological therapy. Radiation may be used to control tumors in certain parts of the body. These treatments are not likely to cure the disease, but they may help improve survival.

Many women with stage IV disease also need supportive care along with anticancer treatments. Anticancer treatments are given to slow the progress of the disease. Supportive care helps manage pain, other symptoms, or side effects (such as nausea). It does not aim to extend a woman's life. Supportive care can help a woman feel better physically and emotionally. Some women with advanced cancer decide to have only supportive care.

Recurrent Breast Cancer

Approximately one in five breast cancer survivors who have completed 5 years of adjuvant therapy experience a recurrence within 10 years after their treatment; recurrence rates are estimated to be 11% at 5 years and 20% at 10 years after completion of adjuvant therapy (Brewster et al., 2008). Recurrence risk increases with higher stage cancers. Five-year recurrence rates are estimated to be 7%, 11%, and 13% for women with stages I, II, and II disease, respectively.

Treatment for the recurrent disease depends mainly on the location and extent of the cancer. Another important consideration is the type of treatment the woman had before. If breast cancer recurs only in the breast after breast-sparing surgery, the woman may have a mastectomy.

If breast cancer recurs in other parts of the body, treatment may involve chemotherapy, hormone therapy, or biological therapy. Typically chemotherapy involves different agents, as the tumor may have become resistant to the chemotherapy agents initially utilized. Radiation therapy may help control cancer that recurs in the chest muscles or in certain other areas of the body that are sensitive to radiation. Treatment is based on the location of the recurrence and prior treatment the woman has received.

Treatment can seldom cure cancer that recurs outside the breast. Supportive care is often an important part of the treatment plan. Treatment to relieve symptoms depends on where the cancer has metastasized. For example, pain due to bone metastases may be treated with external beam radiation therapy and/or bisphosphonates such as pamidronate (Aredia). See Appendix D for further review of nursing diagnoses.

REHABILITATION

A woman recovering from treatment for breast cancer faces some unique challenges. Among these are the need for post-surgery exercises (for patients undergoing mastectomy or lumpectomy), management of lymphedema, and the possibility of further surgery for reconstruction.

Exercises

For mastectomy or lumpectomy patients, exercising the arm and shoulder after surgery can help a woman regain motion, balance, and strength. Properly targeted and paced exercises can reduce pain and stiffness in her neck and back. These exercises typically start slowly within 1 to 2 days after surgery. Often a physical therapist can suggest exercises. In time, exercising can be more active and part of a woman's normal routine.

Lymphedema

Lymphedema is a troubling chronic adverse effect that can occur almost immediately after surgery or years later. It involves swelling of the affected arm and hand. Women should be instructed on how to monitor for this side effect, how to prevent it, and the importance of early intervention if lymphedema occurs.

Strategies to reduce and manage lymphedema include special techniques in massage, wrapping of the extremity with an elastic sleeve or cuff, exercises protecting the limb from injury, and infection control. Special physical therapists coordinate care of lymphedema patients.

Women need to protect the affected arm and hand for the rest of their lives. This includes:

- Avoid wearing tight clothing or jewelry on the affected arm

- Carry a purse or luggage with the other arm

- Use an electric razor to avoid cuts when shaving under the arm

- Have injections, blood tests, and blood pressure measurements on the other arm

- Wear gloves to protect the hands when gardening and when using strong detergents

- Have careful manicures and avoid cutting the cuticles

- Avoid burns or sunburns to the affected arm and hand

Breast Reconstruction

Patients with total mastectomies may choose to pursue reconstructive surgery at the time of the original mastectomy or later, after healing. Though some women are not interested in breast reconstruction, many breast specialists support reconstructive surgery as an important option for patients to consider. Women are encouraged to weigh both the advantages and disadvantages of breast reconstruction with their plastic surgeons and cancer treatment team and make an informed decision based on their own situations. The goal of breast reconstruction is to create breast symmetry when a woman is wearing a bra. When a woman is nude, the reconstructed breast will look different from the unaffected breast, regardless of the type of reconstruction chosen. However, when a woman is wearing a bra, the size and shape of the reconstructed breast should closely resemble the unaffected breast. In some cases breast reconstruction can be completed at the time of the initial surgery. In many cases it is completed after all treatments are finished.

The insertion of breast implants is usually a two-part procedure. The first implant operation involves placing a tissue expander in the intended breast area beneath the skin and chest muscle. The tissue expander is similar to a balloon, and the surgeon will fill the expander with saline solution (usually once a week). After the skin has sufficiently stretched, the surgeon will replace the tissue expander with a permanent implant, usually 3 to 4 months after the first implant surgery. Occasionally, a woman will not need a tissue expander. If this is the case, then the surgeon will proceed directly to permanent implant surgery. Approximately 50% of implants need some type of modification or replacement after 5 or 10 years.

Muscle flap procedures take much longer than implant operations, lasting about 4 to 5 hours, and patients typically stay in the hospital 3 to 4 days. Though the recovery is slower, the breast usually looks and feels more natural to most women. Because muscle flap reconstruction involves the blood vessels, women who smoke or have diabetes, vascular, or connective tissue diseases cannot typically undergo this type of breast reconstruction.

Because many breast cancers involve the nipple, the surgeon usually removes the nipple during mastectomy. After the breast volume has been rebuilt with a tissue expander or muscle flap procedure, the nipple may be recreated. Most nipple recreation takes place 2 to 6 months after the initial breast reconstruction to allow the new breast area ample time to heal. A new nipple may be created from a skin graft from a woman's inner thigh or from the areola (the pigmented region surrounding the nipple) on her unaffected breast. Occasionally after a skin graft, the skin of the newly created nipple turns white. Some surgeons prefer to tattoo the skin graft of the new nipple to ensure that the color matches the color of the nipple on the unaffected breast.

Breast Prosthesis

Women who do not have reconstruction need to use a prosthesis to ensure adequate weight replacement and cosmesis. Many options are available, so women usually need to go through a period of customizing and special fittings of available garments to accommodate their needs.

An external breast prosthesis is an artificial breast form that can be worn after the breast has been surgically removed. There are several different types of prostheses. They may be made from silicone gel, foam, fiberfill or other materials that feel similar to natural tissue. Most are weighted so that they feel the same as the remaining breast (if only one breast has been removed). Some adhere directly to the chest area while others are made to fit into pockets of post-mastectomy bras. Different types of prostheses may also have different features, such as a mock nipple or special shape. In many cases, a woman will be fitted for a prosthesis so that it can be custom-made for her body. Partial prostheses, called equalizers or enhancers, are also available for women who have had part of their breasts removed such as after a lumpectomy

It is very important that a woman be fitted for a prosthesis by a trained fitter. Usually a bra is fit first and then the prosthesis. Women going to a fitting should be encouraged to wear a tight fitting solid color top to the fitting, as it makes it easiest to check for symmetry. The woman should also bring the bras and swim suits she has worn in the past because it is often possible to use these garments with modifications.

If a woman chooses to wear a breast prosthesis that does not adhere directly to the skin, she will need to wear a special post-mastectomy bra with pockets for the breast form. Some very attractive swimsuits are also available and specially designed to hold breast forms. Some women find that special sleep or leisure bras, with or without pockets for a prosthesis, are comfortable to wear overnight.

Sexuality

Breast cancer surgery and treatment affects the woman's sexuality. Chapter 10 reviews some of the issues of sexuality.

Researchers have studied postmastectomy patients, especially related to their sexuality. Body image, not surprisingly, is a major concern of these women. Support and education for these women is key to their rehabilitation and ability to go on with their lives.

CASE STUDY: BREAST CANCER

*B*B is a 65-year-old Hispanic woman who presented to her primary care physician with symptoms of the flu (fever and chills). The physician took a throat swab and sent it to cytology for evaluation. Before BB left, he asked if he could do a CBE. (BB said she had not had a mammogram "for a while.") The physician also ordered a mammogram.

On CBE, the physician noted a fixed, irregular nodule on her outer right breast. Mammogram results came back suspicious for an opaque, irregular mass on the outer right breast.

BB was scheduled for an ultrasound guided fine needle aspiration. Results indicated invasive ductal carcinoma. Further workup included a bone scan, chest X-ray, and MRI.

After weighing her options with her primary physician, a breast surgeon, and radiation oncologist, BB opted to have a lumpectomy, followed by adjunctive radiation therapy. The lumpectomy procedure was unremarkable. (The excised nodule was 4 cm x 2 cm.) Based on sentinel node mapping, BB was found to have no positive nodes. BB's breast cancer was staged at Stage IIB (T2 N1M0). She went home 4 hours after the procedure.

Postoperatively, BB experienced some pain that resolved within a few days. She also had some nausea because of anesthesia, which resolved within 2 days of the procedure. She was instructed to reduce physical activity involving her right side for 7 to 10 days.

Radiation therapy began 4 weeks after surgery. A total of 5000 cGy was given (25 fractions) over 6 weeks (5 times/week). BB complained of skin irritation from the radiation therapy, which started 2 weeks after her therapy began. She was counseled to manage her mild erythema by washing with gentle soap and water, avoiding heat, and using unscented creams on her breast. The erythema resolved about 2 weeks after her treatments ended.

At 3 months postradiation therapy, BB had another mammogram. The results were negative for any new masses. As part of her new vigilance about breast health, BB began to be more conscientious with BSE and had a nurse practitioner provide a CBE every 6 months.

Continued follow-up every 6 months showed no new breast masses. Under a federally-sponsored program, BB had a yearly mammogram.

Additional Information:

BB started menopause at 50. (She believes she started menstruation at 13.) Her other health problems are obesity (50 pounds overweight), hypertension, and gout.

BB loves to cook for her family. She makes traditional Mexican dishes that use oils, fat, and spices for flavor. She also uses medication, which a local "herb" doctor in her neighborhood has recommended.

BB is a widow and the grandmother of seven. She splits her time between living with two of her daughters, who have families but work outside of the home. BB helps with housework and errands for her daughters, but she finds that her energy fades during the day and she does not have the stamina she had before her lumpectomy and radiation therapy.

One of BB's granddaughters has urged BB to ask about ovarian cancer, because the granddaughter says that she had heard that women with breast cancer "can get" ovarian cancer.

She is pleased with her recovery, but states she has second thoughts about whether she should have had her breast removed as treatment. She says some days she believes she should just have both breasts removed. Her physician has prescribed tamoxifen for her (because she was shown to be ER+) but she admits that she forgets some days to take her pills. Since Medicare does not *cover her prescription and BB is on a fixed income, she is reluctant to spend money for medication.*

Family and religion are extremely important to BB. Since her diagnosis of breast cancer was made, she has attended religious services more frequently. She cries easily around her family. She says she has trouble sleeping and cannot concentrate. She says she feels low more days than not.

What are BB's risk factors for breast cancer?

BB is obese and consumes a high fat diet. She does not appear to exercise. Like most women who develop breast cancer, she does not have other major risk factors for developing the disease.

BB questions whether she should undergo an oophorectomy or bilateral mastectomy. What might the nurse respond to her?

In general, if a woman has an identified mutation in BRCA1 or BRCA2 a prophylactic bilateral mastectomy and oophorectomy is recommended. Since BB does not have this risk factor she has received the standard of care.

BB admits to forgetting to take her tamoxifen. What should the nurse do?

Compliance with oral medication can be challenging. It is especially a problem in women who cannot afford the prescriptions. BB could be referred to a social worker who could try to obtain her tamoxifen through a compassionate need program or organization that provides financial assistance. BB needs to understand that tamoxifen is a very important part of her therapy because she has a hormonally sensitive tumor.

SUMMARY

Screening, early detection, and more effective treatments have led to a decline in the death rate for breast cancer. Ideally all breast cancer is detected in a noninvasive or preinvasive state such as DCIS. Early detection is best accomplished with the use of mammography, which is supplemented by CBE and, in some cases, BSE. Definitive risk factors for breast cancer are elusive, but it is known that breast cancer is a disease of aging. Genetic predispositions to breast cancer have also been identified. Early stage breast cancer is treated with surgery and radiation therapy. More advanced cancers follow multimodality protocols that also include chemotherapy, hormone therapies, and biological therapies. With early detection and appropriate therapy, the long-term prognosis for breast cancer is good.

EXAM QUESTIONS

CHAPTER 2
Questions 7-14

Note: Choose the one option that BEST answers each question.

7. The main risk factors for breast cancer are

    a. gender, age, and obesity.
    b. gender, age, and family history of breast cancer.
    c. gender, age, and use of oral contraceptives.
    d. gender, age, and use of hormone replacement therapy.

8. According to the American Cancer Society, breast cancer screening using mammography is routinely recommended for women beginning at age

    a. 20.
    b. 30.
    c. 40.
    d. 50.

9. An initial diagnostic workup for breast cancer might include

    a. clinical breast examination, mammography, ultrasound, and biopsy.
    b. positron emission tomography scan only.
    c. a CA-125 blood test.
    d. stereotactic needle biopsy.

10. If the pathology report states ductal carcinoma in situ, it indicates that

    a. there is involvement of the lymph nodes.
    b. the prognosis is poor.
    c. the malignancy has not metastasized.
    d. the malignant cells have extended beyond the basement membrane.

11. When staging early stage breast cancer, factors that lead to appropriate treatment are

    a. the age of the woman.
    b. family members with breast cancer.
    c. if the patient has smoked.
    d. the number of positive lymph nodes.

12. Neoadjuvant chemotherapy as a treatment for breast cancer is scheduled

    a. before surgery.
    b. during surgery.
    c. after surgery.
    d. as a sole modality.

13. Standard chemotherapy as a treatment for inoperable stage IIIC breast cancer includes

    a. anthracycline, alkylating agent, and taxane.
    b. progressive hormonal therapy.
    c. investigational drugs alone.
    d. watch and wait monitoring.

14. Muscle flap breast reconstruction procedures are usually not used if the patient

    a. has any positive lymph nodes.
    b. is diabetic.
    c. has large breasts.
    d. is uninsured.

REFERENCES

Altekruse, S.F., Kosary, C.L., Krapcho, M., Neyman, N., Aminou, R., Waldron, W., et al. (eds). (n.d.) *SEER Cancer Statistics Review, 1975-2007.* Bethesda, MD: National Cancer Institute. Retrieved from http://seer.cancer.gov/csr/1975_2007/, based on November 2009 SEER data submission, posted to the SEER web site, 2010.

American Cancer Society. (2009a). *Breast cancer: Early detection.* Retrieved July 19, 2010, from http://www.cancer.org/Cancer/BreastCancer/MoreInformation/BreastCancerEarlyDetection/breast-cancer-early-detection-new-screening-technologies

American Cancer Society. (2009b). *Breast cancer facts & figures 2009-2010.* Atlanta, GA: Author. Retrieved from http://our.cancer.org/downloads/STT/F861009_final%209-08-09.pdf

American Cancer Society. (2010a). *Breast cancer: Detailed guide, early detection, diagnosis, and staging.* Retrieved July 16, 2010, from http://www.cancer.org/Cancer/BreastCancer/DetailedGuide/breast-cancer-detection

American Cancer Society. (2010b). *Cancer facts & figures 2010.* Atlanta, GA: Author.

Anderson, G.L., Limacher, M., Assaf, A.R., Bassford, T., Beresford, S.A., Black, H., et al. (2004). Effects of conjugated equine estrogen in postmenopausal women with hysterectomy: The Women's Health Initiative randomized controlled trial. *Journal of the American Medical Association, 291*(14), 1701-1712.

Brandt-Rauf, S.I., Raveis, V.H., Drummond, N.F., Conte, J.A., & Rothman, S.M. (2006). Ashkenazi Jews and breast cancer: The consequences of linking ethnic identity to genetic disease. *American Journal of Public Health, 96*(11), 1979-1988.

Brewster, A.M., Hortobagyi, G.N., Broglio, K.R., Kau, S., Santa-Maria, C.A., Arun, B., et al. (2008). Residual risk of breast cancer recurrence 5 years after adjuvant therapy. *Journal of the National Cancer Institute, 100*(16), 1179-1183.

Centers for Disease Control and Prevention. (2007). *2006/2007 National breast and cervical cancer early detection program fact sheet.* Retrieved December 28, 2008, from http://screening.iarc.fr/doc/0607_nbccedp_fs.pdf

Chavez-MacGregor, M., Elias, S.G., Onland-Moret, N.C., van der Schouw, Y.T., Van Gils, C.H., Monninkhof, E., et al. (2005). Postmenopausal breast cancer risk and cumulative number of menstrual cycles. *Cancer Epidemiology, Biomarkers & Prevention, 14*(4), 799-804.

Claus, E.B., Schildkraut, J.M., Thompson, W.D., & Risch, N. (1996). The genetic attributable risk of breast and ovarian cancer. *Cancer, 77*(11), 2318-2324.

Colditz, G.A. (2005). Epidemiology and prevention of breast cancer. *Cancer Epidemiology, Biomarkers & Prevention, 14*(4), 768-772.

Collaborative Group on Hormonal Factors in Breast Cancer. (2002). Breast cancer and breastfeeding: Collaborative reanalysis of individual data from 47 epidemiological studies in 30 countries, including 50302 women with breast cancer and 96973 women without the disease. *Lancet, 360*(9328), 187-195.

Couch, F.J., DeShano, M.L., Blackwood, M.A., Calzone, K., Stopfer, J., Campeau, L., et al. (1997). BRCA1 mutations in women attending clinics that evaluate the risk of breast cancer. *New England Journal of Medicine, 336*(20), 1409-1415.

Decarli, A., Calza, S., Masala, G., Specchia, C., Palli, D., & Gail, M.H. (2006). Gail Model for prediction of absolute risk of invasive breast cancer: Independent evaluation in the Florence-European Prospective Investigation into cancer and nutrition cohort. *Journal of the National Cancer Institute, 98*(23), 1686-1693.

Dienger, M.J. (2004). Hormonal therapy in advanced and metastatic disease. In K. Dow (Ed.), *Contemporary issues in breast cancer* (2nd ed., pp. 175-186). Sudbury, MA: Jones & Bartlett.

Edge, S.B., Byrd, D.R., Carducci, M., Compton, C.C., Fritz, A.G., Greene, F.L., & Trotti, A. (2010). *AJCC cancer staging manual,* 7th ed., New York: Springer.

Evans, D.G., Eccles, D.M., Rahman, N., Young, K., Bulman, M., Amir, E., et al. (2004). A new scoring system for the chances of identifying a BRCA1/2 mutation outperforms existing models including BRCAPRO. *Journal of Medical Genetics, 41*(6), 474-480.

Frank, T.S., Deffenbaugh, A.M., Reid, J.E., Hulick, M., Ward, B.E., Lingenfelter, B., et al. (2002). Clinical characteristics of individuals with germline mutations in BRCA1 and BRCA2: Analysis of 10,000 individuals. *Journal of Clinical Oncology, 20*(6), 1480-1490.

Gawlick, U., Mone, M.C., Hansen, H.J., Connors, R.C., & Nelson, E.W. (2008). Selective use of intraoperative sentinel lymph node pathological evaluation in breast cancer. *American Journal of Surgery, 196*(6), 851-855.

Guillem, J.G., Wood, W.C., Moley, J.F., Berchuck, A., Karlan, B.Y., Mutch, D.G., et al. (2006). ASCO/SSO review of current role of risk-reducing surgery in common hereditary cancer syndromes. *Journal of Clinical Oncology, 24*(28), 4642-4660.

Gullatte, M.M. (2007). *Clinical guide to antineoplastic therapy: A chemotherapy handbook* (2nd ed.). Pittsburgh, PA: Oncology Nursing Society.

Harris, L., Fritsche, H., Mennel, R., Norton, L., Ravdin, P., Taube, S., et al. (2007). American Society of Clinical Oncology 2007 update of recommendations for the use of tumor markers in breast cancer. *Journal of Clinical Oncology, 25*(33), 5287-312.

Hayes, D.F. & Picard, M.H. (2006). Heart of darkness: The downside of trastuzumab. *Journal of Clinical Oncology, 24*(25), 4056-4058.

Hoskins, K.F., Zwaagstra, A., & Ranz, M. (2006). Validation of a tool for identifying women at high risk for hereditary breast cancer in population-based screening. *Cancer, 107*(8), 1769-1776.

Lynch, H.T., Snyder, C.L., Lynch, J.F., Riley, B.D., & Rubinstein, W.S. (2003). Hereditary breast-ovarian cancer at the bedside: Role of the medical oncologist. *Journal of Clinical Oncology, 21*(4), 740-753.

Marchbanks, P.A., McDonald, J.A., Wilson, H.G., Folger, S.G., Mandel, M.G., Daling, J.R., et al. (2002). Oral contraceptives and the risk of breast cancer. *New England Journal of Medicine, 346*(26), 2025-2032.

National Cancer Institute. (2010). *Breast cancer treatment PDQ.* Retrieved July 19, 2010, from http://www.cancer.gov/cancertopics/pdq/treatment/breast/HealthProfessional/allpages

National Comprehensive Cancer Network. (2010). *NCCN clinical practice guidelines in oncology, genetic testing in hereditary breast and ovarian cancer.* Retrieved July 3, 2010, from http://www.nccn.org

Nesvold, I.L., Dahl, A.A., Løkkevik, E., Marit Mengshoel, A., & Fosså, S.D. (2008). Arm and shoulder morbidity in breast cancer patients after breast-conserving therapy versus mastectomy. *Acta Oncologica, 47*(5), 835-842.

Newcomer, L.M., Newcomb, P.A., Trentham-Dietz, A., Longnecker, M.P., & Greenberg, E.R. (2003). Oral contraceptive use and risk of breast cancer by histologic type. *International Journal of Cancer, 106*(6), 961-964.

Parmigani, G., Chen, S., Iversen, E.S., Jr., Friebel, T.M., Finkelstein, D.M., Anton-Culver, H., et al. (2007). Validity of models for predicting BRCA1 and BRCA2 mutations. *Annals of Internal Medicine, 147*(7), 441-450.

Perun, J. (2004). Radiation therapy. In K. Dow (Ed.), *Contemporary issues in breast cancer* (2nd ed., pp. 110-133). Sudbury, MA: Jones & Bartlett.

Saslow, D., Boetes, C., Burke, W., Harms, S., Leach, M.O., Lehman, C.D., et al. (2007). American Cancer Society guidelines for breast screening with MRI as an adjunct to mammography. *CA: A Cancer Journal for Clinicians, 57*(2), 75-89.

Shattuck-Eidens, D., Oliphant, A., McClure, M., McBride, C., Gupte, J., Rubano, T., et al. (1997). BRCA1 sequence analysis in women at high risk for susceptibility mutations. Risk factor analysis and implications for genetic testing. *Journal of the American Medical Association, 278*(15), 1242-1250.

Singletary, S.E. (2003). Rating the risk factors for breast cancer. *Annals of Surgery, 237*(4), 474-482.

Travis, L.B., Hill, D.A., Dores, G.M., Gospodarowicz, M., van Leeuwen, F.E., Holowaty, E., et al. (2003). Breast cancer following radiotherapy and chemotherapy among young women with Hodgkin disease. *Journal of the American Medical Association, 290*(4), 465-475.

United Nations Population Fund. (2002). *Breast cancer: Increasing incidence, limited options.* Retrieved July 19, 2010, from http://screening.iarc.fr/doc/eol19_4-rev.pdf

Vogel, V.G., Costantino, J.P., Wickerham, D.L., Cronin, W.M., Cecchini, R.S., Atkins, J.N., et al. (2006). Effects of tamoxifen vs raloxifene on the risk of developing invasive breast cancer and other disease outcomes: The NSABP Study of tamoxifen and raloxifene (STAR) P-2 trial. *Journal of the American Medical Association, 295*(23), 2727-2741.

Wood, W.C., Muss, H.B., Solin, L.J., & Olopade, O.I. (2005). Malignant tumors of the breast. In V.T. DeVita, Jr., S. Hellman, & S.A. Rosenberg (Eds.), *Cancer: Principles and practice of oncology* (7th ed., pp. 1415-1477). Philadelphia: Lippincott Williams & Wilkins.

CHAPTER 3

ENDOMETRIAL CANCER

CHAPTER OBJECTIVE

After completing this chapter on endometrial cancer, the reader will be able to discuss the disease's epidemiology, risk factors, prevention and detection strategies, common staging schemas, and treatments.

LEARNING OBJECTIVES

After studying this chapter, the reader will be able to

1. identify the main risk factors for endometrial cancer.

2. describe a hereditary cancer syndrome associated with endometrial cancer

3. list tests included in the diagnostic workup of endometrial cancer.

4. cite terms that describe abnormal endometrial cells or their spread so that the cancer can be staged.

5. discuss treatment strategies for endometrial cancer.

6. identify adverse effects that women may experience after a hysterectomy.

INTRODUCTION

Endometrial cancer is the most common gynecologic cancer and is highly curable if detected early. The chapter will review those factors that increase a woman's risk for endometrial cancer. The standard treatment for endometrial cancer is surgery, sometimes accompanied by radiation therapy or chemotherapy.

EPIDEMIOLOGY

Cancer of the endometrium, or lining of the uterus, is the most common gynecologic malignancy and accounts for 6% of all cancers in women and 3% of all cancer deaths (American Cancer Society [ACS], 2010a). The ACS (2010a) estimates 43,370 new cases and 7950 deaths annually. Endometrial cancer is highly curable and the mortality rate has declined about 25% from 1974 to the present (ACS, 2010a). Box 3-1 contains other epidemiologic data about endometrial cancer

ANATOMY

The uterus is a hollow organ, about the size and shape of a medium-sized pear, that has two main components. The lower end of the uterus extends into the vagina and is referred to as the cervix. The upper part of the uterus is called the body and is known as the corpus (see Figure 3-1).

The body of the uterus has two layers. The inner layer or lining is called the endometrium. The outer layer of muscle is known as the myometrium. This thick layer of muscle is needed to push the

BOX 3-1: FACTS ABOUT ENDOMETRIAL CANCER

- Incidence rates of endometrial cancer have been decreasing by about 0.5% per year since 1997, after a period of increase during the previous decade.

- Death rates from cancer of the uterine corpus have been stable since 1992, after decreasing an average of 1.5% per year from 1975 to1992.

- The 1- and 5-year relative survival rates for uterine corpus cancer are 92% and 83%, respectively.

- The 5-year survival rate is 96%, 67%, and 17%, if the cancer is diagnosed at local, regional, or distant stages, respectively.

- Relative survival for Caucasians exceeds that for African Americans by more than 8 percentage points at every stage.

(ACS, 2010a)

FIGURE 3-1: ANATOMY OF THE UTERUS

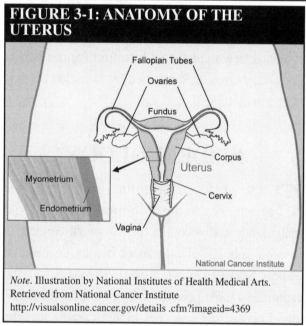

Note. Illustration by National Institutes of Health Medical Arts. Retrieved from National Cancer Institute http://visualsonline.cancer.gov/details .cfm?imageid=4369

baby out during birth. The tissue coating the outside of the uterus is the serosa.

Hormone changes during a woman's menstrual cycle cause the endometrium to change. The ovaries produce estrogens during the early part of the cycle, before they release an egg (ovulation). Estrogen causes the endometrium to thicken so that it can nourish an embryo if pregnancy occurs. If there is no pregnancy, estrogen is produced in lower amounts and more of the hormone called progesterone is made after ovulation. This causes the innermost layer of the lining to prepare to shed. By the end of the cycle, the endometrial lining is shed from the uterus and becomes the menstrual flow. This cycle repeats throughout a woman's life until menopause, unless interrupted for pregnancy.

RISK FACTORS

Table 3-1 reviews known risk factors associated with endometrial cancer. These should be considered as a group of risk factors – usually no one factor carries a supreme risk. However, multiple risk factors combine as cofactors and appear to increase the risks for women. All women are at risk for endometrial cancer and women need to remember that the risk increases steadily with age.

Some women have a hereditary risk for developing endometrial cancer, which is a component of a genetic syndrome known as hereditary nonpolyposis colorectal cancer (HNPCC) or Lynch syndrome. Identification of families with this syndrome is important because screening and prevention strategies are more rigorous than for women in the general population.

Key indicators of HNPCC are shown in Table 3-2. Any woman who presents with such a family history should be referred to a genetics professional for a more thorough evaluation.

The autosomal dominant syndrome known as HNPCC accounts for 3% to 5% of all colorectal cancer (Lynch & de la Chapelle, 2003). Key indicators include a family history of colon, endometrial, ovarian, gastric, bile duct, small bowel, renal pelvis, and ureter cancers (Lynch & Lynch, 2006). The majority of mutations responsible for HNPCC occur in four mismatched repair genes: MSH2, MLH1, PMS2, and MSH6.

TABLE 3-1: RISK FACTORS FOR ENDOMETRIAL CANCER

Risk Factor	Etiology
Hormonal Factors	Many of the risk factors for endometrial cancer affect estrogen levels. Before menopause, the ovaries are the main source of estrogen and progesterone. A shift in the balance of these two hormones toward more estrogen increases a woman's risk of developing endometrial cancer. After menopause, the ovaries stop making these hormones, but a small amount of estrogen is still made naturally in fat tissue. This estrogen has a bigger impact after menopause than it does before menopause.
Estrogen Stimulation	Hormone replacement therapy can reduce hot flashes and improve vaginal dryness that can occur with menopause. Estrogen alone (without progesterone) can lead to endometrial cancer. Progesterone-like drugs must be given along with estrogen to avoid the increased risk of endometrial cancer. This approach is called combination hormone therapy and reduces endometrial cancer risk. Usually this is recommended for less than 5 years.
Total Number of Menstrual Cycles	Having more menstrual cycles during a woman's lifetime raises her risk of endometrial cancer. Menarche before age 12 or going through menopause later in life raises the risk.
Obesity	Although most of a woman's estrogen is produced by her ovaries, fat tissue can change some other hormones into estrogens. Having more fat tissue can increase a woman's estrogen levels and therefore increase her endometrial cancer risk. In comparison with women who maintain a healthy weight, endometrial cancer is twice as common in overweight women, and more than three times as common in obese women.
Tamoxifen Therapy	Tamoxifen can be a very effective treatment for estrogen receptor positive breast cancer. Tamoxifen acts as an anti estrogen in breast tissue, but it acts like an estrogen in the uterus. It can cause the uterine lining to grow, which increases the risk of endometrial cancer. The risk of developing endometrial cancer from tamoxifen is small – about 1 in 500. Women taking tamoxifen must balance this small risk against the value of this drug in treating breast cancer and reducing the chance of cancer in the other breast.
Age	Risk increases with age probably because cells are more sensitive to carcinogenic substances.
Polycystic Ovary Disease	Women with a condition called polycystic ovarian syndrome have abnormal hormone levels, such as higher estrogen levels and lower levels of progesterone. The increase in estrogen relative to progesterone can increase a woman's chance of getting endometrial cancer.
Diabetes	Endometrial cancer may be as much as four times more common in women with diabetes. Although diabetes is more common in people who are overweight, even diabetics who are not overweight have a higher risk of endometrial cancer.
High-Fat Diet	A high-fat diet can increase the risk of several cancers, including endometrial cancer. Because fatty foods are also high-calorie foods, a high-fat diet can lead to obesity, which is a well-known endometrial cancer risk factor. High-fat foods may also have a direct effect on estrogen metabolism, which increases endometrial cancer risk.
Endometrial Hyperplasia	Mild or simple hyperplasia, which is the most common type, has a very small risk of becoming malignant. It may resolve on its own or after treatment with hormone therapy. If the hyperplasia is called "atypical," it has a higher chance of becoming a cancer. Simple atypical hyperplasia turns into cancer in about 8% of cases if it is not treated. Complex atypical hyperplasia has a risk of becoming cancerous if not treated in up to 29% of cases.

(ACS, 2010b; Amant, Moerman, & Neven, 2005)

TABLE 3-2: KEY INDICATORS OF HEREDITARY NONPOLYPOSIS COLORECTAL CANCER (HNPCC)

- Personal history of colorectal or endometrial cancer diagnosed before 50 years of age.

- First-degree relative with colorectal cancer diagnosed before 50 years of age.

- Two or more relatives with colorectal cancer or an HNPCC-associated cancer, which includes endometrial, ovarian, stomach, hepatobiliary, small bowel, renal pelvis, or ureter cancer. The one relative must be a first-degree relative of another.

- Colorectal cancer occurring in two or more generations on the same side of the family.

- A personal history of colorectal cancer and a first-degree relative with adenomas diagnosed before 40 years of age.

- An affected relative with a known HNPCC mutation.

(Guillem et al., 2006; Lindor et al., 2006)

Although not associated with large numbers of polyps, persons with HNPCC who do form colorectal adenomatous polyps are more likely to do so at an earlier age, more likely to develop right-sided colon cancer, and exhibit a very rapid progression to malignancy in 1 to 3 years instead of the 5 to 10 year pattern seen in the general population (Lynch & de la Chapelle, 2003). Persons with HNPCC have a 70% to 80% lifetime risk of developing colorectal cancer, a 60% risk of developing endometrial cancer, 13% risk of developing stomach cancer, and a 12% risk of developing ovarian cancer.

Since HNPCC is associated with increased risks to the endometrium and ovaries, females with the mutation need to consider careful surveillance. This usually includes annual or semi-annual transvaginal ultrasound of the endometrium and ovaries with concurrent endometrial aspiration for pathological evaluation and CA-125 testing (Levin et al., 2006); however, the ultrasound has limited utility in evaluating endometrial thickness in premenopausal women because of cyclic changes. CA-125 is a tumor marker that is routinely utilized to monitor for recurrence in women with documented ovarian cancer; it is sometimes monitored in women with a high risk for ovarian cancer that is associated with HNPCC, as a screening test for ovarian cancer.

Chemoprevention is another strategy sometimes considered in these families. The exact efficacy of

nonsteroidal anti-inflammatory drugs and aspirin in decreasing gastrointestinal cancers is not known (Lindor et al., 2006; Levin et al., 2006). Because oral contraceptive pills have been associated with decreased risk of developing ovarian and endometrial cancer, some women choose to consider this strategy (Lindor et al., 2006).

Prophylactic colectomy in HNPCC is controversial. It is not associated with a large increase in life expectancy over annual colonoscopy (Lynch & de la Chapelle, 2003). It is generally reserved for persons in whom colonoscopy is not technically possible or the individual who refuses regular screening (Guillem et al., 2006).

Because the risks of endometrial and ovarian cancer are substantial and screening may be ineffective, many women will consider a total abdominal hysterectomy with bilateral salpingo-oophorectomy at 35 years of age or older if childbearing is complete (Lindor et al., 2006). These women need to be aware of the risks of a premature menopause and that this surgery typically requires 4 to 8 weeks of recuperation. Table 3-3 lists management recommendations for people with HNPCC.

PREVENTION

For years, surgery – specifically hysterectomy – was the key strategy to prevent endometrial

TABLE 3-3: MANAGEMENT RECOMMENDATIONS FOR PERSONS WITH HEREDITARY NONPOLYPOSIS COLORECTAL CANCER (HNPCC)

Screening Recommendations

- Colonoscopy with removal of polyps annually starting between 20 and 25 years of age
- Consider gastroscopy and upper endoscopy
- Biannual pelvic examination beginning at 25 years of age
- Annual or biannual transvaginal ultrasound with color Doppler beginning at 25 years of age
- Annual or biannual serum CA-125 testing

Prevention Measures

- Consider chemoprevention with aspirin or nonsteroidal anti-inflammatory drugs
- Consider colectomy in patients who cannot or will not undergo regular colonoscopy
- Consider chemoprevention with oral contraceptives
- Prophylactic hysterectomy including bilatleral salpingo oophorectomy between 35 and 40 years of age if childbearing is complete

(Guillem et al., 2006; Lindor et al., 2006)

cancer. However, reducing the risk of endometrial cancer is preferable. Currently, prevention efforts are targeted in ways that reduce risk factors of endometrial cancer.

Risk factor prevention strategies include weight loss, a low-fat diet, and careful use of exogenous estrogen hormones. It is recommended that any woman taking hormone replacement therapy take it with a progestin and for as short of time as necessary. Other prevention strategies include a high assessment alert and follow-through in treating symptoms of abnormal uterine bleeding.

Using oral contraceptives reduces the risk of endometrial cancer (Harris, Wei, Chu, & Acs, 2004). The risk is lowest in women who take the pill for more than 10 years, and the protection continues for at least 10 years after a woman stops taking them. However, it is important to look at all of the risks and benefits when choosing a contraceptive method – endometrial cancer risk is only one factor to be considered. The risk of breast cancer may be increased in women who use oral contraceptives.

BENIGN UTERINE CONDITIONS

The most common type of cancer of the uterus begins in the endometrium. (Frequently uterine cancer and endometrial cancer are used interchangeably). Common benign conditions include fibroids, endometriosis, and endometrial hyperplasia. A diagnostic evaluation is indicated to rule out malignancy.

Benign tumors that form in the uterus are called fibroids. The medical term for a fibroid is leiomyoma, which refers to a proliferation or abnormal growth of smooth muscle tissue. Uterine fibroids arise from the tissue in the muscle layer of the wall of the uterus, called the myometrium and are not malignant. The etiology of why some women develop fibroids is not yet understood. Family history may play a role because there is often a history of fibroids developing in women of the same family. Fibroids are two to three times more common in African American women as compared to Caucasian women. Women who are overweight have an increased risk of fibroids. (Maizlin, Vos, & Cooperberg, 2007).

Most women with fibroids probably go through life not even knowing they have them, because fibroids are often found incidentally during diagnostic or therapeutic procedures. Fibroids are common and may occur to some degree in up to 50% of women.

Most women with uterine fibroids have no symptoms. However, fibroids can cause a number of symptoms, depending on their size, location within the uterus, and how close they are to adjacent pelvic organs. Large fibroids can cause:

- pelvic pressure

- severe, localized pain, particularly when they are deteriorating

- pressure on the bladder with frequent or obstructed urination

- pressure on the rectum with pain during defecation.

Abnormal uterine bleeding is the most common symptom of a fibroid. If the tumors are near the uterine lining, or interfere with the blood flow to the lining, they can cause heavy, painful and prolonged periods or spotting between menses.

Another benign condition of the uterus is endometriosis. Endometrial cells are the same cells that are shed each month during menstruation. The cells of endometriosis attach themselves to tissue outside the uterus and are called endometriosis implants. These implants are most commonly found on the ovaries, the fallopian tubes, outer surfaces of the uterus or intestines, and on the surface lining of the pelvic cavity. They can also be found in the vagina, cervix, and bladder (Speroff & Fritz, 2005).

Endometriosis affects women in their reproductive years. The exact prevalence of endometriosis is not known because many women may have the condition and have no symptoms. Endometriosis is estimated to affect over one million women (estimates range from 3% to 18% of women) in the U.S. (Speroff & Fritz, 2005). It is one of the leading causes of pelvic pain and reasons for laparoscopic surgery and hysterectomy in the U.S. Most cases of endometriosis are diagnosed in women between 25 and 35 years of age. Endometriosis is rare in postmenopausal women and is more commonly found in Caucasian women than in African American and Asian women. Studies further suggest that endometriosis is most common in taller, thin women with a low body mass index. Delaying pregnancy until an older age is also believed to increase the risk of developing endometriosis.

The cause of endometriosis is unknown. One theory is that the endometrial tissue is deposited in unusual locations by the backing up of menstrual flow into the fallopian tubes and the pelvic and abdominal cavity during menstruation (termed retrograde menstruation). The cause of retrograde menstruation is not clearly understood; however, retrograde menstruation cannot be the sole cause of endometriosis. Many women have retrograde menstruation in varying degrees but not all of them develop endometriosis (Guidice & Kao, 2004).

It is also likely that direct transfer of endometrial tissues during surgery may be responsible for the endometriosis implants sometimes seen in surgical scars (for example, episiotomy or cesarean delivery scars). Some studies have shown alterations in the immune response in women with endometriosis, which may affect the body's natural ability to recognize and destroy any misdirected growth of endometrial tissue (Guidice & Kao, 2004).

Most women who have endometriosis do not have symptoms. Of those who do experience symptoms, the common symptoms are pain (usually pelvic) and infertility. Other symptoms related to endometriosis include:

- lower abdominal pain

- diarrhea and constipation

- lower back pain

- irregular or heavy menstrual bleeding

- blood in the urine.

Endometriosis may be suspected by the practitioner because of the woman's pattern of symptoms and may sometimes be found during a physical examination; however, the diagnosis is confirmed by surgery, usually laparoscopy. Treatment of endometriosis includes medication and surgery for pain relief and treatment of infertility, if pregnancy is desired (Guidice & Kao, 2004).

Endometrial hyperplasia is a condition that occurs when the endometrium grows too much. It is a benign condition. In some cases, however, it can lead to cancer of the uterus. Endometrial hyperplasia is more likely to occur in certain women (Ely, Kennedy, Clark, & Bowdler, 2006). Those most at risk are women who:

- are in the years around menopause

- skip menstrual periods or have no periods at all

- are overweight

- have diabetes

- have polycystic ovary syndrome

- take estrogen without progesterone to replace the estrogen their bodies are no longer making and to relieve symptoms of menopause

- are on tamoxifen therapy.

The presence of abnormal vaginal bleeding, which is the most common symptom of endometrial hyperplasia, along with any of the risk factors, should be followed by a diagnostic evaluation with ultrasound, endometrial biopsy, dilatation and curettage, or hysteroscopy. One or more tests may be required.

In most cases, endometrial hyperplasia can be treated with medication that is a form of the hormone progesterone. Taking progesterone will cause the lining to shed and prevent it from building up again. It will often cause vaginal bleeding.

Hysterectomy may be an option if no further pregnancies are desired and the biopsy shows atypical hyperplasia.

Women can take steps to reduce the risk of endometrial hyperplasia. Those who take estrogen after menopause should take a form of progesterone to reduce the risk of endometrial hyperplasia and cancer of the uterus. For those who are overweight, losing weight may help.

SIGNS AND SYMPTOMS

The most common symptom of endometrial cancer is abnormal or unexpected vaginal bleeding, especially after menopause. Up to 20% of women who have abnormal bleeding after menopause will have endometrial cancer (Mutch, 2003).

Abnormal bleeding in women older than 35 years of age who have not started menopause may also be a symptom of endometrial cancer, though this is less common. In rare cases, an unexplained abnormal vaginal discharge may be an early symptom.

Symptoms of more advanced endometrial cancer include:

- difficult or painful urination

- pain in the pelvic area

- a pelvic lump

- weight loss.

Other conditions with similar symptoms include cervical cancer and benign uterine conditions. For this reason, any symptom should be evaluated carefully.

EARLY DETECTION AND DIAGNOSTIC EVALUATION

In most cases, being alert to any signs and symptoms of endometrial cancer, such as abnormal vaginal bleeding or discharge, and reporting them promptly, followed by an appropriate diagnostic evaluation, allows the disease to be diagnosed at an early stage.

At this time, there are no tests or exams that can find endometrial cancer early in women who are at average endometrial cancer risk and have no symptoms. The ACS (2010a) recommends that, at the time of menopause, all women should be told about the risks and symptoms of endometrial cancer and strongly encouraged to report any vaginal bleeding or spotting to their doctors. Women should talk to their doctors about getting regular pelvic exams. Although the pelvic exam can find some cancers, including some advanced uterine cancers, it is not very effective in finding early endometrial cancers. Although the Pap test can find some early endometrial cancers, it is not a good test for this type of cancer. The Pap test is very effective in finding early cancers of the cervix.

The ACS (2010a) recommends that most women at increased risk should be informed of their risk, offered annual screening with endometrial biopsy and/or transvaginal ultrasound, and advised to see their doctors whenever there is any abnormal vaginal bleeding. This includes women whose risk of endometrial cancer is increased due to increasing age, late menopause, never giving birth, infertility, obesity, diabetes, high blood pressure, estrogen treatment, or tamoxifen therapy. Women on tamoxifen therapy need to evaluate if the potential benefit in reducing breast cancer risk is greater than the slightly increased risk of developing endometrial cancer.

A pelvic examination is a routine procedure used to assess the well-being of female patients' lower genito urinary tracts. This is done as part of a usual health screening and prevention tool, and is an element of the total healthcare for the female patient. This is demonstrated in Figure 3-2.

During the bimanual examination, the examiner will place an index and middle finger into the vagina to first examine the vaginal walls for any irregularities or tenderness. The cervix will then be palpated in order to note its shape, consistency, mobility, and any tenderness. The examiner will

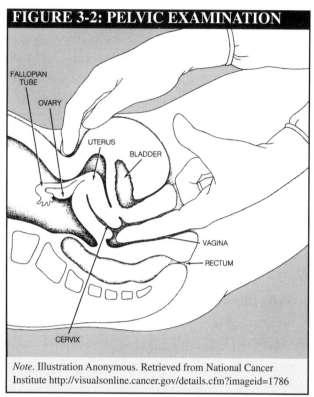

FIGURE 3-2: PELVIC EXAMINATION

FALLOPIAN TUBE
OVARY
UTERUS
BLADDER
VAGINA
RECTUM
CERVIX

Note. Illustration Anonymous. Retrieved from National Cancer Institute http://visualsonline.cancer.gov/details.cfm?imageid=1786

then place his or her other hand on the abdomen and gently push down while pushing the cervix up. This is done to assess the size and shape of the uterus and also to note any tenderness or abnormal lesions. During this time, the ovaries are also checked for any masses or tenderness.

The last part of the pelvic exam is the rectovaginal examination. This allows the clinician to better examine the pelvic organs and structures. The examiner will place an index finger into the vagina and a lubricated, gloved middle finger against the anus. The patient will then be asked to bear down in order for the anal sphincter to relax. As relaxation occurs, the examiner will insert the middle finger into the rectum, enabling the position and shape of the uterus to be better assessed. In addition, any masses or tenderness can be evaluated at this point. The anal canal and rectum can also be examined for polyps or other lesions at this time.

The presence of any unexplained vaginal bleeding requires a diagnostic evaluation to determine if the condition is a benign or malignant one. Table 3-4 provides an overview of the various diagnostic procedures used in such an evaluation. The diagnosis is made after obtaining a tissue sample.

PATHOLOGY

Endometrial cancers start in the cells that line the uterus and belong to the group of cancers called carcinomas. Most endometrial carcinomas are cancers of the cells that form glands in the endometrium. These are called adenocarcinomas and account for about 80% of endometrial cancers. Other rare types of endometrial carcinomas include squamous cell and undifferentiated.

Some endometrial cancers contain squamous cells (squamous cells are flat, thin cells that can be found on the outer surface of the cervix) as well as glandular cells. A cancer with both types of cells is called an adenocarcinoma with squamous differentiation. If, under the microscope, the glandular cells look cancerous but the squamous cells do not, the tumor may be called an adenoacanthoma. If both the squamous cells and the glandular cells look malignant, these tumors can be called adenosquamous carcinomas. There are other types of endometrial cancers, such as secretory carcinoma, ciliated carcinoma, and mucinous adenocarcinoma.

The grade of an endometrial cancer is based on how much the cancer forms glands that look similar to the glands found in normal, healthy endometrium.

* Grade 1 tumors have 95% or more of the cancerous tissue forming glands.

* Grade 2 tumors have between 50% and 94% of the cancerous tissue forming glands.

* Grade 3 tumors have less than half of the cancerous tissue forming glands.

Grade 3 cancers are called "high-grade." They tend to be aggressive and have a poorer outcome than low-grade cancers (grades 1 and 2).

Some less common forms of endometrial adenocarcinoma are clear-cell carcinoma, serous carci-

TABLE 3-4: TESTS USED IN THE DIAGNOSTIC EVALUATION OF ENDOMETRIAL CANCER	
Endometrial Biopsy	An endometrial biopsy is the most commonly performed test for endometrial cancer. It can be done in the doctor's office. In this procedure, a very thin flexible tube is inserted into the uterus through the cervix. Then, using suction, a small amount of endometrium is removed through the tube. The suctioning takes about a minute or less. The discomfort is similar to menstrual cramps and can be helped by taking a nonsteroidal anti-inflammatory drug such as ibuprofen before the procedure. Transvaginal ultrasound is often done before the biopsy. This helps the examiner locate any suspicious areas that should be biopsied.
Hysteroscopy	For this technique a tiny telescope (about 1/6 inch in diameter) is inserted into the uterus through the cervix. To get a better view of the inside of the uterus, the uterus is filled with saline solution. This lets the examiner visualize and biopsy anything that appears abnormal. This is usually done with the patient awake, using a local anesthetic. This is the most accurate way of directly examining for cancer.
Dilitation and Curettage (D&C)	If the endometrial biopsy sample does not provide enough tissue, or if the biopsy suggests cancer but the results are uncertain, a D&C must be done. The opening of the cervix is enlarged (dilated) and a currette is used to scrape tissue from inside the uterus. This may be done with or without a hysteroscopy. The procedure takes about an hour and may require general anesthesia or conscious sedation. A D&C is usually done in an outpatient surgery area. Most women have little discomfort after this procedure.

(ACS, 2010c; Amant, 2005)

noma, and poorly differentiated carcinoma. These cancers are more aggressive than most endometrial cancers. They tend to grow quickly and often have metastasized at the time of diagnosis.

STAGING

The main system used to stage endometrial cancer is called the FIGO (International Federation of Gynecology and Obstetrics) system (FIGO staging for corpus cancer, 1992). This is a surgical staging system, which means that it is based on examination of tissue removed during a surgical procedure. The FIGO system classifies the cancer in stages I through IV, with some of these stages being further divided. A system that is used to stage most cancers is the TNM system of the American Joint Committee on Cancer (AJCC) (Edge et al, 2010). For endometrial cancer, the stages in the TNM system exactly match those in FIGO. This means that stage I in FIGO is the same as the AJCC stage I, stage IIA in FIGO is the same as stage IIA in AJCC, and so on.

A doctor may order tests before surgical staging, such as a transvaginal ultrasound, MRI, or CT scan, to look for signs that a cancer has spread. Although it is not as good as the surgical stage, this information can be helpful in planning surgery and other treatment. These tests may result in the need to refer a patient to a gynecologic oncologist.

The staging system identifies the extent of the malignant disease. Endometrial cancer can spread locally to other parts of the uterus. It can also spread regionally to nearby lymph nodes. The regional lymph nodes are found in the pelvis and more distantly along the aorta. The lymph nodes along the aorta are called para-aortic nodes. Finally, the cancer can metastasize to distant lymph nodes or organs, such as the lung, liver, bone, brain, and others.

TREATMENT

The choice of treatment for endometrial cancer depends on the size of the tumor, the stage of the disease, whether female hormones affect tumor growth, and the tumor grade. The grade determines differences between normal and abnormal cells. Grading the tumor can also indicate how quickly the cells are growing. Low-grade cancers typically grow slower than high-grade tumors.

Staging is key to directing treatment decisions. Table 3-5 lists staging schema for endometrial cancer from two accepted sources – AJCC and FIGO.

Staging also provides prognostic information (ACS, 2010c; Chu, Lin, & Rubin, 2008). Relative 5-year survival rates by stage for endometrial adenocarcinoma are:

- Stage IA: 99%
- Stage IB: 99%
- Stage IC: 92%
- Stage II: 80%
- Stage III: 60%
- Stage IV: 30%

Surgery

The main treatment for endometrial cancer is an operation to remove the uterus and cervix, called a hysterectomy. When the uterus is removed through an incision in the abdomen, it is called a simple or total abdominal hysterectomy. If the uterus is removed through the vagina, it is known as a vaginal hysterectomy. Removal of the ovaries and fallopian tubes is not actually part of a hysterectomy. It is a separate procedure known as a bilateral salpingo-oophorectomy, which is almost always done in the same operation as a hysterectomy. To decide what stage the cancer is in, lymph nodes in the pelvis and around the aorta will also need to be removed. This can be done through the same incision as the abdominal hysterectomy. If a vaginal hysterectomy is done, lymph nodes can be removed by laparoscopy.

TABLE 3-5: ENDOMETRIAL CANCER STAGING SUMMARY

- Stage IA – No or less than half myometrial invasion
- Stage IB – Invasion equal to or more than half of the myometrium
- Stage II – Tumor invades cervical stroma but does not extend beyond the uterus
- Stage III – Local and/or regional spread of the tumor
- Stage IIIA – Tumor invades the serosa of the corpus uteri and/or adnexa
- Stage IIIB – Vaginal metastasis and/or parametrial involvement
- Stage IIIC – Metastases to pelvic and/or para-aortic lymph nodes
- Stage IIIC1 – Positive pelvic nodes
- Stage IIIC2 – Positive para-aortic lymph nodes with or without positive pelvic nodes
- Stage IV – Tumor invasion of bladder and/or bowel mucosa and/or distant metastases
- Stage IVA – Tumor invasion of bladder and/or bowel mucosa
- Stage IVB – Distant metastases, including intra-abdominal and/or inguinal lymph node

(Creasman, 2009; Edge et al., 2010)

A radical hysterectomy is done when endometrial cancer has spread to the cervix or the area around the cervix (the parametrium). In this operation, the entire uterus, both ovaries and fallopian tubes, the tissues next to the uterus (parametrium and uterosacral ligaments), and the upper part of the vagina (next to the cervix) are all removed. This operation is most often done through an incision in the abdomen, but it can also be done through the vagina. When a vaginal approach is used, laparoscopy is used to help safely remove all of the correct tissues.

The pelvic and para-aortic lymph node dissection removes lymph nodes from the pelvis and the area next to the aorta to determine if they contain cancer cells. In women who have had a vaginal hysterectomy, these lymph nodes can be removed through laparoscopic surgery. In a lymph node dissection, most or all of the lymph nodes in a certain area are removed. When only a few of the lymph nodes in an area are removed, it is called lymph node sampling.

In many cases, the surgeon will do a pelvic washing, in which the surgeon "washes" the abdominal and pelvic cavities with saline solution and sends the fluid to the lab to see if it contains cancer cells.

Some patients also have an omentectomy: removal of the layer of fatty tissue that covers the abdominal contents like an apron. Cancer sometimes spreads to this tissue and it is removed during a hysterectomy to see if cancer has spread there.

For an abdominal hysterectomy, the hospital stay is usually from 3 to 7 days. The average hospital stay after a radical hysterectomy is about 5 to 7 days. Complete recovery can take about 4 to 6 weeks. A laparoscopic procedure and vaginal hysterectomy usually require a hospital stay of 1 to 2 days and 2 to 3 weeks for recovery. Complications are unusual but could include excessive bleeding, wound infection, and damage to the urinary or intestinal systems. Common symptoms women experience during the recovery period include gastrointestinal disturbance, fatigue, and incisional pain.

Any hysterectomy causes infertility. For those who were premenopausal before surgery, removing the ovaries will cause menopause. This can lead to symptoms such as hot flashes, night sweats, and vaginal dryness.

Radiation Therapy

Radiation therapy alone is an option when the cancer is localized to cells in a specific area. In earlier stage endometrial cancers, when the cells are considered high-grade, radiation treatment is coupled with surgery. These cancers can be staged at I, II, or III (Mutch 2003). Radiation therapy to the cancerous area can shrink the tumor before or after surgery. This is done in cases when the woman is a poor surgical candidate because of preexisting health problems.

Some patients need external and internal radiation therapies. Both therapies can be used when the tumor is large and fixed to the pelvic wall or other critical structures. Clinicians use two types of radiation therapy to treat endometrial cancer.

External Radiation

In this type of treatment, the radiation is delivered from a source outside of the body. External beam radiation therapy is often given 5 days a week for 4 to 6 weeks. The skin covering the treatment area is carefully marked with permanent ink or injected dye, similar to a tattoo. A mold of the pelvis and lower back is custom made to ensure that the woman is placed in the exact same position for each treatment. Although each treatment takes less than a half-hour, the daily visits to the radiation center may be tiring and inconvenient.

Internal Radiation

For vaginal brachytherapy, a cylinder containing a source of radiation is inserted into the vagina. With this method, the radiation mainly treats the area in contact with the cylinder, such as the vaginal cuff. Nearby structures, such as the bladder and rectum, get less radiation exposure than the area in contact with the cylinder. This procedure is done in the radiation suite of the hospital or care center. About 4 to 6 weeks after the hysterectomy, the surgeon or radiation oncologist inserts a special applicator into the woman's vagina, and pellets of radioactive material are inserted into the applicator.

Side Effects of Radiation Therapy

Common side effects of radiation therapy include tiredness, upset stomach, or loose bowels. Serious fatigue, which may not occur until about 2 weeks after treatment begins, is a common side effect. Diarrhea is common, but can usually be controlled with over-the-counter medicines. Nausea and vomiting may also occur, but can be treated with medication. Side effects tend to be worse when chemotherapy is given with radiation.

Skin changes are also common, with the skin in the treated area looking and feeling sunburned. As the radiation passes through the skin to the cancer, it may damage the skin cells. This can cause irritation ranging from mild temporary redness to permanent discoloration. The skin may release fluid, which can lead to infection, so care must be taken to clean and protect the area exposed to radiation.

Radiation can irritate the bladder and problems with urination may occur. Irritation to the bladder, called radiation cystitis, can result in discomfort and an urge to urinate often.

Radiation can also lead to low blood counts, causing anemia (low red blood cells) and leukopenia (low white blood cells). The blood counts usually return to normal after radiation is stopped.

Pelvic radiation therapy may cause scar tissue to form in the vagina. The scar tissue can make the vagina shorter or more narrow (called vaginal stenosis), which can make vaginal intercourse painful. A woman can help prevent this problem by stretching the walls of her vagina several times a week. This can be done by having sexual intercourse 3 to 4 times per week or by using a vaginal dilator (a plastic or rubber tube used to stretch out the vagina). Nurses can support patients through these adverse effects with appropriate interventions. (See Appendix B, Selected Nursing Diagnoses for Radiation Therapy.)

Hormone Therapy

Hormone therapy is a treatment option when a woman is not a candidate for surgery or radiation therapy. It is also a treatment for metastatic disease.

Progestins

The main hormone treatment for endometrial cancer uses progesterone-like drugs called progestins. The two most commonly used progestins are medroxyprogesterone acetate (Provera) and megestrol acetate (Megace). These work by slowing the growth of endometrial cancer cells. Side effects can include increased blood sugar levels in patients with diabetes. Hot flashes, night sweats, and weight gain may also occur. Rarely, serious blood clots are seen in patients on progestins.

Tamoxifen

Tamoxifen, an antiestrogen drug often used to treat breast cancer, may also be used to treat advanced or recurrent endometrial cancer. The goal of tamoxifen therapy is to prevent any estrogens circulating in the woman's body from stimulating growth of the cancer cells. Even though tamoxifen may prevent estrogen from nourishing the cancer cells, it acts like a weak estrogen in other areas of the body. It does not cause bone loss, but can cause hot flashes and vaginal dryness. Women taking tamoxifen also have an increased risk of serious blood clots in the legs.

Gonadotropin-releasing Hormone Agonists

Most women with endometrial cancer have had their ovaries removed as a part of treatment. In others, radiation treatments have made their ovaries inactive. This reduces the production of estrogen and may also slow the growth of the cancer. Gonadotropin-releasing hormone (GNRH) agonists are another way to lower estrogen levels (Mutch, 2003). These drugs switch off estrogen production by the ovaries in women who are premenopausal. Examples of GNRH agonists include goserelin (Zoladex) and leuprolide (Lupron). These drugs are given every 1 to 3 months by subcuta-neous or intramuscular injection. Side effects can include any of the symptoms of menopause, such as hot flashes and vaginal dryness. If they are taken for a long time (years), these drugs can weaken bones, sometimes leading to osteoporosis.

Aromatase Inhibitors

After the ovaries are removed (or are not functioning), estrogen is still made in fat tissue. This becomes the body's main source of estrogen. Drugs called aromatase inhibitors can stop this estrogen from being formed and lower estrogen levels even further (Chu et al., 2008). Examples of aromatase inhibitors include letrozole (Femara), anastrozole (Arimidex), and exemestane (Aromasin). Side effects can include hot flashes and muscle pain. If they are taken for a long time (years), these drugs can weaken bones, sometimes leading to osteoporosis.

Chemotherapy

Effective chemotherapy treatment options for endometrial cancer are limited. No standard protocol for metastatic uterine cancer has emerged. Drugs used in treating endometrial cancer may include doxorubicin (Adriamycin), cisplatin, carboplatin, and paclitaxel (Taxol). Usually two or more drugs are combined for treatment. The most common combinations include cisplatin and doxorubicin, paclitaxel and doxorubicin, and cisplatin, paclitaxel, and doxorubicin. Side effects of these drugs were shown in Table 2-5 in Chapter 2.

CASE STUDY: ENDOMETRIAL CANCER

CC is a 63-year-old Asian woman who presents to her primary care physician with intermittent vaginal bleeding for 3 months. Occasionally, she said the discharge was yellow and watery. She also reports pain on urination and has had problems with swelling in her abdomen, so that her skirts and pants are tight.

On pelvic examination, her clinician evaluated the size, shape, and consistency of her uterus. She was scheduled for a D&C to obtain a sufficient endometrial biopsy. CC also underwent a vaginal probe ultrasonography, color flow Doppler, chest X-ray, and blood work (complete blood count [CBC]; metabolic, renal, and liver panels; CA-125 levels.) The pathology report indicated that CC has endometrial adenocarcinoma.

CC's surgeon performed a total abdominal hysterectomy, bilateral salpingo-oophorectomy, and lymph node biopsy, where further staging of her tumor followed. Pathologic and staging results indicated T1c disease (AJCC staging) or Stage 1C (FIGO staging). She discussed further treatment with her surgeon and oncologist and opted to have her care team manage her with close observation, rather than add radiation therapy or chemotherapy.

After surgery, CC had periods of diarrhea and fatigue. She also experienced estrogen deficiency, manifested by vaginal dryness (dyspareunia). Her postoperative pain was controlled with Vicodin and a stool softener. Her appetite and energy gradually returned and she was back at work part-time as a 6th grade teacher's aid 4 weeks after surgery.

Following surgery, CC dutifully went to follow-up checks every 2 to 3 months for the next 2 years. During the 3rd year, follow-up was every 6 months. (Checks included a pelvic examination, chest X-ray, CBC, and metabolic panel. Every 6 months for the first year posttreatment, she had a transvaginal ultrasound.)

Additional Information

CC's medical history is remarkable for the use of unopposed estrogens for 10 years, no pregnancies (nulliparity), and menopause, which began after age 55. The challenge of hormone replacement therapy now, is weighing the risks and benefits of treatment for her hot flashes, irritability, and developing osteoporosis compared with the risk of breast cancer. She intends to discuss this issue with

her physician so that she can decide what is best for her.

CC's social network is limited. She lives alone with her cats. She has a niece, who lives nearby and looks in on her every 2 weeks. Her social support group is limited to a few neighbors and some teachers at her school. She plans to retire within the next 4 months and live on a fixed income that is supplemented with Social Security checks. She fears that her medical bills will overwhelm her ability to stay healthy in her post-retirement years.

She says she uses Japanese herbs for her well-being and practices Reiki. In addition, CC has decided to boost her immune system with supplements that she has heard about on late-night television infomercials.

What classic symptom of endometrial cancer does CC have?

Intermittent vaginal bleeding, especially in a postmenopausal woman is an early sign of endometrial cancer. Later symptoms, not necessarily associated with early detection, are pain with urination, vaginal discharge, ascites, and lower extremity swelling

What risk factors for endometrial cancer does CC have?

CC had a history of unopposed estrogen (estrogen without progesterone to protect the uterus) replacement therapy. She is nulliparous and experienced a later menopause. It also is not clear if CC engaged in regular screening that might have resulted in the early detection of endometrial cancer. Sometimes minority patients may be reluctant to engage in early detection or may not be fully informed of the importance of early detection.

What practice of CC might interfere with treatment?

CC uses Japanese herbs and supplements she ordered through a television program. The purity of these substances is not clear. More importantly, it is not clear if these agents will interfere with chemotherapy or other prescribed medications. The nurse needs to assess for these potential interactions.

SUMMARY

Endometrial cancer is a highly curable cancer when detected early. It is the most common of the gynecologic cancers. Atypical pain or uterine bleeding are early symptoms of this cancer. Women especially at increased risk for this cancer usually present with a combination of factors – obesity, nulliparity, and smoking. Standard treatment for endometrial cancer remains surgery, although radiation therapy plays a therapeutic role alone or in combination with surgery and, sometimes, hormonal manipulation. Chemotherapy regimens are used as treatment for advanced stage endometrial cancers.

EXAM QUESTIONS

CHAPTER 3
Questions 15-23

Note: Choose the one option that BEST answers each question.

15. The risk factors for endometrial cancer include

    a. hypotension, early menopause, infertility.

    b. obesity (more than 20 pounds overweight), no children, history of breast or ovarian cancer.

    c. many children, early menopause.

    d. weight loss, early menopause, productive cough.

16. Women who take hormone replacement therapy for menopausal symptoms can reduce their risk of endometrial cancer by taking

    a. estrogen alone.

    b. a combination of estrogen and progesterone for a period of time (less than 5 years).

    c. progesterone 1 day per month.

    d. a combination of estrogen and progesterone intermittently over a period of a year.

17. Tamoxifen is a treatment for breast cancer but has also been linked to an increased risk of endometrial cancer. Cancer specialists have concluded that the

    a. benefits of tamoxifen in preventing recurrence of breast cancer outweigh the risks.

    b. risk of taking tamoxifen outweighs the benefit, therefore tamoxifen should be taken off the market.

    c. risk increases in patients who have had a hysterectomy.

    d. risk is the same for all patients with breast cancer.

18. Key indicators of HNPCC include a family history of

    a. breast and endometrial cancer.

    b. colorectal and liver cancer.

    c. pancreatic, ovarian, and stomach cancer.

    d. endometrial, colon, ovarian, and stomach cancer.

19. The most frequent endometrial cancer cell type is

    a. adenocarcinoma.

    b. uterine papillary serous.

    c. squamous cell.

    d. clear cell.

20. A typical test included in the staging workup for endometrial cancer is the

    a. transvaginal ultrasound.

    b. colonoscopy.

    c. bone scan.

    d. CA-125 blood test.

21. In Stage III endometrial cancer, the tumor has

    a. spread outside the uterus but not to the bladder.

    b. remains confined to the uterus.

    c. invaded the bladder.

    d. spread only to the cervix.

22. A woman recovering from a hysterectomy may typically experience

    a. GI disturbance, pain, and fatigue.

    b. neutropenia, alopecia, and fatigue.

    c. tachycardia, anemia, and insomnia.

    d. hot flashes, pain, and rashes.

23. Radiation therapy for endometrial cancer

    a. can shrink the tumor only if it is administered before surgery.

    b. is the lone modality of therapy.

    c. can only be delivered with external beam radiation.

    d. can be delivered with external beam and/or brachytherapy.

REFERENCES

Amant, F., Moerman, P., Neven, P., Timmerman, D., Van Limbergen, E., & Vergote, I. (2005). Endometrial cancer. *Lancet, 366*(9484), 491-505.

American Cancer Society. (2010a). *Cancer facts & figures 2010*. Atlanta, GA: American Cancer Society.

American Cancer Society. (2010b). *Endometrial cancer: Causes, risk factors and prevention topics*. Retrieved July 16, 2010, from http://www.cancer.org/Cancer/EndometrialCancer/DetailedGuide/endometrial-uterine-cancer-risk-factors

American Cancer Society. (2010c). *Endometrial Cancer: Early detection, diagnosis and staging*. Retrieved July 16, 2010, from http://www.cancer.org/Cancer/EndometrialCancer/DetailedGuide/endometrial-uterine-cancer-diagnosis

Chu, C.S., Lin, L.L., & Rubin, S.C. (2008). Cancers of the uterine body. In V.T. DeVita, Jr., T.S. Lawrence, & S.A. Rosenberg (Eds.), *DeVita, Hellman, and Rosenberg's Cancer: Principles and practice of oncology* (8th ed., pp. 1543-1563). Philadelphia: Lippincott Williams & Wilkins

Creasman, W.T. (2009). Revised FIGO staging for carcinoma of the vulva, cervix and endometrium. *International Journal of Gynecology and Obstetrics, 105*:103-4.

Edge, S.B., Byrd, D.R., Carducci, M., Compton, C.C., Fritz, A.G., Greene, F.L., & Trotti, A. (2010). *AJCC cancer staging manual* (7th ed.), New York: Springer.

Ely, J.W., Kennedy, C.M., Clark, E.C., & Bowdler, N.C. (2006). Abnormal uterine bleeding: A management algorithm. *Journal of the American Board of Family Medicine, 19*(6), 590-602.

FIGO staging for corpus cancer. (1992). *British Journal of Obstetrics & Gynaecology, 99*(5), 440.

Giudice, L.C. & Kao, L.C. (2004). Endometriosis. *Lancet, 364*(9447), 1789-1799.

Guillem, J.C., Wood, W.C., Moley, J.F., Berchuck, A., Karlan, B.Y., Mutch, D.G., et al. (2006). ASCO/SSO review of current role of risk-reducing surgery in common hereditary cancer syndromes. *Journal of Clinical Oncology, 24*(28), 4642-4660.

Harris, E.R., Wei, S.J., Chu, C., & Acs, G. (2004). Cancer of the uterus. In M.D. Abeloff, J.O. Armitage, J.E. Niederhuber, M.B. Kastan, & W.G. McKenna (Eds.), *Clinical oncology* (3rd ed., pp. 2273-2310). Philadelphia: Churchill Livingstone.

Levin, B., Barthel, J.S., Burt, R.W., David, D.S., Ford, J.M., Giardiello, F.M., et al. (2006). Colorectal cancer screening clinical practice guidelines. *Journal of the National Comprehensive Cancer Network, 4*(4), 384-420.

Lindor, N.M., Petersen, G.M., Hadley, D.W., Kinney, A.Y., Miesfeldt, S., Lu, K.H., et al. (2006). Recommendations for the care of individuals with an inherited predisposition to Lynch Syndrome: A systematic review. *Journal of the American Medical Association, 296*(12), 1507-1517.

Lynch, H.T. & de la Chapelle, A. (2003). Genomic medicine: Hereditary colorectal cancer. *New England Journal of Medicine, 348*(10), 919-932.

Lynch, H.T. & Lynch, P.M. (2006). Clinical selection of candidates for mutational testing for cancer susceptibility. *Oncology (Williston Park), 20*(14 Suppl 10), 29-34.

Maizlin, Z.V., Vos, P.M., & Cooperberg, P.L. (2007). Is it a fibroid? Are you sure? Sonography with MRI assistance. *Ultrasound Quarterly, 23*(1), 55-62.

Mutch, D.G. (2003). Uterine cancer. In J.R. Scott, R.S. Gibbs, B.Y. Karlan, & A.F. Haney (Eds.), *Danforth's obstetrics and gynecology* (9th ed., pp. 951-969). Philadelphia: Lippincott Williams and Wilkins.

Speroff, L. & Fritz, M.A. (2005). Endometriosis. In *Clinical gynecologic endocrinology and infertility* (7th ed., pp. 1103–1133). Philadelphia: Lippincott Williams and Wilkins.

CHAPTER 4

OVARIAN CANCER

CHAPTER OBJECTIVE

After completing this chapter, the reader will be able to discuss the epidemiology, risk factors, prevention and detection strategies, common staging schemas, and treatments for ovarian cancer.

LEARNING OBJECTIVES

After studying this chapter, the reader will be able to

1. identify trends in incidence and mortality for ovarian cancer.

2. describe the anatomy and physiology of the ovaries.

3. recognize risk factors for the development ovarian cancer.

4. identify signs and symptoms for ovarian cancer.

5. discuss strengths and limitations of early detection strategies used for ovarian cancer.

6. describe diagnostic tests that are ordered when evaluating ovarian cancer.

7. discuss surgical options for the management of ovarian cancer.

8. discuss chemotherapy agents utilized in the treatment of ovarian cancer.

INTRODUCTION

Ovarian cancer is one of the deadliest gynecological cancers. Unfortunately, there are few early signs and symptoms of ovarian cancer. Frequently, when women present with ovarian cancer, it has progressed to a more advanced stage of malignancy. The focus of this chapter is on the known risks for ovarian cancer and standard treatments. Because of the high morbidity of an ovarian cancer diagnosis, the initial workup and continuing follow-up after treatment are major nursing responsibilities.

EPIDEMIOLOGY

Ovarian cancer remains a challenge in gynecologic cancer. Basic facts about ovarian cancer are listed in Box 4-1. Ovarian cancer remains a deadly cancer because there are few symptoms and most are vague. In addition, there are limited tools for the early detection of ovarian cancer. Although there have been strides in ovarian cancer treatment, especially with chemotherapy, options for treatment still remain somewhat limited and have variable effectiveness (O'Rourke & Mahon, 2003). However, if ovarian cancer is detected early, approximately nine out of ten women will live for at least 5 years with the disease.

BOX 4-1: EPIDEMIOLOGIC FACTS REGARDING OVARIAN CANCER

- Estimated 21,880 new cases expected annually

- Accounts for about 3% of all cancers among women

- Ranks second among gynecologic cancers

- From 2001 to 2006, ovarian cancer incidence declined at a rate of 2.1% per year
  - Estimated 13,850 deaths are expected annually
  - Causes more deaths than any other cancer of the female reproductive system
  - Women younger than 65 years of age are about twice as likely to survive 5 years (57%) following diagnosis as women 65 years of age and older (30%).
  - Overall, the 1- and 5-year relative survival rate of ovarian cancer patients is 75% and 46%, respectively
  - If diagnosed at the localized stage, the 5-year survival rate is 94%; however, only about 15% of all cases are detected at this stage
  - If diagnosed with regional and distant disease, 5-year survival rates are 73% and 28%, respectively
  - The 10-year relative survival rate for all stages combined is 38%.

(ACS, 2010a)

ANATOMY

A woman's ovaries have two roles: to produce eggs and to produce the female hormones – estrogen and progesterone – which are integral to reproduction. In addition to being part of the reproduction process, estrogen and progesterone contribute to the female characteristic changes seen in puberty: development of breasts, body shape, and body hair. These hormones also regulate the menstrual cycle.

Each of the two ovaries lies on adjacent sides of the uterus. The uterus is the hollow sac that holds a growing embryo as it becomes a fetus. (See Figure 4-1.) Each ovary is about the size of an almond. Every month when a woman menstruates, one of the ovaries releases an egg in a process called ovulation. The egg travels from the ovary to the uterus through the fallopian tube.

OVARIAN CYSTS

A s with other cancer cell processes, ovarian cancer cells grow, divide, and produce more cells, creating tumors that can be benign or malignant. Benign tumors do not spread to other parts of the body and do not threaten the woman's life (ACS, 2010a).

FIGURE 4-1: ANATOMY OF OVARIES

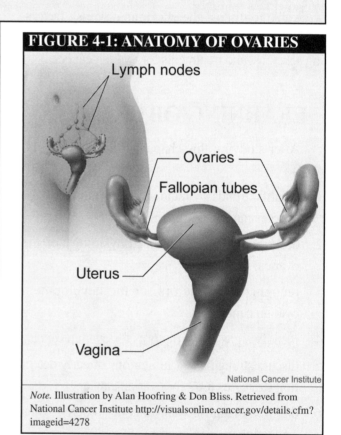

National Cancer Institute

Note. Illustration by Alan Hoofring & Don Bliss. Retrieved from National Cancer Institute http://visualsonline.cancer.gov/details.cfm?imageid=4278

A variation of benign ovarian growth is the ovarian cyst – a fluid filled sac that can form on the surface of the ovary. Cysts usually occur in younger women and often they go away on their own. If they do not, a surgeon may remove them. There are many different types of ovarian cysts (Purcell & Wheeler, 2003).

Functional cysts or simple cysts, are part of the normal process of the menstrual cycle:

- Follicle cysts form when the sac doesn't break open to release the egg, and the sac keeps growing. This type of cyst most often goes away in 1 to 3 months.

- Corpus luteum cysts form if the sac doesn't dissolve. Instead, the sac seals off after the egg is released, followed by a fluid build-up in the sac. Most of these cysts go away after a few weeks but can grow to 8 to 10 cm. They may bleed or twist the ovary and cause pain. They are rarely malignant. Some drugs used to cause ovulation, such as Clomid or Serophene, can increase the risk of getting these cysts.

Other types of ovarian cysts are:

- Endometriomas form in women who have endometriosis. This problem occurs when tissue that looks and acts like the lining of the uterus grows outside the uterus. The tissue may attach to the ovary and form a growth. These cysts can lead to pain during the menstrual cycle and occasionally during intercourse.

- Cystadenomas form from cells on the outer surface of the ovary. They can become large and cause pain.

- Dermoid cysts contain many types of cells. They may be filled with hair, teeth, and other tissues that become part of the cyst. They can become large and cause pain.

- Polycystic ovaries form cysts that are caused when eggs mature within the sacs but are not released. The cycle then repeats. The sacs continue to grow and many cysts form.

RISK FACTORS

Age, demographics, reproductive history, and lifestyle are risk factors for ovarian cancer. The risk of developing ovarian cancer increases with age; it is rare in women younger than 40 years

old and most ovarian cancers develop after menopause. Half of all ovarian cancers are found in women older than 63 years of age (ACS, 2010b).

Nulliparity increases the risk of ovarian cancer. Among the general population, parity decreases the risk of ovarian cancer by 45%, compared to the risk of nulliparous women. After a woman has her first pregnancy, subsequent pregnancies appear to decrease ovarian cancer risk by 15% (ACS, 2010a).

In addition to pregnancy, lactation and the use of oral contraceptives have been associated with a protective effect against ovarian cancer. Estimates show that the risk of developing ovarian cancer is 40% to 60% lower in women who use oral contraceptives, even if they stopped using them 10 to 30 years earlier (O'Rourke & Mahon, 2003). In addition, women who undergo a bilateral tubal ligation or hysterectomy have been shown to reduce their risk of developing ovarian cancer.

Unfortunately, the most striking risk factors for ovarian cancer are linked to heredity and genetic syndromes that are out of the woman's control. This may account for approximately 10% to 15% of all ovarian cancers. Hereditary risk associated with ovarian cancer has been linked to mutations in the BRCA1/2 (see chapter 2) and colon and endometrial cancer, which is also referred to as hereditary nonpolyposis colorectal cancer (HNPCC) (see chapter 3). Lifetime risk of ovarian cancer in women with BRCA1/2 mutations approach 50% and 12% to 15% in women with mutations associated with HNPCC (Guillem et al., 2006). Women with ovarian cancers caused by some of these inherited gene mutations may have a better outlook than patients who do not have a family history of ovarian cancer because of aggressive screening and, most often, because of the implementation of primary prevention strategies.

Studies are investigating whether a diet high in animal fats leads to ovarian cancer. Some evidence suggests such a link (O'Rourke & Mahon, 2003). As with other cancers, researchers suggest that pursuing a diet rich in fruits and vegetables may have a small effect in preventing some ovarian cancers. Studies also advance the idea that supplementation with vitamins A, C, and E may decrease a cancer risk, but no definitive guidelines have emerged. Obesity is associated with increased risk as well as increased mortality (ACS, 2010a, 2010b). No evidence has shown that the use of talc leads to the development of ovarian cancer (O'Rourke & Mahon, 2003.)

SIGNS AND SYMPTOMS

Signs and symptoms of ovarian cancer can be vague. In general, women report symptoms as the ovarian cancer tumor cells grow. These symptoms include

- abdominal swelling or abdominal pain
- vaginal bleeding between periods or after menopause
- bloating, gas, indigestion, or cramps
- pelvic pain
- loss of appetite
- feeling full after a small meal, or feeling full quickly
- changes in bowel or bladder habits
- weight loss or weight gain

(ACS, 2010a).

PREVENTION

Unfortunately, no definitive strategies exist for women to avoid ovarian cancer. General strategies to prevent ovarian cancer match those for other gynecologic malignancies. They include having an annual pelvic examination, reducing dietary fat, increasing dietary intake of vitamin A, and using oral contraceptives for birth control in younger women (ACS, 2010a, 2010b; Karlan, Markman, & Eifel, 2005).

For women with a known mutation in BRCA1/2 or a mutation associated with HNPCC, serious consideration needs to be given to a prophylactic oophorectomy. Most often this is a laprascopic procedure that is offered between 35 and 45 years of age (Guillem et al., 2006). This can confer a risk reduction of over 95% in women with a known mutation. Genetic testing can clarify this risk and is often very helpful for women as they determine if the benefit of an oophorectomy outweighs the risks. A small percentage of women may develop a primary peritoneal carcinoma, similar in appearance to ovarian cancer, after prophylactic oophorectomy (ACS, 2010a; Guillem et al., 2006).

SCREENING/DIAGNOSTIC EVALUATION

To date, no effective approaches to ovarian cancer screening have emerged. For women of average risk (age and demographics), an annual bimanual rectovaginal exam (pelvic examination) is recommended. During a pelvic exam, the healthcare professional feels the ovaries and uterus for size, shape, and consistency. Although a pelvic exam is recommended because it can find some reproductive system cancers at an early stage, most early ovarian tumors are difficult or impossible for even the most skilled examiner to feel. Although the Pap test is effective in detecting cervical cancer early, it is not an effective test for ovarian cancer.

Transvaginal sonography is an ultrasound test that places a small instrument in the vagina. It can help find a mass in the ovary, but it can't actually tell which masses are cancers and which are not. CA-125 is a protein in the blood that is higher in many women with ovarian cancer. The problem with this test is that conditions other than cancer can also cause high levels of CA-125. In addition, someone with ovarian cancer can still have a normal CA-125 level.

In studies of women at average risk for ovarian cancer, these screening tests did not lower the number of deaths caused by ovarian cancer. For this reason, transvaginal sonography and the CA-125 blood test are not recommended for ovarian cancer screening of women without known strong risk factors (ACS, 2010a). These tests are often done in women at high risk, but it is not known how helpful they are.

The most common reason for a physician to suspect ovarian cancer is if a mass is palpated during a pelvic examination. When a pelvic mass is found in a postmenopausal woman or a young girl or teenager who hasn't yet begun menstruating, the female patient needs to undergo a surgical laparotomy to determine the final diagnosis. Chances are extremely high that a pelvic mass in a young girl or teenager who hasn't begun menstruating is malignant (usually a germ cell ovarian cancer). However, only 5% of masses felt on pelvic examination in menstruating women are malignancies. Certain characteristics of the mass – solid, irregular, or fixed – make it more or less likely to be a cancer (ACS, 2010a; Kramer & Greene, 2004).

If the mass is small, has holes (is cystic), is in only one ovary, is freely movable, and has regular contours, then it is unlikely to be a cancer. Follow-up of these masses is by clinical exam. In most cases these masses are ovarian cysts and will disappear on their own. However, if these masses persist or enlarge, further surgical exploration is warranted. And if a mass persists with the woman showing signs of fluid collecting in the abdomen, laporotomy is indicated.

Imaging Procedures

Imaging methods such as CT scans, MRI, and ultrasound studies can confirm whether a pelvic mass is present. Although these studies cannot confirm that the mass is a malignant, they are useful to determine if there is spread of ovarian cancer to other tissues and organs.

Ultrasound

Since ovarian tumors and normal ovarian tissue often reflect sound waves differently, this test may be used to find tumors and determine whether a mass is solid or a fluid-filled cyst.

Computed Tomography Scan

The CT scan can help determine if the cancer has spread into the liver or other organs. CT scans are useful in showing how large the tumor is, what other organs it may be invading, whether lymph nodes are enlarged, and if the kidneys or bladder are affected.

Magnetic Resonance Imaging

An MRI scan is particularly helpful to examine the brain and spinal cord.

Chest X-ray

A chest X-ray may be done to determine whether ovarian cancer has spread (metastasized) to the lungs. This spread may cause one or more tumors in the lungs and often causes fluid to collect around the lungs. This fluid, called a pleural effusion, can be seen with chest X-rays.

Positron Emission Tomography Scan

A PET scan is a nuclear medicine imaging technique. PET scans involve injecting a form of sugar that contains a small amount of radioactive tracer into the blood. This sugar collects in the cancer cells. The radioactivity can show the areas of cancer in the body by producing a three-dimensional image to determine how organs are functioning.

A PET scan can be helpful for spotting small collections of cancer cells. In some instances this test has proved useful in finding ovarian cancer that has spread. It is even more valuable when combined with a CT scan.

Colonoscopy

A colonoscopy is utilized to examine the inside of the large intestine.

Laparoscopy

A laparoscopy uses a thin, lighted tube through which a doctor can look at the ovaries and other pelvic organs and tissues in the area around the bile duct. The tube is inserted through a small incision in the lower abdomen and sends the images of the pelvis or abdomen to a video monitor. Laparoscopy provides a view of organs that can help plan surgery or other treatments and can help doctors confirm the stage of the cancer. Also, doctors can manipulate small instruments through the laparascopic incision to perform biopsies.

Biopsy

The only way to determine for certain if a growth is malignant is to biopsy a sample of the growth from the suspicious area and examine it under a microscope. For ovarian cancer, the biopsy is most commonly done by removing the tumor during surgery. It can be also be done during a laparoscopic procedure or with a needle placed directly into the tumor through the skin of the abdomen. Usually the needle will be guided by an ultrasound or CT scan. A needle biopsy is sometimes used instead of surgery if the patient cannot have surgery because of advanced cancer or some other serious medical condition.

In patients with ascites, samples of fluid can also be used to diagnose the cancer. In this procedure, called paracentesis, a local anesthetic is administered and a needle, attached to a syringe, is passed through the abdomen wall into the fluid in the abdominal cavity. The fluid is aspirated into the syringe and then sent for analysis.

CA-125 Testing

Cancer antigen-125, or CA-125, is a protein that is found at elevated levels in most ovarian cancer cells compared to normal cells. CA-125 is produced on the surface of cells and is released in the blood stream. The CA-125 test is a blood test that assesses the concentration of CA-125 in the blood.

The CA-125 test only returns a true positive result in about 50% of Stage I ovarian cancer patients. The CA-125 test is not an adequate early detection tool when used alone. The CA-125 test has an 80% chance of returning true positive results in stage II, III, and IV ovarian cancer patients. The other 20% of ovarian cancer patients do not show any increase in CA-125 concentrations (Kramer & Greene, 2004). However, several women's reproductive disorders can cause a false positive result. Endometriosis, benign ovarian cysts, first trimester of pregnancy, and pelvic inflammatory disease all produce higher levels of CA-125. A CA-125 test result of greater than 35 U/ml is generally accepted as being elevated.

Screening – Optimal Combination of Tests

Women who carry genetic markers (including BRCA1/2 or mutations increasing risk of HNPCC) that increase their tendency to develop ovarian cancer should follow an aggressive schedule for screening and follow-up. Screening can include a thorough pelvic examination with further evaluation through ultrasound, usually on a biannual basis (O'Rourke & Mahon, 2003). Pelvic examinations have limitations because developing ovarian masses may be too deep to palpate. Therefore, repeat pelvic exams – every 1 to 2 months for suspicious masses – are recommended.

Some women who face increased risk of developing ovarian cancer may consider a prophylactic oophorectomy, which removes the woman's ovaries before they become diseased. However, this procedure does not eliminate the woman's chances of developing ovarian cancer. Such a decision should be preceded by genetic testing and counseling (Guillem et al., 2006).

Standards for routine screening of at risk women remains a dilemma. The ACS (2010a) recommends an annual pelvic examination; the U.S. Preventive Services Task Force (2005) does not feel there is adequate evidence to justify an annual pelvic examination. Research continues toward developing effective ovarian cancer screening tools. Ideally a simple blood test or Pap test equivalent for ovarian cancer is needed.

TYPES OF OVARIAN TUMORS

Many types of tumors can start growing in the ovaries. Most of these are benign and never extend beyond the ovary. Benign tumors are usually treated successfully by removing either the ovary or the part of the ovary that contains the tumor. Ovarian tumors that are not benign are malignant and often quickly metastasize to other parts of the body. Their treatment is more complex.

In general, ovarian tumors are named according to the kind of cells the tumor started from and whether the tumor is benign or malignant. There are three main categories of ovarian tumors (Edge et al., 2010).

- Epithelial tumors start from the cells that cover the outer surface of the ovary. Most ovarian tumors are epithelial cell tumors.

- Germ cell tumors start from the cells that produce the ova (eggs).

- Stromal tumors start from connective tissue cells that hold the ovary together and produce the female hormones estrogen and progesterone.

Epithelial Ovarian Tumors

Benign epithelial tumors: These include serous adenomas, mucinous adenomas, and Brenner tumors.

Tumors of low malignant potential are also known as borderline epithelial ovarian cancer (Kramer & Greene, 2004). These differ from typical ovarian cancers in that they do not grow into the supporting tissue of the ovary. These cancers tend to affect women at a younger age than the typical

ovarian cancers and grow slowly and are less life-threatening than most ovarian cancers.

Malignant epithelial ovarian tumors: About 85% to 90% of ovarian cancers are epithelial ovarian carcinomas (ACS, 2010d). Epithelial ovarian cancers are classified into several types: serous, mucinous, endometrioid, and clear cell. The serous type is by far the most common. If the cells don't look like any of these subtypes, the tumor is called undifferentiated. Undifferentiated epithelial ovarian carcinomas tend to grow and spread more quickly than the other types. In addition to being classified by these subtypes, epithelial ovarian carcinomas are also given a grade and a stage.

The grade classifies the tumor based on how much it looks like normal tissue on a scale of 1, 2, or 3. Grade 1 epithelial ovarian carcinomas look more like normal tissue and tend to have a better prognosis. Grade 3 epithelial ovarian carcinomas look less like normal tissue and usually have a poorer prognosis. The tumor stage describes how far the tumor has spread from where it started in the ovary (ACS, 2010a).

Primary Peritoneal Carcinoma

Primary peritoneal carcinoma (PPC) is a rare cancer closely related to epithelial ovarian cancer (Karlan et al., 2005). PPC develops in cells from the lining of the pelvis and abdomen (the peritoneum). These cells are very similar to the cells on the surface of the ovaries. Like ovarian cancer, PPC tends to spread along the surfaces of the pelvis and abdomen, so it is often difficult to tell exactly where the cancer first started. This type of cancer can occur in women who still have their ovaries, but it is of more concern for women who have had their ovaries removed to prevent ovarian cancer. Symptoms of PPC are similar to those of ovarian cancer, including abdominal pain or bloating, nausea, vomiting, indigestion, and a change in bowel habits. Also, like ovarian cancer, PPC may elevate the blood level of a tumor marker called CA-125.

Fallopian Tube Cancer

Fallopian tube cancer is an extremely rare cancer. It begins in the tube that carries an egg from the ovary to the uterus (the fallopian tube). Like PPC, fallopian tube cancer causes symptoms similar to those seen in women with ovarian cancer (Karlan et al., 2005). The treatment and prognosis is similar to that for ovarian cancer.

Germ Cell Tumors

Germ cells are the cells that usually form the ova or eggs (Karlan et al., 2005). Most germ cell tumors are benign, although some are cancerous and may be life threatening. About 5% of ovarian cancers are germ cell tumors. There are several subtypes of germ cell tumors. The most common germ cell tumors are teratoma, dysgerminoma, endodermal sinus tumor, and choriocarcinoma.

Stromal Tumors

About 5% to 7% of ovarian cancers are ovarian stromal cell tumors. Most of these are granulosa cell tumors (Kramer & Greene, 2004). More than half of stromal tumors are found in women older than 50 years of age; however, about 5% of stromal tumors occur in young girls. The most common symptom of these tumors is abnormal vaginal bleeding. This happens because many of these tumors produce female hormones (like estrogen). These hormones can cause vaginal bleeding to start again after menopause or can cause menstrual periods and breast development in young girls. Less often, stromal tumors make male hormones (like testosterone). If male hormones are produced, the tumors can disrupt normal periods and cause facial and body hair to grow. Another symptom of stromal tumors can be sudden, severe, abdominal pain. This occurs if the tumor starts to bleed.

TREATMENT

Based on the cell of origin established through an initial laparotomy, treatment decisions fol-low. Because ovarian cancer is a complicated and aggressive disease, a team of physicians may be involved in the woman's care – gynecological surgeon, medical oncologist, and radiation oncologist.

Several factors lead to a favorable prognosis. Among them are younger age, good performance status, cell type other than mucinous and clear cell, earlier stage, well-differentiated tumor, smaller disease volume prior to any surgical debulking, absence of ascites, and smaller residual tumor following primary cytoreductive surgery.

Surgery

Surgery for ovarian cancer has two main goals. The first goal is to stage the cancer – to see how far the cancer has spread from the ovary. Usually this means removing the uterus, both ovaries, and both fallopian tubes (a bilateral salpingo-oophorectomy). In addition, the omentum is also removed (omentectomy). Some lymph nodes in the pelvis and abdomen are taken out to determine if they contain cancer spread from the ovary. If there is fluid in the pelvis or abdominal cavity, it will also be removed for analysis. The surgeon may "wash" the abdominal cavity with saline solution and send that fluid for analysis. Staging is very important because ovarian cancers at different stages are treated differently. Table 4-1 highlights staging criteria for ovarian cancer.

The other important goal of surgery is to remove as much of the tumor as possible – called debulking. The aim of debulking surgery is to leave behind no tumors larger than 1 cm. Patients who have had successful debulking surgery have a better outlook than those left with larger tumors after surgery.

Many gynecologists and surgeons are not trained to do the staging and debulking procedures that are necessary in treating ovarian cancer. For this reason, experts recommend that patients see a gynecologic oncologist for surgery. Gynecologic oncologists are specialists who have training and experience in treating ovarian cancer and know

TABLE 4-1: STAGING CRITERIA FOR OVARIAN CANCER
Stage I – Growth limited to the ovaries
• Stage Ia – Growth limited to 1 ovary, no ascites, no tumor on external surface, capsule intact
• Stage Ib – Growth limited to both ovaries, no ascites, no tumor on external surface, capsule intact
• Stage Ic – Tumor either stage Ia or Ib but with tumor on surface of one or both ovaries, ruptured capsule, ascites with malignant cells or positive peritoneal washings
Stage II – Growth involving one or both ovaries, with pelvic extension
• Stage IIa – Extension and/or metastasis to the uterus or fallopian tubes
• Stage IIb – Extension to other pelvic tissues
• Stage IIc – Stage IIa or IIb but with tumor on surface of one or both ovaries, ruptured capsule, ascites with malignant cells or positive peritoneal washings
Stage III – Tumor involving one or both ovaries, with peritoneal implants outside the pelvis and/or positive retroperitoneal or inguinal nodes; superficial liver metastases constitute stage III disease
• Stage IIIa – Tumor grossly limited to pelvis, negative lymph nodes but histological proof of microscopic disease on abdominal peritoneal surfaces
• Stage IIIb – Confirmed implants outside of pelvis in the abdominal peritoneal surface; no implant exceeds 2 cm in diameter and lymph nodes are negative
• Stage IIIc – Abdominal implants larger than 2 cm in diameter and/or positive lymph nodes
Stage IV – Distant metastases; pleural effusion must have a positive cytology to be classified as stage IV; parenchymal liver metastases constitute stage IV disease
Used with permission of the American Joint Committee on Cancer (AJCC), Chicago, Illinois. The original source for this material is the *AJCC Cancer Staging Handbook,* Seventh Edition (2010) published by Springer Science and Business Media, LLC, www.springerlink.com.

how to stage and debulk ovarian cancer properly. Women with ovarian cancer who don't have the correct or adequate surgery the first time may need to go back to the operating room for more surgery later to stage and debulk the cancer.

A complete hysterectomy with bilateral salpingo-oophorectomy and omentectomy is extensive surgery. Most women will stay in the hospital for 3 to 7 days after the operation and can resume their usual activities within 4 to 6 weeks.

If the cancer recurs, a second debulking procedure – usually 1 year after the first surgery – is recommended. Surgery has also been used when palliating symptoms in patients with advanced disease.

Chemotherapy

After surgery, the risk of recurrence is high due to microscopic cancer cells that may remain or due to the high stage of the malignancy. Therefore, chemotherapy protocols have been developed as a component of treatment. The most common combination chemotherapies that treat epithelial ovarian cancer are based with paclitaxel and either cisplatin or carboplatin. Commonly used agents are shown in Table 4-2.

The two-drug combination of carboplatin plus paclitaxel is the current standard regimen for advanced ovarian cancer. Ovarian cancer is chemosensitive. Current treatment with combination chemotherapy results in a clinical complete remission rate in approximately 75% of all patients with advanced ovarian cancer (Ozols, 2006). However, median progression-free survival ranges from 16 to 21 months, depending upon the volume of disease present at the time of chemotherapy initiation.

Since most women with ovarian cancer who obtain a clinical complete remission following induction chemotherapy will ultimately relapse, numerous strategies have been tested in an effort to prevent or delay recurrences. There currently is no evidence that any form of maintenance therapy improves survival in patients who achieve a clinical complete remission following initial therapy (Vasey, 2008).

TABLE 4-2: COMMON CHEMOTHERAPY AGENTS FOR OVARIAN CANCER

Agent (generic)	Administration	Side Effects
Platinol (cisplatin)	I.V. over 30 to 60 minutes Intraperitoneal over 15 minutes with 4 hour dwell time	Nausea and vomiting Acute renal failure Peripheral neuropathy Ototoxicity Anorexia
Paraplatin (carboplatin)	I.V. over 15 to 30 minutes	Hypersensitivity Nausea and vomiting Myelosuppression Alopecia Peripheral neuropathy
Taxol (paclitaxel)	I.V. infusion over 30 minutes	Alopecia Anemia Neutropenia Peripheral neuropathy Diarrhea Nausea and vomiting Myalgias
Alkeran (melphalan)	Oral I.V.	Nausea and vomiting Mucositis Hypersensitivity reactions Delayed myelosuppression
Adriamycin (doxorubicin)	Slow I.V. push or continuous infusion	Nausea and vomiting Anorexia Mucositis Diarrhea Myelosuppression Cardiotoxicity Fatigue

Ovarian cancer patients who undergo chemotherapy may be given one drug or a combination of two or more drugs during treatment. Most physicians believe that combination chemotherapy is most effective for ovarian cancer patients because combination therapy has been shown to provide better cancer cell control with lower doses of individual drugs. With combination chemotherapy, better results may be achieved while causing fewer side effects associated with higher doses of an individual drug. This table shows common first line therapy for ovarian cancer.

(Newton, Hickey, & Marrs, 2009)

Intraperitoneal chemotherapy has been studied for over two decades in patients with ovarian cancer. The primary rationale for intraperitoneal chemotherapy is the fact that ovarian cancer remains primarily an intraperitoneal disease and that administration of drugs directly into the peritoneal cavity will lead to a higher drug concentration (Tropé & Kaern, 2007). There may be some improvement with intraperitoneal therapy; however, it has not been generally accepted as standard therapy for ovarian cancer patients because of the excessive toxicity.

Another major challenge for chemotherapy in ovarian cancer is to develop more effective regimens for treatment of patients with recurrent ovarian cancer. The primary goal of therapy in these patients is symptom management because a cure is essentially not feasible (Liu & Matulonis, 2006). Many compounds are also being investigated in ovarian cancer, including epidermal growth factor receptor and vascular epithelial growth factor (Bhoola & Hoskins, 2006).

At the time of diagnosis, CA-125 has no prognostic significance when measured. For patients whose elevated CA-125 normalizes with chemotherapy, more than one subsequent elevated CA-125 is highly predictive of active disease, but this does not mandate immediate therapy (Kramer & Greene, 2004).

Hormone Therapy

Hormone therapy is sometimes used as an alternative to second or third-line chemotherapy, when the patient cannot tolerate further chemotherapy. It is used for short-term control for a period of time with advanced stages of tumor.

Radiation Therapy

Radiation therapy as treatment for ovarian cancer is rare. In some early stage cases, radiation therapy follows surgery to debulk the disease. In advanced cancers, it can help stop bleeding or palliate pain. Radiation is usually avoided so that it does not affect portions of the bowel and pelvis (Karlan et al., 2005). Radioisotopes (radioactive phosphorus), when used, have been an option to treat Stage I or Stage II disease (ACS, 2010c).

Complications from Ovarian Cancer

Women treated for ovarian cancer may face additional complications stemming from their treatments (surgery and chemotherapy) or the cancer itself. These complications can include ascites, bowel obstruction, pain, pleural effusion, and malnutrition. Nursing interventions to address these complications are highlighted in Nursing Interventions for Complications from Treatment, Appendix D.

CASE STUDY: OVARIAN CANCER

*M*L *is a 55-year-old Caucasian woman, who presents to her primary care physician with mild abdominal bloating for the past 5 months. On examination, her clinician palpated a medium-size mass on her left ovary.*

On ultrasound, the mass was measured at approximately 6 cm x 2.5 cm. (A normal ovary measures 2 cm x 3 cm.) A tubular cystic interface appeared to surround the ovary. The cyst borders appeared irregular. The Doppler examination showed large tortuous vessels within the left ovary. The right ovary was of normal size with no irregularities. In addition to the ovarian tissue measurements, the ultrasound report indicated that the area was suspicious for malignancy.

One week after her pelvic examination, ML had an exploratory laparotomy. During the procedure (and with informed consent before she was anesthetized), ML's surgeon performed a total abdominal hysterectomy, bilateral salpingo-oophorectomy, and lymph node biopsy. Pathologic results indicated Stage IIIC epithelial ovarian cancer based on abdominal metastasis and positive lymph nodes.

After surgery, ML had periods of bleeding and bowel obstruction in the small intestine. (She reported progressing symptoms of cramping, colicky abdominal pain, bloating, and gas.) The obstruction was decompressed with a nasogastric tube, bowel rest, and accompanying analgesics and antiemetics. The nurses caring for ML monitored for signs of infection, worsening symptoms, diet, and comfort.

Following her surgery, ML was treated with three courses of chemotherapy. The agents – paclitaxel and cisplatin – were given intraperitoneally. Course doses were aggressive and ML required the administration of granulocyte colony stimulating factor to increase her neutrophil count. Adverse effects from her treatment were diarrhea, insomnia, nausea and vomiting, and sensory-motor deficits.

After her third course of chemotherapy, ML underwent second-look surgery. No evidence of disease was noted. Maintenance therapy began, which included I.V. doses of paclitaxel and cis-platin. ML had a follow-up appointment every 4 months, which included laboratory tests, a chest x-ray, and an abdominal CT scan.

At 16 months after ovarian cancer was diagnosed, repeat studies showed that her ovarian cancer had returned and that the cancer had spread to her lungs and liver.

ML opted to forego further treatment and have her care managed by a community hospice. Palliative care included pain management and interventions that optimized her quality of life for the final 4 months.

Additional Information:

ML's medical history was remarkable for breast cancer (stage II, left breast) when she was 45 years old. Her breast cancer treatments were lumpectomy, followed by radiation therapy and adjuvant chemotherapy. Because she was estrogen receptor positive, she was also prescribed tamoxifen and took the medication until she was 50 years old. In the last 2 years, it was determined from genetic testing that ML had the BRCA1 or BRCA2 genetic factors.

Before diagnosis, ML was 20 lb overweight. She had been diagnosed with hypertension. Her father was a diabetic and died at the age of 78.

Before her ovarian cancer was diagnosed, ML dutifully had yearly follow-up physical examinations with her physician with CBE, mammograms, and pelvic examinations. For the past 5 years, her pelvic and breast checks had been unremarkable.

ML was divorced, the mother of two daughters, 21 and 25 years of age, and the grandmother of a 1-year-old grandson. As a new mother, she breast-fed both of her daughters until they were 6 months

old. She started menstruation at age 12. Menopause was induced at age 46, when she received her chemotherapy for breast cancer.

ML was also a 20/pack year smoker. (She quit smoking when she was diagnosed with breast cancer.)

From the time she was diagnosed, ML attempted to use complementary and alternative medicines to help her keep a sense of control and help with adverse effects. She got massages every 2 weeks and treated herself occasionally to aromatherapy to help her with her anxiety and nausea.

Throughout her illness and treatment, she was able to journal and practice meditation, which strengthened her spiritually. She was also a member of a cancer support group, which met biweekly at a local community center.

What was ML's most outstanding risk factor for ovarian cancer?

Women with a mutation in BRCA1 or BRCA2 have an approximate 90% lifetime risk for developing breast cancer and up to 50% lifetime risk for developing ovarian cancer. At the time ML was determined to have a BRCA mutation it would have been appropriate to offer a prophylactic oophorectomy.

What symptom of ovarian cancer did ML have?

Ovarian cancer has few early symptoms. Unfortunately many women have vague gastrointestinal symptoms that are not attributed to ovarian cancer. By time they experience bloating or ascites such as ML, the tumor may be large.

SUMMARY

Ovarian cancer remains one of the deadliest gynecological cancers because it typically presents at more advanced stages. Women at risk for ovarian cancer are usually older and can have a personal or family history of cancer. A woman at risk may also be obese and have never been pregnant.

Few effective screening methods exist for women at high risk. Vague symptoms that women present to clinicians are worsening pain and bloating. When possible ovarian cancer is the focus, a workup consists of laporatomy with subsequent trending of CA-125 levels. Standard treatments focus on surgery with adjuvant chemotherapy to eliminate micrometastasis. Areas of study include better screening and diagnostic tools and targeted therapies that can boost the effectiveness of multi-modality therapy.

EXAM QUESTIONS

CHAPTER 4
Questions 24-33

Note: Choose the one option that BEST answers each question.

24. Advanced stage ovarian cancer is

    a. treated with surgery alone.

    b. typically the stage at which women are first diagnosed.

    c. resistant to all chemotherapy regimens.

    d. treated only with radiation.

25. When ovarian cancer is detected as regional disease, the survival rate at 5 years is about

    a. 50%.

    b. 60%.

    c. 70%.

    d. 80%.

26. The purpose of the ovaries is to produce

    a. eggs and only estrogen.

    b. eggs and only progesterone.

    c. only eggs.

    d. eggs, estrogen and progesterone.

27. A woman has an increased risk of ovarian cancer if she

    a. is childless, had an early menarche, and is 40 years old.

    b. had a tubal ligation, had a late menarche, and is 65 years old.

    c. had a BRCA1 mutation, is childless, and is 55 years old.

    d. had three children, had a late menarche, and is 50 years old.

28. Lifetime risk of developing ovarian cancer in a woman with a BRCA1/2 mutation is

    a. 10%.

    b. 50%.

    c. 75%.

    d. 85%.

29. Early signs of ovarian cancer are

    a. productive cough.

    b. headache.

    c. pronounced thirst.

    d. generally nonspecific.

30. Among methods to detect ovarian cancer in a high risk woman, the physician

    a. evalutes a guaiac test.

    b. tests for CA-125 and determines if it is elevated.

    c. orders a bronchoscopy.

    d. evaluates the most recent Pap test.

31. A diagnostic workup of ovarian cancer can include

    a. MRI, transvaginal ultrasound, and surgery.

    b. bone scan, iron levels, surgery.

    c. brain scan, gastric lavage, and surgery.

    d. oophorectomy, mammography, and sentinel node biopsy.

32. One of the goals of surgery for ovarian cancer is

    a.   sterilization.

    b.   debulking.

    c.   reconstruction.

    d.   remove ova for future reproduction.

33. The most common combination chemotherapy
    agents used to treat epithelial ovarian cancer are

    a.   paclitaxel and prednisone.

    b.   carboplatin and paclitaxel.

    c.   cisplatin and prednisone.

    d.   adriamycin and methotrexate.

REFERENCES

American Cancer Society. (2010a). *Cancer facts & figures 2010.* Atlanta, GA: American Cancer Society.

American Cancer Society. (2010b). *Ovarian cancer: Causes, risk factors and prevention.* Retrieved July 16, 2010, from http://www.cancer .org/Cancer/OvarianCancer/OverviewGuide/ ovarian-cancer-overview-what-causes

American Cancer Society. (2010c). *Ovarian cancer: Treating ovarian cancer.* Retrieved July 16, 2010, from http://www.cancer.org/Cancer/ OvarianCancer/DetailedGuide/ovarian-cancer-treating-radiation-therapy

American Cancer Society. (2010d). *Ovarian cancer: What is ovarian cancer?* Retrieved July 16, 2010, from http://www.cancer.org/Cancer/ OvarianCancer/DetailedGuide/ovarian-cancer-what-is-ovarian-cancer

Bhoola, S. & Hoskins, W.J. (2006). Diagnosis and management of epithelial ovarian cancer. *Obstetrics & Gynecology, 107*(6), 1399-1410.

Edge, S.B., Byrd, D.R., Carducci, M., Compton, C.C., Fritz, A.G., Greene, F.L., & Trotti, A. (2010). *AJCC cancer staging manual* (7th ed.), New York : Springer.

Guillem, J.C., Wood, W.C., Moley, J.F., Berchuck, A., Karlan, B.Y., Mutch, D.G., et al. (2006). ASCO/SSO review of current role of risk-reducing surgery in common hereditary cancer syndromes. *Journal of Clinical Oncology, 24*(28), 4642-4660.

Karlan, B.Y., Markman, M.A., & Eifel, P.J. (2005). Ovarian cancer, peritoneal carcinoma, and fallopian tube carcinoma. In V.T. DeVita, Jr., S. Hellman, & S.A. Rosenberg (Eds.), *Cancer: Principles and practice of oncology* (7th ed., 1364-1397). Philadelphia: Lippincott Williams & Wilkins.

Kramer, J.L. & Greene, M.H. (2004). Epidemiology of ovarian, fallopian tube, and primary peritoneal cancers. In D. Gershenson, W. McGuire, M. Gore, M. Quinn, & G. Thomas (Eds.), *Gynecologic cancer: Controversies in management* (pp. 327-340). Philadelphia: Elsevier Churchill Livingstone.

Liu, J. & Matulonis, U. (2006). Rational use of cytotoxic chemotherapy for recurrent ovarian cancer. *Journal of the National Comprehensive Cancer Network, 4*(9), 947-953.

Newton, S., Hickey, M., & Marrs, J. (2009). *Mosby's oncology nursing advisor: A comprehensive guide to clinical practice.* St. Louis, MO: Mosby Elsevier.

O'Rourke, J. & Mahon, S. (2003). A comprehensive look at the early detection of ovarian cancer. *Clinical Journal of Oncology Nursing, 7*(1), 41-47.

Ozols, R.F. (2006). Challenges for chemotherapy in ovarian cancer. *Annals of Oncology 17*(Supplement 5), v181-v187.

Purcell, K. & Wheeler, J.E. (2003). Benign disorders of the ovaries and oviducts. In A.H. DeCherney, L. Nathan (Eds.), *Current obstetric and gynecologic diagnosis and treatment* (9th ed., pp. 708-715). New York: McGraw-Hill.

Shepherd, J.H. (1989). Revised FIGO staging for gynecological cancer. *British Journal of Obstetrics and Gynecology, Aug. 96*(8): 889-892.

Tropé, C. & Kaern, J. (2007). Adjuvant chemotherapy for early-stage ovarian cancer: Review of the literature. *Journal of Clinical Oncology. 25*(20), 2909-2920.

U.S. Preventive Services Task Force. (2005). Screening for ovarian cancer: Recommendation statement. *American Family Physician, 71*(4), 759-762.

Vasey, P.A. (2008). Ovarian cancer: Front-line standard treatment in 2008. *Annals of Oncology, 19*(Suppl 7), vii61-vii66.

CHAPTER 5

CERVICAL CANCER

CHAPTER OBJECTIVE

After completing this chapter on cervical cancer, the reader will be able to discuss the disease's epidemiology, risk factors, prevention and detection strategies, common staging schemas, and treatments.

LEARNING OBJECTIVES

After studying this chapter, the reader will be able to

1. describe the main risk factors for cervical cancer.

2. identify human papilloma viruses (HPVs) associated with cervical cancer.

3. state screening recommendations for cervical cancer.

4. describe classification systems used in the interpretation of Pap tests.

5. describe a diagnostic evaluation for cervical cancer.

6. describe treatment options for Stage 1 cervical cancer.

7. describe treatment options for later stage cervical cancer.

INTRODUCTION

Despite the widespread use of the Pap test, women continue to be diagnosed with cervical cancer. Facts about the disease are shown in Box 5-1. Cervical cancer is the second most common cancer among women worldwide, with significantly higher rates seen in developing countries, especially in Africa, the Caribbean, and Latin America (Parkin, Bray, Ferlay, & Pisani, 2005).

BOX 5-1: CERVICAL CANCER FACTS

- 12,200 estimated new cases anually
- Incidence rates are gradually decreasing in all races
- Widespread utilization of the Pap smear results in more pre-invasive lesions being detected
- 4210 estimated deaths annually
- Five-year survival rate for localized disease is 92%
- Cervical cancer is diagnosed at a localized state in Caucasians at a higher rate (51%) than in African Americans (43%)

(ACS, 2010a)

Cervical cancer is potentially preventable through risk reduction and appropriate screening with the Pap test (American Cancer Society [ACS], 2010a). The Pap test should detect abnormalities of the cervix before they progress to malignancy. The challenge in detecting premalignant cervical lesions is in engaging women in appropriate, consistent screening programs based on their cervical cancer risk profile. Current estimates suggest that 50% of women diagnosed with cervical cancer have never had a Pap test and another 10% have not had a Pap test in the last five years (Nuovo, Melnikow, & Howell, 2001).

EPIDEMIOLOGY

Cervical cancer remains a public health problem in both the United States and the world. During the last 50 years in the U.S., cervical cancer mortality rates have decreased by 74%. Cervical cancer – once considered a highly deadly disease – has now dropped to 15 on the list of cancers that kill women in the U.S. (ACS, 2010a, 2010b).

Cervical cancer tends to occur in midlife. Most cases are found in women younger than 50 years old, and it rarely develops in women younger than 20 years old. Many older women do not realize that the risk of developing cervical cancer remains as they age, but almost 20% of women with cervical cancer are diagnosed when they are older 65 years of age. The 5-year relative survival rate for the earliest stage of invasive cervical cancer is 92%, and the 5-year survival rate overall, all stages combined, is approximately 71% (ACS, 2010b).

Cervical cancer is diagnosed at an early stage more often in Caucasians (51%) than in African Americans (43%) and in women younger than 50 years old (61%) than in women 50 years of age and older (36%) (ACS, 2010a).

ANATOMY

The cervix is the lower part of the uterus. It is sometimes called the uterine cervix. The body of the uterus is where a fetus grows. The cervix connects the body of the uterus to the vagina (birth canal). The opening of the cervix, through which menstrual flow is released, is the os. The part of the cervix closest to the body of the uterus is called the endocervix. The part next to the vagina is the ecto-cervix. The place where these two parts meet is called the transformation zone. Most cervical cancers begin in the transformation zone. Figure 5-1 highlights these areas of the woman's anatomy.

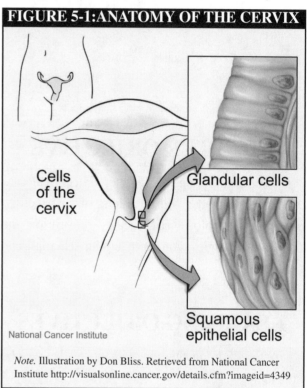

FIGURE 5-1: ANATOMY OF THE CERVIX

Cells of the cervix

Glandular cells

Squamous epithelial cells

National Cancer Institute

Note. Illustration by Don Bliss. Retrieved from National Cancer Institute http://visualsonline.cancer.gov/details.cfm?imageid=4349

RISK FACTORS

The exact etiology of cervical cancer is not yet identified. However, studies suggest that cervical cancer is caused by repeated, chronic injury to the cervical cells (Mehring, 2007). This type of cell injury can occur because of sexual intercourse at an early age, women who have sex with multiple male partners, women who have sex with male partners who themselves have had multiple sex partners, HPV infection, and smoking. Because the risk increases with high-risk sexual behavior, unprotected sex can also be considered a risk factor. Other risk factors are shown in Table 5-1.

In the U.S., HPV is the most common sexually transmitted infection, with an estimated 15% of the population being currently infected, although the lifetime risk of getting HPV is estimated to be as

TABLE 5-1: RISK FACTORS FOR CERVICAL CANCER

Risk Factor	Description
HPV Infection	2 HPV subtypes cause 90% of genital warts and are associated with increased cervical cancer risk.
Sexual History	Women who begin having sexual intercourse at an early age and women who have had many sexual partners are at a greater risk of HPV infection and developing cervical cancer.
Reproductive History	Having a high number of full-term pregnancies (7 or more) increases the risk of cervical cancer.
Oral Contraceptive Use	Long term use of oral contraceptives (5 or more years) increases risk.
Screening History	Women who are screened regularly are more likely to have lesions detected in a premalignant state. Abnormal changes can be treated before cancer develops. Women who are not screened are more likely to progress to cervical cancer.
Smoking	Cigarette smoking is associated with increased risk. Nicotine deposits have been found in cervical tissue.
Dietary Factors	Women with diets low in fruits and vegetables may be at increased risk for cervical cancer. Also, overweight women are more likely to develop this cancer.
Human Immunodeficiency Virus (HIV)	HIV damages the body's immune system and seems to make women more at risk for HPV infections. In women with HIV, a cervical precancerous lesion might develop into an invasive cancer faster than it normally would.

(ACS, 2010a, 2010c; Mehring, 2007)

high as 78% (Altekruse et al., 2003). There are over 100 different types of HPV. Fortunately, most are benign and resolve without treatment.

Low-risk HPV types may cause visible warts known as condylomata acuminate. High-risk HPV types tend to persist and are associated with the development of precancerous lesions and cervical cancer. Approximately 15 high-risk HPV types are associated with the development of cervical cancer, especially HPV types 16, 18, 33, and 45 (ACS, 2010c). More than one-half of cervical cancers are caused by HPV 16 and 18, and these two types are associated with more than a 200-fold increase of developing invasive cervical cancer (Muñoz et al., 2003).

Transmission of HPV occurs by genital contact with an infected partner. The virus enters through a break in the squamous epithelium, where infection stimulates the replication of the epithelium. The time from exposure to infection may be 1 to 8 months (Mehring, 2007).

The risk of acquiring HPV increases with the number of lifetime sexual partners and is not 100% preventable with condom use because the HPV infection can still be transmitted on body surfaces that are not covered by the condom (Bertram, 2004; Smith, et al., 2003).

CERVICAL SCREENING

Cervical cancer can usually be found early by having regular Pap tests. Mortality rates from cervical cancer have decreased over 40% in the past 30 years because of more widespread use of the Pap test. As Pap testing has become more common, pre-invasive lesions (pre-cancers) of the cervix are found far more frequently than invasive cancer. The conventional Pap smear is an inexpensive, widely available test with a reported sensitivity rate as high as 77% in detecting precursor lesions (Andy, Turner, & Neher, 2004). There are various guidelines for cervical screening from different organizations and they sometimes change. A comparison of the cervical screening guidelines from the ACS, American College of Obstetricians and Gynecologists (ACOG), and U.S. Preventive Services Task Force (USPSTF) are shown in Table 5-2.

The Pap test (also called a Pap smear) collects cells from the cervix during the pelvic examination to be analyzed for abnormal cell changes, thus pro-

TABLE 5-2: CERVICAL CANCER SCREENING GUIDELINES

Recommendation	American Cancer Society (2010)	USPSTF (2003)	ACOG (2009)
When to start	Begin screening approximately 3 years after onset of vaginal intercourse or by 21 years of age.	Begin screening within 3 years of onset of sexual activity or 21 years of age (whichever comes first).	Screening should begin at 21 years of age (regardless of sexual history).
Interval	Screen every year with regular Pap tests or every 2 years using liquid-based Pap tests. At or after 30 years of age, women who have had three normal test results in a row may get screened every 2 to 3 years. A healthcare provider may suggest getting the test more frequently in women with risk factors such as HIV infection or a weakened immune system.	Screen at least every 3 years with a conventional Pap smear. Do not recommend for or against liquid-based cytology or HPV testing.	Cervical cytology screening is recommended every 2 years for women between 21 and 29 years of age using either the standard Pap or liquid-based cytology. Women 30 years of age and older who have had three consecutive normal Pap tests can be screened every 3 years. Women with certain risk factors may need to be screened more frequently. These risk factors include HIV positivity; immunosuppression; diethylstilbesterol exposure in utero; or history of treatment for cervical intraepithelial neoplasia (CIN) II, CIN III, or cervical cancer.
When to stop	Women 70 years of age and older who have had three or more normal Pap test results and no abnormal results in the last 10 years may choose to stop cervical cancer screening.	Women 65 years of age and older, if they have had adequate recent screening with normal Pap smears and are not otherwise at high risk for cervical cancer, may choose to stop servical cancer screening.	Women may be able to stop cervical cancer screening at 65 or 70 years of age if they have had three or more normal Pap results in a row and no abnormal Pap in the previous 10 years. Women at high-risk of cervical cancer may need to continue screening beyond this age.
After a hysterectomy	Screening after a total hysterectomy is not necessary unless the surgery was done as a treatment for cervical cancer or precancerous lesion. Women who have had a hysterectomy without removal of the cervix should continue cervical cancer screening at least until 70 years of age.	Recommend against routine Pap smear screening in women who have had a total hysterectomy for benign disease.	Women who have had a total hysterectomy for reasons other than cancer can stop being screened for cervical cancer unless they have a history of high-grade CIN.

(ACS, 2010a; USPSTF, 2003; ACOG, 2009)

viding an early means of detecting precancerous conditions. During the pelvic examination, the clinician also checks the woman's uterus, vagina, ovaries, fallopian tubes, bladder, and rectum and notes any abnormality in their shapes or sizes.

The Pap test was introduced as a cervical cancer screening test in 1943 by Dr. George Papanicolaou. In the United States, about 58 million Pap tests are performed each year, with approximately 3.7 million (8%) reported as abnormal and requiring medical followup (Eltoum & Roberson, 2007). Annual Pap testing has been estimated to reduce mortality in women from cervical cancer from 4 per 1,000 to 4 per 10,000 – a difference of almost 90% (ACS, 2010a).

Regardless of when the last Pap test was completed, women who report any of the following symptoms need a diagnostic evaluation. These include:

- abnormal bleeding (including bleeding after sexual intercourse or between periods, heavier or longer lasting menstrual bleeding, or bleeding after menopause)

- abnormal vaginal discharge (may be foul smelling)

- pelvic or back pain

- pain on urination

- blood in the stool or urine.

Many health organizations have published cervical cancer screening guidelines, although there are some differences between the recommendations, there are general commonalities. Most organizations now recommend initial Pap screening 3 years after the onset of vaginal intercourse or by 21 years of age, whichever comes first. However, the ACOG recommends 21 years of age no matter what the age of sexual onset.

Annual screening is recommended by most organizations although the ACS and ACOG make a distinction between women younger than and older than 30 years of age. According to ACS and ACOG, women older than 30 years of age may be tested every 2 to 3 years if they have three negative Pap results on three consecutive occasions (Saslow, Runowicz, et al., 2002; ACOG, 2003).

Recommendations for stopping screening are not consistent. The ACS (2010a) recommends that women older than 70 years of age can stop screening if they have had normal results in the past 10 years and ACOG (2003) recommends that physicians make decisions based on their individual patients. One important consideration is whether new risk factors have arisen, such as divorce and new sexual partner(s). Pap screening after hysterectomy is generally not recommended if the cervix was removed and if the hysterectomy was for benign disease.

HPV-DNA testing is now U.S. Food and Drug Administration (FDA)-approved for adjunct screening with cytology screening either with conventional screening or with liquid-based technology. The ACS (2010a) recommends HPV-screening but not until women reach 30 years of age. After 30 years of age, the ACS recommends screening every 3 years using conventional or liquid-based cytology, combined with HPV-DNA testing; however, HPV-DNA testing should not be done more frequently than every 3 years (Saslow, Runowicz, et al., 2002).

Since the development of the Pap smear, a variety of devices have been implemented to obtain cells for cytologic evaluation. These fall into two large categories of smear instruments and cervicovaginal lavage devices (Bidus et al., 2005). Most often the smear is taken with a smear device, which may be a cytobrush, swab, broom instrument, sponge, or tampon. These devices are inserted up through the vagina into the cervical opening, where the transformation zone is found, and are either rotated or left in place for a short period of time; then the device is removed. Sampling the transformation zone is very important because that is where the majority of cervical cancers begin to develop. The cells on the device (or the device itself) are placed in a preservative solution or spread on a slide and placed in or sprayed with a preservative, then sent to a laboratory. The liquid-based technologies may result in the transfer of more endocervical cells, which improves the possibility of detecting a cervical abnormality. This is why some organizations recommend screening less frequently with liquid-based technologies.

Unfortunately, 30% of cervical cancers result from errors in sampling and interpretation (Nuovo et al., 2001). These errors include incomplete sampling of the transformation zone, a poorly prepared slide with drying artifact or clumping of cells, and failure of the pathologist or cytotechnologist to detect abnormal cells. If the report shows the presence of endocervical cells, there is a much greater likelihood that the transformation zone was sampled. The overall false negative rate of the Pap for cervical cancer screening is estimated to be 15% to 25%; the overall sensitivity may range from 50% to 77% (Andy et al., 2004).

Common liquid-based technologies include the ThinPrep (Cytyc Corp, Boxborough, MA) and the AutoCyte Prep (TriPath Imaging, Burlington, NC). Liquid-based preparation systems help prevent poor sampling, uneven cell distribution, and improper fixation on the slide. The Pap smear is obtained with either a cytobrush and Ayre spatula or a cervical broom device. With the liquid-based collections, the sample is not smeared directly onto a glass slide but placed in a small bottle containing fixative solution. At the lab, the sample is filtered, centrifuged to remove excess blood and debris, and a thin layer of cells is transferred to the slide. Liquid-based or thin-layer preparations improve the quality of the Pap smear, decrease unsatisfactory smears, and often increase the number of precancerous lesions detected (Schoof & Lawlor, 2004).

Women should be educated about several issues when scheduling and preparing for a Pap smear.

The Pap smear should not be collected during a menstrual cycle. Two weeks after the first day of the last period is the optimal time to have the Pap smear. Women should be instructed not to douche or use vaginal creams during the 3 days before the Pap smear. Finally, the woman should be instructed to abstain from intercourse for 24 hours before the Pap smear because it can cause inaccurate results.

Many women do not get regular Pap smears for a variety of reasons, including an inability to pay for services, fatalistic attitudes, knowledge deficit, and lack of support (Loerzel & Bushy, 2005). While many of these factors may not be easily addressed, women should consistently be offered education and support in finding appropriate resources. The most significant example of this is the National Breast and Cervical Cancer Detection Program administered by the CDC. It provides free or low-cost cervical cancer screening to qualified women. In 2006, the program screened 367,200 women for cervical cancer using the Pap test and detected 5,162 high-grade and invasive cervical lesions (CDC, 2007).

PAP TEST RESULTS

Scales to interpret Pap tests have evolved in their precision. Currently, the Bethesda System offers the most clarity in reporting cytologic results between the clinician and pathologist. The Bethesda System offers a way to correlate colposcopic, cytologic, and histologic data (Solomon et al., 2002). Previous systems included the original Papanicolaou classification – using I to V classes – and the CIN (cervical intraepithelial neoplasia) system. Table 5-3 lists features of the Bethesda System.

The Bethesda System includes three main categories:

1. a statement of specimen adequacy

2. a general categorization of normal or abnormal

3. descriptive diagnoses.

TABLE 5-3: COMPONENTS OF THE BETHESDA SYSTEM FOR REPORTING PAP TEST RESULTS

Bethesda System for Classification of Pap Smears

Unsatisfactory for evaluation – reason will be specified as to why it is unsatisfactory

- Negative for intraepithelial lesion or malignancy
  - vaginal organisms may be mentioned, such as trichomonas, yeast, shift in vaginal flora, actinomyces, herpes simplex
- Other non-neoplastic findings, such as reactive changes associated with inflammation, radiation, or intrauterine device; glandular cells status post hysterectomy; or atrophy
- Other changes such as endometrial cells in a woman older than 40 years of age

Epithelial cell abnormality
- *Squamous Cell*
  - *Atypical squamous cells*
    - o atypical squamous cell changes of undetermined significance ASC-US
    - o cannot exclude high grade intraepithelial lesion ASC-H
  - *LSIL* – low-grade squamous intraepithelial dysplasia
    - o encompassing: HPV/mild dysplasia/CIN I
  - *HSIL* – high-grade squamous intraepithelial dysplasia
    - o encompassing: moderate or severe dysplasia, CIS/CIN II,CIN III
    - o with features suspicious for invasion (if invasion suspected)
  - *Squamous cell carcinoma*
- *Glandular Cell*
  - *Atypical*
    - o endocervical cells
    - o endometrial cells
    - o glandular cells
  - *Endocervical adenocarcinoma in situ*
  - *Adenocarcinoma*
    - o endocervical
    - o endometrial
    - o extrauterine
    - o not otherwise specified

Other malignant neoplasms/cancer

(Solomon et al., 2002)

Epithelial cell abnormalities are divided into low- and high-grade groups. The Bethesda System also provides a means to evaluate hormonal state, infection, reactive and reparative changes, and glandular cell components (Solomon et al., 2002). In some women the Pap test is difficult to interpret.

The Pap test is not only a screening test for cervical cancer, but also a screen that aids in the detection of benign and preinvasive cervical conditions.

Benign Conditions

Squamous intraepithelial lesions (SIL) are considered benign conditions. These tumors are on the surface of the epithelial tissue. They include:

- *Low-grade SIL* – These cells are early in the process of changing in size, shape, and number on the surface of the cervix.

- *High-grade SIL* – These cells are a large number of precancerous cells.

Treatment of SILs and warts includes cryosurgery (freezing the tissue to destroy the wart), laser treatment (destroying the wart with high-intensity light), LEEP (loop electrosurgical excision procedure – the removal of tissue using a hot wire loop), and standard surgery (ACOG, 2005). Chemical treatments for SILs include applying podophyllin, bichloroacetic acid, and trichloroacetic acid. Treatment of these benign conditions is recommended to prevent progression to premalignant more invasive conditions (Wright et al., 2007).

Inflammation often results in mildly abnormal Pap tests. Table 5-4 reviews some of the causes of inflammation. When cervical inflammation is treated and cleared, the tissue repairs itself. Then, in several months, a repeat Pap test will often be normal (ACOG, 2005).

TABLE 5-4: CAUSES OF INFLAMED CERVICAL TISSUE (AFFECTING THE RESULTS OF A PAP SMEAR)

- Viruses, especially herpes infections and condyloma cuminata (warts)
- Yeast or monilia infections
- Trichomonas infections
- Pregnancy, miscarriage, or abortion
- Immunosuppression from chemotherapy agents
- Chemicals (for example, medications)
- Hormonal changes

(ACOG, 2005; Hawkins, Roberto-Nichols, & Stanley-Haney, 2008)

Preinvasive Conditions

Premalignant changes of epithelial cells are referred to as dysplasia. The term cervical intraepithelial neoplasia (CIN) describes many intraepithelial changes that can occur before cells become invasive cervical cancer cells. Preinvasive disease does not penetrate the basement membrane (stroma) as does invasive disease.

Four degrees of classification grade the level of CIN. They are

- CIN I (mild dysplasia; involvement of less than one-third thickness of epithelium)
- CIN II (moderate dysplasia; one-third to two-thirds thickness of epithelium)
- CIN III (severe dysplasia)
- Carcinoma in situ (full thickness involvement of the surface area)

(Solomon et al., 2002).

Mild dysplasia and CIN I typically occur in younger women (25 to 35 years of age). Each year, an estimated 1.2 million women are diagnosed with SIL or CIN changes (Solomon et al., 2002).

When high-grade SILs invade deeper layers of the cervix, becoming severe dysplasia (CIN II or III) or carcinoma in situ, they can become invasive and spread. These lesions are more often identified in women between 30 to 40 years of age. Ultimately, when cervical cancer cells spread to other tissues or organs, the condition is invasive cervical cancer. Invasive cervical cancer is most often seen in women older than 40 years of age (ACOG, 2005; Solomon et al., 2002).

Treatment strategies for CIN can range from observation to ablative therapies, such as electrocautery, cryotherapy, laser vaporization, excisional therapies, and hysterectomy.

If properly managed, dysplasias are nearly 100% curable. A small proportion of mild dysplasias (CIN I or low-grade SIL) will regress without treatment. However, for now, clinicians do not have methods to distinguish between dysplastic areas that will either remain benign or those that will become malignant (Safaeian, Solomon, Wacholder, Schiffman, & Castle, 2007; Solomon et al., 2002; Wright et al., 2007).

The majority of cervical tumors are squamous cell carcinomas. The external surface of the cervix, or ectocervix, is lined with squamous epithelial cells. The transformation zone refers to the area where the columnar epithelium lining the cervical canal joins the squamous epithelium, generally in the area of the cervical os. Most cervical cancers begin as an alteration of the transformation zone and originate from precursor lesions (Silverberg & Ioffe, 2003). Such lesions include atypical squamous cells (ASC) of undetermined significance (ASC-US) that do or do not exclude low-grade or high-grade SIL. Low-grade SIL includes HPV, mild dysplasia, and cervical intraepithelial neoplasia. High-grade SIL includes moderate to severe dysplasia and carcinoma in situ. Glandular cell changes from the cervix can also be atypical (AGC) and are more likely to become neoplastic or cancerous as adenocarcinoma of the endocervix in situ (Hawkins et al., 2008). A summary of the recommendations for follow-up of abnormal Pap smears is found in Table 5-5.

PREVENTION

Cervical cancer is a cancer in which there are direct measures to prevent the disease. These measures are aimed at preventing premalignant lesions. If such lesions develop, the goal becomes to detect and treat the lesions before there is malignant progression. Although cervical cancer is potentially preventable, the time between preinvasive and invasive stages usually is long and screening methods are effective, causing the rate of cancer deaths due to cervical cancer to be high. Therefore, patient education – toward improving primary and secondary prevention – is a key area of nursing influence. Key populations to target for preventive information are adolescents, women testing positive for HIV, and women with multiple sex partners. In addition to information about cervical cancer and safer sex practices, nurses can emphasize the importance of reducing risk factors that are thought to contribute to cervical dysplasia and tumor development. Among those risks is cigarette smoking.

TABLE 5-5: PAP TEST TERMS, FOLLOW-UP, AND TESTING STRATEGIES			
Pap Test Result	**Abbreviation**	**Also Known As**	**Tests and Treatments May Include**
Atypical squamous cells – undetermined signficance	ASC-US		HPV testing repeat Pap test Colposcopy and biopsy Estrogen cream
Atypical squamous cells – cannot exclude HSIL	ASC-H		Colposcopy and biopsy
Atypical glandular cells	AGC		Colposcopy and biopsy and/or endocervical curettage
Endocervical adenocarcinoma in situ	AIS		Colposcopy and biopsy and/or endocervical curettage
Low-grade squamous intraepithelial lesion	LSIL	Mild dysplasia or cervical intraepithelial neoplasia–I (CIN I)	Colposcopy and biopsy
High-grade squamous	HSIL	Moderate dysplasia, Severe dysplasia, CIN II, CIN III, or Carcinoma in situ (CIS)	Colposcopy and biopsy and/or endocervical curettage, further treatment with LEEP, cryotherapy, laser therapy, conization, or hysterectomy

(Solomon et al., 2002; ACOG, 2005)

First, women should avoid exposure to HPV. Most premalignant lesions of the cervix could be prevented by avoiding exposure to HPV (Saslow, Castle, et al., 2007). Certain types of sexual behavior increase a woman's risk of getting HPV infection, such as:

- having sex at an early age

- having many sexual partners

- having a partner who has had many sex partners

- having sex with uncircumcised males

Delaying having sex helps to limit the number of sexual partners and helps to avoid having sex with someone who has had many other sexual partners. It is possible to have HPV for years, yet have no symptoms as it does not always cause warts or any other symptoms. Someone can have the virus and pass it on without knowing it.

Women should avoid smoking. There is a direct link between smoking and cervical cancer (ACS, 2010a). Women who do smoke should engage in a smoking cessation program because this helps reduce the risk.

One of the most effective ways to prevent cervical cancer is to prevent HPV infection through vaccination. Vaccines have been developed that can protect women from HPV infections. There is a vaccine that protects against HPV types 6, 11, 16 and 18 (Gardasil).

Gardasil has been approved for use in this country by the FDA. It requires a series of three injections over a 6-month period. The second injection is given 2 months after the first one, and the third is given 4 months after the second. Side effects are reported to be mild (Saslow, Castle, et al., 2007). The most common one is short-term redness, swelling, and soreness at the injection site. In clinical trials, Gardasil prevented genital warts caused by HPV types 6 and 11 and prevented precancers and cancers of the cervix caused by HPV types 16 and 18. This vaccine only works to pre-vent HPV infection; it will not treat an infection that is already there.

To be most effective, the HPV vaccine should be given before a person starts having sex. The Federal Advisory Committee on Immunization Practices (ACIP) has recommended that the vaccine be given routinely to females 11 to 12 years old. It can be given to younger females (as young as 9 years old) at the discretion of doctors (CDC, 2008). ACIP has also recommended that women 13 to 26 years old, who have not yet been vaccinated, get "catch-up" vaccinations.

The ACS (2010a) also recommends that the vaccine be routinely given to females 11 to 12 years old and as early as 9 years old at the discretion of doctors as well as "catch-up" vaccinations to females 13 to 18 years old. The ACS recommends that women 19 to 26 years old talk with their healthcare providers about their personal risk of previous HPV exposure and potential benefit from vaccination, before deciding to get vaccinated. Research is now being done on using Gardasil in older women and in males.

Gardasil is expensive. The vaccine series costs about $360 (not including any doctor's fee or the cost of giving the injections). It should be covered by most medical insurance plans (if given according to ACIP guidelines). It should also be covered by government programs that pay for vaccinations in children younger than 18 years of age.

It is important to realize that the vaccine doesn't protect against all cancer-causing types of HPV, so routine Pap tests are still necessary. One other benefit of the vaccine is that it protects against the two viruses that cause 90% of genital warts.

CERVICAL CANCER DIAGNOSTIC EVALUATION

Cervical cancer cells are usually squamous cell in origin. As with other malignant tumors, cervical cancer cells can invade and damage tissues and organs near the tumor and can break away from a malignant tumor and move through the lymphatics. Typical areas of spread are to the woman's rectum, bladder, bones of the spine, and lungs (ACS, 2010a). Treatment for CIN, including carcinoma in situ, depends on the type and extent of abnormal changes. Some of the treatments for CIN are also used for early-stage cancer

If the Pap test shows a finding of ASC-H, LSIL, or HSIL, the clinician may perform a colposcopy. This procedure involves the use of an instrument similar to a microscope (called a colposcope) to examine the vagina and the cervix. The colposcope does not enter the body. During a colposcopy, the clinician coats the cervix with a dilute vinegar solution that causes abnormal areas to turn white. During the procedure (called the Shiller test), the clinician can biopsy the tissue.

Another procedure to evaluate abnormal cells is endocervical curettage. This test involves scraping cells from inside the endocervical canal with a small spoon-shaped tool called a curette, then sending the tissue sample for evaluation.

These biopsy procedures may cause some bleeding or other watery discharge, but the area should heal quickly. Women often experience some pain – similar to menstrual cramping.

If under laboratory analysis the abnormal tissue cells are considered at high risk for becoming invasive cancer, further treatment options are needed. Many of these techniques (or a combination of these) can be done in the physician's office or on an out-patient basis. In addition to providing a way to biopsy abnormal tissues, these techniques can also remove the abnormal tissue areas:

- *LEEP* – surgery that uses an electrical current transmitted through a thin wire loop, which acts as a knife.

- *Cryotherapy or cryosurgery* – technique destroys abnormal tissue by freezing it.

- *Cauterization* – burning the tissue.

- *Laser therapy* – technique that uses a narrow beam of intense light to destroy or remove abnormal cells.

- *Conization* – technique that removes a cone-shaped piece of tissue using a knife, laser, or the LEEP technique. Conization sampling allows a view of the tissue beneath the surface of the cervix. It can also be used to remove pre-cancerous lesions.

- *Simple hysterectomy* – removal of the uterus and cervix. If abnormal cells are found inside the opening of the cervix, this is a surgical option when childbearing years are complete. (ACOG 2005).

- *Dilation & curettage* – this method scrapes cells from the endometrium and the cervix, in an attempt to isolate sampling in the suspicious area.

Further treatment decisions are based on staging criteria (Tables 5-6 and 5-7 review the AJCC and FIGO staging systems). After a woman is diagnosed and treated for invasive cervical cancer, follow-up is recommended for 8 to 10 years (ACS, 2010a; ACOG, 2005; National Comprehensive Cancer Network [NCCN] 2010).

TREATMENT

Surgery

For early stage cervical cancer, surgery is the treatment of choice. Surgeries can be simple hysterectomies, coupled with lymphadenectomies (removal of lymph nodes in the pelvis). Depending on the amount of disease, tissue may be removed around the uterus as well as part of the vagina and the fallopian tubes (Benedet, Bender, Jones, Ngan, & Pecorelli, 2000).

TABLE 5-6: AJCC CERVICAL CANCER STAGING

TNM Definitions

(The definitions of the T categories correspond to the several stages accepted by FIGO.)

Primary Tumor (T)

TX: Primary tumor cannot be assessed

T0: No evidence of primary tumor

Tis: Carcinoma in situ

T1/I: Cervical carcinoma confined to uterus (extension to corpus should be disregarded)

T1a/IA: Invasive carcinoma diagnosed only by microscopy. All macroscopically visible lesions – even with superficial invasion – are T1b/IB. Stromal invasion with a maximal depth of 5 mm measured from the base of the epithelium and a horizontal spread of 7 mm or less. Vascular space involvement, venous or lymphatic, does not affect classification.

T1a1/Ia1: Measured stromal invasion 3 mm or less in depth and 7 mm or less in horizontal spread

T1a2/IA2: Measured stromal invasion more than 3 mm and not more than 5 mm with a horizontal spread 7 mm or less

T1b/IB: Clinically visible lesion confined to the cervix or microscopic lesion greater than T1a2/IA2

T1b1/IB1: Clinically visible lesion 4 cm or less in greatest dimension

T1b2/IB2: Clinically visible lesion more than 4 cm in greatest dimension

T2/II: Cervical carcinoma invades beyond uterus but not to pelvic wall or to the lower third of the vagina

T2a/IIa: Tumor without parametrial involvement

T2b/IIb: Tumor with parametrial involvement

T3/III: Tumor extends to the pelvic wall and/or involves the lower third of the vagina, and/or causes hydronephrosis or nonfunctioning kidney

T3a/IIIA: Tumor involves lower third of the vagina, no extension to pelvic wall

T3b/IIIB: Tumor extends to pelvic wall and/or causes hydronephrosis or nonfunctioning kidney

T4/IVA: Tumor invades mucosa of the bladder or rectum, and/or extends beyond true pelvis (bullous edema is not sufficient to classify a tumor as T4)

M1/IVB: Distant metastasis

Regional Lymph Nodes (N)

NX: Regional lymph nodes cannot be assessed

N0: No regional lymph node metastasis

N1: Regional lymph node metastasis

Distant Metastasis (M)

MX: Distant metastasis cannot be assessed

M0: No distant metastasis

M1: Distant metastasis

AJCC Stage Groupings

Stage 0
Stage 0 is carcinoma in situ, intraepithelial carcinoma. There is no stromal invasion.

Tis, N0, M0

Stage 1
T1 N0 M0

Stage IA1
T1a1, N0, M0

Stage IA2
T1a2, N0, M0

Stage IB1
T1b1, N0, M0

Stage IB2
T1b2, N0, M0

Stage IIA
T2a, N0, M0

Stage IIA1
T2a1 N0 M0

Stage IIA2
T2a2 N0M0

Stage IIB
T2b, N0, M0

Stage IIIA
T3a, N0, M0

Stage IIIB
T1, N1, M0

T2, N1, M0

T3a, N1, M0

T3b, Any N, M0

Stage IVA
T4, Any N, M0

Stage IVB
Any T, Any N, M1

TABLE 5-7: FIGO CERVICAL CANCER STAGING

Stage 0 (Tis, N0, M0): The cancer cells are only in the cells on the surface of the cervix (the layer of cells lining the cervix), without growing into (invading) deeper tissues of the cervix. This stage is also called carcinoma in situ (CIS) or cervical intraepithelial neoplasia (CIN) grade III (CIN III). This stage is not included in the FIGO system.

Stage I (T1, N0, M0): In this stage the cancer has grown into (invaded) the cervix, but it is not growing outside the uterus. The cancer has not spread to nearby lymph nodes (N0) or distant sites (M0).

Stage IA (T1a, N0, M0): This is the earliest form of stage I. There is a very small amount of cancer, and it can be seen only under a microscope. The cancer has not spread to nearby lymph nodes (N0) or distant sites (M0).

- **Stage IA1 (T1a1, N0, M0):** The cancer is less than 3 mm (about 1/8-inch) deep and less than 7 mm (about 1/4-inch) wide. The cancer has not spread to nearby lymph nodes (N0) or distant sites (M0).
- **Stage IA2 (T1a2, N0, M0):** The cancer is between 3 mm and 5 mm (about 1/5-inch) deep and less than 7 mm (about 1/4-inch) wide. The cancer has not spread to nearby lymph nodes (N0) or distant sites (M0).

Stage IB (T1b, N0, M0): This stage includes stage I cancers that can be seen without a microscope as well as cancers that can only be seen with a microscope if they have spread deeper than 5 mm (about 1/5 inch) into connective tissue of the cervix or are wider than 7 mm. These cancers have not spread to nearby lymph nodes (N0) or distant sites (M0).

- **Stage IB1 (T1b1, N0, M0):** The cancer can be seen but it is not larger than 4 cm (about 1 3/5 inches). It has not spread to nearby lymph nodes (N0) or distant sites (M0).
- **Stage IB2 (T1b2, N0, M0):** The cancer can be seen and is larger than 4 cm. It has not spread to nearby lymph nodes (N0) or distant sites (M0).

Stage II (T2, N0, M0): In this stage, the cancer has grown beyond the cervix and uterus, but hasn't spread to the walls of the pelvis or the lower part of the vagina.

Stage IIA (T2a, N0, M0): The cancer has not spread into the tissues next to the cervix (called the parametria). The cancer may have grown into the upper part of the vagina. It has not spread to nearby lymph nodes (N0) or distant sites (M0).

- **Stage IIA1 (T2a1, N0, M0):** The cancer can be seen but it is not larger than 4 cm (about 1 3/5 inches). It has not spread to nearby lymph nodes (N0) or distant sites (M0).
- **Stage IIA2 (T2a2, N0, M0):** The cancer can be seen and is larger than 4 cm. It has not spread to nearby lymph nodes (N0) or distant sites (M0).

Stage IIB (T2b, N0, M0): The cancer has spread into the tissues next to the cervix (the parametria). It has not spread to nearby lymph nodes (N0) or distant sites (M0).

Stage III (T3, N0, M0): The cancer has spread to the lower part of the vagina or the walls of the pelvis. The cancer may be blocking the ureters (tubes that carry urine from the kidneys to the bladder). It has not spread to nearby lymph nodes (N0) or distant sites (M0).

Stage IIIA (T3a, N0, M0): The cancer has spread to the lower third of the vagina but not to the walls of the pelvis. It has not spread to nearby lymph nodes (N0) or distant sites (M0).

Stage IIIB (T3b, N0, M0; OR T1-3, N1, M0): either:

- The cancer has grown into the walls of the pelvis and/or has blocked one or both ureters (a condition called hydronephrosis), but has not spread to lymph nodes or distant sites.

OR

- The cancer has spread to lymph nodes in the pelvis (N1) but not to distant sites (M0). The tumor can be any size and may have spread to the lower part of the vagina or walls of the pelvis (T1-T3).

Stage IV: This is the most advanced stage of cervical cancer. The cancer has spread to nearby organs or other parts of the body.

Stage IVA (T4, N0, M0): The cancer has spread to the bladder or rectum, which are organs close to the cervix (T4). It has not spread to nearby lymph nodes (N0) or distant sites (M0).

Stage IVB (any T, any N, M1): The cancer has spread to distant organs beyond the pelvic area, such as the lungs or liver.

(Pecorelli et al., 2009).

A simple hysterectomy is surgery to remove the uterus (the body of the uterus and the cervix). The structures next to the uterus (parametria and uterosacral ligaments) are not removed. The vagina remains entirely intact, and pelvic lymph nodes are not removed. The ovaries and fallopian tubes are usually left in place unless there is some other reason to remove them.

If the uterus is removed through a surgical incision in the front of the abdomen, it is called an abdominal hysterectomy. When the uterus is removed through the vagina, it is called a vaginal hysterectomy. General or epidural (regional) anesthesia is used for both operations. The recovery time and hospital stay tends to be shorter for a vaginal hysterectomy than for an abdominal hysterectomy. For a vaginal hysterectomy, the hospital stay is usually 1 to 2 days followed by a 2 to 3 week recovery period. For an abdominal hysterectomy, a hospital stay of 3 to 5 days is common, and complete recovery takes about 4 to 6 weeks. Any type of hysterectomy results in infertility. Complications are unusual but could include excessive bleeding, wound infection, or damage to the urinary or intestinal systems.

A simple hysterectomy is used to treat stage IA1 cervical cancers. The operation is also used for some stage 0 cancers (carcinoma in situ), if there are cancer cells at the edges of the cone biopsy (positive margins).

In a radical hysterectomy with pelvic node dissection, the surgeon removes more than just the uterus. The tissues next to the uterus (parametria and uterosacral ligaments), the upper part (about 1 inch) of the vagina next to the cervix, and some lymph nodes from the pelvis are also removed. The ovaries and fallopian tubes are not removed unless there is some other medical reason to do so. This surgery is usually performed through an abdominal incision.

Another surgical approach is called laparoscopic-assisted radical vaginal hysterectomy. This operation combines a radical vaginal hysterec-tomy with a laparoscopic pelvic node dissection. Laparoscopy allows the inside of the abdomen and pelvis to be seen through a tube inserted into a very small surgical incision. Small instruments can be controlled through the tube, so the surgeon can remove lymph nodes through the tube without making a large cut in the abdomen. The laparoscope can also make it easier to remove the uterus, ovaries, and fallopian tubes through the vaginal incision.

More tissue is removed in a radical hysterectomy than in a simple one, so the hospital stay can be longer, usually about 5 to 7 days. The surgery results in infertility. Complications are unusual but could include excessive bleeding, wound infection, or damage to the urinary and intestinal systems. A radical hysterectomy and pelvic lymph node dissection are the usual treatment for stages IA2, IB and, less commonly, IIA cervical cancer, especially in young women.

Most women with stage IA2 and stage IB are treated with hysterectomy. Another procedure, known as a radical trachelectomy, allows some young women to be treated without losing their ability to have children. This procedure involves removing the cervix and the upper part of the vagina and placing a "purse-string" stitch to act as an artificial internal opening of the cervix os. The nearby lymph nodes are also removed using laparoscopy. The operation is done either through the vagina or the abdomen. After trachelectomy, some women are able to carry a pregnancy to term and deliver a healthy baby by cesarean section. In one study, the pregnancy rate after 5 years was over 50%, but the risk of miscarriage after this surgery is higher than is seen in normal healthy women. The risk of the cancer coming back after this procedure is low.

A pelvic exenteration is a more extensive operation that may be used to treat recurrent cervical cancer. In this surgery, all of the organs and tissues, as in a radical hysterectomy with pelvic lymph node dissection, are removed. In addition, the bladder, vagina, rectum, and part of the colon may also be removed. This operation is used to treat recurrent cervical cancer.

If the bladder is removed, a urostomy is needed. If the rectum and part of the colon are removed, a colostomy may be needed. If the vagina is removed, a new vagina can be surgically created out of skin, intestinal tissue, or myocutaneous (muscle and skin) grafts. Recovery from total pelvic exenteration takes up to 6 months after surgery. Some say it takes a year or two to adjust completely.

The advantages of surgery over radiation therapy include shorter treatment time, preserving the function of the ovaries, and limited sexual dysfunction. Surgery can also be the more appropriate treatment if the patient had previous radiation therapy, has inflammatory bowel or pelvic disease, or is pregnant (ACOG, 2005; NCCN, 2010).

Radiotherapy

Radiation therapy is an extremely effective treatment option for cervical cancer. Surgery and radiation have been studied as equivalent treatments for early stage cervical cancers. Radiation therapy can be a treatment for early-stage disease or for advanced stage disease. It can be targeted at the main malignant area as well as the lymph nodes. The advantage of radiation therapy is that the woman can avoid surgery if she is too ill or at too high of a risk for surgical anesthesia.

External beam radiation treatment usually takes 6 to 7 weeks to complete. For cervical cancer, this type of radiation therapy is often given along with low doses of chemotherapy with a drug called cisplatin.

Brachytherapy for cervical cancer is commonly utilized. The radioactive material is placed in a cylinder in the vagina. For some cancers, radioactive material may be placed in thin needles that are inserted directly in the tumor. Low-dose brachytherapy is completed in just a few days. During that time, the patient remains in the hospital with instruments holding the radioactive material in place. High-dose rate brachytherapy is done as an outpatient over several treatments. For each treatment, the radioactive material is inserted for a few minutes and then removed. The advantage of high-dose rate is that it does not require prolonged immobilization.

Common side effects of radiation therapy include tiredness, upset stomach, and diarrhea. Some women have problems with nausea and vomiting. These side effects tend to be worse when chemotherapy is given with radiation. Skin changes are also common.

Pelvic radiation therapy may cause scar tissue to form in the vagina. The scar tissue can make the vagina more narrow (vaginal stenosis) or even shorter, which makes vaginal intercourse painful. A woman can help prevent this problem by stretching the walls of her vagina several times a week. This can be done by engaging in sexual intercourse 3 to 4 times per week or by using a vaginal dilator. Vaginal dryness and painful intercourse can be long-term side effects from radiation. Vaginal (local) estrogens may also be used to help with vaginal dryness and atrophy.

Pelvic radiation can damage the ovaries, causing premature menopause. Radiation can irritate the bladder and problems with urination may occur. Radiation to the pelvis can also weaken the bones, leading to fractures. Hip fractures are the most common and may occur 2 to 4 years after radiation. Bone density studies are recommended (Hawkins et al., 2008).

Chemotherapy

Chemotherapy can be used as adjuvant treatment in cervical cancer to reduce the risk of recurrence from microscopic tumor cells; however, its role is limited.

Most patients who are in good medical condition and receiving radiation for stage IIA or higher cervical cancer will be offered chemotherapy in addition to their radiation. Studies have shown that adding chemotherapy to radiation decreases mortality from cervical cancer (ACOG, 2005; NCCN, 2010).

The most common chemotherapy regimens include:

* cisplatin and paclitaxel
* cisplatin and topotecan
* cisplatin and gemcitabine
* carboplatin and paclitaxel

Side effects of these commonly used regimens are shown in Table 5-8.

RECURRENT CERVICAL CANCER

About one-third of patients with invasive cervical cancer will have a recurrence. About two-thirds of those who recur will present with the disease within 2 years after initial treatment (ACOG, 2005; NCCN, 2010). Recurrent disease typically presents as unexplained weight loss, excessive unilateral leg edema, vaginal discharge, and pelvic, thigh, or buttock pain.

Patients with recurrent disease have limited effective options. More surgery may be elected such as a pelvic exenteration, and additional radiation therapy may be necessary.

CASE STUDY: CERVICAL CANCER

JN is a 37-year-old Vietnamese woman, who has not had annual pelvic examinations. At the community clinic, JN reports symptoms of abnormal postcoital bleeding for the past year. She also complains of urinary urgency. Her nurse practitioner

TABLE 5-8: CHEMOTHERAPY AGENTS FOR CERVICAL CANCER (1 OF 2)		
Agent	**Administration**	**Side Effects**
Cisplatin (Platinol)	I.V. The patient should be well hydrated prior to administration of the drug. Poor hydration increases the likelihood of developing side effects. Use with extreme caution (if at all) in patients with kidney dysfunction, impaired hearing, preexisting peripheral neuropathy, or past history of an allergic reaction to this type of medication.	Nausea and vomiting Anaphylactic reactions (consisting of fast heart rate, wheezing, lowered blood pressure and facial edema), kidney damage Nephrotoxicity Ototoxicity Bone marrow suppression with increased risk of bleeding and infection Electrolyte (sodium, potassium, and magnesium) disturbances Cardiac toxicity (manifested by electrocardiogram changes) may be seen
Carboplatin (Paraplatin)	I.V. over 15 minutes or longer	The dose-limiting toxic effect is bone marrow suppression, particularly thrombocytopenia leading to increased risk of bleeding Nausea and vomiting Nephrotoxicity Neurotoxicity, especially tingling and numbness of the hands and feet Ototoxicity

continued on next page

TABLE 5-8: CHEMOTHERAPY AGENTS FOR CERVICAL CANCER (2 OF 2)		
Agent	**Administration**	**Side Effects**
Paclitaxel (Taxol)	I.V. infusion Anaphylactic-like (hypersensitivity) reactions have been seen with administration, characterized by wheezing, shortness of breath, facial flushing, facial swelling, and decreased blood pressure. Premedication with a steroid, Benadryl and Cimetidine will help minimize this adverse effect.	The dose-limiting side effect of Taxol is bone marrow suppression. Decreases in the white count are more predominant than platelet or red blood cell effects. Neuropathy, characterized by numbness, tingling, and pain has also been seen. The neuropathy is typically reversible when the agent is discontinued. Symptom resolution usually occurs over several months. Cardiac side effects include lowing of the heart rate (bradycardia) but is usually short lived. Rarely, the slowing is progressive leading to complete heart block. Other side effects include nausea and vomiting, diarrhea, mouth sores, hair loss, and flu-like symptoms, consisting of joint and muscle aches (arthralgia and myalgia), fever, rash, headache, and fatigue.
Topotecan (Hycamtin)	I.V. infusion	Major side effect is the development of neutropenia. Lowered platelets and anemia have also been noted. 30% of patients experience nausea and vomiting. One-third of patients experience fever greater than 101° F. Microscopic blood in the urine has occurred in 10% to 12% of patients.
Gemcitabine (Gemzar)	I.V. infusion over 30 minutes	Bone marrow suppression is common. Other effects include a reversible skin rash, fever, nausea and vomiting, and the development of a flu-like syndrome.

performs a pelvic examination and Pap test. On examination, her clinician notes lesions in the perineal area that are suspicious for HPV.

JN's Pap test was sent to a local laboratory. The Pap results came back noting HPV and dysplasia. On follow-up colposcopy, additional punch biopsies were taken with results showing CIN II (based on Bethesda System for classification of Pap smears, high-grade SIL).

JN's risk factors include multiple sex partners in her teens and 20s. She is married but she and her husband are now separated. Her husband still returns to have intercourse with her when he is home from his deployments with the Navy.

To treat her CIN, JN returned to the clinic for a cryosurgical procedure to remove the cervical lesions. Postprocedure, she had some abdominal cramping and bleeding, which resolved within 48 hours. She was given Tylenol #3 to help with pain.

She was instructed to return to the clinic for a follow-up pelvic examination in 6 months. A year and a half later, JN presented at the clinic with abnormal vaginal bleeding, dysuria, and hematuria. She had also lost 10 pounds in the last 6 months. Diagnostically, JN had an additional tissue biopsy via curettage. The biopsy indicated that she now had squamous cell cancer of the cervix. Based on clinical data, chest X-ray and a CT scan of the colon and rectum, she was staged at IIA disease (AJCC staging).

JN was scheduled for a total abdominal hysterectomy. Postoperatively, JN experienced bleeding and pain. She also had surgical drains, which were removed on day 2 postoperatively. She was discharged from the hospital on day 3.

Postoperatively, 5 weeks later, JN underwent additional external beam radiotherapy (4,500 cGy over 5 weeks – 5x/week) and intracavitary cesium radiotherapy (2 applications). Postradiation she complained of pain and dryness in her vagina. She also showed signs of vaginitis. She was given a 10-day course of antibiotics and instructed to use a water-soluble lubrication on her perineum for comfort.

Follow-up after her surgery and radiation treatments was scheduled at 3-month intervals during the 1st year, then every 3 to 4 months during the 2nd year. JN was somewhat compliant with her follow-up examinations, returning to the clinic every 5 to 6 months. Two years after surgery, JN continued to be disease free on follow-up exam. (Follow-up exams included chest X-ray, complete blood count, liver function tests, and a CT scan.)

Additional Information:

JN says that since her cancer diagnosis, her husband and she have decided to divorce. She has not seen him for the last year. She continues to work as a check-out clerk at the local warehouse store. She says she previously used a diaphragm as

birth control but no longer requires birth control since her hysterectomy. She says she has had two sexual partners in the past 6 months.

On return visits to her physician, JN is reluctant to discuss any other aspects about her health (such as mammography, colonoscopy). She also has isolated herself from friends and neighbors. Her sons (ages 4 and 10), although appearing to be clean and fed, act out when they are out with her. She looks distressed and tired.

JN does admit to regularly visiting her local Vietnamese market to get ingredients for her own "health" tea, which she says will keep any future cancer away.

What major risk factors does JN have for cervical cancer?

JN has an HPV infection that is associated with higher risk of cervical cancer, which may be due to having multiple sexual partners. She also has not engaged in regular screening, which can often detect cervical cancer at a very early stage.

What side effect of radiation therapy should be addressed with JN?

Radiation therapy to the cervix can result in significant vaginal stenosis, which is associated with vaginal dryness and painful intercourse or speculum examinations. JN might want to consider using a dilator to reduce vaginal stenosis. She may want to use a vaginal moisturizer to decrease vaginal dryness. During intercourse, she may need a lubricant such as K-Y jelly.

SUMMARY

Cervical cancer morbidity has decreased because of widely used detection methods, specifically the Pap smear. Women at risk are usually younger with risk factors of active or unprotected sexual activity and exposure to HPV or other viruses. Morbidity and mortality related to cervical cancer can be traced to clinician vigilance in detecting and treating benign cervical tumors and those in the early stages of cervical cancer. Once diagnosed, patients are usually treated with excision procedures or surgery. Radiation therapy (external and internal) also plays a role in effective treatment protocols.

EXAM QUESTIONS

CHAPTER 5
Questions 34-43

Note: Choose the one option that BEST answers each question.

34. A major risk factor of cervical cancer is

    a. sexual activity (at early age, multiple sex partners).
    b. colon cancer.
    c. estrogen receptor negative (ER–) status.
    d. obesity.

35. Types of human paplilloma viruses associated with cervical cancer are

    a. HPV-6.
    b. HPV-11.
    c. HPV-16.
    d. HPV-31.

36. Mortality rates for cervical cancer have declined 40% in the last 30 years, due in large part to wider and consistent use of

    a. the Pap test.
    b. clinical staging.
    c. hysterectomies.
    d. hormone replacement therapy.

37. A technique or strategy that is thought to improve the interpretation of Pap tests is

    a. immediate refrigeration of slides.
    b. air drying the slide before transport.
    c. liquid-based thin-layer slide preparation.
    d. combing the smear with Betadine.

38. The Bethesda System for interpreting a Pap test includes

    a. CIN grading only.
    b. general categorization of normal or abnormal.
    c. categorization by class.
    d. HPV results.

39. When classifying cervical cellular changes, moderate dysplasia that is one-third to two-thirds thickness of the epithelium, would receive the classification grade of

    a. CIN I.
    b. CIN II.
    c. CIN III.
    d. Carcinoma in situ.

40. Abnormal Pap test results may be reported as

    a. atypical glandular cells.
    b. atypical adipose cells.
    c. atypical HPV.
    d. atypical mucosa.

41. The treatment for a woman with Stage I cervical cancer is typically

    a. surgery.
    b. radiation.
    c. chemotherapy.
    d. hormonal manipulation.

42. Carcinoma in situ of the cervix is staged as

    a. T1a.
    b. Tis.
    c. T1b.
    d. T2.

43. Chemotherapy agents used as a treatment for cervical cancer include

    a. cisplatin and cyclophosphamide.
    b. cisplatin and paclitaxel.
    c. cisplatin and hydroxyurea.
    d. cisplatin and BCNU.

REFERENCES

Altekruse, S.F., Lacey, J.V., Jr., Brinton, L.A., Gravitt, P.E., Silverberg, S.G., Barnes, W.A., Jr., et al. (2003). Comparison of human papillomavirus genotypes, sexual, and reproductive risk factors of cervical adenocarcinoma and squamous cell carcinoma: Northeastern United States. *American Journal of Obstetrics and Gynecology, 188*(3): 657-663.

American Cancer Society. (2010a). *Cancer facts & figures 2010.* Atlanta, GA: American Cancer Society.

American Cancer Society. (2010b). *Cervical cancer: What are the key statistics about cervical cancer?* Retrieved July 16, 2010, from http://www.cancer.org/Cancer/CervicalCancer/Detailed Guide/cervical-cancer-key-statistics

American Cancer Society. (2010c). *Cervical cancer: What are the risk factors for cervical cancer?* Retrieved July 16, 2010, from http://www.cancer.org/Cancer/CervicalCancer/Detailed Guide/cervical-cancer-risk-factors

American College of Obstetricians and Gynecologists (ACOG). (2003). *Cervical cytology screening* (ACOG practice bulletin no. 45). Washington, DC: Author.

American College of Obstetricians and Gynecologists (ACOG). (2005). *Management of abnormal cervical cytology and histology* (ACOG practice bulletin no. 66). Washington, DC: Author.

American College of Obstetricians and Gynecologists (ACOG). (2009). *Clinical management guidelines for obstetrician-gynecologists.* (ACOG practice bulletin no.109). Retrieved June 10, 2010, from http://journals.lww.com/greenjournal/documents/PB109_Cervical_Cytology_Screening.pdf

Andy, C., Turner, L.F., & Neher, J.O. (2004). Clinical inquiries: Is the ThinPrep better than conventional Pap smear at detecting cervical cancer? *Journal of Family Practice, 53*(4), 313-315.

Benedet, J.L., Bender, H., Jones, H., 3rd., Ngan, H.Y., & Pecorelli, S. (2000). FIGO staging classifications and clinical practice guidelines in the management of gynecologic cancers. FIGO Committee on Gynecologic Oncology. *International Journal of Gynaecology and Obstetrics, 70*(2), 209-262.

Bertram, C.C. (2004). Evidence for practice: Oral contraception and risk of cervical cancer. *Journal of the American Academy of Nurse Practitioners, 16*(10), 455-461.

Bidus, M.A., Zahn, C.M., Maxwell, G.L., Rodrigues, M., Elkas, J.C., & Rose, G.S. (2005). The role of self-collection devices for cytology and human papillomavirus DNA testing in cervical cancer screening. *Clinical Obstetrics and Gynecology, 48*(1), 127-132.

Centers for Disease Control and Prevention. (2007). *2006/2007 National breast and cervical cancer early detection program fact sheet.* Accessed December 30, 2008, from http://screening.iarc.fr/doc/0607_nbccedp_fs.pdf

Centers for Disease Control and Prevention. (2008). Human papilloma virus. In W. Atkinson, J. Hamborsky, L. McIntyre, & S. Wolfe (Eds.), *Epidemiology and prevention of vaccine-preventable diseases* (10th ed., 2nd printing, pp. 283-294). Washington, DC: Public Health Foundation.

Edge, S.B., Byrd, D.R., Carducci, M., Compton, C.C., Fritz, A.G., Greene, F.L., & Trotti, A. (2010). *AJCC cancer staging manual* (7th ed.), New York: Springer.

Eltoum, I.A. & Roberson, J. (2007). Impact of HPV testing, HPV vaccine development, and changing screening frequency on national Pap test volume: Projections from the National Health Interview Survey (NHIS). *Cancer, 111*(1), 34-40.

Hawkins, J.W., Roberto-Nichols, D.M., & Stanley-Haney, J.L. (2008). *Guidelines for nurse practitioners in gynecologic settings* (9th ed.). New York: Springer.

Loerzel, V.W. & Bushy, A. (2005). Interventions that address cancer health disparities in women. *Family and Community Health, 28*(1), 79-89.

Mehring, P.M. (2007). Disorders of the female reproductive organs. In C.M. Porth (Ed.), *Essentials of pathophysiology: Concepts of altered health states* (2nd ed., pp. 931-943). Philadelphia: Lippincott Williams & Wilkins.

Muñoz, N., Bosch, F.X., de Sanjosé, S., Herrero, R., Castellsagué, X., Shah, K.V., et al. (2003). Epidemiologic classification of human papillomavirus types associated with cervical cancer. *New England Journal of Medicine, 348*(6), 518-527.

National Comprehensive Cancer Network (NCCN). (2010). *NCCN Clinical practice guidelines in oncology: Cervical cancer* (V.1.2010). Retrieved February 16, 2010, from http://www.nccn.org/professionals/physician_gls/PDF/cervical.pdf

Nuovo, J., Melnikow, J., & Howell, L.P. (2001). New tests for cervical cancer screening. *American Family Physician, 64*(5), 780-786.

Parkin, D.M., Bray, F., Ferlay, J., & Pisani, P. (2005). Global cancer statistics, 2002. *CA: A Cancer Journal for Clinicians, 55*(2), 74-108.

Pecorelli, S., Zigliani, L., & Odicino, F. (2009). Revised FIGO Staging for carcinoma of the cervix. *International Journal of Gynecology and Obstetrics, 105,* 307-308.

Safaeian, M., Solomon, D., Wacholder, S., Schiffman, M., & Castle, P. (2007). Risk of precancer and follow-up management strategies for women with human papillomavirus-negative atypical squamous cells of undetermined significance. *Obstetrics & Gynecology, 109*(6), 1325-1331.

Saslow, D., Castle, P.E., Cox, J.T., Davey, D.D., Einstein, M.H., Ferris, D.G., et al. (2007). American Cancer Society guideline for human papillomavirus (HPV) vaccine use to prevent cervical cancer and its precursors. *CA: A Cancer Journal for Clinicians, 57*(1), 7-28.

Saslow, D., Runowicz, C.D., Solomon, D., Moscicki, A., Smith, R.A., Eyre, H.J., et al. (2002). American Cancer Society guideline for the early detection of cervical neoplasia and cancer. *CA: A Cancer Journal for Clinicians, 52*(6), 342-362.

Schooff, M. & Lawlor, A. (2004). What is the best collection device for screening cervical smears? *American Family Physician, 69*(7), 1661-1662.

Silverberg, S.G. & Ioffe, O.B. (2003). Pathology of cervical cancer. *Cancer Journal, 9*(5), 335-347.

Smith, J.S., Green, J., de Gonzalez, A.B., Appleby, P., Peto, J., Plummer, M., et al. (2003). Cervical cancer and use of hormonal contraceptives: A systematic review. *Lancet, 361*(9364)1, 1159-1167.

Solomon, D., Davey, D., Kurman, R., Moriarty, A., O'Connor, D., Prey, M., et al. (2002). The 2001 Bethesda System: Terminology for reporting results of cervical cytology. *Journal of the American Medical Association, 287*(16), 2114-2119.

U.S. Preventive Services Task Force. (2003). *Screening for cervical cancer.* Retrieved June 10, 2010, from http://www.ahrq.gov/clinic/uspstf/uspscerv.htm

Wright, T.C., Jr., Massad, L.S., Dunton, C.J., Spitzer, M., Wilkinson, E.J., & Solomon, D. (2007). 2006 consensus guidelines for the management of women with abnormal cervical cancer screening tests. *American Journal of Obstetrics & Gynecology, 197*(4), 346-355.

CHAPTER 6

LUNG CANCER

CHAPTER OBJECTIVE

After completing this chapter, the reader will be able to discuss the epidemiology, risk factors, prevention and detection strategies, and main treatments for lung cancer in women.

LEARNING OBJECTIVES

After studying this chapter, the reader will be able to

1. recognize the main risk factors for lung cancer.

2. describe two strategies to help women quit smoking.

3. identify the main symptoms of lung cancer.

4. describe the main modalities for the treatment of lung cancer.

5. recognize chemotherapy agents used to treat lung cancer.

INTRODUCTION

A review of cancer in women typically focuses on the gender-specific cancers unique to women. Yet, the most prevalent cancer in women is lung cancer, a cancer that continues to scorn prevention efforts and spurn the hope promised by new treatments. Lung cancer accounts for 26% of all cancer deaths in women (American Cancer

Society [ACS], 2010a). See Box 6-1 for lung cancer facts.

BOX 6-1: LUNG CANCER FACTS

- 222,520 estimated new cases annually
- Responsible for 15% of all cancer diagnoses
- Incidence rate is decreasing in men; current rate is 1 in 13 men
- Incidence rate in women has reached a plateau after many years of increase; current rate is 1 in 16 women
- 157,300 estimated deaths annually
- Responsible for 14% of new cancers diagnosed in women annually
- Responsible for 26% of all cancer deaths in women
- The mortality rate from lung cancer is slowly dropping with fewer people smoking
- 1 year survival rate is 42%; 5 year survival rate is 16%
- Only 15% of cases are diagnosed at the localized stage

(ACS, 2010a)

Unfortunately, the history of lung cancer has not changed much in the last 20 years. What is renewed are some approaches to treatment – the multidisciplinary approach to care, society's success in showing how deadly tobacco use can be, and promising novel targeted therapies that have modestly extended the still too-short survival rates. This chapter provides a brief review of the well-known challenges of lung cancer and the rays of hope associated with early detection and more strategic treatments.

EPIDEMIOLOGY

Most of the epidemiologic data on lung cancer includes small cell and non-small cell lung cancers. In general, small cell lung cancer (SCLC) accounts for about 10% to 15% of all lung cancers; most are non-small cell lung cancers (NSCLC). Lung cancer is the second most common cancer in both men (after prostate cancer) and women (after breast cancer). It accounts for about 15% of all new cancers (ACS, 2010a). Trends in lung cancer incidence and mortality are shown in Figure 6-1.

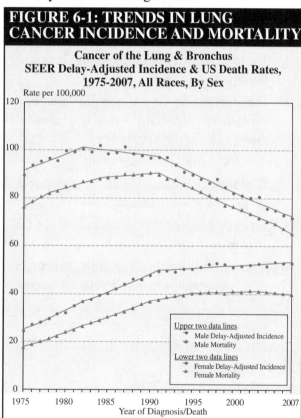

FIGURE 6-1: TRENDS IN LUNG CANCER INCIDENCE AND MORTALITY

Cancer of the Lung & Bronchus
SEER Delay-Adjusted Incidence & US Death Rates,
1975-2007, All Races, By Sex

Upper two data lines
- Male Delay-Adjusted Incidence
- Male Mortality

Lower two data lines
- Female Delay-Adjusted Incidence
- Female Mortality

Source: SEER 9 areas and US Mortality Files (National Center for Health Statistics, CDC).

Rates are age-adjusted to the 2000 US Std Population (19 age groups - Census P25-1103).

Regression lines are calculated using the Joinpoint Regression Program Version 3.4.3, April 2010, National Cancer Institute.

Note. From SEER Cancer Statistics Review, 1975-2007, by S.F. Altekruse, C.L. Kosary, M. Krapcho, N. Neyman, R. Aminou, W. Waldron, et al. (Eds), Bethesda, MD: National Cancer Institute. Retrieved from http://seer.cancer.gov/csr/1975_2007/, based on November 2009 SEER data submission, posted to the SEER web site, 2010.

Lung cancer occurs mainly in older people. About 2 out of every 3 people diagnosed with lung cancer are older than 65 years of age; fewer than 3% of all cases are found in people younger than 45 years of age. The average age at the time of diagnosis is about 71.

MYTHS

There are many myths and misconceptions about lung cancer. These are shown in Table 6-1. Nurses have a major responsibility to educate the public about the facts regarding lung cancer.

RISK FACTORS: SMOKING

Cigarette smoking is the primary risk factor associated with the development of lung cancer. There is a direct causal effect of cigarette smoking. Although cigarette smoking and exposure to tobacco are not absolute causes of lung cancer, 90% of lung cancers can be linked to the patient's tobacco exposure. A smoker's lung cancer risk is between 10 and 20 times higher than that of a non-smoker, depending on how many cigarettes are smoked and how long the person has smoked (ACS, 2009a).

Secondhand smoke also increases the risk for lung cancer. A nonsmoker who lives with a smoker has about a 20% to 30% greater risk of developing lung cancer (ACS, 2009a). Secondhand smoke is the attributed cause of more than 3,400 lung cancer deaths annually (ACS, 2010a).

The longer an individual smokes, and the more packs per day smoked, the greater the risk. People who stop smoking before 50 years of age cut their risk of dying in the next 15 years in half, compared with those who continue to smoke (ACS, 2009a). Individuals who are current smokers also should be informed that the more immediate preventive health priority is the elimination of tobacco use altogether because smoking cessation offers the

TABLE 6-1: MYTHS AND FACTS ABOUT TOBACCO USE

Myth	Fact
Only smokers are at risk.	Most people diagnosed with lung cancer are not current smokers, but are ex-smokers (some of whom have quit a decade or more ago). Additionally, each year approximately 26,000 Americans who never smoked learn that they have lung cancer.
	A smoker's lung cancer risk is between 10 and 20 times higher than that of a nonsmoker, depending on how many cigarettes are smoked and how long the person has smoked.
Men and women are equally susceptible to the effects of lung carcinogens found in tobacco smoke.	Women may have a greater susceptibility to these carcinogens than men.
Once someone begins to smoke, the damage is done, so there's no point in quitting.	When smokers stop, the damage that leads to cancer may heal. Research shows that quitting helps those who already have lung cancer respond better to treatment.
Women need not worry about lung cancer.	Lung cancer is by far the leading cancer killer of women. According to the American Cancer Society, 65,700 American women will die from lung cancer this year, compared to 39,600 from breast cancer.
The first sign of lung cancer is coughing up blood.	Coughing up blood is a common symptom, but it usually appears later. The early signs are vague: fatigue and shortness of breath.
	The signs and symptoms of lung cancer may take years to appear and often are confused with symptoms of less serious conditions. They may not appear until the disease reaches an advanced stage. Depending on which organs are affected, these can include headaches, general weakness, pain, bone fractures, bleeding, or blood clots
Nicotine replacement therapy (NRT) does not work.	NRT can double a smoker's chances of quitting smoking. The likelihood of staying quit for more than 6 months is increased when a smoker uses NRT according to the directions.
The nicotine in cigarettes is the same as the nicotine found in NRT products, so it is just trading one addiction for another.	No, the products are different and the likelihood of long-term addiction to NRT is very low. The nicotine found in NRT is regulated by the U.S. Food and Drug Administration. The amount of nicotine in NRT is less than in cigarettes and it is delivered more slowly. NRT products have a much lower risk of addiction than cigarettes.
With NRT, there are no withdrawal symptoms or cravings from quitting smoking.	NRT does reduce withdrawal symptoms associated with cigarette smoking; however, it may not completely eliminate them. The symptoms most helped by NRT include: irritability, frustration, anger, craving, hunger, anxiety, difficulty concentrating, restlessness, and insomnia.
Many smokers choose "low-tar," "mild," "light," or "ultra-light" cigarettes because they think that these cigarettes may be less harmful to their health than "regular" cigarettes.	Although smoke from light cigarettes may feel smoother and lighter on the throat and chest, light cigarettes are not healthier than regular cigarettes. Light cigarettes do not reduce the health risks of smoking. The only way to reduce a smoker's risk, and the risk to others, is to stop smoking completely.
If a smoker fails to quit the first time, they will continue to be unsuccessful.	On average, it usually takes six attempts before a person actually succeeds in quitting.

(ACS, 2009a, 2010b; Cooley, 2003; Luty, 2002)

most effective means of reducing the risk of premature mortality from lung cancer (Smith, Cokkinides, & Eyre, 2003). Other health benefits of smoking cessation include:

Short-term Benefits

- Blood pressure, pulse, and body temperature, which were abnormally elevated by nicotine, return to normal. Persons taking blood pressure medication should continue doing so until told otherwise by their physicians.

- The body starts to heal itself. Carbon monoxide and oxygen levels in the blood return to normal.

- The risk of having a heart attack decreases.

- Nerve endings start to regenerate. The ability to taste and smell improves.

- Bronchial tubes relax, lung capacity increases, and breathing becomes easier.

- Circulation improves and lungs become stronger, making it easier to walk.

- Cilia in the lungs begins to regrow, increasing the ability of the lungs to handle mucus, to clean themselves, and to reduce infection. Coughing, sinus congestion, fatigue, and shortness of breath decrease.

- Overall energy level increases.

Long-term Benefits

- The risk of dying from lung cancer is less than it would be if the individual continued to smoke.

- The risk of getting cancer of the throat, bladder, kidney, or pancreas also decreases.

- The risk of stroke or heart attack is reduced.

The risk of getting lung cancer due to smoking increases with these factors

- the age at which smoking began

- how long the person has smoked

- the number of cigarettes smoked per day

- how deeply the smoker inhales.

In the USA, there are still about 1 million new smokers per year. Of these, about half will eventually be killed by tobacco if they do not stop, and half these deaths will be in middle age (35 to 69 years old). Around the world, it is estimated that there are currently 30 million who start to smoke every year. It can be expected that the number of tobacco deaths in the world will exceed 10 million every year, unless 20 million current smokers stop (Boyle et al., 2006).

Studies report that approximately 50% of those who smoke and want to quit have difficulty quitting because of the addictive nature of tobacco and nicotine products (Heater, 2010). The Surgeon General's Report on Nicotine Addiction in 1988 was the first study that provided conclusive evidence: Cigarettes and other types of tobacco are addictive. The report underscored the fact that willpower alone could not eliminate smoking as a public health threat (Heater, 2010).

Nicotine creates a physical dependence because nicotine receptors in the brain become saturated during exposure, creating an increased tolerance to nicotine. Studies have suggested that a person's genetics may increase the risk of tobacco dependence (Heater, 2010). These early studies may lead to ways to target those more susceptible to nicotine and smoking behaviors, so that early treatment or cessation interventions are effective.

Smoking behavior is also linked with psychological and social factors. Among those factors are people prone to anxiety and depression. Once again, methods to establish ways to target interventions are being studied. With women, social support has been established as a method to help them quit smoking (Heater, 2010).

Once diagnosed, many of those with lung cancer continue to smoke because their tobacco addiction is well-entrenched. Studies show that with acute illness, most lung cancer patients make attempts to quit (Heater, 2010). Nursing support to help patients quit is an important focus of care. Table 6-2 highlights some well-known strategies to help patients quit smoking.

TABLE 6-2: CONSIDERATIONS FOR SMOKING CESSATION (1 OF 2)

Preparing Yourself for Quitting

- Decide positively that you want to quit.

- List all the reasons you want to quit.

- Develop strong personal reasons, in addition to your health and obligations to others for quitting. For example, think of all the time you waste taking cigarette breaks, rushing out to buy a pack, or hunting for a light.

- Begin to condition yourself physically: Start a modest exercise program, drink more fluids, get plenty of rest, and avoid fatigue.

- Set a firm target date for quitting – perhaps a special day such as your birthday, your anniversary, or the Great American Smokeout.

Knowing What to Expect

- Have realistic expectations.

- Understand that withdrawal symptoms are temporary. They usually last only 1 to 2 weeks.

- Know that most relapses occur in the 1st week after quitting, when withdrawal symptoms are strongest and your body is still dependent on nicotine.

- Mobilize all your personal resources – willpower, family, friends, and the tips – to get you through this critical period successfully.

- Know that most other relapses occur in the first 3 months after quitting, when situational triggers – such as a particularly stressful event – occur unexpectedly.

- Realize that most successful ex-smokers quit for good only after several attempts.

Involving Someone Else

- Ask your friend or spouse to quit with you.

- Tell your family and friends that you're quitting and when.

- Consider joining a smoking cessation class or support group.

- Discuss cessation with your healthcare provider to see if he or she can provide additional support or assistance.

Quitting Tips

- Switch brands.

- Smoke only half of each cigarette.

- Decide beforehand how many cigarettes you'll smoke during the day.

- Change your eating habits to help you cut down.

- Reach for a glass of juice instead of a cigarette for a "pick-me-up."

- Don't empty your ashtrays.

- Make smoking inconvenient; stop buying cigarettes by the carton. Stop carrying cigarettes with you at home or at work.

Making Smoking Unpleasant

- Smoke only under circumstances that aren't especially pleasurable for you. If you like to smoke with others, smoke alone.

- Collect all your cigarette butts in one large glass container as a visual reminder of the filth made by smoking.

continued on next page

TABLE 6-2: CONSIDERATIONS FOR SMOKING CESSATION (2 OF 2)

Avoiding Temptation

- For the first 1 to 3 weeks, avoid situations you strongly associate with the pleasurable aspects of smoking.

- Limit your socializing to healthful, outdoor activities or situations where smoking is not allowed.

- Keep oral substitutes handy. Try carrots, pickles, sunflower seeds, apples, celery, raisins, or sugarless gum instead of a cigarette.

- Take 10 deep breaths and hold the last one while lighting a match.

- Never allow yourself to think that "one won't hurt" – it will.

- Recognize the urge to smoke usually only lasts 3 to 5 minutes – try to wait it out.

Finding New Habits

- Change your habits to make smoking difficult – such as swimming, jogging, or playing tennis or handball.

- Do things that require you to use your hands.

- Find activities that you enjoy – without the need to smoke.

- Make things clean and fresh at home, work, and in the car.

- Use the money saved on cigarettes to buy something as a reward.

- Spend free time in places where smoking is not allowed.

- Drink water and juice. Do not drink alcohol as it can trigger a desire to smoke.

Using Medication and Pharmacology methods

- Nicotine replacement treatments: gum, patch, lozenges, nasal spray, inhaler

- Bupropion (Zyban)

- Varenicline (Chantix)

(ACS, 2010b; Heater, 2010; Luty, 2002)

One simple way to talk to patients about smoking cessation is to use the START method prior to smoking cessation (Tobacco Control Research Branch of the National Cancer Institute, 2009). There are many other helpful resources for smoking cessation at http://smokefree.gov/

- **S** = Set a quit date.

- **T** = Tell family, friends, and coworkers that you plan to quit.

- **A** = Anticipate and plan for the challenges you'll face while quitting.

- **R** = Remove cigarettes and other tobacco products from your home, car, and work.

- **T** = Talk to your doctor about getting help to quit.

Many patients will need additional help to stop smoking. Medications used to assist with smoking cessation are shown in Table 6-3.

Teenagers and Smoking

The overall decline in adult smoking has prompted the tobacco industry to recruit almost 1 million new smokers a year, most of them children and adolescents. Tobacco advertising targets younger smokers, luring them to begin a lifelong addiction before they truly understand the long-term consequences (ACS, 2009c; Jemal et al., 2008).

Many kids start using tobacco by 11 years of age, and many become addicted by 14 years of age (ACS, 2009c). Studies show that a person who does not begin smoking as a child or adolescent is not likely to begin as an adult, with 90% of adult smokers having started smoking at or before 19 years of age (ACS, 2009c).

In order to impact tobacco related mortality, everything must be done to stop children and adoles-

TABLE 6-3: AIDS FOR SMOKING CESSATION (1 OF 2)

Agent	Prescription Needed/Cost	Administration	Benefits	Risks
Nicotine Gum	No Estimated cost is $240 per month.	Chew briefly. Park in mouth for 1 minute. Chew again. Repeat every 30 minutes. Use 2 to 4 mg, or no more than 20 pieces per day. Should take dose over 2 to 3 months. Not recommended for more than 6 months.	Easy to use. Delivers nicotine quickly.	Cannot eat or drink when chewing. Can cause dental problems or oral mucosa irritation.
Nicotine Spray	Yes Cost is about $280 per month.	Spray into each nostril and exhale through mouth. Use every 1 to 2 hours. Taper over 2 to 3 months. Not recommended for more than 6 months.	Very quick delivery of nicotine. Good for reducing sudden craving. May work well for heavy smokers.	Can lead to nasal and sinus irritation.
Nicotine Patch	No Cost is about $120 per month.	The nicotine patch is placed on the skin and supplies a small and steady amount of nicotine into the body. Nicotine patches contain varied concentrations of nicotine (21mg, 14mg, or 7mg). Use over 2 to 3 months with gradual taper. 16 and 24 hour patches are available.	Very easy to use. Less expensive than some of the other methods.	Slower release of nicotine. Can cause skin irritation. Occasionally associated with tachycardia.
Nicotine Inhaler	Yes Cost is about $300 per month.	A nicotine inhaler consists of a cartridge attached to a mouthpiece. Inhaling through the mouthpiece delivers a specific amount of nicotine to the user. At least 6 cartridges are needed for the first 3 to 6 weeks. Taper at 2 to 3 months. Not recommended more than 6 months.	Delivers nicotine very quickly.	May lead to throat irritation or coughing.

continued on next page

TABLE 6-3: AIDS FOR SMOKING CESSATION (2 OF 2)

Agent	Prescription Needed/Cost	Administration	Benefits	Risks
Nicotine Lozenges	No Estimated $240 per month	Nicotine lozenges look like hard candy and are placed between the cheek and gum tissue. The nicotine lozenge (2mg or 4mg dose) releases nicotine as it slowly dissolves in the mouth. Use every 1 to 2 hours over 2 to 3 months. Gradually taper at 3 months. Not recommended beyond 6 months.	Easy to use. Delivers nicotine quickly.	Cannot eat or drink when using. Can cause dental problems or oral mucosa irritation.
Bupropion* (Zyban)	Yes Approximate cost is $120 per month depending on healthcare prescription coverage.	Bupropion helps to reduce nicotine withdrawal symptoms and the urge to smoke. Prescription taper written by physician – usually taken for 7 to 12 weeks. Start taking 2 weeks before quitting.	Bupropion can be used safely with nicotine replacement products.	Contraindicated in persons with seizures or eating disorders. Not safe when pregnant or breast feeding.
Varenicline* (Chantix)	Yes Approximate cost is $120 per month depending on healthcare prescription coverage.	Varenicline, eases nicotine withdrawal symptoms and blocks the effects of nicotine from cigarettes if the user resumes smoking. Start taking 1 week before quitting. Dosage increases slowly during the first week. After day 8, the full dose can be taken for up to 12 weeks.	Eases withdrawal symptoms. Decreases pleasure from smoking.	Can cause nausea.

*See FDA boxed warning for bupropion and varenicline released July 2009 at http://www.fda.gov/NewsEvents/Newsroom/PressAnnouncements/ucm170100.htm
(Corelli & Hudman, 2006)

cents from starting to smoke. This will greatly affect the burden of tobacco-related deaths in the latter half of the 21st century. The major public health gain in the coming 20 to 40 years will come from getting smokers to stop smoking (Boyle et al., 2006).

Women and Smoking

According to the Centers for Disease Control and Prevention (CDC) Office on Smoking and Health, about 24 million adult women and at least 1.9 million adolescent girls smoke cigarettes, despite what they know about death, disease, and addiction caused by smoking (CDC, 2008).

In terms of current smoking, prevalence in women is highest among:

- non-Hispanic whites (24.5%)

- those with a high school education (29.4%)

- those with less than high school education (28.3%)

- divorced, widowed, or separated women (34.7%) (CDC, 2008).

Currently, it's estimated that 24% of all American women smoke. Female smokers typically take up smoking during adolescence, usually before their senior year in high school, often in middle school or junior high. The earlier a young woman begins smoking, the more likely she is to become a heavy smoker as an adult (CDC, 2008).

A sharp increase in smoking initiation occurred among women between 1965 and 1975. This generation of women, born between 1950 and 1960, passed through adolescence and young adulthood at the time when cigarette brands such as Virginia Slims were introduced and marketed intensively to women (Jemal et al., 2008).

All of the 13 states in which the lung cancer death rates increased in women from 1996 through 2005 are located in the South and Midwest where, on average, the prevalence of smoking is higher (Jemal et al., 2008). The annual percentage decrease in current smoking among adult women is also lower in those areas than in the West and Northeast. State variations in smoking prevalence are influenced by several factors, including public awareness about the harmful health effects of tobacco use, social norms about tobacco use, educational levels within the state, racial and ethnic variations among the states, and tobacco control activities at the state and local levels. Most Southern and Midwestern states continue to have a high prevalence of smoking and low excise tax, despite evidence that excise taxes and other components of comprehensive tobacco control can achieve substantial reductions in tobacco use.

With young girls, the temptation to smoke is more striking. Many girls as young as those in the third and fourth grades are already concerned about their weight and body image, and many have already been on diets by the time they enter junior high school. Smoking is perceived as a means to lose weight and look sophisticated, which is a big concern of young women struggling with self-esteem and feeling like they belong.

Evidence suggests that women are less likely to quit smoking than are men. This may reflect differences in nicotine dependence and, more specifically perhaps, nicotine withdrawal and craving. However, there is conflicting research on gender differences on the experience of withdrawal and craving. Menstrual cycle effects may moderate this relationship. Given hormonal changes during the menstrual cycle, abstinence-related symptoms, such as withdrawal and craving, may vary as a function of menstrual phase as well. There may be heightened experiences of withdrawal or craving within the latter days of the menstrual cycle (the luteal phase) (Carpenter, Upadhyaya, LaRowe, Saladin, & Brady, 2006).

OTHER RISK FACTORS

Table 6-4 lists other risk factors of lung cancer. Most lung cancers develop from environmental exposures – carcinogens, viruses, and chemicals. Of note are the risks associated with exposure to asbestos, second hand smoke, air pollutants, and radon.

Researchers have found that genetics seem to play a role in some families with a strong history of lung cancer. People who inherit certain DNA changes in particular chromosomes (chromosomes 6 or 15) are more likely to develop lung cancer, even if they only smoke a little. At this time, routine testing for these changes is not possible (ACS, 2008; NCI, 2004).

TABLE 6-4: RISK FACTORS FOR LUNG CANCER

- Smoking cigarettes, cigars, and pipes
- Exposure to environmental tobacco smoke (secondhand smoke)
- Exposure to radon, the radioactive gas that occurs naturally in soil and rocks
- Exposure to asbestos, naturally occurring minerals used in shipbuilding, asbestos mining and manufacturing, insulation work, and brake repair
- Inhaled chemicals or minerals such as arsenic, beryllium, cadmium, silica, vinyl chloride, nickel compounds, chromium compounds, coal products, mustard gas, and chloromethyl ethers
- Exposure to pollution and certain air pollutants, including by-products of the combustion of diesel and other fossil fuels, such as coal, coke, and soot. Also, exposure to uranium, nickel, arsenic, and cadmium aluminum
- Lung diseases and tuberculosis
- Personal history and previous lung cancer

(ACS, 2009a; CDC, 2008)

ANATOMY OF THE LUNGS

The lungs are two sponge-like organs found in the chest (see Figure 6-2). The right lung is divided into three sections, called lobes. The left lung has two lobes. The left lung is smaller because the heart takes up more room on that side of the body. During inspiration, air enters through the mouth or nose and goes into the lungs through the trachea. The trachea divides into tubes called the bronchi, which divide into smaller branches called bronchioles. At the end of the bronchioles are tiny air sacs known as alveoli.

Many tiny blood vessels run through the alveoli. They absorb oxygen from the inhaled air into the bloodstream and pass carbon dioxide from the body into the alveoli. This is expelled from the body during expiration.

A thin lining layer called the pleura surrounds the lungs. The pleura protects the lungs and helps them slide back and forth as they expand and contract during breathing.

FIGURE 6-2: ANATOMY OF THE LUNGS

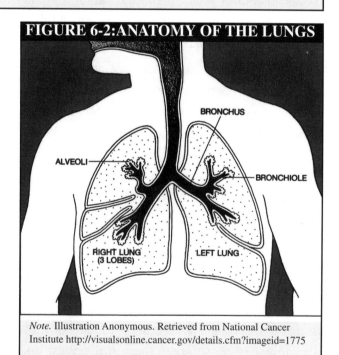

Note. Illustration Anonymous. Retrieved from National Cancer Institute http://visualsonline.cancer.gov/details.cfm?imageid=1775

PREVENTION AND DETECTION STRATEGIES

If a woman stops smoking, her risk of dying of lung cancer decreases. The threshold for reducing risk is notable when the woman has not smoked for at least 10 years. We know this because of the lowered incidence rates of lung cancer in recent years with men after cigarette smoking cessation programs became effective (NCI, 2009).

The mortality rate for female lung cancer has also declined in women younger than 60 years of age. This change prompts a marked slowing of the mortality rate. Previously, overall lung cancer mortality rates among women had shown a steep increase.

In 2008, in an effort to help nicotine-dependent patients and healthcare providers, the Agency for Health Care Policy and Research released clinical smoking-cessation guidelines (Fiore et al., 2008). Highlights of these guidelines include:

- Clinicians must document the tobacco-use status of every patient.

- Every patient using tobacco should be offered one or more of the available effective smoking cessation treatments.

- Tobacco dependence is a chronic disease that often requires repeated intervention and multiple attempts to quit. Effective treatments exist, and continued support and follow-up can significantly increase rates of long-term abstinence.

- Individual, group, and telephone counseling are effective, and their effectiveness increases with treatment intensity. Two components of counseling are especially effective, and clinicians should try to combine these when counseling patients making a quit attempt.

Screening for lung cancer is controversial; in general, it is not included in recommendations for the early detection of cancer. Routine screening with a chest X-ray is not effective as lesions are usually large by time they are seen on a chest X-ray and treatment is not always effective. The Canadian Task Force recommends against screening for lung cancer (Palda & Van Spall, 2003). The U.S. Preventive Services Task Force (2004) concludes that the evidence is insufficient to recommend for or against screening asymptomatic persons for lung cancer. The ACS does not recommend routine lung cancer screening for asymptomatic individuals at risk for lung cancer (ACS, 2010a). However, individual physicians and patients may decide that the evidence is sufficient to warrant the use of screening tests on an individual basis.

The basis of the ACS recommendation comes from research using spiral computed tomography (CT) scan (Smith et al., 2003). This is a relatively new technology with a high rate of positive results. The high rate of false positive results has made it difficult to develop a cost-effective and clinically effective algorithm for working up small nodules. The ACS emphasizes that individuals interested in early detection using spiral CT scanning should be educated about the potential risks and unknowns of the test and also should be encouraged to participate in trials to better evaluate this technology.

SIGNS AND SYMPTOMS

Common Symptoms

Most lung cancers do not cause symptoms until they have metastasized; however, symptoms do occur in some people with early lung cancer (Haas, 2010). The most common symptoms of lung cancer are:

- a cough that does not go away

- chest pain that is often worse with deep breathing, coughing, or laughing

- hoarseness

- weight loss and loss of appetite

- bloody or rust-colored sputum

- shortness of breath

- recurring infections such as bronchitis and pneumonia

- new onset of wheezing.

When lung cancer spreads to distant organs, it may cause:

- bone pain

- neurologic changes (such as headache, weakness or numbness of a limb, dizziness, or recent onset of a seizure)

- jaundice

- lumps near the surface of the body, due to cancer spreading to the skin or to lymph nodes in the neck or above the collarbone

(ACS, 2009b).

Some lung cancers can cause a group of very specific symptoms. These are often described as "syndromes."

Horner Syndrome

Cancer of the top part of the lungs (sometimes called Pancoast tumors) may damage a nerve that passes from the upper chest into the neck. The most common symptom of these tumors is severe shoulder pain. Sometimes they also cause a group of symptoms called Horner syndrome, including:

- drooping or weakness of one eyelid (ptosis)

- having a smaller pupil in the same eye (pupil constriction)

- reduced or absent sweating on the same side of the face.

Conditions other than lung cancer can also cause Horner syndrome.

Paraneoplastic Syndromes

Some lung cancers can make hormone-like substances that enter the bloodstream and cause problems with distant tissues and organs, even though the cancer has not spread to those tissues or organs. These are called paraneoplastic syndromes. These syndromes are sometimes the first symptoms of early lung cancer. Because the symptoms affect other organs, patients and their doctors may suspect at first that diseases other than lung cancer is causing them.

The most common paraneoplastic syndromes caused by non-small cell lung cancer are:

- hypercalcemia, which can cause frequent urination, constipation, weakness, dizziness, confusion, and other nervous system problems

- excess growth of certain bones, especially those in the finger tips, which can be very painful

- blood clots

- gynecomastia in males.

DIAGNOSIS

A number of imaging studies as well as a biopsy and other tests are necessary to both diagnose and stage lung cancer.

Imaging tests

A chest X-ray is often the first test ordered to look for any masses or spots on the lungs. A plain X-ray of the chest can be done in any outpatient setting (see Figure 6-3). If something suspicious is seen, additional tests may be ordered (Ross, 2003).

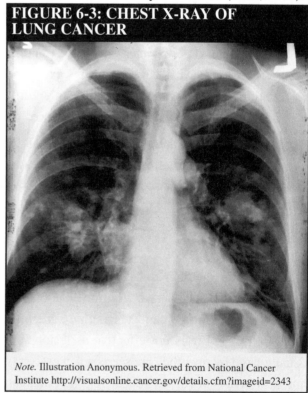

FIGURE 6-3: CHEST X-RAY OF LUNG CANCER

Note. Illustration Anonymous. Retrieved from National Cancer Institute http://visualsonline.cancer.gov/details.cfm?imageid=2343

Next, a CT scan may be ordered (ACS, 2009b, 2010a). It is an X-ray test that produces detailed cross-sectional images of the body. Unlike a regular X-ray, a CT scan creates detailed images of the soft tissues in the body. A contrast agent is often ordered to enhance the image. A CT scan can provide precise information about the size, shape, and position of tumors and can help find enlarged lymph nodes that might contain cancer that has spread from the lung. CT scans are more sensitive than routine chest X-rays in finding early lung cancers. This test can also be used to look for masses in the adrenal glands, brain, and other internal organs that may be affected by the spread of lung cancer.

Like CT scans, MRI provides detailed images of soft tissues in the body; however, an MRI uses radio waves and strong magnets instead of X-rays. A contrast material called gadolinium is often injected into a vein before the MRI to enhance details. MRIs are most often used to look for the possible spread of lung cancer to the brain or spinal cord (National Comprehensive Cancer Network [NCCN], 2010).

Positron emission tomography (PET) scans involve injecting glucose that contains a radioactive tracer into the blood. Because cancer cells in the body are growing rapidly, they absorb large amounts of the radioactive sugar. A special camera can then create a picture of areas of radioactivity in the body. The picture is not finely detailed like a CT scan or MRI, but it provides helpful information about the whole body. A PET scan is also useful if metastasis is suspected and can reveal the spread of cancer to the liver, bones, adrenal glands, and some other organs (NCCN, 2010). It is not as useful when looking at the brain because all brain cells use a lot of glucose. Some newer machines are able to perform PET and CT scans at the same time (PET/CT scan). This allows the doctor to compare areas of higher radioactivity on the PET scan with the appearance of that area on the CT scan.

A bone scan can help show if a cancer has metastasized to the bones (ACS, 2009b). For this test, a small amount of low-level radioactive material is injected intravenously. The substance settles in areas of bone changes throughout the entire skeleton over the course of a couple of hours. This is followed by an imaging procedure. Areas of active bone changes appear as "hot spots" as they attract the radioactivity. These areas may suggest the presence of metastatic cancer; however, arthritis and other bone diseases can also cause the same pattern. To distinguish between these conditions and cancer, other imaging tests such as simple X-rays or an MRI is used to get a better look at the areas that "light up," or a biopsy of the bone may be performed. Because PET scans can usually show the spread of cancer to bones, bone scans aren't needed very often (NCCN, 2010). Bone scans are done mainly when there is reason to believe the cancer may have spread to the bones and other test results are not clear.

Biopsy Strategies

The diagnosis of lung cancer is established by a pathology report that indicates a finding of malignant cells in a tissue sample. There are many approaches that can be used to obtaining a tissue sample.

Sputum cytology is the least invasive of all methods used to obtain tissue samples (ACS, 2009b). A sample of sputum is viewed under a microscope to see if cancer cells are present. The best way to do this is to get early morning samples for 3 days in a row. Often, this test fails to provide adequate information (NCCN, 2010).

A fine needle biopsy can often be used to get a small sample of cells from a suspicious area. For this test, the skin where the needle is to be inserted is first numbed with local anesthesia. A thin, hollow needle is advanced into the suspicious area while looking at the lungs with either fluoroscopy or CT scans. Unlike fluoroscopy, CT scanning doesn't give a continuous picture, so the needle is inserted in the direction of the mass, a CT image is taken, and the direction of the needle is guided based on the image. This is repeated a few times until the needle is within the mass. A tiny sample of the target area is then withdrawn into a syringe and looked at under a microscope to see if cancer cells are present.

A possible complication of CT scans and fluoroscopic procedures is that air may leak out of the lung at the biopsy site and into the space between the lung and the chest wall. This can cause part of the lung to collapse and can cause trouble breathing. This complication, called a pneumothorax, often gets better without any treatment. In some cases, a chest tube is necessary to reinflate the lung.

During bronchoscopy, a lighted, flexible fiber-optic tube (bronchoscope) is passed through the mouth or nose and down into the windpipe and bronchi. The mouth and throat are sprayed first with a local anesthetic. Intravenous sedation is usually utilized. Bronchoscopy can help the doctor find some tumors or obstructions in the lungs. At the same time, small instruments can be passed down the bronchoscope to obtain biopsies. A thin needle can also be inserted through the wall of the trachea or bronchus using a bronchoscope to sample nearby lymph nodes. This procedure, called transtracheal or transbronchial fine needle aspiration, is often used to take samples of lymph nodes around the windpipe and bronchi (ACS, 2009b).

In an endobronchial ultrasound a bronchoscope is fitted with an ultrasound transducer at its tip and passed into the trachea. The transducer can be pointed in different directions to look at lymph nodes and other structures in the mediastinum. If suspicious areas are seen on the ultrasound, a hollow needle can be passed through the bronchoscope and guided by ultrasound into the abnormal structures to obtain a biopsy (NCCN, 2010).

Mediastinoscopy and mediastinotomy allow the doctor to look more directly at and sample the structures in the mediastinum. These procedures are done in an operating room under general anesthesia. The main difference between a mediastinoscopy and a mediastinotomy is in the location and size of the incision (NCCN, 2010).

During mediastinoscopy, a small cut is made in the front of the neck above the sternum and a thin, hollow, lighted tube is inserted behind the sternum. Special instruments can be passed through this tube to obtain tissue samples from the lymph nodes along the windpipe and the major bronchial tube areas.

During mediastinotomy, the surgeon makes a slightly larger incision (usually about 2 inches long) between the left second and third ribs next to the breast bone. This allows the surgeon to reach lymph nodes that are not reached by mediastinoscopy.

Thoracentesis is done to find out whether or not a pleural effusion is the result of cancer spreading to the pleura (ACS, 2009b). For this procedure, the skin is numbed and a needle is placed between the ribs to drain the fluid. The fluid is checked under a microscope to look for cancer cells. Chemical tests of the fluid are also sometimes useful in identifying a malignant pleural effusion from a benign one. If a malignant pleural effusion has been diagnosed, thoracentesis may be repeated to remove more fluid. Fluid build-up can prevent the lungs from filling with air, so thoracentesis can help the patient breathe better (ACS, 2009b).

Thoracoscopy can be done to find out if cancer has spread to the space between the lungs and the chest wall as well as to the linings of these spaces. Most often this procedure is done in the operating room under general anesthesia. The doctor inserts a lighted tube with a small video camera on the end through a small cut made in the chest wall to view the space between the lungs and the chest wall. During this procedure, the doctor can visualize potential cancer deposits on the lung or lining of the chest wall and remove small pieces of tissue for pathology. Thoracoscopy can also be used to sample lymph nodes and fluid and assess whether a tumor is growing into nearby tissues or organs (NCCN, 2010).

Additional Diagnostic Tests

Samples that have been collected during biopsies or other tests are sent to a pathology lab. There, a doctor views the samples under a microscope to find out if they contain cancer and, if so, what type of cancer it is. Special tests may be needed to help classify the cancer. Cancers from other organs can spread to the lungs. It's very important to find out where the cancer started, because treatment is different for different types of cancer.

Immunohistochemistry can often differentiate the specific cell type of the cancer. In some cases, molecular tests may be used to look for specific gene changes in the cancer cells that might affect how they are best treated. For example, the epidermal growth factor receptor (EGFR) is a protein that sometimes appears in high amounts on the surface of cancer cells and helps them grow. Some anticancer drugs target EGFR; however, they only seem to work against certain cancers. Some doctors may test for changes in genes, such as EGFR and K-ras, to determine if these treatments are likely to be helpful (Aberle & McLeskey, 2003). These tests are available in specialized labs and they are not yet widely used.

Blood tests are not used to diagnose lung cancer, but are done to get a sense of a person's overall health. For example, prior to surgery, blood tests can help tell if a person is healthy enough to have an operation or undergo additional therapy. Blood chemistry tests can help spot abnormalities in some organs. If cancer has spread to the liver or bones, it may cause abnormal levels of certain chemicals in the blood.

Pulmonary function tests are often done after a lung cancer diagnosis to see how well the lungs function. This is especially important if surgery is being considered. Because surgical removal of part or all of a lung results in lower lung capacity, it's important to know how well the lungs are functioning before surgery.

STAGING

Most lung cancers start in the bronchi, but can also begin in other areas, such as the trachea, bronchioles, or alveoli. Lung cancers are thought to develop over many years (ACS, 2010a). They may start as areas of precancerous changes in the lung.

The first changes occur within the cells themselves; however, at this point, the cells do not form a mass or tumor. They cannot be seen on an X-ray and they do not cause symptoms. Over time, these precancerous changes may progress to cancer. As a cancer develops, the cancer cells may make chemicals that cause new blood vessels to form nearby. These new blood vessels nourish the cancer cells, which can continue to grow and form a tumor large enough to be seen on imaging tests such as X-rays. At some point, cells from the cancer may break away from the original tumor and spread, or metastasize, to other parts of the body. Lung cancer is a life-threatening disease because it often spreads in this way, even before it can be detected on an imaging test.

Lung cancer cells can enter lymphatic vessels and begin to grow in lymph nodes around the bronchi and in the mediastinum. When lung cancer cells have reached the lymph nodes, they are more likely to have spread to other organs of the body as well. The stage of the cancer and decisions about treatment are based on whether the cancer has spread to the nearby lymph nodes in the mediastinum (ACS, 2010a).

There are 2 major types of lung cancer, including small cell lung cancer (SCLC) and non-small cell lung cancer (NSCLC). If a lung cancer has characteristics of both types it is called a mixed small cell/large cell cancer. This is uncommon.

About 85% to 90% of lung cancers are NSCLC. There are three subtypes of NSCLC. The cells in these subtypes differ in size, shape, and chemical make-up (NCCN, 2010).

- *Squamous cell carcinoma:* About 25% to 30% of all lung cancers are squamous cell carcinomas. They are often linked to a history of smoking and tend to be found in the middle of the lungs, near a bronchus.

- *Adenocarcinoma:* This type accounts for about 40% of lung cancers. It is usually found in the outer region of lung. People with one type of adenocarcinoma, sometimes called bronchi-oloalveolar carcinoma, tend to have a better outlook (prognosis) than those with other types of lung cancer.

- *Large-cell (undifferentiated) carcinoma:* This type of cancer accounts for about 10% to 15% of lung cancers. It may appear in any part of the lung. It tends to grow and spread quickly, which can make it harder to treat effectively.

About 10% to 15% of all lung cancers are SCLC (NCCN, 2010). Other names for SCLC are oat cell cancer, oat cell carcinoma, and small cell undifferentiated carcinoma. SCLC often starts in the bronchi near the center of the chest, and it tends to spread throughout the body fairly early in the course of the disease (usually before it starts to cause symptoms). These cancer cells can multiply quickly, form large tumors, and spread to lymph nodes and other organs, such as the bones, brain, adrenal glands, and liver. SCLC is almost always caused by smoking. It is very rare for someone who has never smoked to have SCLC (ACS, 2010a).

In addition to the two main types of lung cancer, other tumors can occur in the lungs. Carcinoid tumors of the lung account for fewer than 5% of lung tumors. Most are slow-growing tumors that are called typical carcinoid tumors. They are generally cured by surgery. Although some typical carcinoid tumors can spread, they usually have a better prognosis than SCLC or NSCLC. Less common are atypical carcinoid tumors. The outlook for these tumors is somewhere between typical carcinoids and SCLC.

There are other, even more rare, lung tumors, such as adenoid cystic carcinomas, hamartomas, lymphomas, and sarcomas. These tumors are treated differently from the more common lung cancers.

Cancer that starts in other organs (such as the breast, pancreas, kidney, or skin) and metastasizes to the lungs is not the same as lung cancer. For example, cancer that starts in the breast and spreads to the lungs is still breast cancer, not lung cancer. Treatment for metastatic cancer to the lungs depends on the primary cancer site.

Like other cancers, lung cancer is staged using the Tumor Nodes Metastasis system. After the pathology of the tumor is determined, along with the stage, treatment can be planned. Staging of SCLC is typically reported as limited stage (cancer is confined to the lung and lymph nodes in the chest) or extensive stage (cancer has metastasized, usually to the brain, liver, or bone.)

Table 6-5 describes how lung cancer is commonly staged.

PROGNOSIS

The prognosis of a patient diagnosed with NSCLC is determined by

- stage (extent of disease)
- performance status (see Table 6-6)
- weight loss
- gender

(NCCN, 2010; Ross, 2003).

For patients with operable NSCLC, prognosis is adversely influenced by the presence of pulmonary symptoms, large tumor size (greater than 3 centimeters), and presence of the erbB-2 oncoprotein. Other adverse prognostic factors for some patients with NSCLC include mutation of the K-ras gene, vascular invasion, and increased numbers of blood vessels in the tumor specimen (NCCN, 2010).

For NSCLC patients, 25% are diagnosed at Stage I or II, 35% are diagnosed at Stage III, and 38% to 40% are diagnosed at Stage IV (ACS, 2010a; NCCN, 2010). The cure rate for NSCLC at Stage I disease is 70% to 80%. At Stage II, the cure rate is 40% to 50% (ACS, 2010a; NCCN, 2010).

Without treatment, the median survival for patients with SCLC – from diagnosis to death – is only 2 to 4 months. At the time of diagnosis,

TABLE 6-5: REVISED INTERNATIONAL SYSTEM FOR STAGING LUNG CANCER	
Primary tumor (T)	**AJCC stage groupings**
TX: Primary tumor cannot be assessed, or tumor proven by the presence of malignant cells in sputum or bronchial washings but not visualized by imaging or bronchoscopy	*Occult carcinoma* TX, N0, M0
T0: No evidence of primary tumor	*Stage 0* Tis, N0, M0
Tis: Carcinoma in situ	
T1: Divided into T1a (tumor 2 cm or less) and T1b (tumor greater than 2-3 cm)	*Stage IA* T1a, N0, M0 T1b, N0, M0
T2: Divided into T2a (tumor greater than 3-5 cm) and T2b (tumor greater than 5-7 cm)	*Stage IB* T2a, N0, M0
T3: Tumor greater than 7 cm in size	*Stage IIA* T2b, N0, M0
T4: Multiple tumor nodules in the same lung but a different lobe	T1a, N1, M0
Regional lymph nodes (N)	T1b, N1, M0
NX: Regional lymph nodes cannot be assessed	T2a, N1, M0
N0: No regional lymph node metastasis	
N1: Metastasis to ipsilateral peribronchial and/or ipsilateral hilar lymph nodes, and intrapulmonary nodes including involvement by direct extension of the primary tumor	*Stage IIB* T2b, N1, M0 T3, N0, M0
N2: Metastasis to ipsilateral mediastinal and/or subcarinal lymph node(s)	*Stage IIIA* T1a, N2, M0
N3: Metastasis to contralateral mediastinal, contralateral hilar, ipsilateral or contralateral scalene, or supraclavicular lymph node(s)	T1b, N2, M0
Distant Metastasis (M)	T2a, N2, M0
MX: Distant metastasis cannot be assessed	T2b, N2, M0
M0: No distant metastasis	T3, N1, M0
M1: Distant metastasis present. *M1 includes separate tumor nodule(s) in a different lobe (ipsilateral or contralateral) or malignant pleural and pericardial effusions. M1b includes distant metastases*	T3, N2, M0 T4, N0, M0 T4, N1, M0
Specify sites according to the following notations: BRA = brain EYE = eye HEP = hepatic LYM = lymph nodes MAR = bone marrow OSS = osseous OTH = other OVR = ovary PER = peritoneal PLE = pleura PUL = pulmonary SKI = skin	*Stage IIIB* Any T, N3, M0 T4, N2, M0 *Stage IV* Any T, any N, M1a or M1b

approximately 30% of SCLC patients will have a tumor that is confined to the hemithorax of origin, the mediastinum, or the supraclavicular lymph nodes (ACS, 2010a; NCCN, 2010).

TREATMENTS FOR NSCLC

Treatment depends on a number of factors, including the patients general health, the type of lung cancer, and the size, location, and extent of the tumor. Many different treatments and combinations of treatments may be used to control lung cancer, or to improve quality of life by reducing symptoms.

TABLE 6-6: EXAMPLE OF PERFORMANCE STATUS CRITERIA*

- 0 – Asymptomatic (Fully active, able to carry on all predisease activities without restriction)

- 1 – Symptomatic but completely ambulatory (Restricted in physically strenuous activity but ambulatory and able to carry out work of a light or sedentary nature. For example, light housework, office work)

- 2 – Symptomatic, less than 50% in bed during the day (Ambulatory and capable of all self-care but unable to carry out any work activities. Up and about more than 50% of waking hours)

- 3 – Symptomatic, greater than 50% in bed, but not bedbound (Capable of only limited self-care; confined to bed or chair 50% or more of waking hours)

- 4 – Bedbound (Completely disabled. Cannot carry on any self-care. Totally confined to bed or chair)

- 5 – Death

* There are many scales and criteria used by physicians, nurses, and researchers to assess how the disease affects the daily living abilities of the patient, and determine appropriate treatment and prognosis. This scale is one example that is commonly utilized.

(Oken et al., 1982)

Surgery

Depending on the type and stage of a lung cancer, surgery may be used to remove the cancer along with some surrounding lung tissue. Surgery is usually recommended for early stage lung cancers (Stage I and II). If surgery can be done, it provides the best chance to cure NSCLC (Ross, 2003). Pulmonary function tests will be done beforehand to determine whether the patient will have enough healthy lung tissue remaining after surgery.

Several different operations can be used to treat (and possibly cure) non-small cell lung cancer.

- *Pneumonectomy:* The entire lung is removed in this surgery.

- *Lobectomy:* A section (lobe) of the lung is removed in this surgery. Lobectomy is a standard surgical resection used in Stage I disease.

- *Segmentectomy or wedge resection:* Part of a lobe is removed in this surgery.

With any of these operations, lymph nodes are also removed to look for possible spread of the cancer. These operations require general anesthesia and a surgical thoracotomy. Postoperatively most patients spend 5 to 7 days in the hospital after the surgery.

Recently, some doctors have begun to use a less invasive procedure for treating some early stage lung cancers, called video-assisted thoracic surgery (Posther & Harpole, 2006). During this operation, a thin telescopic tube with a tiny video camera on the end is placed through a small hole in the chest to help the surgeon see the chest cavity. One or two other small holes are created in the skin, and long instruments, passed though these holes, are used to remove the tumor. Because only small incisions are needed, there is less pain after the surgery. Another advantage of this surgery is a shorter hospital stay – usually about 4 to 5 days. Most experts recommend that only early stage tumors smaller than 3 to 4 centimeters be treated this way. The cure rate after this surgery seems to be the same as with older techniques. However, it is important that the surgeon performing this procedure is experienced because it requires a great deal of technical skill.

Possible complications depend on the extent of the surgery and a person's health beforehand. Serious complications can include excessive bleeding, wound infections, and pneumonia (Schrump, Giaccone, Kelsey, & Marks, 2008). While it is rare, in some cases people may not survive the surgery, which is why it is important that surgeons select patients carefully. Because the surgeon must spread ribs to get to the lung in patients undergoing a thoracotomy, the incision will hurt for some time after surgery. Activity will be limited for at least 1 to 2 months.

If a pleural effusion occurs, the associated build-up of fluid can interfere with breathing. To remove the fluid and keep it from coming back, doctors sometimes perform a procedure called pleurodesis (Schrump et al., 2008). A small cut is made in the skin of the chest wall and a chest tube is placed into the chest to remove the fluid. Either talc or a drug, such as doxycycline or a chemotherapy drug, is then instilled into the chest cavity. This causes the linings of the lung (visceral pleura) and chest wall (parietal pleural) to stick together, sealing the space and preventing further fluid buildup. The chest tube is generally left in for 1 to 2 days to drain any new fluid that might accumulate.

Radiation Therapy

External beam radiation therapy (EBRT) uses radiation delivered from outside the body that is focused on the cancer. This is the type of radiation therapy most often used to treat a primary lung cancer or its metastases to other organs. Standard (conventional) EBRT is used much less often than in the past (Tyson, 2004). Newer techniques allow doctors to be more accurate in treating lung cancers, while reducing the radiation exposure to nearby healthy tissues. These techniques may offer better chances of increasing the success rate and reducing side effects.

Three-dimensional conformal radiation therapy (3D-CRT) uses special computers to precisely map the location of the tumor (Schrump et al., 2008). Radiation beams are shaped and aimed at the tumor from several directions, which makes it less likely to damage normal tissues. Most doctors now recommend using 3D-CRT when it is available.

Intensity modulated radiation therapy (IMRT) is an advanced form of 3D therapy. It uses a computer-driven machine that moves around the patient as it delivers radiation (Schrump et al., 2008). Along with shaping the beams and aiming them at the tumor from several angles, the intensity (strength) of the beams can be adjusted to minimize the dose reaching the most sensitive normal tissues. This technique is used most often if tumors are near important structures such as the spinal cord. Many major hospitals and cancer centers are now able to provide IMRT.

Stereotactic radiation therapy (SBRT) is a newer form of treatment that is sometimes used to treat very early stage lung cancers (Schrump et al., 2008). Another type of SBRT can sometimes be used instead of surgery for single tumors that have spread to the brain (Tyson, 2004). Using a machine called a Gamma Knife or Cyber Knife, many beams of high-dose radiation are focused on the tumor from different angles over a few minutes to hours. The head is kept in the same position by placing it in a rigid frame.

Brachytherapy is used most often to shrink tumors to relieve symptoms caused by the cancer, although in some cases it may be part of a larger treatment regimen trying to cure the cancer. It involves placing a small source of radioactive material (often in the form of pellets) directly into the cancer or into the airway next to the cancer. This is usually done through a bronchoscope, although it may also be done during surgery. The radiation travels only a short distance from the source, limiting the effects on surrounding healthy tissues. The radiation source is usually removed after a short time. Less often, small radioactive "seeds" are left in place permanently, and the radiation gets weaker over several weeks.

External beam radiation therapy is sometimes used as the main treatment of lung cancer (usually with chemotherapy), especially if the lung tumor cannot be removed by surgery because it is close to large blood vessels or the person's health is too poor. Brachytherapy is most often used to help relieve blockage of large airways by cancer.

After surgery, radiation therapy can be used (alone or with chemotherapy) to try to eliminate very small deposits of cancer that may have been missed by surgery (Tyson, 2004). Radiation therapy can also be used to relieve symptoms of lung cancer, such as pain, bleeding, trouble swallowing, cough, and problems caused by brain metastases.

Side effects of external radiation therapy might include sunburn-like skin problems where the radiation enters the body, nausea, vomiting, and fatigue (Tyson, 2004). Often, these go away after treatment. Radiation might also make the side effects of chemotherapy more intense. Chest radiation therapy may damage the lungs and lead to problems with breathing and shortness of breath. Because the esophagus is located in the middle of the chest, it may be exposed to radiation, which could lead to trouble swallowing during treatment. This usually improves after treatment is over.

Radiation therapy to large areas of the brain can sometimes cause changes in brain function (Schrump et al., 2008). Some people notice memory loss, headache, trouble thinking, or reduced sexual desire. Usually these symptoms are minor compared to those caused by a brain tumor, but they can reduce quality of life. Side effects of radiation therapy to the brain usually become most serious 1 or 2 years after treatment.

Chemotherapy

Depending on the type and stage of NSCLC, chemotherapy may be given as the main (primary) treatment or as an addition (adjuvant) to surgery or radiation therapy. Chemotherapy is given in cycles, with each period of treatment followed by a rest period to allow the body time to recover. Chemotherapy cycles generally last about 3 to 4 weeks, and initial treatment typically involves 4 to 6 cycles. Chemotherapy is often not recommended for patients in poor health; however, advanced age, by itself, is not a barrier to receiving chemotherapy. Most often, initial treatment for advanced NSCLC uses a combination of chemotherapy drugs.

The most common combinations include cisplatin or carboplatin plus one other drug, although some studies have found that using combinations with less severe side effects, such as gemcitabine

with vinorelbine or paclitaxel, may be just as effective for many patients (Tyson, 2004). Single-drug chemotherapy is sometimes used for people who might not be able to tolerate combination chemotherapy such as those in poor overall health. If the initial chemotherapy treatment is no longer working, second-line treatment usually consists of a single drug such as docetaxel (Schrump et al., 2008).

NSCLC and Targeted Therapy

For tumors to grow, they must form new blood vessels to keep them nourished. This process is called angiogenesis and it occurs frequently in NSCLS. Some newer targeted drugs block this new vessel growth.

Bevacizumab (Avastin) is a type of drug known as a monoclonal antibody. It targets vascular endothelial growth factor, a protein that helps new blood vessels to form. This drug has been shown to prolong the survival of patients with advanced lung cancer when it is added to standard chemotherapy regimens as part of first-line treatment (Aberle & McLeskey, 2003). Bevacizumab is given by I.V. infusion every 2 to 3 weeks. The possible side effects of this drug are different from those of chemotherapy drugs. It can cause serious bleeding. It is not used in patients who are coughing up blood, who have cancer that has metastasized to the brain, or who are on medications that increase bleeding time. Other possible effects include high blood pressure, loss of appetite, delayed wound healing, and an increased risk of blood clots.

Epidermal growth factor receptor (EGFR) is a protein found on the surface of cells (Aberle & McLeskey, 2003). It normally receives signals telling the cells to grow and divide. Some lung cancer cells have too many copies of EGFR, which help them grow faster. Erlotinib (Tarceva) is a drug that blocks EGFR from signaling the cell to grow. It has been shown to help keep some lung tumors under control, especially in women and in people who never smoked. It is most often used for advanced lung cancers if initial treatment with chemotherapy is no longer effective. It is taken daily as a pill. The most common side effects of erlotinib include an acne-like rash on the face and chest, diarrhea, loss of appetite, and fatigue.

Cetuximab (Erbitux) is a monoclonal antibody that targets EGFR (Tyson, 2004). For patients with advanced lung cancer, some doctors may add it to standard chemotherapy as part of first-line treatment. Cetuximab is given by I.V. infusion, usually once per week. A rare but serious side effect of cetuximab is an allergic reaction during the first infusion, which could cause problems with breathing and low blood pressure. Other, less serious side effects may include an acne-like rash, headache, tiredness, fever, and diarrhea.

SCLC and Chemotherapy

Because SCLC tends to be more widely disseminated at the time of diagnosis, aggressive chemotherapy is the standard treatment. Chemotherapy for SCLC generally uses a combination of two drugs (Schrump et al., 2008). The drug combinations most often used for initial chemotherapy for SCLC are:

- cisplatin and etoposide

- carboplatin and etoposide

- cisplatin and irinotecan

- carboplatin and irinotecan

- cyclophosphamide, doxorubicin (Adriamycin), and vincristine

If the cancer progresses during treatment or recurs after treatment is completed, different chemotherapy drugs may be tried (Joyce, 2004). The choice of drugs depends to some extent on how soon the cancer begins to grow again. The longer it takes for the cancer to return, the more likely it is to respond to further treatment.

- If the cancer progresses during treatment or relapses within 2 to 3 months of finishing treatment, drugs such as topotecan, ifosfamide,

paclitaxel, docetaxel, irinotecan, or gemcitabine may be tried.

- If the relapse occurs within 2 to 6 months after treatment, topotecan is often the drug of choice. Other drugs that may be tried include irinotecan, cyclophosphamide/doxorubicin/vincristine (known as the CAV regimen), gemcitabine, paclitaxel, docetaxel, oral etoposide, or vinorelbine.

- For relapses 6 or more months after treatment, the original chemotherapy regimen may still be effective and can often be tried again.

COMPLICATIONS

Complications specific to the treatment of lung cancer or the effects of spreading disease include pain, pleural effusions, anxiety, depression, and sleep disturbance. (See Appendix D, Nursing Interventions for Complications from Treatment). In addition to these complications, nurses also need to help patients with lung cancer manage fatigue, pain, loss of appetite, diarrhea, hemoptysis, mucositis, and weight loss. Of special distress to women with lung cancer are dyspnea, coughing, and wheezing (Tyson, 2004).

CASE STUDY: LUNG CANCER

TM is a 59-year-old Black woman, who is a homemaker and was a part-time secretary for a manufacturing plant. She has been a 30/pack year smoker for approximately 10 years, attempting to quit at least twice. She says she now has about five cigarettes per week.

TM visited her primary care physician (PCP) because of a persistent cough (x 2 months), which kept her up at night. Occasionally she saw blood in phlegm from her cough. She tried to quit smoking again 6 weeks before her doctor's visit, using

Nicoderm patches and keeping in contact with a friend, who also was trying to quit smoking.

TM's PCP ordered a chest X-ray. He also started her on a round of antibiotics because she has had bronchial infections in the past. During the office visit, auscultation of TM's right lobe (middle) was muffled. Her PCP obtained a sputum sample and ordered laboratory tests, including a complete blood count and a standard metabolic panel.

Results from the chest X-ray showed an opaque area in the right center of her chest. The following week, TM was scheduled for a CT scan-guided needle biopsy. Results came back as NSCLC (adenocarcinoma).

TM's breathing status continued to worsen with increasing dyspnea and swelling in her neck area. Of concern was the possibility of superior vena cava syndrome and developing pleural effusions; a lobectomy was scheduled for a few days later.

The thoracic surgeon removed TM's right lobe and sampled her lymph nodes. Staging indicated that TM's adenocarcinoma was Stage IIIB, T2, N2, N0, and she was referred to a medical oncologist for further treatment. Three courses of adjuvant chemotherapy began – cisplatin and paclitaxel (every 21 days). Because of severe neutropenia and fatigue, TM delayed the second course of chemotherapy for approximately 6 weeks.

After the latest chemotherapy treatment, she had a repeat chest X-ray, which showed the mass back in her lung and appearing as large as before her surgery. As a second-line treatment, she was enrolled in a Phase II clinical trial, which will look at the effectiveness of gemcitabine, days 1 through 8 and 15 with carboplatin on day 1.

Additional Information

TM's health history is remarkable for two negative breast tissue fine-needle aspirations in the past 10 years, after she detected small masses in her left breast. She is slightly overweight and takes

medication for hypertension; however, in the last 3 months, she has lost 15 lb.

TM has been married 42 years to her husband, a truck driver, who plans to retire in 2 more years. She has two daughters and three sons, who no longer live with her. TM started menopause at age 50. She keeps annual physical examination appointments and has a yearly mammogram. At age 55, she had a sigmoidoscopy.

With her advancing disease, TM complains of dyspnea and profound fatigue. She has quit her job and receives continual oxygen from a nasal cannula. Her husband has cut down on his hours away from home. One of her daughters lives in the area and helps TM with her housekeeping and groceries.

TM, a lifelong Baptist, has found comfort in reading the Bible and listening to inspirational tapes, which her pastor and fellow church members send to her. She says her outlook is "sunny," but she states that she knows her good days are limited. Each week she finds herself staying in bed to rest longer. Her appetite has diminished and she gets about 4 hours of fitful sleep a night.

TM has developed a trust with her PCP's nurse and looks to her for help with her symptom management (dyspnea, fatigue, no appetite) and guidance on what is next in the progression of her illness. TM has said she wants to face the reality of her lung cancer but wants to spare her husband and children the stress of her illness. Her condition is deteriorating and her energy to make decisions is waning. TM has expressed to the nurse that she has become profoundly sad about her condition and finds herself feeling defiant against her faith and family.

What early symptom of lung cancer does TM have?

There really are no early symptoms of lung cancer. Sometimes bloody sputum is associated with early lung cancer, but it can also be a later sign.

What screening methods are recommended for TM?

Currently there are no recommended screening maneuvers for lung cancer. Efforts are usually directed toward smoking cessation.

What might be an important psychosocial intervention with TM?

Because TM finds comfort in reading the Bible, it might be appropriate to offer her a Bible and a visit from a chaplain. The nurse could offer to pray with the patient.

SUMMARY

The incidence and death rates for lung cancer are daunting, especially because the rate of smoking in young people continues to rise. Lung cancer in women is especially disturbing because some data indicates that women have particular susceptibilities to tobacco. Patients continue to ignore the signs and symptoms of lung cancer, delaying treatments that could be much more effective when lung cancer is diagnosed early. Effective treatment is still based on surgery, with some modest inroads when radiation and chemotherapy are added. New chemotherapy agents are being used in clinical trials, with the most effective results found with aggressive dosing, balanced by coordinated symptom management.

EXAM QUESTIONS

CHAPTER 6
Questions 44-49

Note: Choose the one option that BEST answers each question.

44. Non-small cell lung cancer (NSCLC)

    a. is more common than SCLC.

    b. spreads more quickly than SCLC.

    c. is treated with chemotherapy in its early stages.

    d. has a better prognosis in elderly patients.

45. The smoking cessation strategy that does not require a prescription is

    a. bupropion.

    b. a nicotine inhaler.

    c. varenicline.

    d. a nicotine patch.

46. In addition to smoking, additional risk factors for lung cancer are

    a. high-fat diet, sedentary lifestyle, and exposure to second-hand smoke.

    b. exposure to second-hand smoke, air pollution, and radon.

    c. a previous history of colon, lung, or breast cancer.

    d. a well-defined genetic mutation, coupled with a history of tuberculosis.

47. The main signs and symptoms of lung cancer include

    a. a persistent cough that worsens over time, shortness of breath, and nausea.

    b. constant chest pain, especially radiating up the left arm, and a persistent cough that worsens over time.

    c. shortness of breath, a persistent cough that worsens over time, and bloody sputum.

    d. back pain, weight loss, and insomnia.

48. The primary modality to treat NSCLC (Stage I) is

    a. surgery.

    b. 5-fluorouracil.

    c. immunotherapy.

    d. steroids.

49. The agent that is the base for many SCLC chemotherapy protocols is

    a. Decadron and cyclophosphamide.

    b. cisplatin and etoposide.

    c. 5-fluorouracil and cisplatin.

    d. Adriamycin and irinotecan.

REFERENCES

Altekruse, S.F., Kosary, C.L., Krapcho, M., Neyman, N., Aminou, R., Waldron, W., et al. (eds). (n.d.) *SEER Cancer Statistics Review, 1975-2007*. Bethesda, MD: National Cancer Institute. Retrieved from http://seer.cancer.gov/csr/1975_2007/, based on November 2009 SEER data submission, posted to the SEER web site, 2010.

Aberle, M.F. & McLeskey, S.W. (2003). Biology of lung cancer with implications for new therapies. *Oncology Nursing Forum, 30*(2), 273-280.

American Cancer Society. (2008). Researchers identify genetic predictor of lung cancer risk. Retrieved on July 19, 2010, from http://www.cancer.org/Cancer/news/News/researchers-identify-genetic-predictor-of-lung-cancer-risk

American Cancer Society. (2009a). *Lung cancer: Causes, risks factors, and prevention topics*. Retrieved on August 26, 2010, from http://www.cancer.org/Cancer/LungCancer-NonSmallCell/DetailedGuide/non-small-cell-lung-cancer-risk-factors

American Cancer Society. (2009b). *Lung Cancer: Early detection, diagnosis, and staging topics*. Retrieved on August 26, 2010, from http://www.cancer.org/Cancer/LungCancer-NonSmallCell/DetailedGuide/non-small-cell-lung-cancer-detection

American Cancer Society. (2009c). *What causes cancer? Tobacco & cancer: Child and teen tobacco use*. Retrieved on July 19, 2010, from http://www.cancer.org/Cancer/CancerCauses/TobaccoCancer/ChildandTeenTobaccoUse/child-and-teen-tobacco-use

American Cancer Society. (2010a). *Cancer facts & figures – 2010*. Atlanta, GA: American Cancer Society .

American Cancer Society (2010b). *Cancer prevention & early detection facts & figures 2010*. Atlanta, GA: American Cancer Society. Retrieved July 19, 2010, from http://www.cancer.org/acs/groups/content/@epidemiologysurveilance/documents/webcontent/acspc-025759.pdf

Boyle, P., Ariyaratne, M.A.Y., Barrington, R., Bartelink, H., Bartsch, G., Berns, A., et al. (2006). Tobacco: Deadly in any form or disguise. *Lancet, 367*(9524), 1710-1711.

Carpenter, M., Upadhyaya, H., LaRowe, S., Saladin, M., & Brady, K. (2006). Menstrual cycle phase effects on nicotine withdrawal and cigarette craving: A review. *Nicotine & Tobacco Research, 8*(5), 627-638.

Centers for Disease Control and Prevention. (2008). Smoking prevalence among women of reproductive age – United States 2006. *Morbidity and Mortality Weekly Report, 57*(31), 849-52.

Corelli, R.L. & Hudmon, K.S. (2006). Pharmacologic interventions for smoking cessation. *Critical Care Nursing Clinics of North America, 18*(1), 39-51.

Edge, S.B., Byrd, D.R., Carducci, M., Compton, C.C., Fritz, A.G., Greene, F.L., & Trotti, A. (2010). *AJCC cancer staging manual* (7th ed.), New York: Springer.

Fiore, M.C., Jaén, C.R., Baker, T.B., Bailey, W.C., Benowitz, N.L., Curry, S.J., et al. (2008). Treating tobacco use and dependence: 2008 update. U.S. Public Health Service Clinical Practice Guideline executive summary. *Respiratory Care, 53*(9), 1217-1222.

Haas, M. (2010). Controversies in detection and screening. In M. Haas (Ed.), *Contemporary issues in lung cancer: A nursing perspective* (pp. 33-44). Sudbury, MA: Jones & Bartlett .

Heater, M.L. (2010). Understanding and treating tobacco dependence in adults with lung cancer. In M. Haas (Ed.), *Contemporary issues in lung cancer: A nursing perspective* (pp. 283-300). Sudbury, MA: Jones & Bartlett

Jemal, A., Thun, M.J., Ries, L.A., Howe, H.L., Weir, H.K., Center, M.M., et al. (2008). Annual report to the nation on the status of cancer, 1975-2005, featuring trends in lung cancer, tobacco use, and tobacco control. *Journal of the National Cancer Institute, 100*(23), 1672-1794.

Joyce, M. (2004). Small cell lung cancer. In N.G. Houlihan (Ed.), *Site-specific cancer series: Lung cancer* (pp. 73-82). Pittsburgh, PA: Oncology Nursing Society.

Luty, J. (2002). Nicotine addiction and smoking cessation treatments. *Advances in Psychiatric Treatment, 8*(1), 42-48.

National Cancer Institute (NCI). (2004). *Location of potential familial lung cancer gene discovered.* Retrieved July 19, 2010, from http://www.cancer.gov/newscenter/pressreleases/lungcancerlocus

National Cancer Institute (NCI). (2009). *Lung cancer. Prevention (PDQ). Evidence of benefit.* Retrieved June 14, 2010, from http://www.cancer.gov/cancertopics/pdq/prevention/lung/HealthProfessional/page4

National Comprehensive Cancer Network (NCCN) Guideline. (2010). *Nonsmall cell lung cancer.* (Version V.1.2010). National Comprehensive Cancer Network, Inc. Retrieved July 3, 2009, from http://www.nccn.org.

Oken, M.M., Creech, R.H., Tormey, D.C., Horton, J., Davis, T.E., McFadden, E.T., et al. (1982). Toxicity and response criteria of the Eastern Cooperative Oncology Group. *American Journal of Clinical Oncology, 5*(6), 649-655.

Palda, V.A. & Van Spall, H.G.C. (2003). Screening for lung cancer: Updated recommendations from the Canadian Task Force on Preventive Health Care. Retrieved June 11, 2010, from http://www.canadiantaskforce.ca/docs/CTF_Lung_Ca_Screen_Aug03.pdf

Posther, K.E. & Harpole, D.H., Jr. (2006). The surgical management of lung cancer. *Cancer Investigation, 24*(1), 56-67.

Ross, J. (2003). Biology of lung cancer. In M. Hass (Ed.), *Contemporary issues in lung cancer: A nursing perspective* (pp. 11-23). Sudbury, MA: Jones & Bartlett.

Schrump, D.S., Giaccone, G., Kelsey, C.R., & Marks, M.B. (2008). Non-small cell lung cancer. In V.T. DeVita, Jr., T.S. Lawrence, & S.A. Rosenberg (Eds.), *DeVita, Hellman, & Rosenberg's Cancer: Principles and practice of oncology* (8th ed., pp. 896-946). Philadelphia, PA: Lippincott Williams & Wilkins.

Smith, R.A., Cokkinides, V., & Eyre, H.J. (2003). American Cancer Society guidelines for the early detection of cancer, 2003. *CA: A Cancer Journal for Clinicians, 53*(1), 27-43.

Tobacco Control Research Branch of the National Cancer Institute. (n.d.). SmokeFree.gov. Retrieved January 7, 2009, from http://smokefree.gov

Tyson, L.B. (2004). Non-small cell lung cancer. In N.G. Houlilhan (Ed.), *Site-specific cancer series: Lung cancer* (pp. 83-102). Pittsburgh, PA: Oncology Nursing Society.

U.S. Preventive Services Task Force. (2004). Lung cancer screening: Recommendation statement. *Annals of Internal Medicine, 140*(9), 738-739.

CHAPTER 7

COLORECTAL CANCER

CHAPTER OBJECTIVE

After completing this chapter, the reader will be able to discuss the epidemiology, risk factors, prevention and detection strategies, and main treatments for colorectal cancer (CRC) in women.

LEARNING OBJECTIVES

After studying this chapter the reader will be able to

1. Recognize main risk factors of CRC.

2. Identify main symptoms of CRC.

3. List detection methods to determine early stage CRC.

4. List a method for staging CRC.

5. Cite the main modalities used in the treatment for CRC.

6. Recognize adjuvant chemotherapy agents used to treat CRC.

7. Identify elements of a teaching plan for a new ostomy patient.

INTRODUCTION

This chapter provides an overview of CRC, with an emphasis on the disease in women. Colorectal cancer remains a major public health challenge despite documented evidence that screening results in the prevention and early detection of the disease, ultimately reducing the morbidity and mortality associated with CRC. Unfortunately, the public's lack of symptom recognition and desire to seek regular, thorough follow-up care, are major barriers.

Myths about CRC continue – it is only a disease of elderly patients (it is not), that only men get it (women are nearly equal in incidence rates), that it is a disease of Caucasians (CRC incidence affects all races and ethnic groups), and that there is little that can be done to prevent the disease (screening can remove polyps). With so many widespread myths about CRC, educating patients with correct information should be a constant focus for nurses in clinical practice.

EPIDEMIOLOGY

Colorectal cancer remains a feared and significant problem in the U.S. as shown in Box 7-1. In the U.S., the cumulative lifetime risk of developing colorectal cancer is about 6%. Early detection and removal of adenomatous polyps through regular screening could reduce the CRC mortality rate by 50% (American Cancer Society [ACS], 2010b).

Colorectal cancer affects men and women of all races equally, although there is a slightly higher risk in African Americans (Figure 7-1). A personal or family history of colorectal polyps, CRC, or inflammatory bowel disease leads to an increased risk above that of the general population. The rate

BOX 7-1: FACTS ABOUT COLORECTAL CANCER

- 102,900 estimated new cases colon cancer annually

- 39,670 estimated new cases rectal cancer annually

- Third most common cancer in men and women

- Incidence rates have dropped in the past two decades which is attributed to increased screening and removal of colorectal polyps

- Lifetime risk is 1 in 19 men and 1 in 20 women

- 51,370 estimated deaths annually

- Accounts for 9% of all cancer deaths

- Five year survival rate for localized cancer is 91% but only 39% of cancers are diagnosed at this stage

- Five year survival rate for metastatic disease is 11%

(ACS, 2010a)

FIGURE 7-1: TRENDS IN INCIDENCE AND MORTALITY FOR COLORECTAL CANCER

SEER Incidence and US Death Rates[a]
Cancer of the Colon and Rectum, Both Sexes
Joinpoint Analyses for Whites and Blacks from 1975-2007
and for Asian/Pacific Islanders, American Indians/Alaska Natives and Hispanics from 1992-2007

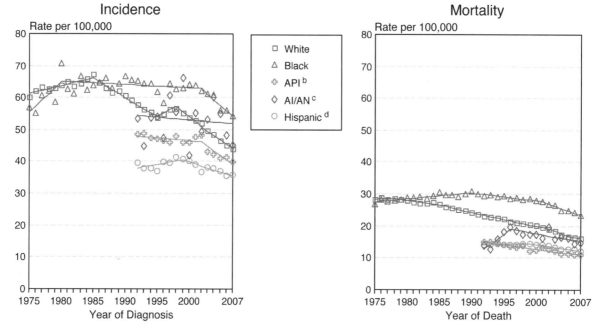

Source: Incidence data for whites and blacks are from the SEER 9 areas (San Francisco, Connecticut, Detroit, Hawaii, Iowa, New Mexico, Seattle, Utah, Atlanta). Incidence data for Asian/Pacific Islanders, American Indians/Alaska Natives and Hispanics are from the SEER 13 Areas (SEER 9 Areas, San Jose-Monterey, Los Angeles, Alaska Native Registry and Rural Georgia). Mortality data are from US Mortality Files, National Center for Health Statistics, CDC.
[a] Rates are age-adjusted to the 2000 US Std Population (19 age groups - Census P25-1103).
Regression lines are calculated using the Joinpoint Regression Program Version 3.4.3, April 2010, National Cancer Institute. Joinpoint analyses for Whites and Blacks during the 1975-2007 period allow a maximum of 4 joinpoints. Analyses for other ethnic groups during the period 1992-2007 allow a maximum of 2 joinpoints.
[b] API = Asian/Pacific Islander.
[c] AI/AN = American Indian/Alaska Native. Rates for American Indian/Alaska Native are based on the CHSDA(Contract Health Service Delivery Area) counties.
[d] Hispanic is not mutually exclusive from whites, blacks, Asian/Pacific Islanders, and American Indians/Alaska Natives. Incidence data for Hispanics are based on NHIA and exclude cases from the Alaska Native Registry. Mortality data for Hispanics exclude cases from Connecticut, the District of Columbia, Maine, Maryland, Minnesota, New Hampshire, New York, North Dakota, Oklahoma, and Vermont.

Note. From SEER Cancer Statistics Review, 1975-2007, by S.F. Altekruse, C.L. Kosary, M. Krapcho, N. Neyman, R. Aminou, W. Waldron, et al. (Eds), Bethesda, MD: National Cancer Institute. Retrieved from http://seer.cancer.gov/csr/1975_2007/, based on November 2009 SEER data submission, posted to the SEER web site, 2010.

of CRC increases significantly in the sixth decade of life in average-risk individuals. For this reason, screening should begin by 50 years of age (Lieberman, 2005). This is the basis for various screening protocols for CRC. Worldwide, CRC is more prevalent in industrialized countries. Those areas with the highest incidence are in Eastern and Western Europe, the Scandinavian countries, New Zealand, Australia, Canada, and the United States (ACS, 2010a).

Based on data gathered about cancer in women internationally, CRC has the third highest incidence. In the U.S. it is the third leading cause of death in men and women. Most frequently, CRC is diagnosed when people are older than 50 years of age. In fact, 90% of CRC patients are older than 50 years of age (ACS, 2010c). The highest incidence rate for CRC is between 65 and 74 years of age.

The probability of developing CRC in the two genders is similar (see Table 7-1). CRC accounts for 10% of all new cancer cases in women and 9% of all cancer deaths in women (ACS, 2010a). Colon cancer is more common than rectal cancer in women. The ACS estimates approximately 53,430 new cases of colon cancer occurred (compared to 49,470 new cases in men). Furthermore, the ACS estimates 17,050 new cases of rectal cancer in women (compared to 22,620 cases in men). A woman has an estimated cumulative lifetime risk of developing CRC of 1 in 20 (ACS, 2010a).

ANATOMY

The upper portion of digestive system processes food for energy, whereas the lower portion (the colon and rectum) removes solid waste (fecal matter or stool) from the body. After food is chewed and swallowed, it travels through the esophagus to the stomach. There, it is partly broken down and then sent to the small intestine. The diameter of the small intestine is narrower than that of the colon and rectum. The small intestine is the longest segment of the digestive system measuring about 20 feet. The small intestine continues breaking down the food and absorbs most of the nutrients. The small intestine joins the colon in the right lower abdomen. The colon is a muscular tube about 5 feet long. The colon absorbs water and sodium from the food matter and serves as a storage place for waste matter. Figure 7-2 shows the colon's anatomy.

The walls of the colon and rectum are made up of several layers of tissue. Colorectal cancer starts in the innermost layer and can grow through some or all of the other layers. These layers, from the inner to the outer, include:

- the inner lining (mucosa)
- a thin muscle layer (muscularis mucosa)
- the fibrous tissue beneath this muscle layer (submucosa)
- a thick muscle layer (muscularis propria) that contracts to force the contents of the intestines along

TABLE 7-1: PROBABILITY OF DEVELOPING INVASIVE COLORECTAL CANCER OVER SELECTED AGE INTERVALS BY SEX, US, 2004-2006

Age	Male	Female
Birth to 39	0.08 (1 in 1,269)	0.08 (1 in 1,300)
40 to 59	0.91 (1 in 110)	0.72 (1 in 139)
60 to 69	1.48 (1 in 67)	1.07 (1 in 94)
70 and Older	4.50 (1 in 22)	4.09 (1 in 24)
Birth to Death	5.39 (1 in 19)	5.03 (1 in 20)

(ACS, 2010a; NCCN, 2010)

FIGURE 7-2: ANATOMY OF THE COLON AND RECTUM

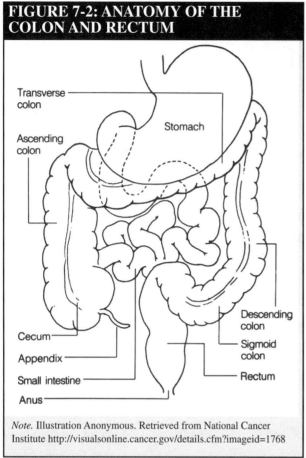

Note. Illustration Anonymous. Retrieved from National Cancer Institute http://visualsonline.cancer.gov/details.cfm?imageid=1768

- the thin, outermost layers of connective tissue (subserosa and serosa) that cover most of the colon but not the rectum.

  There are four different parts of the colon:

- The *ascending colon* starts with the cecum, which is a small pouch. This is where the small intestine attaches to the colon, and it extends upward on the right side of the abdomen. The cecum is where the appendix attaches to the colon. An estimated 9% of CRCs occur in the ascending colon and 13% in the cecum.

- The *transverse colon* goes across the body, from the right to the left side, in the upper abdomen. Approximately 11% of CRCs develop in the transverse colon.

- The *descending colon* continues downward on the left side. Approximately 6% of CRCs occur in the descending colon.

- The *sigmoid colon* is the final portion of the colon. Approximately 25% of CRCs arise in the sigmoid.

The waste matter that is left after going through the colon is known as feces or stool. It goes into the rectum, the final 6 inches of the digestive system. Approximately 30% of CRCs arise in the rectum. From the rectum, the feces pass out of the body through the anus.

PATHOPHYSIOLOGY

In most people, CRC develops slowly over a period of several years. Before a cancer develops, a growth of tissue or tumor usually begins as a non-cancerous polyp on the inner lining of the colon or rectum (see Figure 7-3). Some polyps can change into cancer but many never do. The probability of developing into a cancer depends upon the kind of polyp (NCCN, 2010). There are two general categories of polyps.

- *Adenomatous polyps* (adenomas) are polyps that have the potential to change into cancer. Because of this, adenomas are considered a precursor of cancer. Theoretically, removing the polyp prevents the cancer from developing.

- *Hyperplastic polyps* and inflammatory polyps, in general, are not premalignant. Hyperplastic

FIGURE 7-3: COLORECTAL POLYP

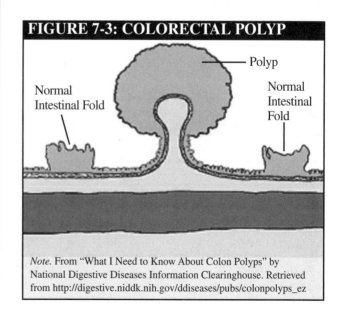

Note. From "What I Need to Know About Colon Polyps" by National Digestive Diseases Information Clearinghouse. Retrieved from http://digestive.niddk.nih.gov/ddiseases/pubs/colonpolyps_ez

polyps can be associated with having a greater risk of developing adenomas and cancer, particularly when these polyps develop in the ascending colon.

In most cases, CRC arises from adenomatous polyps. This occurs during a multistep process involving the inactivation of multiple genes that suppress tumors and repair DNA and the simultaneous activation of oncogenes (Winawer et al., 2006). When gene function is altered there can be a transformation from normal colonic epithelium, to an adenomatous polyp, to invasive colorectal cancer. This multistep process allows a window of time for screening to detect premalignant lesions and potentially prevent disease. In most sporadic cancers it takes 7 to 10 years for a polyp to develop and progress to CRC. These mutations are usually sporadic and nonhereditary; however, in approximately 10% of the cases they are related to hereditary cancer syndromes (ACS, 2010a; NCCN, 2010).

If cancer forms within a polyp, it can eventually begin to grow into the wall of the colon or rectum. When cancer cells are in the wall, they can then grow into blood vessels or lymph vessels. Lymph vessels are thin, tiny channels that carry away waste and fluid. They first drain into nearby lymph nodes, which are bean-shaped structures that help fight against infections. When cancer cells spread into blood or lymph vessels, they can travel to distant parts of the body, such as the liver. This process of spread is called metastasis.

RISK FACTORS

Table 7-2 reviews risk factors for CRC. Increasing age is the greatest risk factor for sporadic colorectal cancer. Statistics show that 99% of cases occur in people older than 40 years of age and 85% in those older than 60 years of age (ACS 2010b; 2010c). The much higher incidence of CRC in more affluent and

TABLE 7-2: RISK STRATIFICATION FOR COLORECTAL CANCER

Average Risk Factors
- *Age:* 90% of CRCs occur after 50 years of age.
- *Ethnic Background:* Risk may be higher in persons of Ashkenazi Jewish heritage.
- *Race:* Incidence and mortality is highest in African Americans.
- *Diet:* Risk is increased in persons who consume a diet high in animal fat, red meat, and processed meats.
- *Lack of exercise:* Risk is increased in inactive persons.
- *Overweight:* Risk is increased in overweight and obese persons.
- *Smoking:* Smoking increases risk 30% to 40%.
- *Alcohol:* Risk is higher in those who drink more than one alcoholic beverage per day.
- *Diabetes:* Risk is increased by 30%.

Moderate Risk Factors
- *Personal History of Colorectal Cancer:* Even if completely resected, the risk of a second primary CRC is increased, especially if the diagnosis is before 60 years of age.
- *Personal History of Polyps:* Risk is higher in persons with large dysplastic or hyperplastic polyps.
- *Personal History of Bowel Disease:* Risk is higher in persons with ulcerative colitis or Crohn's disease.
- *Family History of Colorectal Cancer:* Risk is higher if a first-degree relative has CRC.

High Risk Factors
- Hereditary Nonpolyposis Colorectal Cancer Risk is approximately 85%.
- Familial Adenomatous Polyposis Risk is nearly 100%.

(ACS, 2010c; NCCN, 2010)

industrialized countries, compared with developed countries, is also associated with lifestyle factors, such as obesity and the consumption of processed meat, and an inverse relationship with physical activity and consumption of fruit and vegetables (Kushi et al., 2006; ACS, 2010b; 2010c).

Genetic Factors

About 10% to 20% of patients describe a family history of CRC, but the pattern of inheritance and clinical features are not consistent with one of these syndromes. Screening of individuals with this type of medical history should begin at 40 years of age, or 10 years earlier than the youngest family member at the time of his or her cancer diagnosis (Hawk & Levin, 2005).

Approximately 10% of the mutations are germline (inherited) and associated with Hereditary Nonpolyposis Colorectal Cancer (HNPCC), Familial Adenomatous Polyposis (FAP), and other unusual syndromes. HNPCC is characterized by early onset CRC (before age 50) and endometrial, ovarian, small intestine, and renal cancers in the family. Usually, there are not an excessive number of polyps. The interval from polyp to cancer is very short, often 12 to 18 months. FAP is characterized by the development of hundreds to thousands of adenomatous polyps in the colon and development of CRC and other cancers in the third and fourth decade of life. FAP and HNPCC are the most common of the familial cancer syndromes, but together these two syndromes account for fewer than 5% of cases. Screening for persons with HNPCC usually begins at 25 years of age with annual colonoscopy; for those with FAP, screening often begins at 10 years of age.

History of Polyps

Polyps are precursors to CRC. They are most common as people age – approximately 30% of individuals in their 50s produce polyps. About 50% of individuals in their 70s produce polyps (Dadoly, 2000).

Approximately 70% of polyps are adenomatous with malignant potential. Nevertheless, most polyps do not become cancerous (only 5% become malignant) (Winawer et al., 2006). Most polyps are pedunculated (stalked or tubular), rather than flat, or a combination of stalked and flat. Polyps that develop into cancerous cells develop over several years, starting with growing larger, and then forming an adenoma that can become carcinoma in situ.

Polyps that are more likely to become cancerous are a higher grade and severely dysplastic. Patients who develop more than one polyp increase the likelihood five to eight times that they will develop a malignancy (Winawer et al., 2006). When detected, the smaller the polyp, the less likely that it will become malignant. For those who undergo regular polypectomy for recurring polyps, the incidence of developing CRC decreases by 93% (Winawer et al., 2006).

Personal History

Inherited genetic factors and previous cancers increase the risk for some patients. Those who were previously diagnosed with colon cancer are at higher risk. Women with breast, endometrial, and ovarian cancer are at higher risk for developing CRCs. (See Chapters 2, 3, and 4.) People with a family history of colon cancer are at increased risk.

For example, colon cancer risk increases in women who have been diagnosed with ovarian cancer. In turn, colon cancer increases the risk of a woman developing ovarian cancer, especially if the cancer was diagnosed before 50 years of age (O'Rourke & Mahon, 2003). Most women with ovarian cancer will not survive long enough to develop colon cancer. These risks may be based on hormonal and nutritional interactions and their relationship to Hereditary Nonpolyposis Colorectal Cancer (HNPCC) syndrome.

Family History

A family history of CRC involving a first-degree relative increases the risk of developing colon cancer two to three fold. The risk is higher when the relative was diagnosed before 50 years of age or if there are many family members who were diagnosed with CRC.

The genetic syndromes HNPCC and FAP increase the risk 70% and 100% respectively (NCCN, 2010). These syndromes create a condition whereby family members develop polyps that advance to adenomas and possible malignancies and account for about 5% of all CRC. Key indicators of these hereditary cancer syndromes are shown in Table 7-3.

Familial Adenomatous Polyposis

Familial adenomatous polyposis is caused by mutations in the APC gene that a person inherits from his or her parents. About 1% of all CRCs are due to FAP.

People with this disease typically develop hundreds or thousands of polyps in their colons and rectums, usually in their teens or early adulthood. Cancer usually develops in one or more of these polyps as early as 20 years of age. By 40 years of age, almost all people with this disorder will have developed cancer if a prophylactic colectomy is not done (Lynch & de la Chappelle, 2003). FAP is sometimes associated with Gardner syndrome, a condition that involves benign (non-cancerous) tumors of the skin, soft connective tissue, and bones.

A less severe form of FAP, called attenuated familial adenomatous polyposis (AFAP), is characterized by less than 100 polyps (usually about 20) at presentation and later onset of CRC (Lynch & Lynch, 2006). There are over 800 mutations in the APC gene associated with FAP (Burt & Neklason, 2005). There is also an autosomal recessive gene on chromosome 1, called MYH, that is associated with polyposis. Approximately 25% of individuals with FAP are the first person in their family with the hereditary mutation for FAP. This is referred to as a de novo mutation. Future generations are at risk for inheriting the mutation.

Hereditary Nonpolyposis Colorectal Cancer

Hereditary nonpolyposis colorectal cancer, also known as Lynch syndrome, is another clearly defined colon genetic syndrome. It accounts for

---

TABLE 7-3: KEY INDICATORS OF HEREDITARY CANCER SYNDROMES

Hereditary Nonpolyposis Colorectal Cancer (HNPCC)

- Personal history of CRC diagnosed before 50 years of age.
- Personal history of endometrial cancer diagnosed before 50 years of age.
- First-degree relative with CRC diagnosed before 50 years of age.
- Two or more relatives with CRC or an HNPCC associated cancer, including endometrial, ovarian, gastric, hepatobiliary, small bowel, renal pelvis, or ureter cancer. The first relative must be a first-degree relative of the others.
- CRC occurring in two or more generations on the same side of the family.
- A personal history of CRC and a first-degree relative with adenomas diagnosed before 40 years of age.
- An affected relative with a known HNPCC mutation.

Familial Adenomatous Polyposis (FAP)

- Patient has a clinical diagnosis of FAP (100 or more polyps).
- Patient has suspected FAP or attenuated FAP (AFAP) (15 to 99 polyps).
- Patient is a first-degree relative of FAP or AFAP patient.
- Patient has an affected relative with a known FAP or MYH mutation.
- Patient with any number of adenomas in a family with FAP.

(Lynch & de la Chapelle, 2003; NCCN, 2010)

about 3% to 5% of all colorectal cancers. HNPCC can be caused by inherited changes in a number of different genes that normally help repair DNA damage. This syndrome also develops when people are relatively young.

People with HNPCC have polyps, but they only have a few, not hundreds as in FAP. The lifetime risk of CRC in people with this condition may be as high as 70% to 80% (Lynch & Lynch, 2006). The majority of mutations responsible for HNPCC occur in four mismatch repair genes, MSH2, MLH1, PMS2, and MSH6. Patients with a mutation in MLH1 and MSH2 have an 80% lifetime risk of developing CRC as compared with a 6% risk in the general population (Lynch & Lynch, 2006). Women with this condition also have a very high risk of developing cancer of the endometrium. Other cancers linked with HNPCC include cancer of the ovary, stomach, small bowel, pancreas, kidney, ureters, and bile duct. Women with mutations in these genes have a 60% lifetime risk for developing endometrial cancer and a 12% lifetime risk for developing ovarian cancer (Lynch & Lynch, 2006).

Although not associated with large numbers of polyps, persons with HNPCC who do form adeno-matous polyps are more likely to do so at an earlier age, more likely to develop right-sided colon cancer, and exhibit a very rapid progression to malignancy in 1 to 3 years instead of the 5- to 10-year pattern seen in the general population (Hendriks et al., 2006).

Taking an accurate family history is the key to identifying families with an HNPCC mutation. There are several considerations in identifying these patients and any suspected family should be referred to a genetics professional to identify the most cost-effective and efficient strategy for genetic testing. The Amsterdam and Bethesda criteria assess the number of relatives affected by CRC or other HNPCC-related cancers with particular emphasis on the age of onset. The components of these criteria are shown in Table 7-4. Individuals who fulfill Amsterdam or Bethesda criteria can go directly to genetic testing for HNPCC. Additional immunohistochemistry studies are often done on tumor tissue to determine which gene might be affected and further guide testing.

About 90% of tumors from people who have HNPCC show microsatellite instability. Microsatellites are repeated sequences of DNA.

TABLE 7-4: AMSTERDAM AND BETHESDA CRITERIA

Amsterdam Criteria

- At least one person was diagnosed before 50 years of age.
- There are at least three relatives with an HNPCC-related cancer (large bowel, endometrium, ureter, or renal pelvis – does not include stomach, ovary brain, bladder, or skin.
- FAP has been excluded.
- At least two successive generations are affected.

Bethesda Criteria

- CRC diagnosed in a patient who is younger than 50 years of age.
- Presence of synchronous, metachronous colorectal, or other HNPCC-associated tumors, regardless of age. These tumors would include colorectal, endometrial, stomach, ovarian, pancreas, ureter and renal pelvis, biliary tract, and brain.
- CRC with the MSI-High pathology diagnosed in a patient who is younger than 60 years of age.
- CRC diagnosed in one or more first-degree relatives with an HNPCC-related tumor, with one of the cancers being diagnosed before 50 years of age.

(Umar et al., 2004; Vasen, Watson, Mecklin, & Lynch, 1999)

Although the length of these microsatellites is highly variable from person to person, each individual has microsatellites of a set length. These repeated sequences are common and normal. In cells with mutations in DNA repair genes, some of these sequences accumulate errors and become longer or shorter. The appearance of abnormally long or short microsatellites in an individual's DNA is referred to as microsatellite instability.

Tests are available that detect microsatellite instability in tumor cells, and finding numerous longer or shorter microsatellite regions in these cells suggests the presence of a mutated DNA mismatch repair gene with HNPCC. Thus, testing a tumor sample for microsatellite instability can often provide a helpful way to determine whether genetic testing for HNPCC is appropriate. If a patient's tumor cells show no evidence of microsatellite instability, it's unlikely that he or she has a mutated mismatch repair gene. In such cases, genetic tests are unlikely to yield useful information and are rarely worth the time and money they entail.

Referral to a Genetics Professional

Identifying families with these inherited syndromes is important because it allows doctors to recommend specific steps, such as screening and other preventive measures, at an early age. Often, CRC screening begins in the teenage years for persons with a known mutation in FAP. When polyps begin to develop, a prophylactic colectomy is recommended. For persons with a known mutation in HNPCC, screening begins between 20 and 25 years of age and is done on an annual basis because polyps will often progress to a CRC in 12 to 18 months. Women with a known HNPCC are usually advised to have their uterus and ovaries removed (total hysterectomy) at about 40 years of age because of their high risk of developing these cancers (60% lifetime risk for endometrial cancer and 12% for ovarian cancer). Because the testing and management strategies are complex for the patient with a hereditary cancer syndrome, he or she should be referred to genetics professional.

Other Lifestyle Risk Factors

For those without a genetic predisposition, there are no specific and unique risks for CRC. However, together, many risk factors can put an individual at risk (NCI, 2010).

Epidemiologic, experimental (animal), and clinical investigations suggest that diets high in total fat (saturated and monounsaturated), protein, calories, alcohol, and meat (both red and white), and low in calcium and foliate (vegetables), are associated with an increased incidence of CRC. The risk is 2 to 2.5 times higher for those who follow a high-fat diet compared to those with low-fat diets (Kushi et al., 2006).

Colon cancer rates have been shown to be high in populations with high total fat intake and are lower in those populations where people consume less fat. This means that Western countries – with high-fat diets – have been shown to have more CRC (ACS, 2010c).

Inflammatory Bowel Disease

Inflammatory bowel disease, which includes ulcerative colitis and Crohn's disease, is a condition in which the colon is inflamed over a long period of time. For those with inflammatory bowel disease the risk of developing colorectal cancer is increased (ACS, 2010a). These individuals need to be screened for CRC on a more frequent basis. Often, the first sign that cancer may be developing is dysplasia found in areas of irritation. Inflammatory bowel disease is different than irritable bowel syndrome, which does not carry an increased risk for CRC.

SIGNS AND SYMPTOMS

Colon cancer may not produce symptoms until the tumor is well advanced. Signs and symptoms of CRC are

- rectal bleeding

- blood in the stool

- abdominal cramping or pain

- change in bowel habits lasting more than a few days

- narrowing of the stool

- fatigue

- urge to defecate after defecating.

Unfortunately, these symptoms are also associated with many more benign gastrointestinal problems that necessitate a diagnostic evaluation. A change in bowel habits is a more common presenting symptom for left-sided cancers and are caused by a progressive narrowing of the bowel lumen, with diarrhea, a change in stool form and, eventually, intestinal obstruction (ACS, 2010d). About 10% of patients with iron deficiency have CRC, most commonly on the right side. Thus, iron deficiency in men and women who are not menstruating is an indication for immediate evaluation to rule out CRC (NCCN, 2010). The first symptom that is recognized by the patient is often blood in or on the stool.

Blood in or on the stool does not absolutely mean CRC is present; bleeding could be related to hemorrhoids, ulcers, a tear, or inflammatory bowel disease. Bleeding, however, when related to CRC, is seldom associated with the early detection of colorectal cancer. Ideally, screening should begin before symptoms arise, if possible. Waiting for symptoms to occur may be too late to prevent CRC.

PREVENTION

Lifestyle Risk Factors

Direct efforts need to be made to prevent CRC. Evidence shows that 12% of CRC deaths are attributed to smoking (Zisman, Nickolov, Brand, Gorchow, & Roy, 2006). The carcinogens found in tobacco increase cancer growth in the colon and rectum and increase the risk of being diagnosed

with this cancer. Efforts at smoking prevention and cessation should not be underestimated.

Maintaining a healthy diet and being physically active are important components of CRC prevention. The amount of fat and fiber in the diet has been examined extensively as risk factors associated with CRC. A diet high in fiber and low in fat, which for adults is 20 to 35 grams of fiber per day and about 30% or less of their total daily calories from fat, along with limited consumption of red meat, helps reduce the risk of CRC (ACS, 2010c). It is also recommended that men and women regularly eat fruits and cruciferous vegetables and consume calcium to decrease the risk of CRC.

Additionally, recent evidence supported by the International Agency for Research on Cancer indicates that inactivity can be associated with CRC (Meyerhardt et al., 2006). The lack of physical activity in daily routines can also be attributed to the increased incidence of obesity in men and women, another factor associated with CRC (ACS, 2010c). Therefore, regular physical activity and a healthy diet can help decrease the risk of CRC.

Alcohol consumption is a factor in the diagnosis of CRC at a younger age as well as an increase of CRC in the distal colon. As with smoking, the regular consumption of alcohol causes a two-fold increased risk of developing CRC and limiting alcohol intake is recommended (Zisman et al., 2006).

Chemoprevention

Many studies have found that people who regularly use aspirin and other non-steroidal anti-inflammatory drugs (NSAIDs), such as ibuprofen (Motrin, Advil) and naproxen (Aleve), have a lower risk of CRC and adenomatous polyps (Dube et al., 2007; Rostom et al. 2007). Aspirin can prevent the growth of polyps in people who were previously treated for early stages of CRC or who previously had polyps removed (NCCN, 2010). Because NSAIDs can cause serious or life-threatening bleeding from stomach irritation, they are not recommended as a cancer prevention strategy for people at average risk of developing CRC.

Polypectomy

Regular CRC screening or testing is one of the most effective means in preventing CRC. From the time the first abnormal cells start to grow, it usually takes about 10 to 15 years for them to develop into CRC (ACS, 2010b; 2010d). Regular CRC screening can, in many cases, prevent CRC altogether. This is because some polyps, or growths, can be found and removed before they have the chance to turn into cancer. Colorectal cancer is a very preventable cancer. Detection and removal of adenomatous polyps, from which more than 95% of CRCs arise, reduce the risk of being diagnosed with or dying from this disease (Hawk & Levin, 2005). Polyps at highest risk of becoming malignant include those greater than 1 cm in size, those with high-grade dysplastic features on histology, and those that are removed in pieces (Levin, Lieberman et al., 2008). See Table 7-5 for recommendations for follow-up colonoscopy after polypectomy.

SCREENING AND DETECTION

Screening for CRC has changed in the last 20 years. Recommendations have included combinations of digital rectal examination, sigmoidoscopy, colonoscopy, barium enema, and fecal occult blood testing (FOBT). All scoping methods require full preparation of the bowel with oral laxatives and, sometimes, enemas. The diagnostic yield of the examination depends on adequate preparation. Early detection and removal of adenomatous polyps through regular screening could reduce the CRC mortality rate by 50% (Winawer et al., 2006). Currently, recommendations for CRC screening fall into two broad categories:

- *Tests that can find both colorectal polyps and cancer:* These tests look at the structure of the colon itself to find any abnormal areas. This is done either with a scope inserted into the rectum or with special imaging tests. Polyps found before they turn cancerous can be removed, so these tests may prevent CRC. Because of this, these tests are

TABLE 7-5: RECOMMENDATIONS FOR FOLLOW-UP SCREENING FOLLOWING POLYPECTOMY

Finding	Screening Recommendation
Small hyperplastic rectal polyp	10 years
< 2 tubular adenomas (<1 cm) with low grade dysplasia	5-10 years
3-10 low grade adenomas or any adenoma with high grade dysplasia	5 years
10 or more adenomas on one examination	< 3 years and referral for evaluation for hereditary cancer syndrome
Sessile adenomas removed in pieces	2-6 months to complete removal; when complete (both clinically and by pathology), at the descretion of the endoscopist
Persons with a known mutation for HNPCC or FAP	Annually
Persons with CRC	1 year after resection; if normal, repeat in 3 years, and then 5 years

(Levin et al., 2008; Winawer et al., 2006)

preferred if they are available and the patient is willing to have them.

- *Tests that mainly find cancer:* These involve testing the stool for signs that cancer may be present. These tests are less invasive and easier to have done, but they are less likely to detect polyps.

All guidelines for CRC screening require risk assessment as a first step. The approach to screening differs significantly based on risk category (average, increased, or high risk). The key element of a CRC screening recommendation is to suggest the right test beginning at the correct age for individuals at each risk level (ACS, 2010b). Screening should also be repeated at the proper interval, depending on risk level. High-risk patients with hereditary CRC syndromes or inflammatory bowel disease should be referred to specialists early in life. Those with a suspected hereditary cancer syndrome need to be referred to a genetics expert for genetic testing to clarify risk. Those who test positive for a deleterious mutation should be managed by a clinician with expertise in these syndromes. Screening will be required on an annual basis beginning at a young age. Membersof these families may also want to consider enrolling in chemoprevention trials.

Regular screening for the average-risk person should begin by 50 years of age with FOBT and either a sigmoidoscopy every five years or colonoscopy every ten years (ACS, 2010b). Table 7-6 details screening tests used to identify CRC.

Fecal Occult Blood Testing

The goal of FOBT is to examine the stool for hidden blood that occasionally sheds from adenomatous polyps and cancer. One disadvantage of this screening method is that, often, polyps do not bleed. This test should be done every year by obtaining a three-sample card from a primary care provider; the patient takes the card home to obtain the stool samples for testing. Dietary guidelines must be followed before and during this test; if not

done properly, the test can result in a false outcome. Additionally, negative FOBT results do not necessarily mean there are no polyps or cancer present, just that no blood was detected in the stool. Conversely, positive FOBT does not indicate cancer, only that further screening should be administered to locate the bleeding. Any FOBT that was administered by a doctor using a small stool sample on a single card is inadequate and not recommended as a CRC screening method (NCCN, 2010).

Flexible Sigmoidoscopy

The flexible sigmoidoscopy is an inexpensive procedure that can be done in a physician's office and requires no sedation. The day before the procedure the patient is placed on a clear liquid diet and given a prescription for a bowel prep. The flexible sigmoidoscopy is recommended every 5 years along with an annual FOBT (ACS, 2010b). The primary disadvantage of flexible sigmoidoscopy is that only a portion of the distal colon can be examined. Using a 60 cm flexible sigmoidoscope, approximately 65%-75% of adenomatous polyps and 40%-65% of colorectal cancers are within its reach, whereas with colonoscopy the entire length of the colon can be visualized (Hawk & Levin, 2005).

Colonoscopy

The colonoscopy is a more thorough exam and is becoming the preferred method of screening. Figure 7-4 demonstrates the recent increase in the utilization of colonoscopy. This is especially true because Medicare and most major insurers cover a significant portion of the costs. During a colonoscopy, a thin, lighted tube, which has a small camera attached, is inserted into the rectum. The colonoscope is guided through the rectum and colon and if any polyps are found, they can be removed and biopsied. For patients who cannot tolerate colonoscopy, barium enema is sometimes utilized.

TABLE 7-6: SCREENING TESTS FOR COLORECTAL CANCER

Flexible Sigmoidscopy
Interval: Every 5 years

Preparation: Partial bowel prep with laxatives and enemas; sedation usually not used

Accuracy: 45%-50% sensitivity

Risks/Limitations: Only evaluates lower-third of colon

Patient Teaching: A positive screen requires follow-up with colonosocopy; may cause some discomfort; very small risk of bleeding, infection, or perforation

Colonoscopy
Interval: Every 10 years

Preparation: Complete bowel prep; requires conscious sedation

Accuracy: Up to 95% sensitivity; can usually view entire colon, biopsy and remove polyps, and diagnose other diseases

Risks/Limitations: Perforation and bleeding; risk is increased with polypectomy

Patient Teaching: Will need to miss a day of work and need someone to provide transportation to and from appointment

Double Contrast Barium Enema
Interval: Every 5 years

Preparation: Complete bowel prep; no sedation needed

Accuracy: 48%-73% sensitivity

Risk/Limitations: Rare cases of perforation; cannot biopsy polyps

Patient Education: A positive screen requires follow-up with colonoscopy

Virtual Colonoscopy
Interval: Every 5 years

Preparation: Complete bowel prep; no sedation

Accuracy: 55%-59% sensitivity for large polyps

Risk/Limitations: Rare cases of perforation

Patient Education: Costly – may not be covered by insurance; a positive screen necessitates the need for colonoscopy; if not available on the same day, a second prep will be required; may detect other problems outside of the colon that need evaluation

Fecal Occult Blood Testing
Interval: Annually

Preparation: Foods to avoid 48 hours prior to and during collection include aspirin, NSAIDs, vitamin C, red meat, poultry, fish, raw vegetables

Accuracy: 37%-79% sensitivity

Patient Education: A positive screen requires further evaluation with colonoscopy

Fecal Immunochemical Test
Interval: Annually

Preparation: Special sample collection instructions and transportation to lab

Accuracy: 29%-94% sensitivity

Patient Education: One time testing is likely to be ineffective; a positive screen requires follow-up with colonoscopy

Stool DNA
Interval: None specified

Preparation: Requires collection of an adequate sample and proper preservation and shipping to laboratory

Accuracy: 26%-59% sensitivity

Patient Education: A positive screen requires follow-up with colonoscopy

(Levin et al., 2008)

Virtual Colonoscopy

Virtual colonoscopy is a relatively new screening option to detect CRC (Levin et al., 2006). In 2008, the ACS approved it as a technique to screen for early detection of CRC (Levin et al., 2008). Virtual colonoscopy produces a dual or tri-dimensional colorectal image that is generated using data from a spiral CT scan. This screening method is appealing to many people because it is noninvasive and requires no sedation and a view of the entire colon and rectum is visible. The preparation for this procedure does require the same

FIGURE 7-4: TRENDS IN ENDOSCOPY FOR THE EARLY DETECTION OF COLORECTAL CANCER

Percentage of adults aged 50 years and older who ever had a colorectal endoscopy, by race/ethnicity: 1987-2005

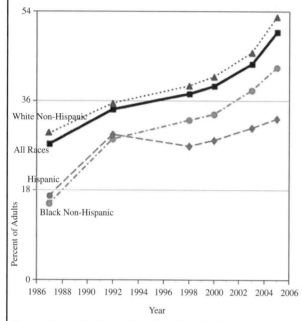

Source: Centers For Disease Control And Prevention, National Center For Health Statistics. National Health Interview Survey.

Data are age-adjusted to the 2000 standard using age groups: 50-64, 65+. analysis uses the 2000 Standard Population as defined by NCHS (http://www.cdc.gov/nchs/data/statnt/statnt20.pdf

Note. From Ries, L.A.G., Melbert, D., Krapcho, M., Stinchcomb, D.G., Howlader, N., Horner, M.J., Mariotto, A., Miller, B.A., Feuer, E.J., Altekruse, S.F., Lewis, D.R., Clegg, L., Eisner, M.P., Reichman, M., Edwards, B.K. (eds). *SEER Cancer Statistics Review, 1975-2005*, National Cancer Institute. Bethesda, MD, http://seer.cancer.gov/csr/1975_2005/, based on November 2007 SEER data submission, posted to the SEER web site, 2008.

dietary restrictions and bowel cleansing as the colonoscopy, and air insufflation is needed for a clear view of the colon. Many people may prefer this screening method to flexible sigmoidoscopy or colonoscopy, but they need to be clearly informed that if any polyps are visible on the scan, the patient will then have to undergo a colonoscopy for further evaluation. If the facility cannot accommodate immediate colonoscopy, the patient will have to repeat the prep at a later point.

Stool DNA

Stool DNA (sDNA) tests do not look for blood in the stool. These tests look for specific abnormal sections of DNA from cancer or polyp cells. Colorectal cancer cells often contain DNA mutations in certain genes such as APC, K-ras, and p53. Cells from CRCs or polyps with these mutations are often shed into the stool, where tests may be able to detect them.

There is no specific interval for how often the test needs to be done (Levin et al., 2008) This test is also much more expensive than other forms of stool testing. It does not require any special preparation. If the results are positive, a colonoscopy is required to investigate further.

People having this test will receive a kit with detailed instructions from their doctor's office or clinic on how to collect the specimen. sDNA requires an entire stool sample. It is obtained using a special container which is placed in a bracket that stretches across the seat of the toilet. The specimen must be shipped to the lab within 24 hours of having the bowel movement in a special kit with ice.

Fecal Immunochemical Test

The fecal immunochemical test (FIT) is a test that detects occult blood in the stool. This test reacts to part of the hemoglobin molecule, which is found on red blood cells. The FIT is done essentially the same way as the FOBT, but some people may find it easier to use because there are no drug or dietary restrictions and sample collection may take less effort. This test is also less likely to react to bleeding from the upper digestive tract, such as from the stomach.

As with the FOBT, the FIT may not detect a tumor that is not bleeding, so multiple stool samples should be tested. If the results are positive for hidden blood, a colonoscopy is required to investigate further (Levin et al., 2008). In order to be beneficial the test must be repeated every year. It requires special mailing to the lab.

Patient Education

Educating the public about the epidemiology, risk factors, symptoms, and screening options for CRC enables individuals to become advocates for their own health. Typically, individuals in the community setting have many misconceptions about CRC. For instance, many people do not know the difference between a sigmoidoscopy and a colonoscopy or that FOBT should be done every year to increase the efficiency of sigmoidoscopy and help decrease the risk of CRC (ACS, 2010b). Many individuals believe that CRC inevitably ends in a colostomy. Many do not realize that polypectomy can prevent a colon cancer from developing. Correction of these misconceptions is critical to motivate individuals to engage in CRC screening. As health educators, nurses need to work to alter these perceptions and arm individuals with the correct information. The goal of the health education is to promote healthy living and to encourage individuals to engage in practices and behaviors that are beneficial to long-term health.

STAGING AND DIAGNOSIS

If colon cancer is suspected, diagnostic tests may include

- chest X-ray
- CT scan of the abdomen or pelvis, with or without a needle biopsy
- PET scan
- abdominal ultrasound
- transrectal ultrasound
- MRI
- blood tests (CBC, serum chemistry, and liver studies)
  serum carcinoembryonic antigen (CEA), a tumor-associated marker for cancer (normal, <2.5 ng/ml)
- bone scan.

After all of the data is gathered, the patient is assigned to a stage, based on the size of the tumor, presence or absence of lymph node involvement, and presence or absence of metastasis. Highlights of the staging schema for CRC are listed in Table 7-7 (Edge et al., 2010).

If cancer forms within a polyp, it can eventually begin to grow into the wall of the colon or rectum. When cancer cells are in the wall, they can then grow into blood vessels or lymph vessels. When cancer cells spread into blood or lymph vessels, they can metastasize to distant parts of the body, such as the liver.

There are several types of cancer of the colon and rectum.

- *Adenocarcinomas:* More than 95% of CRCs are a type of cancer known as adenocarcinomas. These are cancers that start in cells that form glands that make mucus to lubricate the inside of the colon and rectum. (ACS, 2010f)

- *Carcinoid tumors:* These tumors develop from specialized hormone-producing cells of the intestine.

- *Gastrointestinal stromal tumors:* These tumors develop from specialized cells in the wall of the colon called the "interstitial cells of Cajal." Some are benign; others are malignant.

- *Lymphomas:* These are cancers of immune system cells that typically develop in lymph nodes, but they may also start in the colon and rectum or other organs.

PROGNOSIS

The overall survival for CRC is demonstrated in Figure 7-5. Survival is quite variable depending on the stage at diagnosis as shown in Table 7-8. Another factor that can affect the prognosis for CRC is the grade of the tumor (Edge et al., 2010). Grade is a description of how closely the cancer resembles normal colorectal tissue microscopically.

TABLE 7-7: STAGING FOR COLORECTAL CANCER

Stage 0

Tis, N0, M0: The cancer is in the earliest stage. It has not grown beyond the inner layer (mucosa) of the colon or rectum. This stage is also known as carcinoma in situ or intramucosal carcinoma.

Stage I

T1, N0, M0 or T2, N0, M0: The cancer has grown through the muscularis mucosa into the submucosa (T1) or it may also have grown into the muscularis propria (T2). It has not spread to nearby lymph nodes or distant sites.

Stage IIA

T3, N0, M0: The cancer has grown into the outermost layers of the colon or rectum but has not reached nearby organs. It has not yet spread to the nearby lymph nodes or distant sites.

Stage IIB

T4a, N0, M0: The cancer has grown through the wall of the colon or rectum and into other nearby tissues or organs. It has not yet spread to the nearby lymph nodes or distant sites.

Stage IIC

T4b, N0, M0: The cancer directly invades or is histologically adherent to other organs. It has not yet spread to the nearby lymph nodes or distant sites.

Stage IIIA

T1, N1, M0 or T2, N1, M0: The cancer has grown through the mucosa into the submucosa (T1) or it may also have grown into the muscularis propria (T2). It has spread to 1 to 3 nearby lymph nodes but not to distant sites.

Stage IIIB

T3, N1, M0 or T4, N1, M0: The cancer has grown into the outermost layers of the colon or rectum but has not reached nearby organs (T3) or the cancer has grown through the wall of the colon or rectum and into other nearby tissues or organs (T4). It has spread to 1 to 3 nearby lymph nodes but not distant sites.

Stage IIIC

Any T, N2, M0: The cancer may or may not have grown through the wall of the colon or rectum, but it has spread to 4 or more nearby lymph nodes. It has not spread to distant sites.

Stage IV

Any T, Any N, Any M1: The cancer may or may not have grown through the wall of the colon or rectum, and it may or may not have spread to nearby lymph nodes. It has spread to distant sites such as the liver, lung, peritoneum (the membrane lining the abdominal cavity), or ovary. M1a is a single metastatic site and M1b refers to multiple metastatic sites.

Used with permission of the American Joint Committee on Cancer (AJCC), Chicago, Illinois. The original source for this material is the *AJCC Cancer Staging Handbook,* Seventh Edition (2010) published by Springer Science and Business Media, LLC, www.springerlink.com.

The scale used for grading CRC goes from G1 (where the cancer looks much like normal colorectal tissue) to G4 (where the cancer looks very abnormal). The grades G2 and G3 fall somewhere in between. The grade is often simplified as either "low-grade" (G1 or G2) or "high-grade" (G3 or G4). In general, the prognosis is not as good for high-grade cancers as it is for low-grade cancers. This distinction is considered when determining whether a patient should get adjuvant therapy with chemotherapy after surgery.

TREATMENTS

Treatment for CRC depends on the size, location, and extent of the tumor, and on the patient's general health. Clinical staging of the tumor is the most important prognosticator.

FIGURE 7-5: SURVIVAL FOR COLORECTAL CANCER

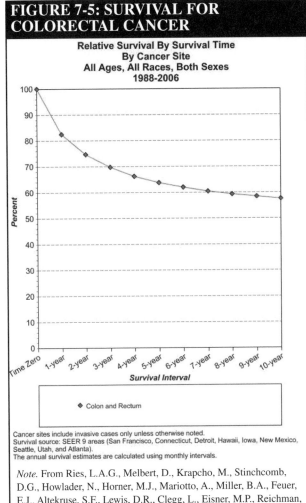

Relative Survival By Survival Time By Cancer Site
All Ages, All Races, Both Sexes
1988-2006

◆ Colon and Rectum

Cancer sites include invasive cases only unless otherwise noted.
Survival source: SEER 9 areas (San Francisco, Connecticut, Detroit, Hawaii, Iowa, New Mexico, Seattle, Utah, and Atlanta).
The annual survival estimates are calculated using monthly intervals.

Note. From Ries, L.A.G., Melbert, D., Krapcho, M., Stinchcomb, D.G., Howlader, N., Horner, M.J., Mariotto, A., Miller, B.A., Feuer, E.J., Altekruse, S.F., Lewis, D.R., Clegg, L., Eisner, M.P., Reichman, M., Edwards, B.K. (eds). *SEER Cancer Statistics Review, 1975-2005*, National Cancer Institute. Bethesda, MD, http://seer.cancer.gov/csr/1975_2005/, based on November 2007 SEER data submission, posted to the SEER web site, 2008.

Areas of metastasis include the liver, lymph nodes, peritoneal cavity, lungs, bones, and adrenal glands. At diagnosis, approximately 39% of colon cancer cells and 50% to 60% of rectal cancer cells have metastasized to regional lymph nodes (ACS, 2010e).

Approximately 50% of colon cancer patients will be diagnosed with hepatic metastases, either at the time of initial presentation or as a result of disease recurrence. Although only a small proportion of patients with hepatic metastases are candidates for surgical resection, advances in tumor ablation techniques and in regional and systemic chemotherapy administration provide for a number of treatment options.

TABLE 7-8: 5-YEAR SURVIVAL RATE FOR CRC BY STAGE GROUPING

Stage I	94%
Stage IIA	79%
Stage IIB	62%
Stage IIIA	85%
Stage IIIB	65%
Stage IIIC	45%
Stage IV	8%

(Edge et al., 2010)

For patients with hepatic metastasis that is considered to be resectable (based on limited number of lesions, intrahepatic locations of lesions, lack of major vascular involvement, absent or limited extrahepatic disease, and sufficient functional hepatic reserve), a negative margin resection has resulted in 5-year survival rates of 25% to 40% (Leonard, Brenner, & Kemeny, 2005). Patients with hepatic metastases that are deemed unresectable will occasionally become candidates for resection if they have a good response to chemotherapy. These patients have 5-year survival rates similar to patients who initially had resectable disease.

Surgery

Surgery is often the main treatment for earlier stage colon cancers (Libutti, Salz et al., 2005). Surgery is usually the main treatment for rectal cancer, although radiation and chemotherapy will often be given before or after surgery (Libutti, Tepper, Salz, & Rustgi, 2005). Several surgical methods are used for removing or destroying rectal cancers.

Colon Cancer

- *Polypectomy and local excision:* Some early colon cancers (stage 0 and some early stage I tumors) or polyps can be removed by surgery through a colonoscope avoiding an abdominal incision. For a polypectomy, the cancer is cut out across the base of the polyp's stalk. Local excision removes superficial cancers and a small amount of nearby tissue.

- *Colectomy:* A colectomy involves removing part of the colon as well as nearby lymph nodes through an abdominal incision. Typically, about one-fourth to one-third of the colon is removed; however, more or less tissue may be removed, depending on the exact size and location of the tumor. The remaining sections are reattached. Nearby lymph nodes are removed at this time as well.

- *Laparoscopic-assisted colectomy:* This is a newer approach to removing part of the colon and nearby lymph nodes, which may be an option for some earlier stage cancers. Instead of making one long incision in the abdomen, the surgeon makes several smaller incisions. A laprascope is used to remove part of the colon and lymph nodes. One of the instruments has a small video camera on the end, which allows the surgeon to see inside the abdomen. After the diseased part of the colon has been freed, one of the incisions is made larger to allow for its removal.

Because the incisions are smaller than with a standard colectomy, they usually heal faster. Patients may recover slightly faster and have less pain than they do after standard colon surgery.

Laparoscopic-assisted surgery appears to be about as curative as the standard approach for earlier stage cancers. However, the surgery requires special expertise and training.

Rectal Cancer

- *Polypectomy and local excision:* As in colon surgery, polypectomy can be used to remove superficial cancers or polyps. This is done with instruments inserted through the anus, without making a surgical opening in the skin of the abdomen.

- *Local transanal resection:* This is a full thickness resection. A local transanal resection is done with instruments inserted through the anus, without making an opening in the skin of the abdomen. This operation involves cutting through all layers of the rectum to remove invasive cancer as well as some surrounding normal rectal tissue. This procedure can be used to remove some stage I rectal cancers that are relatively small and not too far from the anus.

- *Low anterior resection:* Some stage I rectal cancers and most stage II or III cancers in the upper two-thirds of the rectum can be removed with this procedure in which the tumor is removed without affecting the anus. After low anterior resection, the colon will be attached to the anus and the waste will leave the body in the usual way through the anus. It requires an abdominal incision.

- *Abdominoperineal resection:* This operation can be used to treat some stage I cancers and most stage II or III rectal cancers in the lower one-third of the rectum, close to the sphincter muscle. There is one incision in the abdomen, and another in the perineal area around the anus. This incision allows the surgeon to remove the anus and the tissues surrounding it, including the sphincter muscle. Because the anus is removed, a permanent colostomy is made to allow stool a path out of the body. Nursing care for an ostomy patient is shown in Table 7-9.

Chemotherapy

Chemotherapy may be given for two different reasons (Elsevier, 2006). Adjuvant chemotherapy is the use of chemotherapy after surgery with the intent to increase the survival rate for patients with some stages of colon cancer and rectal cancer. It is given when there is no evidence of cancer but there may be microscopic disease putting the patient at risk for recurrence. For some cancers, especially rectal cancers, chemotherapy is given (along with radiation) before surgery to try to shrink the cancer and make surgery more effective. This is referred to as neoadju-

TABLE 7-9: IMPORTANT ASPECTS OF OSTOMY MANAGEMENT
• Early participation in care is key to self-care after surgery. Teaching should begin as soon as possible before surgery.
• A one-piece system is placed immediately after surgery to allow healing; then the appliance is changed to a 2-piece.
• Initial drainage after surgery is liquid with blood. Then with increased diet, the discharge becomes solid. Final consistency depends on the placement of the stoma along the colon. The proximal portion of the colon returns to normal 3 to 5 days postoperatively.
• Flatulence begins through the stoma and occasional venting of appliance needs to be done throughout the day.
• Appliance choice depends on the location of the stoma.
• Appliance fit is key to prevent fecal leakage.
• Flange (faceplates) vary in size, shape, adhesive, pre-cut, or customized.
• Skin barriers also vary.
• Pay attention to signs of infection, prompted by adhesive and appliance materials.
• Changing the appliance requires systematic cleaning, airing, and replacement of the bag. A routine schedule is encouraged.
• Adapting colostomy needs to lifestyle – Returning to physical activities, work schedule, and sexual activities creates fear and apprehension. Open discussion is essential for healthy coping.

vant treatment. Chemotherapy agents typically used in the treatment of CRC are detailed in Table 7-10.

Targeted Therapy

Newer drugs have been developed that specifically target the genetic and protein changes in cells that cause cancer. These targeted drugs work differently than standard chemotherapy drugs. They often have different and, sometimes, less severe side effects. In general, targeted therapies are combined with a chemotherapeutic agent or used as single agents if chemotherapy is no longer effective. Targeted therapies used in the treatment of CRC are shown in Table 7-11.

Radiation Therapy

Radiation therapy in people with colon cancer is mainly used when the cancer has attached to an internal organ or the lining of the abdomen. Radiation therapy may also be used to kill any cancer cells remaining after surgery. Radiation therapy is seldom used to treat metastatic colon cancer because of side effects, which limit the dose that can be used.

For rectal cancer, radiation therapy is usually given to help prevent the cancer from coming back in the pelvis. It may be given either before or after surgery; however, recently, doctors have begun to favor preoperative treatment, along with chemotherapy (Libutti, Tepper et al., 2005). If a rectal cancer's size or position make surgery difficult, radiation may be used before surgery to shrink the tumor. Radiation therapy can also be given to help control rectal cancers in people who are not healthy enough for surgery.

Radiation may also be used to palliate symptoms in people with advanced cancer that is causing intestinal blockage, bleeding, or pain.

Colon and Rectal Cancer Treatment by Stage

Depending on the stage of the colon or rectal cancer, a variety of treatment options may be presented to the patient. Careful staging is important because it helps to ensure that proper treatment is selected.

TABLE 7-10: CHEMOTHERAPY FOR COLORECTAL CANCER

Agent	Administration	Other Considerations/ Indications	Side Effects
Fluorouracil (5-FU)	It may be given as an infusion over 2 hours. It may be given I.V. push followed by continuous infusion over 1 or 2 days. For most chemotherapy regimens, treatment with 5-FU is repeated every 2 weeks, over a period of 6 months to 1 year.	It is often given together with another drug called leucovorin (or folinic acid), which increases its effectiveness.	Nausea, anorexia, mouth sores, diarrhea, myelosuppression, and photosensitivity are possible. A syndrome of hand and foot redness that is sometimes accompanied by blistering or skin peeling may also occur.
Capecitabine (Xeloda)	Capecitabine is an oral chemotherapy agent that is usually taken twice a day for 2 weeks, followed by 1 week off.	Once in the body, it is changed to 5-FU when it gets to the tumor site. This drug seems to be about as effective as giving continuous I.V. 5-FU.	The possible side effects are similar to those listed for 5-FU. Although most of the side effects seem to be less common with this drug than with 5-FU, problems with the hands and feet are more common and severe.
Irinotecan (Camptosar)	It is given as an I.V. infusion over 30 minutes to 2 hours.	Some people are unable to break down the drug, so it stays in the body and causes severe side effects. This is due to an inherited genetic variation that can be tested for. The simplest test is to measure the blood level of bilirubin. If it is slightly elevated, this can be a sign of the genetic variation that makes people sensitive to irinotecan. Most doctors do not routinely test for the genetic variant. In some cases it may be used as a single agent as a second-line treatment if other chemotherapy drugs are no longer effective. This drug is often combined with 5-FU and leucovorin (known as the FOLFIRI regimen) as a first-line treatment for advanced CRC.	Severe diarrhea, myleosupression, and nausea are possible. A diarrhea prophylaxis regimen is recommended and patients need to report any diarrhea promptly as it is a dose-limiting and potentially fatal side effect in compromised patients.
Oxaliplatin (Eloxatin)	Oxaliplatin is given as an I.V. infusion over 2 hours, usually once every 2 or 3 weeks.	This drug is usually combined with 5-FU and leucovorin (known as the FOLFOX regimen) or with capecitabine (known as the CapeOX regimen) as a first- or second-line treatment for advanced CRC. It may also be used as adjuvant therapy after surgery for earlier stage cancers.	Oxaliplatin can affect peripheral nerves, which can cause numbness, tingling, and intense sensitivity to temperature in the extremities, especially the hands and feet. This goes away after treatment has stopped in most patients, but in some cases it can cause long-lasting nerve damage.

(Balch, De Meo, & Guillem, 2006; Elsevier, 2006; Libutti, Salz, Rustgi, & Tepper, 2005; Libutti, Tepper et al., 2005)

TABLE 7-11: TARGETED THERAPY FOR COLORECTAL CANCER

Agent	Administration	Indications/Other Considerations	Side Effects
Bevacizumab (Avastin)	I.V. infusion, usually once every 2 or 3 weeks	Bevacizumab is a manmade version of an immune system protein called a monoclonal antibody. This is an antibody that targets vascular endothelial growth factor, a protein that helps tumors form new blood vessels to get nutrients (angiogenesis). Bevacizumab is most often used along with chemotherapy as a first- or second-line treatment for metastatic CRC.	Rare but serious side effects include blood clots, colon perforation, and delayed wound healing. More common side effects include hypertension, fatigue, neutropenia, headaches, mouth sores, anorexia, and diarrhea.
Cetuximab (Erbitux)	I.V. infusion, usually once a week	This is an monoclonal antibody that specifically attacks the epidermal growth factor receptor (EGFR), which is a molecule that often appears in high amounts on the surface of cancer cells and helps them grow. Cetuximab is used in metastatic CRC, usually after other treatments have been tried. It can be used with irinotecan or as a single agent for those that cannot tolerate irinotecan or whose cancer is no longer responding to it.	A rare but serious side effect is an allergic reaction during the first infusion, which could cause respiratory distress and hypotension. Premedication may alleviate this side effect. Less serious side effects may include an acne-like rash, headache, fatigue, fever, and diarrhea.
Panitumumab (Vectibix)	I.V. infusion, usually once every 2 weeks	Panitumumab is a monoclonal antibody that attacks CRC cells. It targets the EGFR protein. It is used by itself to treat metastatic CRC after other treatments have been tried	Most people develop skin problems such as a rash during treatment, which in some cases can lead to infections. Other possible side effects are lung scarring and allergic reactions to the drug. Sensitivity to sunlight, fatigue, diarrhea, and changes in fingernails and toenails are also possible.

(Libutti, Salz et al., 2005; Odham & Dillman, 2008; Schmidt & Wood, 2003)

CASE STUDY: CRC

*A*P is a 62-year-old Caucasian woman, who visited her physician, complaining of cramping and bloating for 1 month. She noted that she thought she saw blood in her stool. She also complained of crushing fatigue, which seemed to have started a few months prior.

AP worked as a waitress for many years but retired from her job several years ago. She now provides childcare for her grandchildren, while her daughter works.

AP commented that her aunt had "cancer of the bowel." While waiting for the physician to see her, she revealed that she enjoys eating blue-plate specials with her husband of 40 years. She smoked until she was 50 years of age, but quit with the help of a support group. She also said that she enjoys a mixed cocktail twice a week.

Two years ago, AP's physician removed benign polyps from her colon. However, because of a lapse in her insurance, she had not been to the physician for 2 years.

On digital rectal exam, AP's physician did not note any masses but was concerned about her symptoms because of her past polypectomies. Her physician immediately scheduled her for a colonoscopy. Based on her symptoms and history, the physician also ordered a CBC and CEA.

During AP's colonoscopy, biopsies were taken of three lesions found in her left and sigmoid colon. The biopsy results came back as adenocarcinoma in the sigmoid colon. Her CBC indicated anemia and her CEA was 5.0 mg/nl.

A sigmoid colectomy was scheduled. In preparation for her surgery, her physician ordered a chest X-ray, CT scan of the pelvis, and bone scan. As part of surgery preparation, the procedure was reviewed with AP and preoperative teaching about her colostomy began. She was told that depending on the spread of the cancer to regional lymph nodes, she might need postoperative chemotherapy.

Postoperatively, while she recovered in the hospital, nurses continued to teach AP how to take care of her colostomy. Because her cancer had spread to regional lymph nodes, AP was referred to a medical oncologist for adjuvant chemotherapy.

Three weeks after surgery, AP began a chemotherapy protocol that included 5-FU, leucovorin, and CPT-11 (Days 1, 8, 15, 22) every 6 weeks. Adverse effects from the chemotherapy included diarrhea, stomatitis, and leukopenia, which the nurses managed with antidiarrheals, good hygiene (perineum and mouth care), and monitoring for infection (AP received two courses of antibiotics).

Six months after her surgery, a repeat CT scan, bone scan, and chest X-ray were ordered. All test results were negative. Her CEA level was unchanged.

While in the hospital after her surgery and during her chemotherapy treatments, AP had been made aware that her colon cancer may be associated with a hereditary syndrome. She was encouraged to proceed with genetic counseling and encourage family members to be checked regularly for polyp formation.

Additional Information

AP continues to do well after her colectomy and adjuvant chemotherapy treatments. She returns to her physician for checks every 3 to 6 months. Because of stability during the final years of her husband's job as a police dispatcher, her insurance remains intact.

AP has also worked to accept her colostomy, but grieves that she no longer can wear certain clothes and must schedule her day around her colostomy care. She states that her husband and children have been supportive since she was first diagnosed, but that she senses they distance themselves from her – either because of her appliances or because they fear her colon cancer and the seriousness of her illness.

What late symptoms of CRC does AP display?

Blood in the stool, cramping, bloating, and abdominal pain are all typically late symptoms of CRC.

What risk factors does AP have for CRC?

AP has an aunt with a history of CRC. She consumes a high-fat diet. She consumes some alcohol. She has a history of polyps.

What might have resulted in prevention of her CRC?

Regular colonoscopy is probably the best means to prevent colon cancer. Polyps can be removed before they progress to CRC.

SUMMARY

Progress continues in the detection, screening, and treatment of CRC. Women share a similar incidence and mortality rate as men for CRC. Polyp identification and removal are cornerstones in the successful early treatment of CRC. Hereditary conditions, such as familial polyposis, HNPCC, and ulcerative colitis, have been determined to be risk factors. Screening efforts include attention to signs, symptoms, genetic histories, and follow-up to find pre-cancerous conditions early, when treatment is most effective. Surgery is the main treatment modality, although radiation therapy, targeted therapy, and chemotherapy play an important role in advanced CRCs. When CRC has spread to the liver, treatment to control additional tumor spread focuses on surgery and ablative therapies.

EXAM QUESTIONS

CHAPTER 7
Questions 50-58

Note: Choose the one option that BEST answers each question.

50. Risk factors of colorectal cancer are

    a. being younger than 50 years of age.

    b. eating a low-fat, low-calorie, and low-fiber diet.

    c. polyp formation or history of polyps.

    d. history of thyroid or skin cancer.

51. Genetic predisposition to colorectal cancer is associated with

    a. BRCA1.

    b. BRCA2.

    c. CA-125.

    d. HNPCC and FAP.

52. The main signs and symptoms of colorectal cancer include

    a. a change in bowel habits, diarrhea, constipation, and blood in the stool.

    b. weight gain, constipation, and anxiety.

    c. specific abdominal discomfort.

    d. shortness of breath, fatigue, and loss of appetite.

53. For persons at average risk for developing colorectal cancer, the ACS recommends colonoscopy, beginning at 50 years of age every

    a. 3 years.

    b. 5 years.

    c. 7 years.

    d. 10 years.

54. The most accurate method to screen for colorectal cancer is

    a. colonoscopy.

    b. double contrast barium enema.

    c. fecal occult blood test.

    d. sigmoidoscopy.

55. When colorectal cancer has spread to nearby lymph nodes, the cancer is staged as

    a. Stage I.

    b. Stage II.

    c. Stage III.

    d. Stage IV.

56. The main treatment of choice for early-stage colorectal cancer is

    a. radiation.

    b. surgery.

    c. multimodality therapy.

    d. chemotherapy.

57. Teaching a colorectal patient about her ostomy care should begin

    a. as soon as possible, before surgery.

    b. the day of surgery.

    c. postoperatively on day 2.

    d. 2 weeks after surgery.

continued on next page

159

58. An adjuvant chemotherapy regimen for colorectal cancer is

    a. Rituxan and interferon.

    b. bleomycin and etoposide.

    c. 5-fluorouracil and leucovorin.

    d. tamoxifen and docetaxel.

REFERENCES

Altekruse, S.F., Kosary, C.L., Krapcho, M., Neyman, N., Aminou, R., Waldron, W., Ruhl, J., Howlader, N., Tatalovich, Z., Cho, H., Mariotto, A., Eisner, M.P., Lewis, D.R., Cronin, K., Chen, H.S., Feuer, E.J., Stinchcomb, D.G., & Edwards, B.K. (eds). *SEER Cancer Statistics Review, 1975-2007,* National Cancer Institute. Bethesda, MD, http://seer.cancer.gov/csr/1975_2007, based on November 2009 SEER data submission, posted to the SEER web site, 2010.

American Cancer Society. (2010a). *Cancer facts & figures – 2010.* Atlanta, GA:American Cancer Society.

American Cancer Society (2010b). *Cancer prevention & early detection facts & figures 2010.* Atlanta, GA: American Cancer Society. Retrieved July 19, 2010, from http://www.cancer.org/acs/groups/content/@epidemiologysurveilance/documents/webcontent/acspc-025759.pdf

American Cancer Society. (2010c). *Colorectal cancer: Causes, risk factors, and prevention topics.* Retrieved July 19, 2010, from http://www.cancer.org/Cancer/ColonandRectumCancer/DetailedGuide/colorectal-cancer-risk-factors

American Cancer Society. (2010d). *Colorectal cancer: Early detection, diagnosis, and staging topics.* Retrieved July 19, 2010. from http://www.cancer.org/Cancer/ColonandRectumCancer/DetailedGuide/colorectal-cancer-detection

American Cancer Society. (2010e). *Colorectal cancer: Treating colon/rectum cancer topics.* Retrieved July 19, 2010, from http://www.cancer.org/Cancer/ColonandRectumCancer/DetailedGuide/colorectal-cancer-treating-general-info

American Cancer Society. (2010f). *Colorectal cancer: What is colon/rectum cancer?* Retrieved July 19, 2010, from http://www.cancer.org/Cancer/ColonandRectumCancer/DetailedGuide/colorectal-cancer-what-is-colorectal-cancer

Balch, G.C., De Meo, A., & Guillem, J.G. (2006). Modern management of rectal cancer: A 2006 update. *World Journal of Gastroenterology, 12*(20), 3186-3195.

Burt, R. & Neklason, D.W. (2005). Genetic testing for inherited colon cancer. *Gastroenterology, 128*(6), 1696-1716.

Dadoly, A.M. (2000). Moving into the spotlight. *Harvard Pilgrim Health Care: Your Health.* (Fall), 8-12.

Dubé, C., Rostom, A., Lewin, G., Tsertsvadze, A., Barrowman, N., Code, C., et al. (2007). The use of aspirin for primary prevention of colorectal cancer: A systematic review prepared for the U.S. Preventive Services Task Force. *Annals of Internal Medicine, 146*(5), 365-375.

Edge, S.B., Byrd, D.R., Carducci, M., Compton, C.C., Fritz, A.G,, Greene, F.L. & Trotti, A. (2010). *AJCC Cancer Staging Manual,* 7th Edition, New York : Springer.

Elsevier. (2006). *The Elsevier guide to oncology drugs and regimens.* New York: Elsevier.

Hawk, E.T. & Levin, B. (2005). Colorectal cancer prevention. *Journal of Clinical Oncology, 23*(2), 378-391.

Hendriks, Y.M., de Jong, A.E., Morreau, H., Tops, C.M., Vasen, H.F., Wijnen, J.T., et al. (2006). Diagnostic approach and management of Lynch Syndrome (hereditary nonpolyposis colorectal carcinoma): A guide for clinicians. *CA: A Cancer Journal for Clinicians, 56*(4), 213-225.

Kushi, L.H., Byers, T., Doyle, C., Bandera, E.V., McCullough, M., McTiernan, A., et al. (2006). American Cancer Society guidelines on nutrition and physical activity for cancer prevention: Reducing the risk of cancer with healthy food choices and physical activity. *CA: A Cancer Journal for Clinicians, 56*(5), 254-281.

Leonard, G.D., Brenner, B., & Kemeny, N.E. (2005). Neoadjuvant chemotherapy before liver resection for patients with unresectable liver metastases from colorectal carcinoma. *Journal of Clinical Oncology, 23*(9), 2038-2048.

Levin, B., Barthel, J.S., Burt, R.W., David, D.S., Ford, J.M., Giardiello, F.M., et al. (2006). Colorectal cancer screening clinical practice guidelines. *Journal of the National Comprehensive Cancer Network, 4*(4), 384-420.

Levin, B., Lieberman, D.A., McFarland, B., Smith, R.A., Brooks, D., Andrews, K.S., et al. (2008). Screening and surveillance for the early detection of colorectal cancer and adenomatous polyps, 2008: A joint guideline from the American Cancer Society, the US Multi-Society Task Force on Colorectal Cancer, and the American College of Radiology. *CA: A Cancer Journal for Clinicians, 58*(3), 130-160.

Libutti, S.K., Salz, L.B., Rustgi, A.K., & Tepper, J.E. (2005). Cancer of the colon. In V.T. DeVita, Jr., S. Hellman, & S.A. Rosenberg (Eds.), *Cancer: Principles and practice of oncology* (7th ed., pp. 1061-1109). Philadelphia: Lippincott Williams & Wilkins.

Libutti, S.K., Tepper, J.E., Salz, L.B., & Rustgi, A.K. (2005). Cancer of the rectum. In V.T. DeVita, Jr., S. Hellman, & S.A. Rosenberg (Eds.), *Cancer: Principles and practice of oncology* (7th ed., pp. 1110-1124). Philadelphia: Lippincott Williams & Wilkins.

Lieberman, D. (2005). Race, gender, and colorectal cancer screening. *American Journal of Gastroenterology, 100*(12), 2756–2758.

Lynch, H.T. & de la Chapelle, A. (2003). Genomic medicine: Hereditary colorectal cancer. *New England Journal of Medicine, 348*(10), 919-932.

Lynch, H.T. & Lynch, P.M. (2006) Clinical selection of candidates for mutational testing for cancer susceptibility. *Oncology (Williston Park), 20*(14 Suppl 10), 29-34.

Meyerhardt, J.A., Giovannucci, E.L., Holmes, M.D., Chan, A.T., Chan, J.A., Colditz, G.A., et al. (2006). Physical activity and survival after colorectal cancer diagnosis. *Journal of Clinical Oncology, 24*(22), 3527–3534.

National Cancer Institute (NCI). (2010). *Genetics of Colorectal Cancer (PDQ)*. Retrieved July 19, 2010, from http://www.cancer.gov/cancertopics/pdq/genetics/colorectal/healthprofessional

National Comprehensive Cancer Network (NCCN). (2010). *NCCN Clinical practice guidelines in oncology: Colorectal cancer* (V.2.2010). Retrieved February 25, 2010, from http://www.nccn.org/professionals/physician_gls/PDF/colon.pdf

O'Rourke, J. & Mahon S.M. (2003). A comprehensive look at the early detection of ovarian cancer. *Clinical Journal of Oncology Nursing, 7*(1), 41-47.

Odham, R. & Dillman, R. (2008). Monoclonal antibodies in cancer therapy: 25 years of progress. *Journal of Clinical Oncology, 26*(11), 1774-1777.

Ries, L.A.G., Melbert, D., Krapcho, M., Stinchcomb, D.G., Howlader, N., Horner, M.J., Mariotto, A., Miller, B.A., Feuer, E.J., Altekruse, S.F., Lewis, D.R., Clegg, L., Eisner, M.P., Reichman, M., Edwards, B.K. (eds). *SEER Cancer Statistics Review, 1975-2005,* National Cancer Institute. Bethesda, MD, http://seer.cancer.gov/csr/1975_2005/, based on November 2007 SEER data submission, posted to the SEER web site, 2008.

Rostom, A., Dubé, C., Lewin, G., Tsertsvadze, A., Barrowman, N., Code C., et al. (2007). Nonsteroidal anti-inflammatory drugs and cyclooxygenase-2 inhibitors for primary prevention of colorectal cancer: A systematic review prepared for the U.S. Preventive Services Task Force. *Annals of Internal Medicine, 146*(5), 376-389.

Schmidt, K.V. & Wood, B.A. (2003). Trends in cancer therapy: role of monoclonal antibodies. *Seminars in Oncology Nursing, 19*(7), 169-179.

Umar, A., Boland, C.R., Terdiman, J.P., Syngal, S., de la Chapelle, A., Rüschoff, J., et al. (2004). Revised Bethesda guidelines for hereditary nonpolyposis colorectal cancer (Lynch Syndrome) and microsatellite instability. *Journal of the National Cancer Institute, 96*(4), 261-268.

Vasen, H.F.A., Watson, P., Mecklin, J.P., & Lynch, H.T. (1999). New clinical criteria for hereditary nonpolyposis colorectal cancer (HNPCC, Lynch Syndrome) proposed by the International Collaborative Group on HNPCC. *Gastroenterology, 116*(6), 1453-1456.

Winawer, S.J., Zauber, A.G., Fletcher, R.H., Stillman, J.S., O'Brien, M.J., Levin, B., et al. (2006). Guidelines for colonoscopy surveillance after polypectomy: A consensus update by the US Multi-Society Task Force on Colorectal Cancer and the American Cancer Society. *CA: A Cancer Journal for Clinicians, 56*(3), 143-159.

Zisman, A.L., Nickolov, A., Brand, R.E., Gorchow, A., & Roy, H.K. (2006). Associations between the age at diagnosis and location of colorectal cancer and the use of alcohol and tobacco: Implications for screening. *Archives of Internal Medicine, 166*(6), 629-634.

CHAPTER 8

SKIN CANCER

CHAPTER OBJECTIVE

After completing this chapter, the reader will be able to discuss the epidemiology, risk factors, prevention and detection strategies, and main treatments for skin cancer in women.

LEARNING OBJECTIVES

After studying this chapter, the reader will be able to

1. identify the main risk factors for developing skin cancer.

2. distinguish between nonmelanoma and melanoma skin cancers.

3. describe at least three means to prevent skin cancer.

4. describe prognostic indicators used in the diagnosis of skin cancer.

5. describe the main modalities for the treatment of nonmelanoma skin cancer.

6. describe the main modalities for the treatment of melanoma skin cancer.

INTRODUCTION

Skin cancer is a broad term that describes several types of malignancies that occur in the skin. Basal cell carcinoma and squamous cell carcinoma are often combined into the term nonmelanoma skin cancer. Malignant melanoma is usually addressed separately because of the differences in this malignancy when compared to nonmelanoma skin cancer in terms of treatment and prognosis.

EPIDEMIOLOGY

Skin cancer is a major public health problem in both the United States and the world. Facts about skin cancer and melanoma can be found in Box 8-1. Skin cancers account for approximately one-third of all diagnosed cancers (American Cancer Society [ACS], 2010a). The lifetime risk of a woman developing malignant melanoma is one in 61. The skin is a visible organ; early detection is feasible. More importantly, most if not all of the nonmelanoma skin cancers could be prevented by reducing ultraviolet radiation (UVR) exposure.

Of great concern is the increasing incidence of malignant melanoma (see Figure 8-1). Figure 8-2 demonstrates that although the incidence has increased steadily, the mortality has not increased as quickly. This may be due to improved earlier detection of malignant melanoma. Unfortunately, malignant melanoma is associated with the highest risk of recurrence or metastasis.

ANATOMY

The skin is the largest organ in the body. It does several different things:

BOX 8-1: EPIDEMIOLOGY – SKIN CANCER

- More than 2 million unreported cases of nonmelanoma skin cancer annually.

- 68,130 new cases of malignant melanoma annually.

- During the1970s, the incidence rate of melanoma increased rapidly by about 6% per year. From 1981-2000, the rate of increase slowed to 3% per year and since 2000 malignant melanoma incidence has been stable.

- Malignant melanoma primarily occurs in Caucasians; rates are more than 10 times higher in Caucasians than in African Americans.

- 8700 deaths annually from malignant melanoma.

- 3090 deaths annually from nonmelanoma skin cancer.

- The death rate for malignant melanoma has been decreasing rapidly in Cauasians younger than 50, by 3.0% per year since 1991. In those older than 50, rates have been stable since 1998.

- Most nonmelanoma skin cancers can be cured if the cancer is detected and treated early.

- The overall 5 year relative survival rates for persons with melanoma is 91%.

- For localized melanoma, the 5-year survival rate is 98% (84% of malignant melanomas are detected at this stage).

- For regional stage disease the 5-year relative survival rate is 62%.

- For distant stage diseases the 5-year relative survival rate is 15%.

(ACS, 2010a)

- covers the internal organs and protects them from injury

- serves as a barrier to germs such as bacteria

- prevents the loss of too much water and other fluids

- helps control body temperature.

The skin has 3 layers, including the epidermis, dermis, and subcutis. Figure 8-3 demonstrates the layers of the skin.

Epidermis

The top layer of skin is the epidermis. The two main types of skin cancer, melanomas and non-melanomas, begin in the epidermis (Chu, 2008). The epidermis is very thin, averaging only 0.2 millimeters thick (about 1/100 of an inch). It protects the deeper layers of skin and the organs of the body from the environment.

Keratinocytes are the main cell type of the epidermis. These cells make an important protein called keratin. Keratin contributes to the skin's ability to protect the rest of the body.

The outermost part of the epidermis is called the stratum corneum, or horny layer. It is composed of keratinocytes that are no longer living. The cells in this layer are called squamous cells because of their flat shape. These cells are continually shed as new ones form. Living keratinocytes are found below the stratum corneum. These cells have moved here from the lowest part of the epidermis, the basal layer. The keratinocytes of the basal layer, called basal cells, continually divide to form new keratinocytes. These replace the older keratinocytes that wear off the skin's surface.

Melanocytes, the cells that can become melanoma, are also present in the epidermis. These skin cells make the protective brown pigment called melanin, which makes skin tan or brown. Melanin protects the deeper layers of the skin from the harmful effects of the sun.

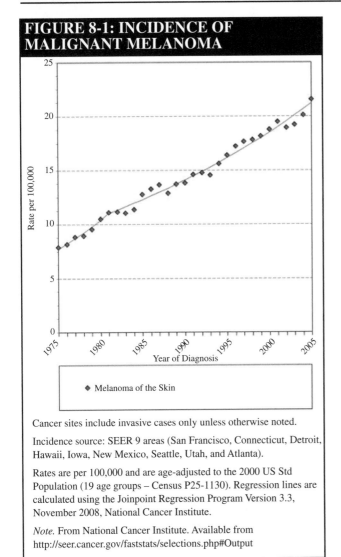

FIGURE 8-1: INCIDENCE OF MALIGNANT MELANOMA

Cancer sites include invasive cases only unless otherwise noted.

Incidence source: SEER 9 areas (San Francisco, Connecticut, Detroit, Hawaii, Iowa, New Mexico, Seattle, Utah, and Atlanta).

Rates are per 100,000 and are age-adjusted to the 2000 US Std Population (19 age groups – Census P25-1130). Regression lines are calculated using the Joinpoint Regression Program Version 3.3, November 2008, National Cancer Institute.

Note. From National Cancer Institute. Available from http://seer.cancer.gov/faststats/selections.php#Output

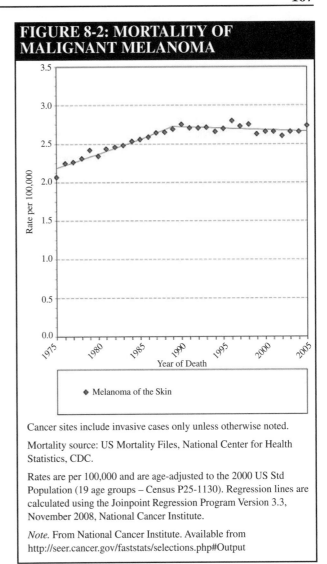

FIGURE 8-2: MORTALITY OF MALIGNANT MELANOMA

Cancer sites include invasive cases only unless otherwise noted.

Mortality source: US Mortality Files, National Center for Health Statistics, CDC.

Rates are per 100,000 and are age-adjusted to the 2000 US Std Population (19 age groups – Census P25-1130). Regression lines are calculated using the Joinpoint Regression Program Version 3.3, November 2008, National Cancer Institute.

Note. From National Cancer Institute. Available from http://seer.cancer.gov/faststats/selections.php#Output

The epidermis is separated from the deeper layers of skin by the basement membrane. The basement membrane is an important structure because, when a cancer becomes more advanced, it generally grows through this barrier.

Dermis

The middle layer of the skin is called the dermis. The dermis is much thicker than the epidermis. It contains hair follicles, sweat glands, blood vessels, and nerves that are held in place by a protein called collagen. Collagen, made by cells called fibroblasts, gives the skin its resilience and strength.

Subcutis

The last and deepest layer of the skin is called the subcutis. The subcutis and the lowest part of the

dermis form a network of collagen and fat cells. The subcutis conserves heat and has a shock-absorbing effect that helps protect the body's organs from injury.

RISK FACTORS

Everyone has some risk for developing skin cancer and melanoma. Clearly the risk is higher in lighter or fair complected individuals. Risk factors for melanoma are shown in Table 8-1. Those with a significant family history of melanoma should be referred to a genetics professional for additional testing and education. Individuals who come from high-risk families often require more extensive and frequent monitoring. Because the prognosis can be favorable when melanoma is detected early, it is

FIGURE 8-3: ANATOMY OF THE SKIN

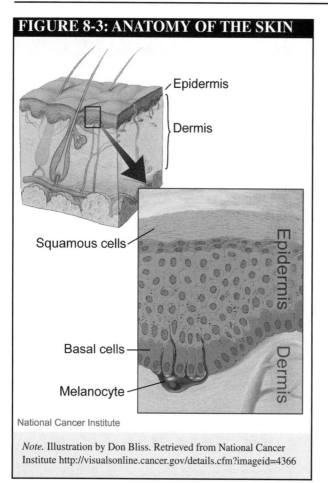

National Cancer Institute

Note. Illustration by Don Bliss. Retrieved from National Cancer Institute http://visualsonline.cancer.gov/details.cfm?imageid=4366

important for individuals and healthcare providers to be aware of the early signs and symptoms of melanoma.

Ultraviolet Light Exposure

Frequent and prolonged exposure to UVR over a period of years will induce cellular changes in human skin. Sun exposure adds up on a daily basis in everyday activities, including walking back and forth from the car. Most individuals underestimate the cumulative effect of this exposure. Episodic high exposure resulting in sunburn, especially when it occurs in childhood, may be critical (ACS, 2010b, 2010c). Skin cancer risk begins at an early age. It is estimated that 80% of total lifetime UVR exposure occurs before 20 years of age (Maselis, Vandaele, & De Boulle, 2005). Risk is also higher in child athletes who repeatedly expose their skin to UVR.

UVR leads to direct skin damage. The effects of UVR are both acute and chronic. Acute changes include sunburn and discomfort (ACS, 2010b,

TABLE 8-1: RISK FACTORS FOR SKIN CANCER

Risk Factor	Etiologic Facts
Past history of malignant melanoma or nonmelanoma skin cancer	A person who has already had a malignant melanoma or non-melanoma skin cancer is at much higher risk of another skin cancer because of lifetime exposure to UVR.
Sunlight (UVR) exposure	Risk comes from both natural and artificial sources such as tanning booths.
Moles	Irregular, dysplastic, or multiple nevi increase risk.
Fair skin	People with fair skin, freckles, or red or blond hair have a higher risk of malignant melanoma or nonmelanoma skin cancer. Persons with red hair have the highest risk.
Family history	Approximately 10% of people with melanoma have a first degree relative with malignant melanoma.
Weakened immune system	Persons who have been treated with medicines that suppress the immune system, such as transplant patients, have an increased risk of developing both nonmelanoma skin cancer and malignant melanoma.
Age	Risk is higher with aging, but malignant melanoma may occur in younger persons.
Gender	Men have a higher rate of malignant melanoma and nonmelanoma skin cancer than women.

(ACS, 2010b)

2010c). Chronic effects include photoaging, premalignant and malignant growths, and immunosuppression.

Data suggest that nonmelanoma skin cancers are associated with cumulative sun exposure, whereas malignant melanoma is associated with short, intense episodes of sun exposure, especially those involving sunburns (Cummins et al., 2006). A history of severe and painful sunburn, especially repeated sunburn, is associated with upper extremity melanoma.

High sun exposure at certain times of life is associated with higher risks of developing different types of skin cancer. Early sun exposure, particularly in childhood and adolescence, is associated with a much higher risk of developing basal cell carcinoma and is estimated to confer a tenfold elevated risk for developing squamous cell carcinoma (Boukamp, 2005). Sun exposure in the 10 years prior to diagnosis may be important in accounting for many cases of squamous cell carcinoma and is associated with a 2.5-fold increased risk when compared to those without this exposure (ACS, 2010b)

Sun exposure during childhood and adolescence also seems to have a substantial influence on the risk of developing malignant melanoma (ACS, 2010b) Approximately 80% of lifetime sun exposure occurs before 20 years of age. During this time, melanocytes may be more sensitive to the sun, resulting in an alteration of their DNA and possibly leading to the formation of unstable moles that have a greater potential to become malignant. Sunlight exposure and blistering sunburns during youth may be more intense than those incurred later in life because of the recreation patterns of children.

The eyes can also be affected by UVR (ACS. 2010b) Repeated and prolonged exposure of the conjunctiva will lead to thickening and hypervascularity. There also appears to be a positive correlation between increased cataract formation, decreased latitude, increased ultraviolet B (UVB), and total sunlight exposure.

Genetic Factors

Skin color is one of the most important genotypic features that places a person at risk for developing skin cancer. Malignant melanoma is very rare in African Americans (ACS, 2010a, 2010b). Persons who are light or fair complected, have a tendency to freckle, or burn easily are at higher risk. The development of melanocytic nevi in childhood is strongly related to characteristics of pigmentation associated with poor sun tolerance (Cummins et al., 2006)

The epidermis of African Americans has been shown to have a natural sun protection factor (SPF) of 13.4, with the melanin in the epidermis filtering twice as much UVB as the epidermis of a white person (Cummins et al., 2006). This protection, however, is not complete and both nonmelanoma skin cancer and malignant melanoma can develop in African Americans. As many as 67% of malignant melanomas in the African American population arise in non-sun-exposed skin such as on the palmer and plantar surfaces and even the mucous membranes.

Large congenital melanocytic nevi (moles) are also considered a significant risk factor associated with the development of malignant melanoma and are estimated to occur in 1% of newborns (Naeyaert & Brochez, 2003). This increase in risk has been reported to range from 0% to 42%. The larger the nevus, the higher the lifetime risk. Surgical removal of these large nevi is thought to decrease the risk of developing malignant melanoma.

The number of moles is correlated with risk. The total number of moles is an indicator or risk; persons with over 100 nevi have a relative risk of 7.6 compared to persons with 10 or fewer moles (Cummins et al., 2006).

Dysplastic nevi may develop throughout life and show clinical features similar to normal moles and malignant melanomas. These features include a size greater than 6 to 8 mm, irregular borders, variable pigmentation, and irregular surface characteristics. The identification of truly dysplastic nevi is difficult to perform clinically.

Approximately 10% of patients with malignant melanoma describe a history of an affected family member (Cummins et al., 2006). People who have a family history of malignant melanoma or dysplastic nevi, or who have a large number of nevi themselves, are at a very high risk (100+ fold increase) for developing malignant melanoma over their lifetime. Persons with a history of melanoma in a first-degree relative have twice the risk of developing malignant melanoma than those without a family history (Markovic et al., 2007).

A hereditary predisposition to malignant melanoma is sometimes associated with an earlier age of onset (Markovic et al., 2007). Sex distribution between males and females is usually about equal to those without a hereditary predisposition to malignant melanoma. Hereditary melanoma should be suspected in patients with a family history of pancreatic cancer or astrocytoma. Patients from these families are, however, often diagnosed with thinner lesions and generally have a better prognosis. This better outcome may be related to heightened awareness and increased surveillance. A second primary malignant melanoma does develop in 17% to 20% of patients from these families who survive their first malignant melanoma (Cummins et al., 2006).

These families often have mutations in the CDKN2A gene and less commonly in the CDK4 gene. Genetic testing is commercially available for some CDKN2A mutations commercially, although the clinical usefulness is not completely clear (Cummins et al., 2006). As genetic testing becomes available and the ramifications of testing are better understood, a number of education and counseling issues will emerge.

Several inherited syndromes are associated with basal cell carcinoma and squamous cell carcinoma, including zeroderma pigmentosum, nevoid

BCC syndrome, epidermodysplasia verruciformis, and albinism. Persons with xeroderma pigmentosum have over a 90% risk of developing multiple nonmelanoma skin cancers (Boukamp, 2005). Most of these syndromes are associated with other physical abnormalities and these individuals should be referred to genetics and specialty clinics because of their high risk of developing malignancy and other complications.

Personal History of Skin Cancer

A personal history of basal cell carinoma or squamous cell carcinoma is associated with a much higher risk of malignant melanoma (ACS, 2010b, 2010c). A personal history of a nonmelanoma skin cancer is associated with a much higher risk of developing a second nonmelanoma skin cancer, especially in persons with a history of significant sun exposure.

Persons with chronic immunosuppression are at higher risk for developing malignant melanoma (Markovic et al., 2007). This includes renal transplant patients and persons with HPV and HIV infections. Age, itself, is a risk factor for both nonmelanoma skin cancers and malignant melanomas. It is difficult to separate the interaction of age and other genetic factors from cumulative exposure to sunlight.

SIGNS AND SYMPTOMS

Basal cell carcinomas often appear as flat, firm, pale areas or small, raised, pink or red, translucent, shiny, waxy areas that may bleed after a minor injury (see Figure 8-4). They may have one or more visible abnormal blood vessels, a depressed area in their center, and/or blue, brown, or black areas. A wide range of colors may be present, from pearly white to pink to red. Telangiectasias may or may not be present on the surface. Some lesions will have scaling plaques. As lesions progress, the center usually ulcerates and the borders develop a raised or

FIGURE 8-4: BASAL CELL CARCINOMA

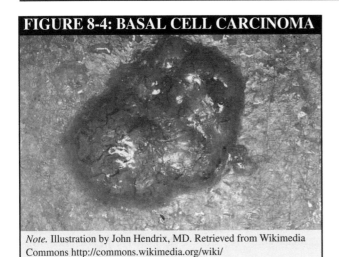

Note. Illustration by John Hendrix, MD. Retrieved from Wikimedia Commons http://commons.wikimedia.org/wiki/ File:Basal_cell_carcinoma.jpg

rolled appearance. Large basal cell carcinomas may have oozing or crusted areas.

Squamous cell carcinomas may appear as growing lumps, often with a rough surface, or as flat reddish patches in the skin that grow slowly (see Figure 8-5). They often begin as a red, raised, firm papule. Crusting and ulceration is often seen. It is not uncommon for the patient to report that the lesion is tender or painful.

A wide range of clinical characteristics may be noted in malignant melanoma (see Figure 8-6). It is often difficult to distinguish a dysplastic nevus from an malignant melanoma. A good way to remember the physical characteristics of melanoma is the ABCDE rule (see Table 8-2).

FIGURE 8-5: SQUAMOUS CELL SKIN CANCER

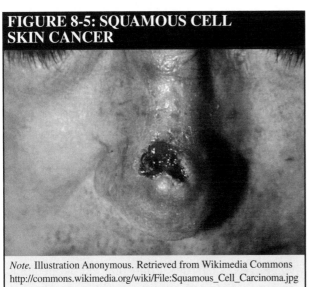

Note. Illustration Anonymous. Retrieved from Wikimedia Commons http://commons.wikimedia.org/wiki/File:Squamous_Cell_Carcinoma.jpg

FIGURE 8-6: ABNORMAL MOLE

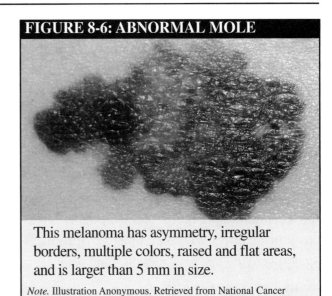

This melanoma has asymmetry, irregular borders, multiple colors, raised and flat areas, and is larger than 5 mm in size.

Note. Illustration Anonymous. Retrieved from National Cancer Institute http://visualsonline.cancer.gov/details.cfm?imageid=2184

TABLE 8-2: ABCDE FOR MALIGNANT MELANOMA

- **A**symmetrical
- **B**orders that are jagged or faded
- **C**olor characteristics of the lesion, such as two or more colors or a lesion that is a different color than the rest of the pigmented lesions on a patient
- **D**iameter greater than 5 mm
- **E**levation: nodular surface characteristics, bleeding or ulceration

PREVENTION

Clearly preventing skin cancer is best. The effectiveness of the regular use of a broad spectrum sunscreen with an SPF of 15, reduction of UVR exposure, and protective clothing should not be underestimated. Regular sunscreen use can reduce the incidence of solar or actinic keratoses (precursors of squamous cell carcinoma). The relationship between UVR exposure and cutaneous melanoma is less clear (ACS, 2010b, 2010c). In melanoma, it seems that intermittent acute sun exposure leading to sunburn in childhood or adolescence may be particularly important (Cummins et al., 2006).

One way to gauge the intensity of and risk for UV exposure is to know the UV index for the geographic locale. The UV Index is a number from 0 to 10+ that indicates the amount of UV radiation reaching the Earth's surface during the hour around noon. The higher the number, the greater the exposure to UV radiation outdoors. The National Weather Service forecasts the UV Index daily in 58 U.S. cities, based on local predicted conditions. The index covers about a 30-mile radius from each city. The information can also be accessed through the local newspaper or TV and radio news broadcasts or at http://www.cpc.noaa.gov/products/stratosphere/uv_index/uv_current.shtml

Public Health Initiatives

The Healthy People 2010 Guidelines are a government initiative that aims to decrease the U.S. mortality rate from malignant melanoma from 2.8 deaths per 100,000 persons to 2.5 deaths per 100,000 persons during the next 10 years (U.S. Department of Health and Human Services, 2000). This objective was proposed for retenetion in the Healthy People 2020 Guidelines, which, at the time this publication went to press, had not been finalized. The Guidelines also seek to increase the proportion of people using skin cancer primary prevention strategies, which include at least one of the following protective measures:

- avoiding the sun between 10 a.m. and 4 p.m when the UVR is most intense

- wearing sun-protective clothing

- using sunscreen with an SPF of 15 or higher

- decreasing or avoiding UVR exposure.

Approximately 47% of the U.S. population 18 years of age and older currently use at least one of these protective measures. The goal is to increase this proportion to 75%. An interim analysis suggests that significant progress has been made in some areas as the age-adjusted proportion of adults 18 years of age and older who took protective measures (e.g., use of sunscreens) against sun exposure to reduce the risk of skin cancer increased from 59% in 2000 to 71% in 2005. The target is

85% (http://www.healthypeople.gov/Data/2010 prog/focus03). For updates on the Healthy People 2020 Guidelines, go to http://www.healthypeople.gov/hp2020.

To reap the most benefits, public education programs need to be started early in a child's life, with the goal of having the individual adopt attitudes and practices that minimize UVR exposure. A number of such programs have demonstrated that even preschoolers can learn and practice behaviors that reduce UVR exposure (ACS, 2010b) Evidence suggests that to get children to change their practices and attitudes, their parents must first adopt more healthy behaviors. (Olson et al. 2007). Despite educational programs and knowledge about the dangers of exposure to UVR, many individuals fail to practice primary prevention strategies. Some believe that fear of skin cancer is not a deterrent to sun-seeking behaviors and that, until it becomes culturally acceptable to have untanned skin in the U.S., there will not be a major decrease in malignant melanoma and nonmelanoma skin cancer incidence and mortality rates. Some groups advocate that public messages should try to change this social norm and emphasize the photoaging effects of excessive UVR exposure. Recently at least 25 states have imposed laws that limit and restrict teen access to indoor tanning (Whitworth, 2006).

Sunscreen

There are two types of sunscreens: chemical and physical. Chemical sunscreens provide protection by absorbing UVR and physical sunscreens block UVR from reaching the skin. Chemical sunscreens have been available since the 1920's with the introduction of para-aminobenzoic acid (PABA) based sunscreens. The importance of sunscreen should not be underestimated as it has clearly been shown to prevent sunburn, and regular use can retard or prevent the development of skin changes (ACS, 2010b). Educating the public about sunscreen is more complicated than it appears. Controversies continue regarding the labeling,

TABLE 8-3: PATIENT EDUCATION ABOUT SUNSCREEN

What is Sunscreen?
- Sunscreen absorbs, reflects, or scatters UVR – invisible rays from the sun that can cause sunburn and other skin damage. UVR is divided into three wavelength bands – ultraviolet A (UVA), ultraviolet B (UVB) and ultraviolet C (UVC). Only UVA and UVB rays reach the earth.
- Physical sunscreens form an opaque film that reflects or scatters UV light before it can penetrate the skin. These sunscreens contain ingredients, such as zinc oxide and titanium dioxide, which protect against both UVA and UVB rays. Original formulations of physical sunscreens remained white when applied to the skin. Newer formulations blend more with skin tone and are less noticeable.
- Chemical sunscreens absorb UV rays before they can cause any damage. They contain one or more ingredients, such as avobenzone or oxybenzone, which absorb UVA or UVB rays. For broad protection, chemical sunscreens often contain more than one ingredient to protect against both UVA and UVB rays.
- It is recommended that any time an individual is outdoors during daylight hours that sunscreen be used.
- Children are especially susceptible to the harmful effects of the sun, so take extra steps to protect their skin and to prevent sunburns. Children or teenagers who experience at least two blistering sunburns are at increased risk of developing skin cancer later in life. Regular sunscreen use is important in this population.
- Babies younger than 6 months should be kept out of direct sunlight because their skin is even more fragile. Use sunscreen on an infant only if one is unable to keep him or her out of the sun and are unable to cover exposed skin. Use a small amount on uncovered areas, such as on the hands or ears, and check for any skin reactions.

What is an SPF?
- All sunscreens products include an SPF, which stands for sun protection factor. The SPF number is a measurement of the amount of UVB protection – the higher the number, the greater the protection. Currently, there's no standard rating system that measures UVA protection.
- SPF is not an indication of how much time one can spend in the sun.

When To Apply Sunscreen
- Apply sunscreen approximately 30 minutes before being in the sun (for best results) so that it can be absorbed by the skin and will be less likely to wash off with perspiration.
- Reapply sunscreen after swimming or strenuous exercise at least every 90 minutes.

How To Apply Sunscreen
- Shake well before use to mix particles that might be clumped up in the container. Consider using the new spray-on or stick types of sunscreen.
- Be sure to apply enough sunscreen. As a rule of thumb, use an ounce (a handful) to cover the entire body.
- Use on all parts of skin exposed to the sun, including the ears, back, shoulders, and the back of the knees and legs.
- Don't forget the back of the neck which is commonly missed and exposed to UVR.
- Apply thickly and thoroughly.
- Be careful when applying sunscreen around the eyes.

What To Look for When Buying Sunscreen
- Pick a broad-spectrum sunscreen that protects against UVA and UVB rays and has a SPF of at least 15.
- Read product labels. Look for a waterproof brand if one will be sweating or swimming.
- Buy a nonstinging product or one specifically formulated for the face.
- Buy a brand that does not contain PABA if one is sensitive to that ingredient.
- Use a water-based sunscreen if one has oily skin or is prone to acne.
- Be aware that more expensive does not mean better. Although a costly brand might feel or smell better, it is not necessarily more effective than a cheaper product.
- Be aware of the expiration date because some sunscreen ingredients might degrade over time.
- Sunscreens are designed to remain stable and at original strength for up to three years. This means that one can use leftover sunscreen from one summer to the next. Keep in mind, however, that if one uses sunscreen frequently and liberally, a bottle of sunscreen shouldn't last that long.

(ACS, 2010b; Bauer, Buttner, Wiecker, Luther, & Garbe, 2005; Wiggs, 2007) application, and effectiveness of these agents. Patient education regarding sunscreen is shown in Table 8-3.

The primary goal of protecting the skin from UVR is not just to avoid sunburn. Studies demonstrate that incremental damage occurs with each exposure to UVR, regardless of whether there is clinical evidence of redness or burn (Cummins et al., 2006) It is impractical and impossible to think that humans can avoid sun exposure completely; therefore, prevention with sunscreens and other protective clothing is necessary.

Epidemiologic studies suggest that recent UVR exposure may be more important than cumulative UVR exposure. Thus, even older individuals and those with high cumulative sun-exposure histories can benefit from sunscreen use by preventing the promoting influence of recent sun exposure and by avoiding new initiating mutations. Sunscreen clearly reduces further actinic damage in patients with such damage when used consistently and adequately. These results can be evident in as few as 2 years (ACS, 2010b).

Currently, sunscreens are rated or classified by their sun protection factor (SPF). The SPF numbers that appear on a sunscreen's label refer to the product's ability to absorb, reflect, or scatter UVB. No uniformly acceptable standardized method currently exists to measure a sunscreen's ability to provide protection from UVA. UVA has a longer wavelength than UVB, which allows it to penetrate deeper into the skin.

Chemical sunscreens are designed to be applied generously to all exposed skin. Depending on the chemicals used, a laboratory SPF can range from 2 to 60. Sunscreens are rated for their UVR absorption under strict and ideal laboratory conditions. In a laboratory, a sunscreen with an SPF of 15 will absorb 92% of UVB, an SPF of 30 will absorb 96.7% of UVB, and an SPF of 40 will absorb 97.5% of UVB (Wiggs, 2007). The effectiveness of a particular sunscreen agent is affected

by an individual's body site of application, degree of normal skin color, thickness of the epidermis, time of day, time of year, cloud cover, ozone levels, reflection, and UVR scatter. A sunscreen of SPF-15 is adequate if it is applied in the amount of $2mg/cm^2$ (Wiggs et al., 2007). Because most individuals typically apply less sunscreen than is used in laboratories to establish the SPF number, the actual SPF protection is often 20% to 50% of the number on the label.

Protective Clothing and Hats

The effectiveness of hats and shirts as a primary prevention measure should not be underestimated. A brim size of 10 cm can lead to a reduction of 73% of UVR exposure to the head and neck (ACS, 2010b, 2010c).

The weave of the material used in hats and clothing is very important. In general, synthetic materials provide better protection against UVA than cotton materials. Densely woven material provides a reflective barrier to UVR. Clothes designed to cover the most skin provide the most protection. Long-sleeved shirts with collars, long pants, and shoes and socks provide more coverage than tank tops, shorts, and sandals. In general, synthetic materials provide better protection against UVA than cotton materials (Cummins et al., 2006) Darker materials provide more protection. Most clothes, such as hats and summer wear, offer an SPF of 2 to 6.5, although sun-protective clothing is available that offers an SPF of up to 30 (Cummins et al., 2006).

Nurses can educate patients about ways to assess the effectiveness of fabric as a sun protectant. This is a very important means to reduce UVR exposure that is consistently underestimated. A simple test of efficacy is to hold the material up to strong light and see whether it casts a dense shadow or whether it is easy to distinguish objects through the shadow (Yoder, 2005). Nurses should also educate patients that virtually all garments lose about one-third of their sun-protective ability when wet (Cummins et al., 2006).

Eye Protection

Protection of the ocular structures is also important. Some sunglasses can offer protection against both UVA and UVB (Kullavanijaya & Lim, 2005). Consumers need to be instructed to read labels correctly and carefully before purchasing sunglasses to assure that they actually offer UVR protection. The label should state "blocks 99% of UVR." Some manufacturers state "UVR up to 400 nm," which is equivalent to 100% UVR absorption. The color and degree of darkness do not provide any information about the ability of the lenses to block UVR. Detailed patient handouts from the American Optometric Association are available at http://www.aoa.org/documents/SunglassShoppingGuide0805.pdf.

Strategies to Reduce Ultraviolet Exposure

Approximately 60% of the total UVB exposure is received from 10 a.m. to 2 p.m. When possible, avoiding prolonged exposure during this time is recommended. Shade from trees and canopies can further reduce this exposure (ACS, 2010b).

Indoor tanning represents a relatively new area that public education programs need to target. Preliminary evidence suggests that there is an increase in malignant melanoma risk for persons who regularly use artificial sources of UVA (Cummins et al., 2006). People who use artificial tanning expose their skin to 2.5-fold and 1.5-fold greater chances of developing squamous cell carcinoma and basal cell carcinoma, respectively (Markovic et al., 2007). Patient education points regarding indoor tanning are shown in Table 8-4.

EARLY DETECTION

Early detection of basal cell carcinoma and squamous cell carcinoma is important to prevent the disfiguring effects of these tumors and their treatment. Early detection of malignant melanoma is an approach to control that, if used effectively and consistently, can have a relatively rapid impact on decreasing the mortality rate from this disease (ACS, 2010a, 2010b).

The United States Preventive Services Task Force (USPSTF, 2003) recommends that clincians

---

TABLE 8-4: PATIENT EDUCATION REGARDING INDOOR TANNING

- Nearly 30 million Americans, including a growing number of teenage girls, visit tanning parlors annually.
- Indoor tanning is a profitable industry grossing more than 5 million dollars annually.
- About half of the states in the U.S. have no tanning-parlor regulations.
- Many facilities offer tanning packages, which encourage frequent tanning.
- Tanning might stimulate secretion of mood-boosting endorphins, which might have an addicting reinforcing effect.
- Any tan indicates that skin has undergone some cellular damage, which is what triggers the melanin production. No one knows how many times one can tan before the damage becomes visible, but it's cumulative and largely irreversible.
- Long-term exposure to artificial sources of ultraviolet rays like tanning beds (or to the sun's natural rays) increases the risk of developing skin cancer.
- Exposure to tanning salon rays increases damage caused by sunlight because ultraviolet light actually thins the skin, making it less able to heal.
- Women who use tanning beds more than once a month are 55% more likely to develop malignant melanoma, the most deadly form of skin cancer.

(ACS, 2010b; Kullavanijaya & Lim, 2005; Wiggs, 2007)

1. be aware that fair-skinned men and women 65 years of age and older and people with atypical moles or more than 50 moles, are at greater risk for developing melanoma

2. remain alert for skin abnormalities when conducting physical examinations for other purposes.

The ACS (2010a, 2010b) also recommends routine inspection of the skin as part of an annual cancer-related check-up. High-risk individuals may

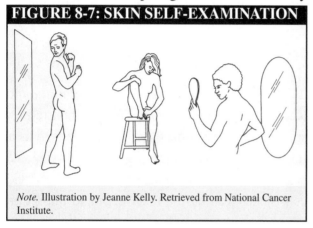

FIGURE 8-7: SKIN SELF-EXAMINATION

Note. Illustration by Jeanne Kelly. Retrieved from National Cancer Institute.

be encouraged to do skin self-examination to monitor for early changes (see Figure 8-7).

Basal cell and squamous cell cancers are most often found in areas that get exposed to a lot of sun, such as the head, neck, and arms, but they can also occur elsewhere. Melanomas can occur anywhere on the skin, but are more likely to start in certain locations. The trunk is the most common site in men. The legs are the most commonly affected site in women. The neck and face are other common sites.

Once diagnosed with skin cancer, the risk of a subsequent nonmelanoma skin cancer or malignant melanoma is considerably higher. These individuals need evaluation and screening on a regular basis to monitor for new lesions.

DIAGNOSTIC EVALUATION

There are many benign and malignant tumors of the skin. There are many types of benign tumors that can develop from different types of skin cells. The diagnostic evaluation determines if the suspicious lesion is benign or malignant.

Examples of benign lesions:

- *Moles (nevi)* are benign skin tumors that develop from melanocytes. Nearly all moles are harmless but having some types may increase the risk of melanoma.

- *seborrheic keratoses:* tan, brown, or black raised spots with a "waxy" texture or rough surface

- *hemangiomas:* benign blood vessel growths often called cherry or strawberry spots, or port wine stains

- *lipomas:* soft growths of benign fat cells

- *warts:* rough-surfaced growths caused by a virus

Examples of malignant lesions

- *Basal cell skin cancer:* malignant tumors that often appear as flat, firm, pale areas or small, raised, pink or red, translucent, shiny, waxy areas that may bleed after a minor injury. They may have one or more visible abnormal blood vessels, a depressed area in their center, as well as blue, brown, or black areas. Large basal cell carcinomas may have oozing or crusted areas.

- *Squamous cell carcinomas:* malignant tumors that may appear as growing lump or bump. They often have a rough surface, or appear as flat reddish patches in the skin that grow slowly.

- *Melanoma:* malignant tumor arising from a mole that changes in size, shape color, or is larger than 5 mm.

History and Physical Exam

The first step in a diagnostic evaluation for skin cancer is a medical history and information about changes in any skin lesions. This is followed by a physical examination. During the physical exam, the doctor will note the size, shape, color, and texture of the areas in question and whether there is bleeding or scaling. The rest of the body should be systematically checked for spots and moles that may be related to skin cancer. Nearby lymph nodes are also assessed.

Along with a standard physical exam, some dermatologists use a technique called dermatoscopy (also called epiluminescence microscopy) to see spots on the skin more clearly (Johr, Argenziano, & Zalaudek, 2005). This involves the use of a dermatoscope, which is a special magnifying lens and light source held near the skin. Sometimes a thin layer of oil is used with this instrument. A photographic image of the spot may be taken.

Skin Biopsy

If the doctor thinks that an area might be skin cancer, he or she will take a sample of skin from the suspicious area to look at under a microscope. This is called a skin biopsy. Different methods can be used for a skin biopsy. The choice depends on the suspected type of skin cancer, where it is on the body, and the size of the affected area. Any biopsy is likely to leave a scar. Potential complications from biopsies include infection, bleeding, hyperpigmentation, hypopigmentation, adhesions, scarring, and problems with wound closure.

For nonmelanoma skin cancer and squamous cell carcinoma, a shave, punch, or incisional or excisional biopsy might be appropriate. For melanoma, an excisional biopsy is preferred because it makes staging the depth of tumor invasion much more accurate (Edge et al., 2010).

- A shave biopsy is one of the simplest ways to take a skin biopsy. After numbing the area with a local anesthetic, the doctor "shaves" off the top layers of the skin (the epidermis and the most superficial part of the dermis) with a surgical blade.

- A punch biopsy removes a deeper sample of skin. The doctor uses a punch biopsy tool that looks like a tiny round cookie cutter. Once the skin is numbed with a local anesthetic, the doc-

tor rotates the punch biopsy tool on the surface of the skin until it cuts through all the layers of the skin, including the dermis, epidermis, and the upper parts of the subcutis.

- If the doctor has to examine a tumor that may have grown into deeper layers of the skin, he or she will use an incisional or excisional biopsy technique. Incisional biopsy involves removing only a portion of the tumor. Removal of the entire tumor is called an excisional biopsy. A surgical knife is used to cut through the full thickness of skin. A wedge or ellipse of skin is removed for further examination, and the edges of the wound are sewn together. Both of these types of biopsies can be done using local anesthesia.

Pathology

The skin sample is sent to a pathologist. In many large academic centers there are dermatopathologists who exclusively examine skin specimens. Often, this is done at the time of resection to determine if free margins have been obtained, decreasing the need for subsequent resections. (ACS, 2010d).

Lymph Node Biopsy

If the doctor feels lymph nodes that are too large or too firm, a lymph node biopsy may be done to determine whether cancer has spread from the skin to the lymph nodes. There are several types of biopsies used with squamous cell carcinoma and basal cell carcinoma (National Comprehensive Cancer Network [NCCN], 2010a).

- A fine needle aspiration biopsy uses a syringe with a thin needle to remove very small tissue fragments from a tumor. A local anesthetic is sometimes used to numb the area. This test rarely causes much discomfort and does not leave a scar. A fine needle aspiration biopsy is not used to diagnose a suspicious skin tumor; however, it may be used to biopsy large lymph nodes near a skin cancer to find out if the cancer has spread to them.

- If the doctor suspects spread of cancer to a lymph node but the needle biopsy result is negative or is not clear, the lymph node should be removed by surgery and examined. This can often be done using local anesthesia in a doctor's office or outpatient surgical center and will leave a small scar.

In melanoma, additional staging tests are needed. These include lymph node evaluation and additional imaging tests

Sentinel Lymph Node Mapping and Biopsy

Sentinel lymph node biopsy has become a common procedure to determine if melanoma has spread to the lymph nodes (Aasi & Leffell, 2005). This procedure can find the lymph nodes that drain lymph fluid from the area of the skin where the melanoma started. If the melanoma has spread, these lymph nodes are usually the first place it will go.

To map the sentinel lymph node (or nodes), some time before surgery, the doctor injects a small amount of radioactive material and usually a blue dye into the area of the melanoma. By checking various lymph node areas with a radioactivity detector, the doctor can see what group of lymph nodes the melanoma is most likely to travel to. The surgeon makes a small incision in the identified lymph node area, and the lymph nodes are then checked to find which one(s) turned blue or became radioactive. When the sentinel node has been found, it is removed and looked at under a microscope. If the sentinel node does not contain melanoma cells, no more lymph node surgery is needed because it is very unlikely the melanoma would have spread beyond this point. If melanoma cells are found in the sentinel node, the remaining lymph nodes in this area are removed and looked at as well. This is known as a lymph node dissection.

Imaging Tests

Imaging tests may be ordered if metastasis is suspected and to better stage the tumor. A chest X-ray may be done to help determine whether melanoma has spread to the lungs. CT scan can help tell if any lymph nodes or organs such as the liver are enlarged, which might be due to the spread of melanoma.

STAGING

Nonmelanoma skin cancer and malignant melanoma are staged using the Tumor Node Metastasis (TNM) staging system from the American Joint Committee on Cancer (Edge et al., 2010). The staging schemas and stage groupings are shown in Table 8-5 and Table 8-6.

Prognostic Indicators for Nonmelanoma Skin Cancer

Basal cell carcinoma is usually slow growing. Complete excision of a primary basal cell carcinoma suggests a 95% cure rate (ACS, 2010a). Primary lesions that are large and involve underlying structures, although rare, are more likely to have metastasized, in which case the prognosis is poorer. Extensive local invasion from basal cell carcinoma may cause significant cosmetic defects depending on the anatomical location of the lesion. For metastatic lesions, the one-year survival rate is less than 20%; the five-year survival rate is 10% (ACS, 2010a)

The course of squamous cell carcinoma is variable and ranges along a continuum from slow-growing, locally invasive tumors, to rapidly growing, widely invasive ones. Overall, the five-year survival rate for squamous cell carcinoma is 90% and its metastatic rate is 3%-6%. Dermal invasion and vertical tumor thickness are important prognostic indicators.

Prognostic Indicators for Malignant Melanoma

There are some special staging considerations with malignant melanoma. The pathologist looking at the skin biopsy measures the thickness of the

TABLE 8-5: AJCC STAGING FOR NONMELANOMA SKIN CANCER

The possible values for T are:

- **TX:** Primary tumor cannot be assessed.

- **T0:** No evidence of primary tumor.

- **Tis:** Carcinoma in situ (tumor is still confined to the epidermis).

- **T1:** The tumor is 2 centimeters (cm) across (about 4/5 inch) or smaller and has less than two high risk features.

- **T2:** Tumor is larger than 2 cm across but smaller than 5 cm (about 2 inches) or a tumor of any size with two more high risk features.

- **T3:** Tumor with invasion into the maxilla, mandible orbit or temporal bone.

- **T4:** Tumor of any size that invades the skeleton or perineural invasion of skull base.

The possible values for N are:

- **NX:** Nearby lymph nodes cannot be assessed.

- **N0:** No spread to nearby lymph nodes.

- **N1:** Spread to a single lymph node 3 cm or less in greatest dimension.

- **N2a:** Spread to a single ipsilateral lymph node more than 3 cm but less than 6 cm in greatest dimension.

- **N2b:** Spread to multiple ipsilateral lymph nodes none more than 6 cm in greatest dimension.

- **N2c:** Spread to bilateral or contralateral lymph nodes none more than 6 cm in greatest dimension.

- **N3:** Spread to a lymph node more than 6 cm in greatest dimension.

The M values are:

- **MX:** Presence of distant metastasis cannot be assessed.

- **M0:** No distant metastasis.

- **M1:** Distant metastasis is present.

The stages are described using the number 0 and Roman numerals from I to IV. In general, patients with lower stage cancers tend to have a better prognosis for a cure or long-term survival.

Stage 0
Tis, N0, M0: Squamous cell carcinoma in situ, also called Bowen disease, is the earliest stage of squamous cell skin carcinoma. The cancer involves only the epidermis and has not spread to the dermis. In contrast, higher stage cancers involve both the epidermis and dermis.

Stage I
T1, N0, M0: The cancer is no larger than 2 centimeters across (about 4/5 inch). It does not invade deeply into muscle, cartilage, or bone and has not spread to nearby lymph nodes or other organs.

Stage II
T2, N0, M0: The cancer is larger than 2 cm across. It does not invade deeply into muscle, cartilage, or bone and has not spread to nearby lymph nodes or other organs.

Stage III
T3, N0, M0 or Any T, N1, M0: The cancer has grown into tissues beneath the skin (such as muscle, bone, or cartilage) and/or it has spread to nearby lymph nodes. The cancer has not spread to other organs such as the lungs or brain.

Stage IV
Any T, Any N, M1: The cancer can be any size and may or may not have spread to local lymph nodes. It has spread to other organs such as the lungs or brain.

High risk features include a depth of more than 2mm or Clark level greater than 4, perinueral invasion, a primary site of the ear or non-hair-bearing lip or a poorly or undifferentiated tumor.

TABLE 8-6: AJCC STAGING FOR MELANOMA (1 OF 2)

The possible values for T are:

- **TX:** Primary tumor cannot be assessed.

- **T0:** No evidence of primary tumor.

- **Tis:** Melanoma in situ (Clark level I - it remains in the epidermis).

- **T1a:** The melanoma is less than or equal to 1.0 mm thick (1.0 mm = 1/25 of an inch), without ulceration and Clark level II or III.

- **T1b:** The melanoma is less than or equal to 1.0 mm thick, Clark level IV or V, or with ulceration.

- **T2a:** The melanoma is between 1.01 and 2.0 mm thick without ulceration.

- **T2b:** The melanoma is between 1.01 and 2.0 mm thick with ulceration.

- **T3a:** The melanoma is between 2.01 and 4.0 mm thick without ulceration.

- **T3b:** The melanoma is between 2.01 and 4.0 mm thick with ulceration.

- **T4a:** The melanoma is thicker than 4.0 mm without ulceration.

- **T4b:** The melanoma is thicker than 4.0 mm with ulceration.

The possible values for N

- **Any Na** (N1a, N2a, etc.) means that the melanoma in the lymph node is only seen under the microscope.

- **Any Nb** (N1b, N2b, etc.) means that the melanoma in the lymph node is visible to the naked eye.

- **N2c** means the melanoma has spread to very small areas of nearby skin (satellite tumors) or has spread to skin lymphatic channels around the tumor (without reaching the lymph nodes).

- **N3** means 4 or more metastatic nodes or matted nodes or satellite tumors with metastic node(s).

The M values are:

- **MX:** Presence of distant metastasis cannot be assessed.

- **M0:** No distant metastasis.

- **M1a:** Distant metastases to skin or subcutaneous (below the skin) tissue or distant lymph nodes.

- **M1b:** Metastases to lung.

- **M1c:** Metastases to other organs, OR distant spread to any site along with an elevated blood LDH level.

continued on next page

melanoma under the microscope with a device called a micrometer. This technique is called the Breslow measurement (Aasi & Leffell, 2005). The thinner the melanoma, the better the prognosis. In general, melanomas less than 1 millimeter (mm) in depth (about ⅒₅ of an inch or the diameter of a period or a comma) have a very small chance of spreading. As the melanoma becomes thicker, it has a greater chance of spreading.

Another technique, called the Clark level, describes how far a melanoma has penetrated into the skin instead of actually measuring it (Aasi & Leffell, 2005). The Clark level of a melanoma uses a scale of I to V (with higher numbers indicating a deeper melanoma) to describe whether:

- the cancer stays in the epidermis (Clark level I)

- the cancer has begun to invade the upper dermis (Clark level II)

- the cancer involves most of the upper dermis (Clark level III)

- the cancer has reached the lower dermis (Clark level IV)

- the cancer has invaded to the subcutis (Clark level V).

The Breslow measurement of thickness is generally thought to be more useful than the Clark level of penetration in determining a patient's prognosis. The thickness is easier to measure and depends less on the pathologist's judgment, and the Clark level sometimes

TABLE 8-6: AJCC STAGING FOR MELANOMA (2 OF 2)

Stage Grouping

Stage 0

Tis, N0, M0: The melanoma is in situ, meaning that it involves the epidermis but has not spread to the dermis (lower layer). This is also called Clark level I.

Stage IA

T1a, N0, M0: The melanoma is less than 1.0 mm in thickness and Clark level II or III. It is not ulcerated, appears to be localized in the skin, and has not been found in lymph nodes or distant organs.

Stage IB

T1b or T2a, N0, M0: The melanoma is less than 1.0 mm in thickness and is ulcerated or Clark level IV or V, or it is between 1.01 and 2.0 mm and is not ulcerated. It appears to be localized in the skin and has not been found in lymph nodes or distant organs.

Stage IIA

T2b or T3a, N0, M0: The melanoma is between 1.01 mm and 2.0 mm in thickness and is ulcerated, or it is between 2.01 and 4.0 mm and is not ulcerated. It appears to be localized in the skin and has not been found in lymph nodes or distant organs.

Stage IIB

T3b or T4a, N0, M0: The melanoma is between 2.01 mm and 4.0 mm in thickness and is ulcerated, or it is thicker than 4.0 mm and is not ulcerated. It appears to be localized in the skin and has not been found in lymph nodes or distant organs.

Stage IIC

T4b, N0, M0: The melanoma is thicker than 4.0 mm and is ulcerated. It appears to be localized in the skin and has not been found in lymph nodes or distant organs.

Stage IIIA

T1a-4a, N1a or N2a, M0: The melanoma is not ulcerated. It has spread to 1 to 3 lymph nodes near the affected skin area, but the nodes are not enlarged and the melanoma is found only when they are viewed under the microscope. There is no distant spread. The thickness of the melanoma is not a factor, although it is usually thick in people with stage III melanoma.

Stage IIIB

T1b-4b, N1a or N2a, M0: The melanoma is ulcerated. It has spread to 1 to 3 lymph nodes near the affected skin area, but the nodes are not enlarged and the melanoma is found only when they are viewed under the microscope. There is no distant spread.

T1a-4a, N1b or N2b, M0: The melanoma is not ulcerated. It has spread to 1 to 3 lymph nodes near the affected skin area. The nodes are enlarged because of the melanoma. There is no distant spread.

T1a/b-4a/b, N2c, M0: The melanoma can be ulcerated or not. It has spread to small areas of nearby skin or lymphatic channels around the original tumor, but the nodes do not contain melanoma. There is no distant spread.

Stage IIIC

T1b-4b, N1b or N2b, M0: The melanoma is ulcerated. It has spread to 1 to 3 lymph nodes near the affected skin area. The nodes are enlarged because of the melanoma. There is no distant spread.

Any T, N3, M0: The melanoma can be ulcerated or not. It has spread to 4 or more nearby lymph nodes, OR to nearby lymph nodes that are clumped together, OR it has spread to nearby skin or lymphatic channels around the original tumor and to nearby lymph nodes. The nodes are enlarged because of the melanoma. There is no distant spread.

Stage IV

Any T, Any N, M1: The melanoma has spread beyond the original area of skin and nearby lymph nodes to other organs such as the lung, liver, or brain, or to distant areas of the skin or lymph nodes. Neither the lymph node status nor thickness is considered, but typically the melanoma is thick and has also spread to lymph nodes.

shows that a melanoma is more advanced than doctors may think it is from the Breslow measurement. The Clark level is, however, more useful in staging thin melanomas. The prognostic indicators by TNM stage grouping for malignant melanoma are shown in Table 8-7.

TABLE 8-7: PROGNOSTIC DATA FOR MELANOMA BY STAGE GROUPING

Stage IA: The 5-year survival rate is about 99%. The 10-year survival is about 97%.

Stage IB: The 5-year survival rate is about 92%. The 10-year survival is about 86%.

Stage IIA: The 5-year survival rate is about 78%. The 10-year survival is about 66%.

Stage IIB: The 5-year survival rate is about 68%. The 10-year survival is about 60%.

Stage IIC: The 5-year survival rate is about 56%. The 10-year survival is about 48%.

Stage IIIA: The 5-year survival rate is about 50%. The 10-year survival is about 44%.

Stage IIIB: The 5-year survival rate ranges from about 50% to about 69%. The 10-year survival ranges from about 44% to about 61%.

Stage IIIC: The 5-year survival rate ranges from about 27% to about 52%. The 10-year survival ranges from about 22% to about 37%.

Stage IV: The 5-year survival rate for stage IV melanoma is about 18%. The 10-year survival is 14%. It is higher if the spread is to skin or distant lymph nodes, rather than to other organs.

(ACS, 2010a; NCCN, 2010b)

There are four subtypes of malignant melanoma. The characteristics and prognostic information about these subtypes is shown in Table 8-8. The risk of recurrence is higher in malignant melanoma than in squamous cell or basal cell carcinoma.

TREATMENT

Nonmelanoma Skin Cancers

In most cases, basal cell and squamous cell carcinomas can be completely cured by fairly minor surgery. There are many different kinds of surgery for these cancers. The type of treatment chosen depends on how large the cancer is, where it is found on the body, and the specific type of skin cancer. For certain squamous cell cancers with a high risk of spreading, surgery may sometimes be followed by radiation or chemotherapy (Aasi & Leffell, 2005).

- A simple excision is similar to an excisional biopsy; although, in this case the diagnosis is already known (often this follows a shave or punch biopsy). For this procedure, the skin is first numbed with a local anesthetic. The tumor is then cut out with a surgical knife, along with some surrounding normal skin. The remaining skin is carefully stitched back together, leaving a small scar.

- Curettage and electrodesiccation removes the cancer by scraping it with a curette, then treating the area where the tumor was located with an electrode to destroy any remaining cancer cells. This process is often repeated. Curettage and electrodesiccation is a good treatment for small basal cell and squamous cell cancers. It will leave a scar.

- Mohs surgery is often used to assure a better cosmetic outcome. Using the Mohs technique, the surgeon removes a thin layer of the skin that the tumor may have invaded and then checks the sample under a microscope. If cancer cells are seen, deeper layers are removed and examined until the skin samples are found to be free of cancer cells. This process is slow, but it means that more normal skin near the tumor can be saved. This is a highly specialized technique that requires much surgical training.

Occasionally, radiation therapy is used for very large squamous cell carcinoma or when the patient cannot tolerate a surgical procedure. For metastatic disease, systemic chemotherapy is sometimes used. One or more chemotherapy drugs may be used to treat squamous cell carcinoma, including cisplatin, doxorubicin, fluorouracil (5-FU), and mitomycin

TABLE 8-8: CHARACTERISTICS OF MALIGNANT MELANOMA SUBTYPES

Characteristic	Superficial spreading melanoma	Nodular melanoma	Lentigo maligna melanoma	Acral lentiginous melanoma
Percent of Melanoma cases	70%	15%	10%	5%
Male to Female ratio	Slightly more common in females.	Occurs more commonly in males.	Occurs most commonly in elderly people; equally in males and females.	Most common form of melanoma in Asians, African Americans, and people with dark skin, accounting for 50% of melanomas that occur in people with these skin types.
Distributions	In females, it most commonly appears on the legs. In males, it is more likely to develop between the neck and pelvis.	There is no specific distribution.	Typically occurs on sun-damaged skin, especially the face.	Commonly develops on the palms, soles, mucous membranes (such as those that line the mouth, nose, and female genitals), and underneath or near fingernails and toenails.
Appearance	It appears with irregular borders and various shades of black, brown, gray, blue, pink, red, or white. Within the lesion there can be a remarkable variation in color involving white, pink, brown, and black.	It is most often darkly pigmented; however, some lesions can be light brown or even colorless (non-pigmented). An ulcerated and bleeding lesion is common.	It begins as a spreading, flat, patch with irregular borders and variable colors of brown.	It often looks like a bruise or nail streak.
Progression	It can progress quickly after a longer radial phase.	It tends to have a rapid radial phase, followed by a rapid vertical phase. Instead of arising from a pre-existing mole, it may appear in a spot where a lesion did not previously exist.	This spreading brownish patch may grow slowly for years.	Can appear to progress quickly. The lesion may have been present for longer periods of time before being detected.
Age	It can occur in young persons.	The average age is 60 years.	The average age is 55 years.	There is no obvious age distribution.

(Cummins et al., 2006; NCCN, 2010b)

(Aasi & Leffell, 2005). They can often slow the spread of these cancers and relieve some symptoms. In some cases, they may shrink tumors enough so that other treatments, such as surgery or radiation therapy, may be used.

Melanoma Skin Cancers

Surgery

Thin melanomas can be completely cured by a wide excision. The tumor is cut out, along with a small amount of normal non-cancerous skin at the edges. The normal, healthy skin around the edges of the cancer is referred to as the margin. The margins should be anywhere from 0.5 centimeter (cm) (about ¼ inch) to about 2½ cm (about 1 inch) depending on the thickness of the tumor. Thicker tumors call for larger margins.

Chemotherapy

There have been various protocols for treatment of malignant melanoma (NCCN, 2010b). Some more commonly used combinations are:

- Dacarbazine (DTIC)
- Dacarbazine, carmustine (BCNU), cisplatin, tamoxifen (Dartmouth Regimen)
- Temozolomide (Temodar)
- Cisplatin, vinblastine, and DTIC (CVD Regimen)
- Paclitaxel
- Paclitaxel and cisplatin
- Paclitaxel and carboplatin

Immunotherapy

Several types of immunotherapy can be used in treating patients with advanced malignant melanoma. Cytokines boost the immune system. Two man-made versions of natural cytokines, interferon-alpha and interleukin-2, are sometimes used in patients with metastatic malignant melanoma. Both drugs can help shrink advanced (stage III and IV) melanomas in about 10% to 20% of patients, when used alone (Aasi & Leffell, 2005).

Side effects of immunotherapy may include fever, chills, aches, severe tiredness, drowsiness, and myelosuppression. Interleukin-2, particularly in high doses, can cause capillary leak syndrome and other significant problems with fluid retention as well as hypotension (NCCN, 2010b).

CASE STUDY: SKIN CANCER

Mrs. S is a 70-year-old female who presented to her primary care for a routine follow-up examination for essential hypertension. She has never had major surgery. She had 2 pregnancies and deliveries without complications. She has been treated eight times for basal cell carcinoma. On routine assessment of her blood pressure, a 4 mm pearly, shiny lesion was noted on her nose. The center had telangiectasia.

Mrs. S is a retired school teacher. Hobbies include gardening, fishing, and reading. She is married and enjoys spending time with her four grandchildren.

This patient is typical in that she is fair, freckled, and red-headed. She lives her life with the results of many sunburns in her youth and young adult years. She used "suntan lotion" years ago for protection, but still suffered numerous blistering sunburns.

Mrs. S was first diagnosed with basal cell carcinoma in 1978. The first spot was sore, and a shave biopsy was done. She frequently verbalizes frustration that she now has red skin, scars from the excisional biopsies, blotchy spots, and areas of less pigment. She states "I'm always concerned with the look of my skin. I usually wear long-sleeve shirts and long pants whenever possible."

Because of the location of the lesion, Mrs. S was referred for Moh's surgery. It was confirmed by the dermopathologist to be basal cell carcinoma. The procedure took over 6 hours because a total of 5 resections were needed to ensure clear margins. Her recovery was uneventful and after 3 months a scar was barely visible.

Mrs. S now faithfully uses sunscreen with an SPF of 15 and wears protective clothing and eyewear. She is also vigilant about these measures with her grandchildren. She realizes that these measures may offer her some benefit in reducing or delaying the development of another basal cell carcinoma. She is also aware that she will need to have continued follow-up with a dermatologist on a regular basis because of her history of previous basal cell carcinoma and the damage in her skin.

What classic symptom of basal cell skin cancer does Mrs. S have?

A white, pearly-colored lesion with telangiectasia is one of the most classic presentations of skin cancer. Typically they occur on the face or sun exposed areas, as is the case with Mrs. S.

What risk factors for skin cancer does Mrs. S have?

Mrs. S is at risk for skin cancer because she is fair, freckled, and red-headed. She has a long history of ultraviolet light exposure and sunburns. She has previously been treated for skin cancer.

What follow-up will be recommended for Mrs. S?

Mrs. S will need lifetime follow-up with a dermatologist. This will probably include a full body examination twice a year with prophylactic removal of suspicious lesions. Her risk for additional skin cancers is substantial.

What prevention measures might benefit Mrs. S?

Mrs. S needs to be sure she regularly uses sunscreen with an SPF of 15 and wears protective clothing and eyewear.

SUMMARY

The management of patients with skin cancer provides many challenges for oncology nurses. Some patients delay seeking treatment because they have a misconception that all cancer is uniformly fatal, despite the excellent prognosis for nonmetastastic nonmelanoma skin cancer. When detected early, the prognosis for malignant melanoma is also excellent.

Clearly, more efforts need to be made to prevent skin cancer. Reducing UVR exposure from both natural and artificial sources is a key prevention measure. If exposure cannot be avoided, direct efforts need to be taken to wear protective clothing and eyewear, seek shade, and use sunscreen appropriately. Prevention efforts are the key to reducing the morbidity and mortality associated with skin cancer.

EXAM QUESTIONS

CHAPTER 8
Questions 59-70

Note: Choose the one option that BEST answers each question.

59. The skin cancer with the highest risk of recurrence or metastasis is

    a. basal cell.

    b. merkel cell.

    c. squamous cell.

    d. malignant melanoma.

60. Which one of the following people would have the highest risk for developing skin cancer?

    a. 15-year-old African American student

    b. 30-year-old Asian teacher

    c. 70-year-old Hispanic factory worker

    d. 75-year-old wheat farmer from the Midwest

61. Chemical sunscreen is given an SPF for its ability to protect against

    a. UVR-B.

    b. UVR-C.

    c. UVR-D.

    d. UVR-E.

62. Providing information on skin cancer prevention should target

    a. office workers.

    b. mothers of children.

    c. persons treated for lung cancer.

    d. factory workers.

63. Sunscreen should be applied

    a. 10 minutes before exposure.

    b. 30 minutes before exposure.

    c. every 3 hours.

    d. once a day.

64. When using sunscreen, an area that is frequently missed is the

    a. face.

    b. back of the neck.

    c. hands.

    d. legs.

65. Which of the following would provide the best protection from UVR?

    a. baseball cap

    b. sleeveless shirt

    c. wide-brimmed hat

    d. loosely woven shirt

66. Appropriate follow-up care for an individual who has been treated for skin cancer includes

    a. use of sunscreen and protective clothing only during the summer months.

    b. limiting sun exposure to 2 hours during the summer months.

    c. screening by a healthcare professional at regular intervals.

    d. daily thorough skin self-examination.

67. Which of the following is most helpful in predicting the prognosis of malignant melanoma?

    a. age of the patient

    b. Clark's level

    c. Breslow's Measurement

    d. location of the lesion

68. The primary treatment for nonmelanoma skin cancer is

    a. surgery.

    b. radiation.

    c. chemotherapy.

    d. immunotherapy.

69. The most common subtype of malignant melanoma that occurs in Asians and African Americans is

    a. superficial spreading melanoma.

    b. nodular melanoma.

    c. lentigo maligna melanoma.

    d. acral lentiginous melanoma.

70. Immunotherapy agents used in the treatment of advanced malignant melanoma include interferon-alpha and

    a. Adriamycin.

    b. 5-FU.

    c. Cytoxan.

    d. interleukin-2.

REFERENCES

Aasi, S.Z. & Leffell, D.J. (2005). Cancer of the skin. In V.T. DeVita, Jr., S. Hellman, & S.A. Rosenberg (Eds.), *Cancer: Principles and practice of oncology* (7th ed., pp. 1717-1744). Philadelphia: Lippincott Williams & Wilkins.

American Cancer Society. (2010a). *Cancer facts & figures – 2010*. Atlanta, GA: American Cancer Society.

American Cancer Society. (2010b). *Cancer prevention & early detection facts & figures 2010*. Atlanta, GA: American Cancer Society. Retrieved July 19, 2010, from http://www.cancer.org/acs/groups/content/@epidemiologysurveilance/documents/webcontent/acspc-025759.pdf

American Cancer Society. (2010c). Melanoma skin cancer: Causes, risk factors, and prevention topics. Retrieved July 19, 2010, from http://www.cancer.org/Cancer/SkinCancerMelanoma/DetailedGuide/melanoma-skin-cancer-risk-factors

American Cancer Society. (2010d). *Melanoma skin cancer: Early detection, diagnosis, and staging topics*. Retrieved July 19, 2010, from http://www.cancer.org/Cancer/SkinCancer-Melanoma/DetailedGuide/melanoma-skin-cancer-diagnosed

Bauer, J., Büttner, P., Wiecker, T.S. Luther, H., & Garbe, C. (2005). Effect of sunscreen and clothing on the number of melanocytic nevi in 1,812 German children attending day care. *American Journal of Epidemiology, 161*(7), 620-627.

Boukamp, P. (2005). Non-melanoma skin cancer: What drives tumor development and progression? *Carcinogenesis, 26*(10),1657-1667.

Chu, D.H. (2008). Development and structure of skin. In K. Wolff, L.A. Goldsmith, S.I. Katz, B.A. Gilchrest, A.S. Paller, & D.J. Leffell (Eds.), *Fitzpatrick's dermatology in general medicine* (7th ed., pp. 57-73). New York: McGraw-Hill.

Cummins, D.L., Cummins, J.M., Pantle, H., Silverman, M.A., Leonard, AL., & Chanmugam, A. (2006). Cutaneous malignant melanoma. *Mayo Clinic Proceedings, 81*(4), 500-507.

Edge, S.B., Byrd, D.R., Carducci, M., Compton, C.C., Fritz, A.G., Greene, F.L., & Trotti, A. (2010). *AJCC cancer staging manual* (7th ed.), New York: Springer.

Johr, R.H., Argenziano, G., & Zalaudek, I. (2005). The use of dermoscopy in the diagnosis of skin cancer. In D.S. Rigel, R.J. Friedman, L.M. Dzubow, D. Reintgen, J. Bystryn, & R. Marks (Eds.), *Cancer of the skin* (pp. 433-448). Philadelphia: Saunders.

Kullavanijaya, P. & Lim, H.W. (2005). Photoprotection. *Journal of the American Academy of Dermatology, 52*(6), 937-958.

Markovic, S.N., Erickson, L.A., Rao, R.D., Weenig, R.H., Pockaj, B.A., Bardia, A., et al. (2007). Malignant melanoma in the 21st century, part 1: Epidemiology, risk factors, screening, prevention, and diagnosis. *Mayo Clinic Proceedings, 82*(3), 364-380.

Maselis, T.J., Vandaele, M., & De Boulle, K. (2005). Behaviour and motives of adolescents towards skin cancer. *European Journal of Cancer Prevention, 14*(2), 83-84.

Naeyaert, J.M. & Brochez, L. (2003). Dysplastic nevi. *New England Journal of Medicine, 349*(23), 2233-2240.

National Comprehensive Cancer Network (NCCN). (2010a). *Practice guidelines in oncology: Basal cell and squamous cell skin cancers.* Version 1.2010. Retrieved August 27, 2010, from www.nccn.org/professionals/physician_gls/f_guidelines.asp

National Comprehensive Cancer Network. (2010b). *Practice guidelines in oncology: Melanoma.* Version 1.2010. Retrieved July 3, 2010 from, www.nccn.org/professionals/physician_gls/PDF/nmsc.pd

Olson, A.L., Gaffney, C., Starr, P., Gibson, J.J., Cole, B.F., & Dietrich, A.J. (2007). SunSafe in the middle school years: A community-wide intervention to change early-adolescent sun protection. *Pediatrics, 119*(1), e247-256.

Ries, L.A.G., Melbert, D., Krapcho, M., Stinchcomb, D.G., Howlader, N., Horner, M.J., et al., (Eds). *SEER Cancer Statistics Review, 1975-2005.* Bethesda, MD: National Cancer Institute. Retrieved from http://seer.cancer.gov/csr/1975_2005/, based on November 2007 SEER data submission, posted to the SEER web site, 2008.

U.S. Department of Health and Human Services. (2000). *Healthy People 2010.* Available at http://www.healthypeople.gov/Sitemap

U.S. Preventive Services Task Force. (2003). Counseling to prevent skin cancer: Recommendations and rationale of the U.S. Preventive Services Task Force. *MMWR Recommendations and Report, 52*(RR-15), 13-17.

Whitworth, A. (2006). Legislators combat melanoma, restrict teen tanning. *Journal of the National Cancer Institute, 98*(22), 1594-1596.

Wiggs, W.P. (2007). Playing it safe in the sun: Primary prevention of skin cancer for sun-exposed athletes. *Dermatology Nursing, 19*(6), 555-560.

Yoder, L.H. (2005). Be sun safe! Understand skin cancer prevention and detection. *Medsurg Nursing, 14*(4), 254-256.

CHAPTER 9

PSYCHOSOCIAL ISSUES

CHAPTER OBJECTIVE

After completing this chapter, the reader will be able to discuss the psychosocial concerns that may accompany a diagnosis of cancer.

LEARNING OBJECTIVES

After studying this chapter, the reader will be able to

1. identify specific psychosocial needs at various stages of the cancer trajectory.

2. identify physiologic responses to distress.

3. identify two symptoms of depression.

4. describe a scale to evaluate psychosocial distress.

5. identify a major adverse effect of antidepressants.

6. describe at least two psychosocial interventions.

INTRODUCTION

Adjusting to the many physical changes associated with cancer and its treatment is a complex process. The diagnosis of cancer and its treatment is also associated with changes in the emotional state, body image, and life roles. This chapter will identify areas of concern and explore ways the healthcare professional can support the woman with cancer and her family and significant others.

PSYCHOSOCIAL DISTRESS

Definitions

A diagnosis of cancer is a stressful event and is often accompanied by increasing anxiety and depression (Jacobson & Jim, 2008). For example, women diagnosed with breast cancer consistently score lower on quality of life measures during their cancer diagnosis and treatment and for as long as a year following treatment (Schou, Ekeberg, Sandvik, Hjermstad, & Ruland, 2005). Not only is the diagnosis period stressful, but treatment and follow-up also have potential negative psychological consequences. Nurses need to be aware of the salient psychosocial aspects of diagnosis, treatment, and survival and implement appropriate strategies to assist the patient and family to cope.

Psychosocial distress is commonly associated with a diagnosis of cancer. Distress is a broad term commonly defined as an unpleasant emotional experience that might impact psychological, social, or spiritual aspects of well-being (Hewitt, Herdman, & Holland, 2004). Distress exists on a continuum beginning with "normal" reactions to the diagnosis and its associated treatment to severe, disabling psychiatric problems. Estimates suggest that approximately 30% of women with cancer show significant distress at some point during the illness and its treatment (Hewitt et al., 2004). Everyone reacts to the diagnosis differently. Despite the diversity of reactions, there are some common themes and psychosocial reactions to a diagnosis of cancer. These are shown in Table 9-1.

TABLE 9-1: PSYCHOSOCIAL CONCERNS ASSOCIATED WITH A CANCER DIAGNOSIS

- Physical symptoms including fatigue, sleep disturbances, nausea, and pain
- Body image changes including those related to surgery, weight, skin, and hair
- Sexual dysfunction (painful intercourse, vaginal dryness, early menopause, decreased libido)
- Fear of recurrence
- Stress
- Informational needs regarding treatment
- Treatment related anxieties
- Emotional distress (cognitive dysfunction, anxiety, depression, grief, helplessness, anger, low self-esteem)
- Persistent anxiety or intrusive distressing thoughts about body and illness
- Marital or partner communication issues
- Concerns regarding minor children or aging parents
- Social isolation or difficulty communicating with friends
- Fears of vulnerability
- Difficulties completing duties associated with career or other roles
- Financial and insurance concerns
- Existential and related fears of death

Management of distress should be a priority in cancer care (National Comprehensive Cancer Network [NCCN], 2010a). According to the NCCN, all individuals should be assessed for psychosocial distress and have access to competent multidisciplinary psychosocial care. Surveys have found that 20% to 40% of patients show a significant level of distress; however, less than 10% of patients are actually identified and referred for psychosocial care. The NCCN has established a broad goal of establishing standards of care so that all patients experiencing psychosocial distress will be accurately and routinely identified, recognized, and treated. These guidelines include recommendations for screening, triage, and initial evaluation as well as referral and treatment guidelines for each participating profession: mental health (psychology and psychiatry), social work, palliative care, and pastoral care. Screening methods and assessment provide the foundation for the patient to be properly identified and treated.

Physiologic Response

A person's response to a stressful input mobilizes a neuroendocrine response, which differs somewhat with each individual, depending on the stressor, perception of the stressor, and other variables. Variables that can affect the response are the person's mood, coping styles, and personality as well as his or her reaction to social support (Jacobson & Jim, 2008; NCCN, 2010a).

Researchers have identified a wide range of stressors that can induce maladaptive psychoneuroimmune responses. These stressors move along pathways that involve the hypothalamus, the pituitary gland, and the sympathetic nervous system (NCCN, 2010a). Moreover, physiological responses differ, depending on whether the stressor is acute or chronic in nature and the way in which the person copes or adapts to the stressor.

If a patient's exposure to the stressor becomes more long-term, the physiological responses can change from being an acute response to one of habituation. For example, initial increased pulse and sweat rates may gradually resolve and be replaced by increased basal muscle tension. When responding to a stressor during an acute period, individuals may respond in an exaggerated way and have difficulty returning to the prestress state of relaxation (Golden-Kreutz et al., 2005). Over time these individuals may exhibit higher blood pressures, increased sweating, and increased respiratory rates and epinephrine levels when compared to nonstressed individuals. Also, they may develop mood changes, such as anxiety, depression, and more serious reactions (NCCN, 2010a).

Because stress can have a negative effect on the body and healing, direct efforts need to be taken to decrease stress. For this reason the NCCN (2010a) has made the assessment and management of distress a priority in oncology care.

PSYCHOSOCIAL ISSUES ACROSS THE TRAJECTORY

Psychologically, a significant proportion of women will experience at least some degree of depression and anxiety (Hewitt et al., 2004). These symptoms may be brief adjustment reactions, which decrease as the patient receives more information about the diagnosis and treatment, or they may be present intermittently or long-term throughout the cancer continuum. The diagnosis is almost always a threat to one's security and order in life.

The psychological functioning of patients should be addressed throughout all phases of the cancer trajectory. Psychosocial health impacts quality of life as well as treatment outcomes. Better disease status and longer survival have been documented in patients with fewer psychosocial disturbances (Aukst-Margetić, Jakovljević, Margetić, Bisćan, & Samija, 2005).

Distress extends along a continuum ranging from common normal feelings of vulnerability, sadness, and fears to problems that become disabilities, such as depression, anxiety, panic, social isolation, and existential and spiritual crisis (Hewitt et al., 2004). Distress impacts family life, employment, and psychosocial functioning. Distress can occur at any phase of the cancer trajectory; however, each phase of the trajectory is associated with some specific stressors.

Biopsy

The diagnostic period can be an extremely anxiety-provoking time for a woman. Depending on the clinical presentation of the cancer, a woman may or may not be surprised or unprepared for a diagnosis of cancer.

With increased screening, especially for breast and colorectal cancer, many women will experience an abnormal screen that results in additional diagnostic procedures and biopsies. An estimated 10% to 20% of breast biopsies are positive, which means that over 2 million women annually will undergo some procedure to evaluate a breast change, most of which will prove to be negative (Chappy, 2004). The psychosocial needs of the group of women in this phase of the cancer trajectory should not be overlooked. Finding a lump or other symptom of cancer can be a frightening experience, as can an undefined or suspicious finding on a routine screening examination such as a mammogram. This leads to additional appointments for more radiologic studies and, often, a biopsy. Often a period of days to a week or more can separate each phase of the diagnostic process. This can be a period of great anxiety and fear for women.

Women undergoing any type of biopsy may have escalated feelings of uncertainty and anxiety because of the potential diagnosis and its implications for relationships, mortality, and sexuality. Often this may be the first significant experience a woman has with healthcare or surgical procedures. Care during this time can be very fragmented, as a woman may be seen by a radiologist, technicians, or a surgeon. Specific psychosocial care services are very limited during this phase.

During a stressful illness such as cancer, patients and family members often become anxious. They may be afraid of what the future will bring or worry about the illness. These are normal reactions that may last from a few days to a few weeks. A more intense anxiety, beyond ordinary worry, can develop over time and keep people from doing things that are important to them. Symptoms of anxiety include

- tiring easily, yet having trouble sleeping

- constant body tension

- racing thoughts

- the inability to control how much time is spent worrying

- frequent aches and pains that can't be traced to physical illness

- being irritable most of the time

- trembling or shaking

- a racing heart, dry mouth, excess sweating, or shortness of breath

- an overwhelming belief that the worst will happen

(Jacobsen & Jim, 2008).

Some worries are normal for persons with a diagnosis of cancer and it is not uncommon for individuals to experience one or two of the symptoms for a short time (less than 2 weeks). It is important for the individual to be instructed to seek professional care if anxious feelings are strong, if there are fearful thoughts, or if the individual cannot accomplish ordinary, daily activities. Often, anxiety can be managed with a variety of techniques. The nurse can facilitate adjustment by:

- promoting discussion of fears.

- encouraging the sharing of feelings and fears with a healthcare provider or in a support group.

- listening carefully, offering support, but not denying or discounting feelings.

- providing assurance that it is normal to feel sad and frustrated at times.

- encouraging the use of prayer or other types of spiritual support, especially if the woman has found it helpful in the past.

- providing education on breathing and relaxation exercises. This might include to close eyes, breathe deeply, focus on each body part and relax it, starting with the toes and working up to the head. When relaxed the woman should try to think of a pleasant place, such as a beach in the morning or a sunny field on a spring day.

- talking with a doctor about using anti-anxiety or anti-depressant medicines.

Waiting for the results of a pathological diagnosis can be extremely difficult. It often takes nearly a week for a final report to become available, during which time a woman often feels that her life is "on hold." While a great many women eventually receive good news that their biopsy was benign, a portion of women will receive a diagnosis of malignancy. Assisting women to find a supportive environment and supportive individual during this phase is critical, especially when the diagnosis is malignancy. Women who are less informed or uninformed as to what to expect during a biopsy usually have much higher levels of anxiety (Chappy, 2004).

Stress can be increased with scheduling problems, as well as long waits for appointments, and test results. For this reason, all efforts should be made to reduce time, and provide continuity of care with an identified provider who can answer questions and provide guidance along each step of the way.

Reactions to the Diagnosis

Although most of the population fears a diagnosis of cancer, the initial response when the diagnosis is confirmed and disclosed is often one of shock and disbelief (Hewitt et al., 2004). A diagnosis of cancer is perceived as a shock for most individuals as well as for their families or significant others, despite the fact that they may have been given information about risk and are undergoing a screening examination.

A cancer diagnosis at any point in a woman's life can be very stressful, very sudden, and unexpected. Without warning or choice, a woman is forced to abandon her current identified life to attend doctors' appointments and undergo tests, which are usually unfamiliar and uncomfortable. Often, a woman feels she has lost control of her life after she receives a diagnosis of malignancy. A woman diagnosed with cancer may experience any combination of the following emotions and thoughts:

- uncertainty
- anger
- a feeling of lack of control
- sadness
- fear
- frustration
- guilt
- mood swings
- much stronger and intense feelings
- a sense of being disconnected or isolated from others
- loneliness
- resentment.

Positive reactions that a woman might also experience at the time of diagnosis include:

- a greater sense of resilience or strength
- peace, or a feeling of being at ease
- a clearer idea of her priorities in life
- more appreciation for her quality of life and the people she loves

(Jacobson & Jim, 2008).

Informing women that these can be common reactions is the first step in facilitating adjustment to the diagnosis and its treatment.

Denial is a common reaction. The disbelief that the diagnosis has been made is actually psychologically protective unless it persists for extended periods of time or impairs decisions regarding, or engaging

in, appropriate treatment. Short-term denial can be helpful because it provides time for the woman and her family to adjust to the diagnosis. Most patients work through the denial fairly quickly and have some acceptance of the fact they have cancer by the time treatment begins.

Anger is another reaction that must be acknowledged and, in some cases, dealt with. Patients and families may be angry about the diagnosis, specific incidents involving healthcare providers and healthcare, family, friends, and sometimes an existential power. Encouraging individuals to discuss their feelings of anger is often an effective tool for dealing with anger.

The diagnosis of cancer can be accompanied by a wide range of fears and concerns. Patients and families most often are initially fearful of existential concerns and mortality. As the reality of the diagnosis surfaces, fears may center on pain, alopecia, nausea and vomiting, surgery, unknown healthcare procedures, fatigue, managing day-to-day activities for the family, paying for the costs of treatment, and keeping a job. There may also be fears and concerns about how to discuss the diagnosis with friends and others. Identification of specific fears and developing concrete strategies to manage each specific problem can be very effective in reducing stress.

It is normal to grieve over the changes that cancer brings to a person's life. The future is suddenly uncertain. Some dreams and plans may be lost forever. Reactive depression commonly occurs when the diagnosis is initially made. For some, the depression lasts longer. It is estimated that up to one in four individuals with cancer have clinical depression (Gorman, 2006). Clinical depression causes great distress, impairs functioning, and may make the person with cancer less able to follow her cancer treatment plan. The good news is that clinical depression can be treated.

Signs of depression include:

- feelings of helplessness

- hopelessness

- loss of interest in family, friends, and activities

- loss of appetite

- changes in energy level, extreme fatigue or loss of energy

- ongoing sad or "empty" mood for most of the day

- major weight loss (when not dieting) or weight gain

- trouble sleeping with early waking, sleeping too much, or not being able to sleep

- trouble focusing thoughts, remembering, or making decisions

- feeling guilty, worthless, or helpless

(Jacobsen & Jim, 2008).

The observation or report of the presence of five or more of these symptoms nearly every day for 2 weeks or more may indicate the need for professional help. If the symptoms are severe enough to interfere with normal activities, an evaluation for clinical depression by a qualified health or mental health professional is indicated (Gorman, 2006).

Depending on the seriousness of depression and the length of obvious symptoms, short, or long-term intervention may be indicated. Women and their families need to be instructed that these interventions are not being delivered because the person is "weak," but to improve quality of life and to help facilitate better tolerance of the treatment. Any suicidal thoughts require immediate intervention, and the patient and family should be instructed on this point. Indications of suicidal thoughts include:

- thoughts of suicide (or of hurting herself)

- inability to eat or sleep

- lack of interest in usual activities for many days

- inability to find pleasure in anything

- emotions that interfere with daily activities and last more than a few days

- confusion

- trouble breathing

- sweating

- severe restlessness

- new or unusual symptoms that cause concern.

Because the signs of suicidal thought are often vague or difficult to discern from depression, it is often necessary to inquire directly with the patient if she is having suicidal thoughts (Jacobson & Jim, 2008).

Guilt is another common reaction to the diagnosis of cancer. Some women feel guilt related to prior use of hormone replacement therapy or birth control pills. Others feel guilt if they believe they have a hereditary predisposition for developing breast cancer and fear they have passed the susceptibility gene on to a child. Women with cervical cancer may think prior sexual practices, which resulted in an HPV infection, caused the cancer. Others with later detected cancers may feel guilty for ignoring symptoms or failing to engage in regular screening. For individuals with lung cancer, there may be guilt because of years of tobacco usage. Women with skin cancer may feel guilty for failing to utilize practices that reduce ultraviolet light exposure. Others feel guilty because they perceive themselves to be a burden to others. Acknowledging that these feelings are common and encouraging patients to discuss them may be helpful.

Information Seeking and Treatment Decisions

After the diagnosis of cancer has been made, the patient, family, and physicians will begin to discuss treatment. Most women are unprepared for the diagnosis and even less prepared for the array of medical consultants they will be scheduled to see in a relatively short period of time and the number of treatment decisions they will have to make. Lives and work schedules are usually abruptly interrupted for the woman as well as those supporting her during the decision-making and treatment process.

The first few days and weeks after the biopsy or primary surgical procedure typically involve more diagnostic work-ups, which can be a frightening and unfamiliar experience for the woman. This is necessary to determine the stage of disease and other prognostic factors, so an effective treatment plan can be formulated. This information can be technically complex. Many times, healthcare providers have difficulty explaining the details of the pathology reports and patients can have significant difficulty understanding the findings. This can lead to more anxiety and distress for the woman and those supporting her. Providing patients with a copy of the pathology report and explaining each term, such as stage, grade, and tumor prognostic markers can be very helpful to some patients.

Following the discussion of the pathological findings comes one regarding treatment choices. This can be a very overwhelming experience. Often, there is more than one treatment discussed or suggested, which may require the patient to make a choice about the best treatment for her. In some cases there are few choices; in other cases, such as with breast cancer, there are multiple options to consider. Women with breast cancer are frequently asked to decide about type of treatment (such as mastectomy, with or without reconstruction, or lumpectomy with radiation) and adjuvant treatment (standard or investigational).

Essentially, the woman is being asked to make decisions about life-saving treatments for which she usually has little knowledge and background. Whereas some patients find that this decision-making process restores a sense of control, others find it very stressful. The ability to make informed decisions may be influenced by the patient's education level, stress level, family and social support systems, and previous experiences with the healthcare system. Women need to be reminded that although

a decision is needed, they should not be too hasty, resulting in decisions that are later regretted (Hewitt et al., 2004). It is not inappropriate to encourage a woman to get a second opinion with another group of specialists to ensure that treatment decisions are appropriate (Jacobson & Jim, 2008).

Communication and patient education can be challenging because of the shock of the diagnosis. Shock and anxiety can limit the woman's ability to comprehend information (Engel et al., 2003). For this reason, it is recommended that women bring a supportive person to appointments who is also learning about the options. The woman should also be encouraged to write down questions as they occur because they are often forgotten at the time the woman is seeing the healthcare provider. Acceptance of the disease and its treatment comes at different rates for different individuals. Lack of information increases anxiety, and information can provide individuals with a sense of control. Striking a balance is important.

The decision for treatment lies with the patient but must be made based on information from the physician, nurse, and other resources. Some treatment alternatives are based on the size or location of the tumor, prognostic markers, and pre-existing or co-morbid conditions.

Psychosocial distress may also be increased during this time, because women may have to deal with multiple specialists. Although these providers are ideally seen as a team, usually women must go from office to office or different departments. Fragmentation of care can be a source of additional psychosocial distress (Hewitt et al., 2004).

Active Treatment

After the treatment plan is determined, a woman may feel some sense of relief because there is a plan; however, new fears and concerns usually surface related to the treatment.

The shift toward outpatient and short-stay surgical procedures adds to the psychosocial distress for some families. Depending on the surgical procedure, women can be discharged with drains and dressings and may have limited mobility initially. This means someone must be available to help with household tasks and the management of the incision. Careful assessment of the support system available to the woman is necessary for successful care. Often, those who assist the woman also have psychosocial concerns that need to be addressed.

Following the initial adjustment to the diagnosis of cancer, the patient begins the journey of treatment. Treatment may include any combination of surgery, chemotherapy, radiation therapy, hormonal therapy, targeted therapy, or close follow-up, depending on the tumor type, stage at diagnosis, and other factors. Treatment almost always results in a change in physical health, which also affects the psychosocial health of the patient. This includes side effects from therapy, role changes, and body image alterations.

Depression and anxiety can increase as side effects worsen, which in turn can intensify the physical symptoms. Depression can lead to an increase in anxiety and pain, cause difficulty with concentration, and can result in insomnia. Early identification of anxiety and depression is important so interventions can be delivered. If depression or anxiety becomes too severe, there can be delays in treatment of the tumor, which can ultimately decrease long-term survival (Jacobson & Jim, 2008).

Long-Term Survivors

The end of treatment can be a time of mixed emotions for many women (Engel et al., 2003). The stress associated with the transition is often underestimated. There is joy in completing treatment but there is also the fear of leaving the close monitoring of the healthcare team. There is a sense of comfort in having chemotherapy or radiation therapy that will fight the cancer. When the treatment is over, the sense of control over the cancer, in some patients, is also taken away. Talking with others who have completed treatment may help to normalize these feelings.

Many survivors are also unprepared for the lingering effects of therapy, including fatigue, cognitive dysfunction, and premature menopause (Ganz et al., 2004). Although much time is spent preparing patients for the acute toxicities of treatment (such as nausea, vomiting, fatigue, or alopecia), much less time is devoted to what to expect in the pattern of recovery and adjustment following active treatment. Appropriately, in many cases, nurses may tell patients it takes as much time to recover as it did to complete the therapy, although little specifically is known about how this recovery takes place (Jacobsen & Jim, 2008).

Throughout the diagnosis and treatment period it is common for a woman to identify herself as a patient with cancer. Other roles, such as wife, mother, or career woman, are put on hold and cancer becomes the main focus. Although often difficult, it is important for women with cancer to learn to integrate the cancer and related treatments into their lives. Some patients may find strength in groups where other women discuss how they returned to new normal (without cancer) lives, whereas others may prefer individual counseling to help them understand the meaning of the illness and return to a normal life. The ultimate goal is to understand the effects of the cancer on the individual and the best ways to move forward with life. For some this may mean a change in career, whereas others may find they have a different perspective on life, having experienced a serious illness.

Following the end of treatment, some women may find the possibility of a recurrence frightening and almost paralyzing. For some this fear is manifested as an increased dependence on the healthcare team. Fears of recurrence are a well documented concern among long-term survivors (Ganz et al., 2004). Acknowledging that this is a common response that is exacerbated at follow-up visits and exams can be helpful for some women.

Long-term survivorship can be influenced by healthy living habits following diagnosis and treatment for cancer. Exercise has been associated with higher quality of life at least 10 years after cancer diagnosis (Kendall, Mahue-Giangreco, Carpenter, Ganz, & Bernstein, 2005) as well as decreasing long-term fatigue, which is often felt following treatment for cancer (Bower, 2005). Encouraging a healthy lifestyle may help reduce or prevent distress during this phase of the trajectory.

Recurrent or Advanced Disease

Although the overall prognosis for cancer may be good, especially for those who have early detection, many women will experience a recurrence of cancer or never really have a response to initial treatment, especially if their cancer was diagnosed at a later stage. Recurrence is defined as the return of the disease after an initial course of treatment with a disease-free period. Although recurrence does not necessarily lead to terminal illness, patients with recurrent disease are usually much more aware of the reality of and potential mortality of their diagnosis. Often, this event occurs years or decades after the initial diagnosis. For many it is considered a failure by both the patient and treatment team. Because recurrence is frequently associated with clinical symptoms from the cancer, including increased pain, cough, headaches, or other changes, the woman has a tangible constant reminder that her condition is serious and perhaps life-limiting. This can lead to enormous stress for the patient and her family.

Recurrent disease may be treated with the same, similar, or completely new treatments than the primary treatment. Women may feel overwhelmed by the treatment and their potential mortality. Women with recurrent cancer may have more anxiety about treatment because of previous experiences as well as more symptom distress, including fatigue and pain. Patients may also have anger, self-blame, and regret about prior treatment choices. Women may be less hopeful, as the first treatment did not completely irradicate the disease.

As the disease progresses, attention to symptom and pain relief becomes paramount. This phase of the illness is also often accompanied by concerns related to spiritual and existential matters that should be addressed. There are many fears in the terminal phases of disease, including fear of the unknown, pain, suffering, abandonment, loss of control, loss of identify, loss of body image, loss of loved ones, and loss of hope (Gorman, 2006). Acknowledgement of these fears and stressors, and that they are a common reaction, is often the first step in helping patients to cope with these overwhelming feelings. Open communication with family and significant others may decrease some distress and offer an opportunity for closure for the patient and those involved in her care.

At many different times during treatment and recovery, women with cancer may be fearful and anxious. For most people with cancer, diagnosis and recurrence cause the most anxiety and fear. Fear of treatment, doctor visits, and tests may also cause apprehension. Women may be afraid of uncontrolled pain, dying, or what happens after death, including what may happen to loved ones. Sometimes, despite having the symptoms, the person may deny having these feelings. Symptoms of anxiety and fear include

- anxious facial expression
- uncontrolled worry
- trouble solving problems and focusing thoughts
- muscle tension (looks tense or uptight)
- trembling, shaking, and other signs of restlessness
- dry mouth
- angry outbursts
- irritability

(NCCN, 2010a).

If a person has these symptoms, and they are interfering with her life, a mental health evaluation may be helpful. Therapy can often help as well as helpful interventions, which may include:

- encouraging the woman to talk about her fears and feelings

- listening carefully to what the woman is saying

- offering support, but not denying or discounting her feelings

- considering a support group

- using prayer or other types of spiritual support

- trying deep breathing and relaxation exercises

- considering the use of anti-anxiety agents or anti-depressants

(Jacobsen & Jim, 2008).

SPECIAL PSYCHOSOCIAL PROBLEMS

People who have physical symptoms, such as pain or fatigue, also seem more likely to have emotional distress (Jacobson & Jim, 2008). Most of the time, these physical symptoms can be controlled with medicines – but it may take more than one try to find the right drug or combination of drugs.

Cancer can be very unpredictable. Someone with cancer can feel good one day and terrible the next. Learning to live with uncertainty is part of learning to live with cancer, for the patient and her significant others. There may be times when the uncertainty and fear cause the person with cancer to seem angry, depressed, or withdrawn. This is normal and is a part of the process of grieving and adjusting to the diagnosis. Over time, most people are able to adjust to the new reality in their lives and go forward. Many patients, families, and caregivers face some degree of depression, anxiety, and fear when cancer becomes part of their lives. These feelings are normal responses to such a life-changing experience.

Fatigue

The fatigue associated with cancer is different from the fatigue of everyday life. Everyday, normal fatigue is most often a short-term problem that gets better with rest. Cancer-related fatigue is worse and it causes more distress. Rest does not necessarily make it go away. For some people, this kind of fatigue can cause even more distress than pain, nausea, vomiting, or depression. Cancer-related fatigue can be overwhelming and greatly affects quality of life with family and friends as well as completing a treatment plan.

Cancer-related fatigue is the most common side effect of cancer and cancer treatment. Research suggests that approximatley 70% to 100% of cancer patients receiving treatment experience fatigue (NCCN, 2010b). In addition, about 30% to 50% of cancer survivors have reported fatigue that lasts for months or even years after they finish treatment. Signs of fatigue include:

- feelings of tiredness are recurrent or they becomes severe

- feeling more tired than usual during or after an activity

- feeling tired when it is not related to an activity

- fatigue not getting better with rest or sleep

- sleeping more than usual

- becoming confused or the inability to concentrate or focus thoughts

- complaining of complete lack of energy

- being unable to get out of bed for more than 24 hours

- disruptions in work, social life, or daily routine

- lack of desire to do the things one would normally do

- feeling negative, sad, or irritable

(NCCN, 2010b).

Cancer itself can cause fatigue directly, by spreading to the bone marrow and causing anemia, or indirectly, by forming toxic substances in the body that change the way normal cells function (NCCN, 2010b). Fatigue is also very common with many cancer treatments, such as chemotherapy, radiation therapy, and immunotherapy. Cancer treatments often kill fast-growing healthy cells, especially the red blood cells, resulting in an anemia. Treatments can kill normal cells and cancer cells, which leads to a build-up of cell waste. The body needs extra energy to clean up this waste and repair damaged tissue (Carroll, Kohli, Mustian, Roscoe, & Morrow, 2007).

There are some other factors that often worsen fatigue and should be considered in an assessment of fatigue. Managing these factors can greatly help reduce the fatigue:

- anemia
- pain
- emotional distress (including depression and anxiety)
- sleep problems
- medicines that worsen symptoms (including antidepressants)
- other medical problems (such as infection, low thyroid function, and heart, lung, liver, kidney, or nervous system disease)
- nutrition problems
- low level of physical activity.

Fatigue is often caused by more than one problem. Treating an underlying cause is very important (Jacobsen, Donovan, Vadaparampil, & Small, 2007). Strategies that may be helpful for managing fatigue include:

- engaging in distraction
- engaging in attention-restoring activities, such as walking on a beach, sitting in a peaceful setting, gardening, doing volunteer activities not related to illness, or bird watching
- reducing stress

- participating in support groups, mental health counseling, stress management training, and relaxation exercises
- joining a supervised exercise program
- nutritional counseling
- evaluating sleep patterns and making changes to get uninterrupted sleep
- asking for help and having other people assist with tasks when possible
- placing things that are frequently used within easy reach
- setting up and following a structured daily routine keeping as normal a level of activity as possible.
- balancing rest and activity
- scheduling activities around rest periods (shorter rest periods are reported to be better than one long one)
- learning ways to deal with stress and trying to reduce it by using things like deep breathing, imagery, meditation, prayer, talking with others, reading, listening to music, and painting.

PAIN

Cancer pain is a significant source of distress and most patients with cancer experience pain at some point during the trajectory of the disease (Dy et al., 2008). Accurate assessment of pain is important because the experience is unique for each individual. Management of this symptom is critical to improve quality of life and decrease distress. Unfortunately, cancer pain frequently is assessed and treated inadequately (NCCN, 2010c).

There are many ways to assess pain. Patients should be asked to describe the location, sensation, and aggravating and relieving factors. Intensity can be easily measured using a 1 to 10 scale, in which the patient rates the pain, with 1 being the least pain and 10 the worst pain. (See Table 9-2). This way the patient serves as the anchor and it is feasible to evaluate the effectiveness of an intervention (Bruera et al., 2005).

TABLE 9-2: PAIN ASSESSMENT

Pain assessment should include:

- Location
- What the pain feels like – for instance, sharp, dull, throbbing, gnawing, burning, shooting, steady
- Intensity (using the 0 to 10 scale below)
- Duration
- Relieving factors
- Exacerbating factors
- Impact of pain on daily life
- Current medications for pain and their effectiveness

Using a pain scale is helpful in describing the intensity of pain. To use the Pain Intensity Scale below, the patient should be instructed to try to assign a number from 0 to 10 to the pain level. If there is no pain, use a 0. As the numbers increase, they stand for pain that is getting worse. A 10 means it is the worst pain one can imagine.

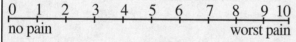

The rating scale can be used to describe:

- how bad the pain is at its worst
- how bad the pain is most of the time
- how bad the pain is at its least
- how the pain changes with treatment or medication

(NCCN, 2010c; Wiffen & McQuay, 2007)

Excellent pain management is almost always the result of the thoughtful development of a pain management treatment plan. Patients and healthcare professionals should work together to develop this plan, the cornerstone of effective pain management. Pharmacologic management of pain should be given on a "round the clock" basis with additional agents for break-through pain (Foley, 2005).

Suggested pharmacologic agents used in the management of pain are shown in Table 9-3.

TABLE 9-3: PHARMACOLOGIC MANAGEMENT OF PAIN

For mild to moderate pain

Non-opioids (no prescription is needed)

- Acetaminophen (Tylenol)
- Nonsteroidal anti-inflammatory drugs (NSAIDs), such as aspirin and ibuprofen are often used.

For moderate to severe pain

Opioids (a prescription is required) – may be combined in non-opioids

- Morphine
- Fentanyl
- Hydromorphone
- Oxycodone
- Codeine

For breakthrough pain

Rapid-onset opioids (prescription is required)

- Fast acting oral morphine
- Fentanyl in a lozenge or "sucker" form.
- A short-acting opioid, which relieves breakthrough pain quickly, and is often used with a long-acting opioid for chronic pain.

For tingling and burning pain

Antidepressants (prescription is required):

- Amitriptyline
- Nortriptyline
- Desipramine

Anti-convulsants (prescription is required):

- Carbamazepine
- Gabapentin
- Phenytoin

For pain caused by swelling or pressure

Steroids (prescription is required):

- Prednisone
- Dexamethasone

(NCCN, 2010c; Pharo & Zhou, 2005)

ASSESSMENT OF PSYCHOSOCIAL FUNCTIONING

The assessment of psychosocial distress is important because it is so prevalent. An estimated one-third to one-half of women diagnosed with breast cancer experience significant levels of distress (Hewitt et al., 2004). Predictors of increased psychosocial stress and problems in women with cancer include younger age at diagnosis and poor prior psychosocial functioning. Weak social support systems and lower socioeconomic status are also risk factors for significant psychosocial distress.

Younger Women

A diagnosis of cancer in women younger than 40 years of age, can be particularly challenging and puts these women at increased risk for psychosocial distress (Ganz et al., 2003). If the diagnosis is made during a pregnancy or shortly after a delivery, a woman must not only confront the diagnosis but also manage the demands of a young family and infant. The threat of early menopause, or infertility, is also associated with increased psychological distress. Additionally, younger women are challenged by trying to juggle work and career development. Protection of fertility is a significant concern that cannot be underestimated. Supporting spouses, friends, and children will ultimately build a better support system for the patient.

Prior Psychosocial Functioning

It is beneficial to assess the patient's past psychosocial history. The diagnosis and treatment of cancer is stressful and could potentially exacerbate preexisting conditions which have been under control. For instance, a patient with a longstanding history of clinical depression may find the diagnosis of cancer increases the depression and she may require more intensive interventions. Assessment and understanding past effective coping strategies may provide insight into how to manage the multiple stressors that accompany a diagnosis of breast cancer.

Assessment of Family Support

Supporting the patient also means supporting the family. It is helpful to assess the needs of the family at the time of diagnosis. Issues such as intimacy and sexuality, femininity, role changes, child care needs, and ways to talk to a partner or children about the diagnosis are areas that require assessment and, frequently, intervention.

Family and friends also play a critical role in a patient's decision regarding treatment. As part of the initial assessment, it is important for the healthcare team to determine if the patient has any preconceived ideas, based on reports from other patients, family members, or friends. This will provide an opportunity for the healthcare team to dispel any misconceptions regarding the patient's diagnosis and provides an estimate of the baseline information the woman and her family have about the diagnosis and its treatment.

The diagnosis of cancer in mothers with children living at home is disruptive to the routines in the home and especially to the accessibility and availability of mothers to children. Ultimately, this often results in negative effects on overall tension in the home and marriage (Davis Kirsch, Brandt, & Lewis, 2003). Cancer brings change to any family, whether it is a young couple, couple with children, older couple, single person, widowed person, or individual living in a nontraditional relationship. Healthcare providers need to assess the impact of the diagnosis and its subsequent change in each specific situation. This includes an assessment of finances (including whether the patient can work during treatment), living arrangements (so there is someone available to assist the patient), and how daily activities will be managed (this can be especially important in families with children). A clear and thorough assessment may help identify potential problems so interventions can be delivered early.

Assessment Instruments

A 1-10 scale is an easy way to assess a patient's symptoms (pain, distress, anxiety etc.) and this can be easily communicated to the rest of the healthcare team. This scale can be used at each appointment to track changes and allow for additional consultation as needed. A score of 5 or more may alert the need for specific referrals to mental health professionals (NCCN, 2010a). The tool is also effective because it can be used repeatedly to help assess improvements and new problems with distress.

INTERVENTIONS TO PROMOTE PSYCHOSOCIAL FUNCTIONING

Communication with Children

Parents with children can experience particular psychosocial challenges with a diagnosis of cancer. It is important to discuss the cancer diagnosis in developmentally appropriate ways (Harpham, 2004). Young children may believe a parent's illness is a result of their behaviors and that they are being punished. The child may also have questions about how an individual contracts cancer and how it is spread or they may be curious about why mom is losing her hair. It is important to create an environment where children are able to ask questions and receive age-appropriate answers. In many communities there are support groups that target the psychological needs of young children, teenagers, and partners.

Families with child rearing concerns or children with concerns often benefit from services that are tailored to these needs. Mutual disclosure of fears, anxieties, and hopes between mothers, significant others, and children appear to have benefits for both the woman and her family (Sigal, Perry, Robbins, Gagné, & Nassif, 2003). Teenage children can have particular challenges and difficulty accepting and adjusting to the diagnosis of cancer

in a mother. Verbalizing their feelings and concerns with their parents, significant others and, perhaps, another trusted adult, may be very helpful.

Children and teens should be encouraged to go to school, complete homework, and continue to participate in extracurricular activities and sports. Parents may need to rely on the assistance of others from time to time to enable children to continue to participate in these activities. If a woman is unable to attend an activity with a child, she should make every effort to find out about it when the child comes home. It may be possible to videotape a sports event or other activity to enable the parent to share in the activity with the child at a later point. Helpful interventions include preparing the children for what is going to happen in the immediate future and what the more distant future holds.

For some, relationships are strengthened by the challenges imposed by cancer and its treatment. Open communication with children and honest answers to emotionally laden questions, including questions about death, in age-appropriate terms, is important. Parents may need coaching and assistance with these issues. Open communication helps the parents to understand the child's worries and thoughts and can lead to increased understanding. Support should provide concrete strategies that are child-appropriate and child-oriented. Specific suggestions for talking with children are provided in Table 9-4.

Family Relationships

Relationships are tested and challenged throughout the diagnosis, treatment, and survival in cancer. Relationships that are already fraught with conflict may experience an exacerbation of problems with the diagnosis. Even caring, committed relationships will be stressed by the diagnosis. Emotional distance may surface because of the inability to discuss feelings about grief, loss, change, and potential loss; significant changes in body images or a sense of loss of femininity; and partners wanting to protect a woman from other dis-

TABLE 9-4: TALKING WITH CHILDREN ABOUT CANCER

- Always be honest with the child. If he or she asks a difficult question, think, and then reply in an honest, but as nonthreatening way as possible.
- Assure your children that they will be cared for, no matter what happens during or as a result of treatment.
- Remind them that cancer is not universally fatal and try to give them concrete examples of people they know and can relate to who are long-term survivors of the disease with good prognostic factors.
- Assure children of all ages that there is nothing they could have said, done, or thought that led to the development of the cancer.
- Assure children that it is quite normal to be angry, scared, or sad when someone they love is diagnosed with cancer.
- Assure them that even though the appearance of their mother may change during treatment, they cannot "catch" the cancer.
- It is sometimes helpful for children to participate in a support group with other children so they realize they are not the only family experiencing a diagnosis of cancer.
- Help them to understand how and to what extent they should disclose about what is happening in their family to others.
- Inform them that others may be reluctant to talk with them or, conversely, seem like they are overly kind and generous. Tell them this is a normal reaction, because they might not be sure what to do or they may be really sad about the diagnosis as well.
- Be honest that home routines will probably be disrupted and that they may need to assume some extra responsibilities for a period of time and, possibly, permanently.
- Remind children that even if a parent cannot attend a sports event or other activity, it does not mean that the parent is not interested. Remind the child that it usually saddens parents as well when they have to miss those types of events. Try to send someone else.
- Remind children that they are still expected to keep up with studies and participate in extracurricular activities. The diagnosis is not an excuse to not study.

tressing situations or information. Women without a partner, supportive friends or family may have significant distress because of a lack of support.

Strategies that might be helpful with families:

- Clarify the diagnosis, treatment options and side effects. Take time to ensure that the patient understands each issue.
- Explain that cancer has a trajectory and that needs change over time. Assure the patient and the family that they will receive support during each phase as needed.
- Remind the patient that psychosocial health is just as important as physical health. Explain that this is why psychosocial assessment is conducted regularly.

- Acknowledge that distress is common, expected points when distress might increase, and that the patient needs to communicate about distress in addition to the healthcare provider assessing for distress.
- Suggest concrete recommendations for coping with distress, including journaling, speaking with a trained counselor (psychologist, nurse, chaplain, social worker etc.), and joining a support group.
- Coordinate resources and make referrals as indicated.
- Manage symptoms promptly. Assess effectiveness of interventions.

Financial, Employment and Legal Concerns

All women, regardless of their socioeconomic situation, may eventually have financial, employment, and legal issues that are related to the diagnosis of cancer. Addressing these issues often improves quality of life for these women. The costs associated with cancer treatment can be staggering. In addition to healthcare costs for surgery, chemotherapy, and radiotherapy, there are many hidden costs. These include co-pays, transportation costs when going to treatment, parking costs at treatment, time away from work for the patient and perhaps a significant other, increased childcare costs, and other nonreimbursable charges. Unemployment or time away from work can result in an inability to meet regular living expenses. These costs can easily and quickly deplete savings. In many cases there are agencies and social service resources that can assist families with these needs. Patients are often unaware of these resources. Ongoing assessment in this area is essential with prompt referral when problems become evident. Table 9-5 lists some resources that patients may or may not be aware of related to meeting the costs of cancer care.

Some women face multiple issues in the workplace, whereas others do not. Some women benefit from coaching and anticipatory preparation of what to expect when returning to work. Co-workers may not know how to approach a person who is newly diagnosed or returning to work after an absence.

Sometimes employers may be unsure of how much a patient can or cannot do. They may not be aware of lingering fatigue, even after treatment is complete. Women with cancer need to anticipate what problems might occur and be prepared to address these issues.

Depression

The exact prevalence of depression and other mental health problems in women with cancer is not fully understood. It may be as high as twice the incidence seen in the general population (Gorman, 2006).

Antidepressants may help patients who feel extreme sadness, hopelessness, or a lack of interest in activities. Medications may also be used to help patients sleep, relax, and begin to cope with the diagnosis. As with any medication, it is important to discuss potential side effects and interactions that may occur with current medications and medical treatments. Common side effects of anti-depressants and anti-anxiety medications include

- nausea
- weight gain
- sexual dysfunction
- fatigue or insomnia
- dry mouth
- blurred vision
- constipation
- dizziness
- mental slowing.

TABLE 9-5: TIPS AND RESOURCES FOR MANAGING FINANCIAL CONCERNS (1 OF 2)

Instruct the patient to keep records of the following:
- medical bills from all healthcare providers
- claims filed
- reimbursements (payments from insurance companies) received and explanations of benefits
- dates, names, and outcomes of contacts made with insurers and others
- non-reimbursed or outstanding medical and related costs
- meals and lodging expenses
- travel (including gas and parking)
- admissions, clinic visits, lab work, diagnostic tests, procedures, treatments
- drugs given and prescriptions filled.

continued on next page

TABLE 9-5: TIPS AND RESOURCES FOR MANAGING FINANCIAL CONCERNS (2 OF 2)
Instruct the patient on legislation for insurance coverage and employment
• *COBRA (Consolidated Omnibus Budget and Reconciliation Act of 1986)* – COBRA gives people the right to temporarily continue health insurance coverage at the employer's group rates, but these rates are usually much higher than those paid when employed. This coverage is available when coverage is lost due to certain "qualifying events," such as stopping work, reducing work hours, divorce or legal separation, the covered person becoming entitled to Medicare, a dependent child no longer considered to be dependent according to the terms of the plan, or the death of the employee. COBRA allows people to continue coverage of their group medical insurance for a certain period of time, depending on the qualifying event.
• *The Health Insurance Portability and Accountability Act of 1996 (HIPAA)* – Allows a person who has had health insurance for at least 12 months with no long loss of coverage (usually more than 63 days) to change jobs and be guaranteed other coverage with a new employer who also offers group insurance. In this situation there may be no waiting period and the pre-existing condition exclusion may be reduced or not applied. The act also guarantees the availability of group insurance coverage for employers of small businesses of 2 to 50 people.
• *The Family and Medical Leave Act of 1993 (FMLA)* – This act requires employers (with at least 50 employees) to provide up to 12 weeks of unpaid, job-protected leave to eligible employees for certain family and medical reasons. Employees are eligible if they have worked for a covered employer for at least 1250 hours in the previous 12 months. For the time period of the FMLA leave, the employer must maintain the employee's medical insurance coverage under company group health plan.
• *The Americans with Disabilities Act of 1990 (ADA)* – This act offers protection against discrimination in the workplace to anyone who has, or has had, certain disabilities, including any diagnosis of cancer. It requires private employers who employ 15 or more people, labor unions, employment agencies, and government agencies to treat employees equally, including the benefits offered them, without regard to their disabling condition or medical history.

See Table 9-6 for examples of commonly used antidepressants. Other interventions that might be helpful for the woman with depression include:

• Encouraging the depressed woman to continue treatment until symptoms improve or to talk to the doctor about a different treatment if there is no improvement after 2 or 3 weeks.

TABLE 9-6: COMMON ANTIDEPRESSANTS	
Tricyclic Antidepressants • amitriptyline (Elavil) • clomipramine (Anafranil) • desipramine (Norpramin) • doxepin (Sinequan) • imipramine (Tofranil) • nortriptyline (Pamelor) ***Selective Serotonin Reuptake Inhibitors (SSRIs)*** • citalopram (Celexa) • fluoxetine (Prozac) • fluvoxamine (Luvox) • paroxetine (Paxil) • sertraline (Zoloft)	***Monoamine Oxidase Inhibitors (MAOIs)*** • tranylcypromine (Parnate) • phenelzine (Nardil) ***Atypical Antidepressants*** • bupropion (Wellbutrin) • trazodone (Desyrel) • nefazodone (Serzone) • mirtazapine (Remeron) • maprotiline (Ludiomil) • venlafaxine (Effexor)

- Promote any form of physical activity, especially mild exercise such as daily walks.

- Help the patient make appointments for mental health treatment, if needed.

- Provide assistance or arrange for transportation for treatment, if needed.

- Keep in mind that caregivers and family members can also become depressed. Encourage family members to take time to get the help and support they need (Rodin et al., 2007).

Support for Long-Term Survivors

Long-term survivors continue to need support as they move forward with their lives. Although there is a tendency to assume that if the individual is disease-free, they will not have psychosocial concerns, that is not necessarily the case. Table 9-7 provides interventions that are helpful with this population.

Interventions to Promote Adjustment Across the Trajectory

Hope is important throughout the cancer trajectory. Hope may change throughout the trajectory, but there is a need to continually help patients and families identify hope in different situations. For the newly diagnosed, it might mean hope that the therapy will be effective. For the survivor, it might mean hope for a new normalcy in her life. For someone in the terminal phases, it might mean hope for good symptom management, finishing projects, or experiencing closure with loved ones.

Quality of life is also improved when problems are assessed and confronted directly. Nurses need to assess for symptoms that can be managed such as pain, psychosocial distress, or fatigue. Nurses need to try to explain to the patient why the symptom is occurring, if it is a common one, and what concrete steps are going to be taken to decrease the negative effects of the symptoms. When symptoms are decreased, quality of life usually is improved.

Support groups often help individuals to realize that many others share similar feelings and concerns. Support groups can also be an excellent and efficient way to provide patient education. Before referring a patient to a support group, it is important to understand the focus of the support group, ground rules, biases of the facilitator, and how acute emotional distress is managed. If the group's philosophy is congruent with the healthcare team and the patient's value system, it may be a useful adjunct to improve quality of life. Cancer support groups are often another place where people can receive education. Support groups can have a number of purposes and approaches. They offer a way for people with cancer and, in many cases, their significant others to come together and talk with others facing similar problems and challenges. Support groups often have an educational component or lecture, in addition to sharing. When the educational component is delivered by a professional with expertise on the subject, it can be a very effective means to communicate about and educate persons on issues related to cancer treatment.

A referral to a cancer information or resource center can also be a therapeutic strategy. An information center is usually staffed by a registered nurse who provides education and support. Resource centers often distribute brochures, videos, educational models, wigs, head coverings, and temporary prostheses, which all help facilitate psychosocial adjustment. Nurses can often provide guidance on internet searches and answer specific questions. The continuity of the same nurses, no matter what services the patient is receiving (ie chemotherapy, surgery, radiotherapy, etc) can be very helpful and decrease the sense of fragmentation in care. Many institutions now offer such services and healthcare providers should encourage and refer patients to utilize such services.

Psychosocial Providers

Psychosocial services should be provided by oncology caregivers as part of total medical care.

TABLE 9-7: STRATEGIES AND INTERVENTIONS TO PREPARE INDIVIDUALS AND FAMILIES FOR LONG-TERM SURVIVORSHIP

- Give patients and families a range of what to expect in terms of prognosis, physical symptoms, emotional concerns, and sexual function.

- Remind patients and significant others that they may never return to "normal" and that they may need to establish a new normalcy.

- Specifically define what symptoms should promptly be reported for further evaluation.

- Describe the anticipated follow-up schedule for office visits, scans, and laboratory work with the rationale for the proposed schedule.

- Teach the patient what tertiary prevention is and what specific tertiary screening measures will be recommended; for example, colon screening, bone densitometry, gynecologic screening.

- Develop a wellness plan that includes a specific strategy for exercise, diet, skin cancer prevention, and smoking cessation when indicated.

- Remind the patient and significant others that it is not uncommon to have "trigger" events that are upsetting, such as the anniversary of diagnosis, the diagnosis of a loved one with a similar disease, or feelings of anxiety surrounding things that remind the patient of unpleasant aspects of treatment.

- Discuss that recovery from treatment is a gradual process and it may take a year or more before full energy returns.

- Assess the patient for mental health problems, and manage depression and anxiety early. Remind patients and family members that it may not be uncommon to have some feelings of depression, anxiety, or being overwhelmed, even though treatment is completed. Discuss that there are treatments to manage these symptoms and that it is important for the patient to bring these concerns to the attention of the healthcare provider to explore the best means to improve this aspect of quality of life.

- Acknowledge that the patient may need to adopt a new self-image in terms of energy, physical appearance, and sexuality. For many, staying active and exploring new hobbies and activities helps develop a new self-image.

- Assess for financial problems. Survivors may be paying for the costs of care long after care is complete. If appropriate, remind the patient that social services may be able to assist.

- Discuss the need to try to maintain healthcare coverage. If the patient or family member carrying the insurance wants to switch jobs or something else occurs that would lead to a lapse in coverage, it is important to consider a referral to social services.

- The patient and significant others may want to consider becoming advocates for others with cancer or volunteer in some other way. Some individuals find benefit from continued participation in a support group.

- Some patients experience problems or changes with memory or concentration after chemotherapy. Instruct patients to let their healthcare providers know about this, as sometimes there are strategies to decrease the impact of these problems.

- If the family history suggests hereditary susceptibility for developing the cancer and the family has not yet received counseling about genetic testing, it is appropriate to consider learning more about genetic risk.

- When meeting new people or dating it can be awkward to know when to disclose that the individual has completed cancer treatment. Talking with other survivors can help make persons more comfortable with how and when to disclose. Survivors should be instructed that they may need to plan what to disclose, how to disclose it, and how much to disclose.

- Recognize that there may still be challenges in the workplace related to follow-up care, energy levels, or other health-related concerns. Encourage the patient to discuss these needs with her employer. If problems cannot be resolved, a referral to social services, local cancer advocacy services or, perhaps legal resources, may be indicated.

This responsibility initially falls to oncologists and oncology nurses. Often, referrals to specialists in psycho-oncology are indicated. Table 9-8 provides an overview of healthcare providers who contribute to promoting psychosocial health in oncology patients and their families.

TABLE 9-8: ONCOLOGY TEAM MEMBERS WHO CONTRIBUTE TO PSYCHOSOCIAL CARE (1 OF 2)

Medical Oncologist: The oncologist directs care related to chemotherapy and targeted therapy. The oncologist may take responsibility for referrals for psychosocial care. Often the oncologist will prescribe pharmacologic agents to help mange psychological problems and other symptoms causing psychosocial distress.

Radiation Oncologist: The radiation oncologist plans all treatment with radiation therapy.

Radiation Oncology Technologist: The radiation oncology technologist delivers the radiation dose as prescribed by the radiation oncologist. The technologist sees the patient on a daily basis and assesses for complications and tolerance of therapy.

Surgical Oncologist: The surgeon provides surgical care, including removal of tumor, and often assists with the placement of implanted ports and other infusion devices.

Plastic Surgeon: The plastic surgeon provides all plastic and reconstructive surgery and services.

Nurse: Oncology nurses provide ongoing assessment and psychosocial support for patients undergoing active treatment as well as for long-term survivors. They may recommend interventions to facilitate psychosocial adjustment, and they also help communicate concerns to other members of the oncology team. They typically work with medical oncologists, radiation oncologists, surgeons, and plastic surgeons and also deliver chemotherapy according to the medical oncologist's prescription.

Pharmacist: Pharmacists fill prescriptions and dispense drugs and are also a great source of information. They educate healthcare professionals and patients about the expected effects and side effects of pharmacologic agents.

Dietician: Dieticians work with patients who are having difficulty eating and help other patients to establish appropriate dietary programs. They can help long-term survivors develop healthy habits.

Social Worker: Oncology social workers can have diverse job responsibilities that may include helping individuals to find support groups, dealing directly with financial issues, providing guidance for how to deal with workplace issues, and assisting with paperwork, such as advance directives or living wills. They also provide direct support through counseling and finding ways to assist with transportation to office visits, nutritional supplements, wigs, or prosthetics.

Psychologist: Psychologists can help patients and families by talking with them and identifying specific psychosocial problems. Once identified, they can help develop a concrete plan for how to deal with psychosocial problems.

Psychiatrist: Psychiatrists can be particularly helpful with patients and families who have underlying mental illness concerns that may have existed prior to the diagnosis of cancer or have been exacerbated by the diagnosis and treatment. They can provide supportive therapy as well as prescribe medications for these disorders.

Patient Educator: Many institutions and medical practices have nurses who serve as patient educators. Their primary responsibility is to provide individual and group education on cancer and its treatment. They often work in information centers and help patients select other appropriate materials such as videos, pamphlets, internet sites, and other educational tools. They may offer regular classes on cancer related topics. They often provide individualized education as well as facilitate support groups.

Prosthetics Fitter: Prosthetics fitters are certified and trained to assist with fitting bras and other prosthetics for women undergoing breast surgery, such as mastectomy, lumpectomy, and reconstruction. They provide extensive psychosocial support and assist women with adapting to the body image changes associated with breast surgery.

continued on next page

TABLE 9-8: ONCOLOGY TEAM MEMBERS WHO CONTRIBUTE TO PSYCHOSOCIAL CARE (2 OF 2)

Enterstomal Therapist: An enterstomal therapist is a nurse with specialized training in managing ostomies. They often provide extensive psychosocial and psychosexual care to patients and their partners to assist them in managing an ostomy.

Genetics Counselor: Families with a hereditary susceptibility for developing cancer should be referred to genetics counselors or advanced practice nurses who are credentialed in genetics to explore the risks and benefits of genetic testing for their particular families.

Home Care Nurse: Some patients may need assistance with healthcare needs at home, including wound care or infusion services. While in the home setting, home care nurses often identify psychosocial issues and can either manage these issues or refer the patient to other members of the healthcare team.

Occupational Therapist: Occupational therapists can help patients regain, develop, or relearn skills needed for independent living. Many breast cancer patients with lymphedema utilize the services of these professionals.

Physical Therapist: Physical therapists often work with occupational therapists to help patients learn exercises and instruct on ways to regain strength and mobility. They may also help with lymphedema services.

Hospice Workers: Hospice workers provide care to the patient and family in the terminal phase of the illness. This includes a team of nurses, aides, and other members.

Chaplain: Chaplains assist patients and families with the spiritual aspects of their care. They may pray with the patient, discuss existential concerns, and provide supportive counseling. They may be based in the institution or patients may know them from their own religious institutions.

Barriers to Providing Comprehensive Psychosocial Care

There are several barriers that prevent women from receiving adequate psychosocial care (Hewitt et al., 2004). Care has gradually shifted from inpatient to outpatient care. Many outpatient clinics lack a full complement of specialists in psychosocial care. Furthermore, mental health services are often limited in insurance coverage, and many women lack the financial means to afford such specialty care. Busy clinical settings also discourage women from discussing psychosocial concerns, as they may have stigma, or be perceived as unnecessary extras. Table 9-9 provides an overview of the barriers to assessing and promoting psychosocial care. When such barriers are identified in a care setting, direct efforts need to be taken to address and remove the barrier.

TABLE 9-9: BARRIERS TO APPROPRIATE USE OF PSYCHOSOCIAL SERVICES

- Poor access to services due to the lack of readily available providers in some settings
- Healthcare provider lack of awareness of community services
- Reluctance of the patient and family to ask for help
- Lack of communication between the healthcare provider and patient about psychosocial concerns
- Poor health insurance coverage for psychosocial services
- Expense of cancer care is staggering; many lack financial resources for additional services such as psychosocial care
- Fragmentation among care providers
- Lack of a systematic method to routinely assess for psychosocial distress
- Lack of time to assess for difficulties
- Lack of widespread adoption of clinical practice guidelines to promote psychosocial functioning
- Perception that psychosocial services are secondary to treatment needs
- General misconceptions about mental health care and psychological functioning
- Inadequate quality assurance and accountability for psychosocial care

SUMMARY

Psychosocial issues are important elements of the cancer experience for a woman, affecting her outlook and ability to cope with her diagnosis and treatment. A patient needs enough information to make informed decisions that are congruent with her values and family's needs. This means information that is culturally sensitive and at an appropriate level to be comprehended. After a decision is made, the patient and family need to be supported in the decision, regardless of whether the healthcare provider personally agrees with the decision. Comprehensive care that includes psychosocial assessment and intervention promotes adjustment to a diagnosis of cancer and associated treatment and ultimately results in improved quality of life.

EXAM QUESTIONS

CHAPTER 9
Questions 71-82

Note: Choose the one option that BEST answers each question.

71. When responding to a stressor during an acute period, individuals may respond with

    a. higher blood pressure but lower respiratory rates.

    b. higher blood pressure and higher respiratory rates.

    c. lower epinephrine levels and higher blood pressure.

    d. higher epinephrine levels and lower respiratory rates.

72. During a biopsy, a woman is often overwhelmed by

    a. healthcare providers.

    b. uncertainty.

    c. lack of family support.

    d. denial.

73. Two symptoms of anxiety are

    a. slow breathing and excessive sleeping.

    b. irritability and trembling.

    c. the inability to absorb information and a slow pulse.

    d. constipation and binge eating.

74. When assessing a cancer patient for depression, an appropriate question is

    a. "Have you felt like you have a lump in your throat?"

    b. "Tell me about your sleep problems."

    c. "Do you have trouble breathing?"

    d. "Where is your leg pain?"

75. A marker of depression is

    a. anemia.

    b. slow, even respirations.

    c. intolerance to cold.

    d. loss of interest in daily activities.

76. In general, women with depressive symptoms may need professional help when their symptoms have lasted

    a. 4 days.

    b. 2 weeks.

    c. 4 months.

    d. 2 years.

77. Strategies to combat fatigue include

    a. sleeping.

    b. engaging in a supervised exercise program.

    c. taking sleep medication.

    d. taking antidepressants.

78. A risk factor for significant psychosocial distress, which suggests a need for further evaluation in cancer patients, is

    a. developmental stage.

    b. fever.

    c. abdominal pain.

    d. weak social support system.

continued on next page

213

79. An appropriate choice to manage moderate
    pain might be

    a. oxycodone.

    b. amitriptyline.

    c. Desipramine.

    d. Gabapentin.

80. The assessment instrument that can be used to
    evaluate pain, anxiety, and distress is the

    a. Brief Symptom Inventory.

    b. Karnofosy Scale.

    c. One to Ten Scale.

    d. Facing Cancer Symptoms Scale.

81. A common side effect of antidepressants is

    a. diarrhea.

    b. weight gain.

    c. weight loss.

    d. drooling.

82. An effective intervention for a cancer patient
    who is feeling all alone with her diagnosis and
    overwhelmed with her lack of knowledge
    about how to manage her illness is to

    a. create some small tasks for her to do.

    b. tell her to stop feeling sorry for herself.

    c. refer her to a cancer support group.

    d. find out what television shows she enjoys.

REFERENCES

Aukst-Margeti, B., Jakovljevi, M., Margeti, B., Bisan, M., & Samija, M. (2005). Religiosity, depression, and pain in patients with breast cancer. *General Hospital Psychiatry, 27*(4), 250-255.

Bower, J.E. (2005). Fatigue in cancer patients and survivors: Mechanisms and treatment. *Primary Psychiatry, 12*(5), 53-57.

Bruera, E., Willey, J.S., Ewert-Flannagan, P.A., Cline, M.K., Kaur, G., Shen, L., et al. (2005). Pain intensity assessment by bedside nurses and palliative care consultants: A retrospective study. *Supportive Care in Cancer, 13*(4), 228-231.

Carroll, J.K., Kohli, S., Mustian, K.M., Roscoe, J.A., & Morrow, G.R. (2007). Pharmacologic treatment of cancer-related fatigue. *Oncologist, 12*(Suppl 1), 43-51.

Chappy, S.L. (2004). Women's experience with breast biopsy. *AORN Journal, 80*(5), 885-901.

Davis Kirsch, S.E., Brandt, P.A., & Lewis, F.M. (2003). Making the most of the moment: When a child's mother has breast cancer. *Cancer Nursing, 26*(1), 47-54.

Dy, S.M., Asch, S.M., Naeim, A., Sanati, H., Walling, A., & Lorenz, K.A. (2008). Evidence-based standards for cancer pain management. *Journal of Clinical Oncology, 26*(23), 3879-3885.

Engel, J., Kerr, J., Schlesinger-Raab, A., Eckel, R., Sauer, H., & Hölzel, D. (2003). Predictors of quality of life of breast cancer patients. *Acta Oncologica, 42*(7), 710-718.

Foley, K.M. (2005). Management of cancer pain. In V.T. DeVita, Jr., S. Hellman, & S.A. Rosenberg (Eds.), *Cancer: Principles and practice of oncology* (7th ed., pp 2615-2649). Philadelphia: Lippincott Williams & Wilkins.

Ganz, P.A., Kwan, L., Stanton, A.L., Krupnick, J.L., Rowland, J.H., Meyerowitz, B.E., et al. (2004). Quality of life at the end of primary treatment of breast cancer: First results from the Moving Beyond Cancer randomized trial. *Journal of the National Cancer Institute, 96*(5), 376-387.

Golden-Kreutz, D.M., Thornton, L.M., Wells-Di Gregorio, S., Frierson, G.M., Jim, H.S., Carpenter, K.M., et al. (2005). Traumatic stress, perceived global stress, and life events: Prospectively predicting quality of life in breast cancer patients. *Health Psychology, 24*(3), 288-296.

Gorman, L.M. (2006). The psychosocial impact of cancer on the individual, family, and society. In R.M. Carroll-Johnson, L.M. Gorman, & N.J. Bush (Eds.), *Psychosocial nursing care along the cancer continuum* (2nd ed., pp. 3-23). Pittsburgh, PA: Oncology Nursing Society.

Harpham, W.S. (2004). *When a parent has cancer: A guide to caring for your children.* New York: HarperCollins.

Hewitt, M., Herdman, R., & Holland, J. (Eds.). (2004). *Meeting psychosocial needs of women with breast cancer.* Washington, DC: National Academies Press.

Jacobsen, P.B., Donovan, K.A., Vadaparampil, S.T., & Small, B.J. (2007). Systematic review and meta-analysis of psychological and activity-based interventions for cancer-related fatigue. *Health Psychology, 26*(6), 660-667.

Jacobsen, P.B. & Jim, H.S. (2008). Psychosocial interventions for anxiety and depression in adult cancer patients: Achievements and challenges. *CA: A Cancer Journal for Clinicians, 58*(4), 214-230.

Kendall, A., Mahue-Giangreco, M., Carpenter, C., Ganz, P., & Bernstein, L. (2005). Influence of exercise activity on quality of life in long-term breast cancer survivors. *Quality of Life Research, 14*(2), 361-371.

National Comprehensive Cancer Network. (2010a) Distress management (Version V.1.2010) National Comprehensive Cancer Network, Inc. Retrieved July 3, 2010, from http://www .nccn.org

National Comprehensive Cancer Network. (2010b) *Clinical practice guidelines in oncology. Cancer-related fatigue.* (Version 1.2010). Retrieved July 3, 2010, from www.nccn.org/ professionals/physician_gls/PDF/fatigue.pdf

National Comprehensive Cancer Network. (2010c). *Pain management.* (VersionV.1.2010). National Comprehensive Cancer Network, Inc. Retrieved July 3, 2010, from http://www .nccn.org

Pharo, G.H. & Zhou, L. (2005). Pharmacologic management of cancer pain. *Journal of the American Osteopathic Association, 105*(11, Suppl. 5), S21-S28.

Rodin, G., Lloyd, N., Katz, M., Green, E., Mackay, J.A., & Wong, R.K. (2007). The treatment of depression in cancer patients: A systematic review. *Supportive Care in Cancer, 15*(2), 123-36.

Schou, I., Ekeberg, Ø., Sandvik, L., Hjermstad, M., & Ruland, C. (2005). Multiple predictors of health-related quality of life in early stage breast cancer. Data from a year follow-up study compared with the general population. *Quality of Life Research, 14*(8), 1813-1823.

Sigal, J.J., Perry, J.C., Robbins, J.M., Gagné, M., & Nassif, E. (2003). Maternal preoccupation and parenting as predictors of emotional and behavioral problems in children of women with breast cancer. *Journal of Clinical Oncology, 21*(6), 1155-1160.

Wiffen, P.J. & McQuay, H.J. (2007). Oral morphine for cancer pain. *Cochrane Database of Systematic Reviews,* (4), CD003868.

CHAPTER 10

SEXUALITY:
WOMEN WITH CANCER

CHAPTER OBJECTIVE

After completing this chapter on sexuality issues, the reader will be able to discuss psychologic, functioning, and fertility issues associated with sexuality in women with cancer and identify interventions to address these issues.

LEARNING OBJECTIVES

After studying this chapter, the reader will be able to

1. describe at least two physical and psychological changes that affect a woman's sexuality when she is diagnosed with cancer.

2. discuss the effect of cancer treatment modalities on the woman's sexual functioning and fertility.

3. identify components of a sexual history.

4. identify strategies to promote sexual integrity.

INTRODUCTION

Sexuality is defined by each patient and partner within a context of gender, age, personal attitudes, and religious and cultural values (Katz, 2007). It is an important component to quality of life no matter the patient's age, experience, or status in life. When a woman faces a serious illness such as cancer, her sexuality is affected in many ways. The experience of each woman is unique.

Sex and sexuality are important components of everyday life. The difference between sex and sexuality is that sex or sexual intercourse is considered an activity shared between two individuals. Sexuality is more about the way an individual feels and is linked to human needs for caring, closeness, and touch.

Sexuality affects quality of life, self-image, and relationships with others. Patients and healthcare providers routinely exchange information about how treatment will affect nutrition, pain, and ability to return to work. Despite the profound impact of sexuality on daily life, it is often overlooked or not discussed as a woman receives treatment for cancer. Many patients and healthcare providers feel uncomfortable discussing sexuality. Others feel it is "less important" than other aspects of cancer treatment.

There are many myths associated with sexuality. It is normal for individuals to be interested in sex and have sexual feelings throughout their lives. Many cancers occur more commonly in people older than 50 years of age. Popular culture and media often suggest that sex and sexuality is only a concern or need for the young and that older people universally experience decreased libido and sexual dysfunction. Those beliefs are largely myths.

Many men and women can and do stay sexually active until the end of life. It is true that sexual response and function may change with aging (Katz, 2007). These changes may occur before a diagnosis of cancer. A decrease in sexual desire and problems with vaginal dryness may increase during and after menopause.

As with any issue that patients face, nurses can support them by approaching sexual assessment in a competent, open, and caring manner. This chapter will review strategies of assessment and review interventions that can help patients face sexuality issues.

PHYSIOLOGY

Sexuality encompasses all that an individual is as a human being. Sexuality impacts gender identities and roles, sexual orientation, feelings of pleasure and intimacy, and reproductive processes. Sexuality is expressed in many ways, including thoughts, dress, attitudes, values, roles, and relationships. A person's views of sexuality often are framed by his or her gender identity, culture, religion, and life experiences.

Sexual Response

In general there are four phases in the sexual response. A person usually goes through the phases in the same order; however, the sexual response can be stopped at any phase. The phases are outlined in Table 10-1.

Menopause

The ovaries usually stop producing eggs and greatly reduce their hormone output at about 50 years of age, although the age for menopause varies among women. Many women fear that their sexual desire will go away with menopause; however, for many women the drop in ovarian hormones does not lessen sexual desire at all.

Estrogens and androgens are the hormones that help a woman feel desire (Hawkins, Roberto-Nichols, & Stanley-Haney, 2008). Androgens are thought of as "male" hormones, but women's bodies also make small amounts of androgen. About half of the androgens in women are made in the adrenal glands. The ovaries make the rest of a woman's androgen. When a woman goes through menopause, the adrenal glands continue secreting hormones. There is usually enough androgen, even after the ovaries stop making it, to feel sexual desire.

The Role of Estrogen

Estrogen helps keep the vagina moist and flexible and helps it change during sexual arousal (Wilmoth, 2006a). When a woman is not excited, her vagina is not an open cavity. It stays relaxed and folded together so that its walls touch each other. As a woman starts to feel aroused, the vagina gets longer and wider. The cells lining the vagina

TABLE 10-1: PHASES OF THE SEXUAL RESPONSE

- Desire is an interest in sex. This might include thoughts about sex or attractions to another individual. Sexual desire is a normal part of life from the teenage years onward.

- Excitement is the phase when arousal occurs. Touching and stroking feel much more intense when an individual is aroused. Excitement also results from sexual fantasies and sensual sights, sounds, scents, and tastes. Physically, excitement can cause increased pulse and heart rate, increased blood pressure, increased vaginal lubrication, and increased body temperature.

- Orgasm is the sexual climax. The nervous system creates intense pleasure in the genitals. The muscles around the genitals contract in rhythm, sending waves of feeling through the body. This is associated with feelings of pleasure and satisfaction.

- Resolution occurs within a few minutes after an orgasm. The body returns to its unexcited state. Heartbeat and breathing slow down. The extra blood drains out of the genital area. Mental excitement subsides.

(Katz, 2007)

"sweat" droplets of fluid that make the vagina slippery. Changes in the vagina depend on the hormone estrogen. If a woman's estrogen levels are low, as they might be after menopause, these changes in the vagina may take place more slowly (Katz, 2007). The drop in estrogen at menopause results in

- thinning of the vaginal lining
- decreased elasticity of the vaginal walls
- vaginal atrophy.

Overall Impact of Treatment

Lack of Desire

Both men and women often lose interest in sexual intercourse during cancer treatment, at least for a time (Katz, 2007). At first, concern for survival is so great that sexual issues are often lower on the hierarchy of needs. When women are in active treatment, loss of desire may result from worry, uncertainty, depression, grief, nausea, pain, or fatigue. Any emotion or thought that keeps a woman from feeling excited can interfere with desire for sex. Distracting thoughts can keep her from getting aroused (Wilmoth, 2006b).

Many women who have cancer worry that a partner will find her unattractive because of changes in her body or other stressors. These worries can also affect desire.

Pain

Pain during intercourse is a common problem for women in active cancer treatment. It is often related to changes in the vagina's size or moistness. These changes can occur following pelvic surgery, radiation therapy, menopause, or treatment that has affected a woman's hormones (Stead, 2003).

Sometimes the pain exacerbates a phenomenon known as vaginismus. If a woman has vaginismus, the muscles around the opening of the vagina become tense without the woman being aware of it (Katz, 2007). Her partner cannot penetrate the vagina. Pushing harder increases the woman's pain

because her vaginal muscles are clenched in a spasm. Vaginismus can be treated with counseling and some special relaxation training.

Premature Menopause

Premature menopause can also affect sexuality. Symptoms are often more severe than the slow changes that happen during a natural menopause, including increased and more severe mood swings, increased hot flashes, and vaginal dryness (Graziottin & Basson, 2004). Presently, most women without a diagnosis of cancer can expect to live at least one-third of their lives in the postmenopausal state. For younger women treated aggressively for cancer, its duration can be significantly longer. The risk of premature menopause for women receiving chemotherapy is significant for woman between 35 and 45 years of age (Rogers & Kristjanson, 2002).

Vaginal Dryness

Vaginal dryness is an often overlooked concern that is related to both premature menopause as well as some of the therapies utilized to treat cancer (Stead, 2003). Cancer treatments as well as menopause commonly reduce the amount of moisture that the vagina produces during sexual excitement.

Women often need extra lubrication to make intercourse comfortable and pleasurable. Initially, they can be instructed to use a water-based vaginal lubricant that has no perfumes, coloring, spermicide, or flavors added, as these chemicals can irritate genital tissues (Levine, Williams, & Hartmann, 2008). Lubricants can usually be found near the birth control or feminine hygiene products in drug stores or grocery stores. Common brands include K-Y Jelly and Astroglide. Warming gels can cause burning in some women, so they should be advised to avoid using them.

For some women, lubricants are not enough to replace vaginal moisture. Replens and K-Y Liquibeads are vaginal moisturizers that can be used two or three times a week to help keep the vagina moist and at a more normal acid balance (pH). The effects of these products last longer than those of lubricants, and they can be bought without a prescription. Lubrin and Astroglide Silken Secret are other moisturizers that are marketed as longer lasting than typical lubricants. Women can be encouraged to try different products to see which is most effective (Levine et al., 2008).

Some women do well with local vaginal hormones to help vaginal dryness. These hormones are applied to and absorbed into the genital area, rather than taken by mouth. They come in gel, cream, ring, and tablet forms. Most are put into the vagina, although some creams can be applied to the vulva. Local vaginal hormones must be prescribed by a doctor. The use of these agents is sometimes controversial in women with hormonally based breast cancers (Schultz, Klein, Beck, Stava, & Sellin, 2005).

Petroleum jelly (Vaseline), skin lotions, and other oil-based lubricants are not good choices for vaginal lubrication. In some women, they may raise the risk of a yeast or other vaginal infection (Levine et al., 2008). If latex condoms are used, they can also be damaged by petroleum products and lotions. Similarly, condoms or gels that contain nonoxynol-9 can irritate the vagina, especially if the tissues are already dry or fragile.

Before intercourse, women should be instructed to put some lubricant around and inside the entrance of the vagina. Some lubricant can also be spread on the partner's penis or fingers. This helps get the lubricant inside the vagina. Many couples treat this as a part of foreplay. Depending on how long intercourse lasts and the severity of the vaginal dryness, it may be necessary to stop briefly and smooth on some extra lubricant. Even if a woman uses vaginal moisturizers every few days, it may still be necessary to use gel lubricant before and during intercourse (Wilmoth, 2006a).

Hot Flashes

Hot flashes are a commonly occurring symptom in menopause. They may be more pronounced in women with a premature menopause. Hot flashes seem to be an especially common problem for women being treated for breast cancer, but they can occur in any woman experiencing a premature menopause. Hot flashes may be more troublesome to younger women diagnosed with breast cancer (Schultz et al., 2005). An estimated 53% to 89% of premenopausal women experience ovarian failure and premature menopause after receiving chemotherapy (Rogers & Kristjanson, 2002).

In some women, the intensity of hot flashes can be reduced with hormone replacement therapy. For many women, especially women being treated for breast cancer, this may be contraindicated. In fact, most postmenopausal women taking hormone replacement therapy at the time of their breast cancer diagnosis are immediately taken off of hormone replacement therapy and experience significant hot flashes. Because hormone replacement therapy is not an option for most breast cancer patients, other options need to be considered.

Hot flashes may be triggered by such stimuli as spicy food, hairdryers, or anxiety. Some women find it helpful to dress in layers so that clothes can easily be removed during hot flashes, to wear natural fibers, and use cold packs intermittently. For individual women, identifying potential triggers to hot flashes in a hot flash diary may help in modifying future symptoms. Lifestyle modifications, such as exercise, achieving a healthy weight, and stopping smoking will sometimes improve hot flashes.

Hot flashes can also be treated in other ways, such as by taking medicines that control the nervous system's reaction to a lack of estrogen. Some drugs that are commonly used this way are the antidepressants called serotonin reuptake inhibitors, such as venlafaxine (Effexor), fluoxetine (Prozac), and paroxetine (Paxil). Many women with milder hot flashes may do well with exercise and relaxation techniques alone.

Skin Changes

Some patients may experience skin changes from treatment. Radiation therapy can cause redness and irritation of the skin. Redness may occur early in the treatment, whereas dry or moist desquamation occurs nearer the end of the scheduled treatment. Both may continue following treatment (Camporeale, 2008). Hyperpigmentation may also occur during radiation therapy and the darker pigmentation may remain following treatment. Radiated skin is more sensitive to exposure to ultraviolet light and skin protection must continue indefinitely.

Skin changes can be very distressing to women and are another reminder of the malignancy and its treatment (Boehmke & Dickerson, 2005). These changes can adversely affect body image and lead to feelings of being unattractive. Encouraging women to share their feelings about these changes can be helpful. Changes in pigmentation can sometimes be addressed with make-up. The "Look Good…Feel Better" program can often help women address these issues. For women experiencing skin reactions from targeted therapy, early intervention can be important.

Fatigue

A common side effect associated with radiation therapy is fatigue (Camporeale, 2008). It can also be a significant side effect of chemotherapy. Fatigue can be especially bothersome in the later weeks of treatment. Women who experience fatigue should be instructed to get plenty of rest and try to maintain an active lifestyle. Although many patients can still work and participate in normal activities during radiation therapy, some patients find it necessary to limit their work or activities until treatment has been completed. Fatigue can also decrease libido (Poirier, 2007). Some women need to rest prior to sexual inter-course. Open communication with a partner about fatigue is important.

Concerns of the Partner

In addition, the woman's partner brings his or her own issues of concern, including fear of losing the partner to cancer, coping with physical changes, concern about getting the cancer from the woman during intercourse, and general attitudes toward the changes that a cancer diagnosis brings to the situation (changing roles, income, attitudes). Strained relations before the woman was diagnosed with cancer can only be exacerbated with a cancer diagnosis, affecting the patient's sexual health (Katz, 2007; Wilmoth, 2006a).

In addition to a partner losing interest in sex, the woman and her partner may believe, although incorrectly, that past sexual activity, an extramarital affair, a sexually transmitted disease, or an abortion has caused their cancer. Some believe, again incorrectly, that sexual activity may promote a recurrence of their cancer (Katz, 2007, Wilmoth, 2006b).

This misconception is especially common in individuals with a malignancy of the pelvic or genital area. For example, women with squamous cell carcinoma of the cervix have read or been told that this cancer is associated with the sexually transmitted human papilloma virus. (See Chapter 5, Cervical Cancer.) Information is the best antidote to this guilt – in this case, the emphasis on accuracy is important because the virus is transmittable through sexual contact, not the cancer (Hawkins et al., 2008; Stead, 2003).

Depression

Depression can be prevalent in cancer patients (estimated to occur at some point in at least 50% of all persons diagnosed with cancer) (Wedding et al., 2007). With depression, a common presenting symptom is loss of sexual desire. In some cases, patients will identify sexual dysfunction as the problem, when it is a secondary effect of depression. Thus, appropriate assessment and treatment of the patient's condition should follow; if it is depression, that should be treated.

CONCERNS RELATED TO SPECIFIC TREATMENTS

It is normal for people with cancer to experience decreased libido at times. Doubts and fears, along with cancer and the side effects associated with cancer treatment can have a negative impact on libido as well as how one perceives sexuality. At times, concern about health may be much greater than interest in sex. Once a woman returns to her normal routines or establishes a new normalcy, interest in sex may begin to return. Patient education prior to initiating these treatments should include a discussion of the impact of the treatment on sexuality. Throughout treatment and into long-term survivorship, women may need assistance and encouragement as they cope with changes in their sexuality related to the treatment.

Chemotherapy

Some chemotherapy drugs irritate all mucous membranes in the body. This includes the lining of the vagina, which may become dry and inflamed. Yeast infections are common during chemotherapy, especially in women taking steroids or antibiotics to treat or prevent bacterial infections. Chemotherapy can also lead to an exacerbation of genital herpes or genital warts if a woman has had them in the past.

Any infection can lead to serious problems because of immune suppression. Yeast infections can often be prevented by not wearing pantyhose, nylon panties, or tight pants. Women should be encouraged to wear loose clothing and cotton panties to avoid trapping moisture in the vaginal area. It is also important to remind the woman to wipe front to back after emptying the bladder and not douche.

Women who are receiving chemotherapy often notice decreased libido. Physical side effects, such as upset stomach, nausea, tiredness, and weakness, may leave little energy for relationships. Sexual desire often returns when a woman feels better. If a woman is getting chemotherapy every 2 to 3 weeks, her sexual interest might only come back a few days before she is due for her next treatment.

Women getting chemotherapy also tend to feel unattractive. Hair loss, weight loss or gain and sometimes, infusion catheters or ports can make it challenging to have a positive sexual image.

Alopecia

Alopecia is a side effect that can cause great distress during treatment for women with cancer. Although some women embrace hair loss as a symbol of their fight against the disease, most feel self-conscious. The loss of hair can be a traumatic event and preparing a patient for this occurrence may help ease the adjustment (Boehmke & Dickerson, 2005). Some women want to keep their own hair for as long as possible, preferring that it falls out gradually. Other patients adjust better to cutting the hair short prior to the time they will begin to lose it. Both of these choices can help the patient to gain a little control over what feels like, and basically is, an uncontrollable event.

There are many options for hair covering, including wigs, scarves, and hats. A patient may find it hard to see herself without hair and some women will wear a head covering even while alone. There are many resources available to help women adjust to the hair loss of cancer therapy as well as some of the other physical changes they may experience. "Look Good…Feel Better" is a free program sponsored by the Cosmetic, Toiletry, and Fragrance Association in partnership with the American Cancer Society and the National Cosmetology Association. The web site (www.lookgoodfeelbetter.org) has helpful tips for hair and makeup as well as a program finder for classes where women can learn hair and makeup tips while undergoing cancer treatment. The information is available in English and Spanish and specific information is available for teens.

Weight Changes

For most people, food is a source of joy and comfort. However, for the patient experiencing nausea, vomiting, and diarrhea, food can become a source of frustration. The question of "what did you eat today" can become a source of stress for the patient, the family, and the healthcare team. When weight loss occurs it serves as a visual reminder of the stress of eating and resulting changes in body image, which can contribute to feelings of anxiety, depression, and decreased libido. Nutritional supplements are available to improve calorie and protein intake for patients who are having difficulties with eating. A nutritional consultation may be helpful for women experiencing difficulty eating and weight loss. Correction of nutritional imbalances can improve quality of life and eliminate or reduce psychosocial and sexual problems (Boehmke & Dickerson, 2005).

Weight gain can also occur as a result of treatment for breast cancer and can have a negative impact on body image. Medications, such as steroids used as part of a chemotherapy regimen, can cause increased hunger and weight gain. Hormonal manipulation, especially in breast cancer treatment, can lead to weight gain. An average weight gain of 5 to 14 pounds has been observed in women being treated for breast cancer (Wilmoth, Coleman, Smith, & Davis, 2004). At a time when the patient may already have difficulty with body image due to the diagnosis of cancer, weight gain may add more stress and lead to sexual distress.

Radiation Therapy

Radiation to the pelvic area often affects a woman's sexuality. If the ovaries get a large radiation dose, they probably will cease functioning. Sometimes this occurs for a limited period of time, but most often it is permanent.

If a woman has already gone through menopause, she may notice little or no change because her ovaries have already stopped making hormones. However, if she has not reached menopause the radiation may cause an abrupt menopause, followed by significant hot flashes and vaginal dryness.

With larger doses of radiation therapy, such as those used for cervical cancer, the damage is almost always permanent (Frumovitz et al., 2005). Women who get radiation to the pelvis often become infertile. No matter what the radiation dose, women younger than 50 years old should talk with their doctors before stopping birth control because it may be possible to become pregnant.

During radiation, tissues in the treatment area get pink and inflamed, and may look sunburned (Hogle, 2003). A woman's vagina may feel tender during radiation treatment and for several weeks following therapy. As the irritation heals, scarring may occur. The thick walls of the vagina may become fibrous and tough. This means the walls may not stretch out as much during sexual excitement and intercourse. Radiation damage to the vagina can also make the lining thin and fragile. Many women notice some light bleeding after intercourse, although they felt no pain at the time. A few women get ulcers, or open sores, in their vaginas, which may take several months to heal after radiation therapy ends.

The scarring that normally occurs after pelvic radiation can shorten or narrow the vagina and decrease the elasticity of the tissue (Watkins-Bruner, Haas, & Gosselin-Acomb, 2005). A woman can often keep tight scar tissue from forming by stretching the walls of her vagina with sexual intercourse at least three or four times a week or using a vaginal dilator on a regular basis. A vaginal dilator is a plastic or rubber tube used to stretch out the vagina. It feels much like putting in a large tampon for a few minutes. Even if a woman is not interested in staying sexually active, keeping her vagina normal in size allows more comfortable gynecologic exams, which is an important and frequent component of long-term follow-up

As long as a woman is not bleeding heavily from a tumor in her bladder, rectum, uterus, cervix, or vagina, she can usually have sex during pelvic radiation therapy. The outer genitals and vagina are just as sensitive as before radiation therapy. Unless intercourse or touching is painful, a woman should still be able to reach orgasm.

A woman should receive education about intercourse during radiation therapy. External radiation does not leave any radiation in the body, so a partner will not come in contact with it. Generally there is restriction on intercourse during external radiation therapy. Some women are treated with an implant. An implant is a radiation source put inside the bladder, uterus, or vagina for a few days. Intercourse will not be allowed while the implant is in place. Women treated with this type of radiation do not transmit radiation after the implant is removed.

Surgery

Breast Surgery

Restoration of the breast is an important aspect in the care and rehabilitation of women with breast cancer. For most women diagnosed with breast cancer, some surgical treatment is usually necessary; many of these women will require at least some degree of breast restoration to improve body image and to prevent physical problems.

Women need to realize that the decision to use a prosthesis or have reconstructive surgery is a personal one (Resnick & Belcher, 2002). There is not necessarily a right or wrong answer for any one woman. The woman needs to feel supported in her decision. Research suggests that women who explore their options carefully prior to surgery, are well educated about all options feel they have a major role in all aspects of the decision-making process, and tend to be more satisfied with whatever choice they make for breast restoration.

Breast restoration might include surgical procedures to reconstruct a breast as well as the use of prosthetics. Prostheses and expertly fitted bras are also extremely useful in correcting breast disparities that are due to extensive or multiple surgical biopsies, atrophy occurring long-term following lumpectomy and radiation and, in some cases, to improve the outcome of reconstructive surgery.

Unlike the past, there are now many different options available for women who will need breast restoration. Although a prosthesis or breast reconstruction will never completely replace what was lost with surgery, it can make an enormous difference in how a woman ultimately adjusts to the diagnosis of cancer and the changes in her body image. This is also an important step in helping the woman to reintegrate her body image with a healthy sexual identity.

Breast restoration is central to restoring and improving body image after the surgical management of breast cancer. Adjustments to changes or disturbances in body image contribute to the quality of life in those diagnosed with cancer. Nurses who provide education and information about breast restoration can ultimately help to improve the quality of life in breast cancer survivors. Breast restoration helps reduce or remove the constant reminder that a woman has faced a life-threatening diagnosis. It can allow a woman to wear attractive clothes comfortably, which ultimately results in improved self-image and sexual function.

Prosthetics – Breast prosthetics are an excellent option for breast restoration for many women. Women considering this option should be referred to a reputable fitter.

It takes a tremendous amount of courage for a woman to have a breast prosthesis fitted; women need support and encouragement as they go through the fitting process. Research suggests that the fitting for a prosthetic can be as difficult and emotionally upsetting as the surgical procedure or diagnosis of cancer itself (Roberts, Livingston, White, & Gibbs, 2003).

Although research is extremely limited, as many as 30% of women are dissatisfied with the external prosthetic for which they have been fitted (Roberts et al., 2003). Dissatisfaction is often linked to the fitting experience, including insufficient time, lack of privacy, fitting by a man, incorrect fit, and attitude of the fitter. Dissatisfaction is also felt when the prosthesis is uncomfortable to wear or clothing and lingerie choices are extremely limited. For this reason, before referring a woman for a fitting, the nurse should be familiar with the fitter and provide the woman with information about what to expect during the fitting.

A temporary prosthesis may be given to a woman through the American Cancer Society's (ACS) Reach to Recovery program, which also typically includes a visit from a breast cancer survivor and literature (ACS, 2010). A temporary prosthesis is a lightweight fiber-filled prosthesis that can be worn immediately following surgery. Most women are ready to be fit for a permanent prosthesis 4 to 6 weeks following a mastectomy. Waiting for this period of time allows for postoperative swelling and skin sensitivity to resolve.

Permanent prostheses come in a variety of shapes and sizes. These include nonattachable prostheses that are traditionally used in the pocket of a bra. Traditional prostheses are made from silicone, which is encased in polyurethane. They are molded into various shapes, densities, weights, and sizes (Mahon & Casey, 2003).

There are also two types of attachable prostheses. One attachable version of breast prosthesis can be applied with the use of Velcro and ostomy tape. A piece of ostomy tape is applied to the chest wall which has Velcro attached to it. The prosthesis is attached by the Velcro to the chest wall and can be worn with any fitted bra. This prosthesis can be worn while swimming and during strenuous athletic activities. Women can shower with the ostomy tape in place because it dries quickly. Generally women must change the tape every 2 to 4 weeks. Some women, for a variety of reasons, prefer this prosthesis. In addition to feeling more secure when participating in some activities, it can be worn to bed as well as with bras and swimsuits worn prior to surgery.

The other type of attachable prosthesis is a breast form with a rejuvenating silicone on the back of the prosthesis. The silicone sticks directly to the chest wall. The woman must be willing to care for this prosthesis on a daily basis. It does not work well for women with a lot of perspiration or those experiencing hot flashes. It cannot be worn while swimming.

There are also partial prostheses available for women who have had lumpectomies, reconstruction, multiple biopsies, and congenital disparities. These come in varying shapes, thicknesses, and sizes. Some fitters will even custom design with fiber-filled pads or foam breast cups. Many times a well-fit, supportive bra can disguise the disparity and is all that is needed. These principles are also helpful to women undergoing reconstruction using expanders, during which time their prosthesis needs change. Occasionally after surgical reconstruction, some disparity or asymmetry is still evident, which can often be camouflaged with a well-fit bra and sometimes a partial prosthesis. Patient education considerations related to breast prosthetics are shown in Table 10-2.

Breast Reconstruction

The most common method of reconstructive breast surgery in the United States is using expanders and breast implants. This is a two-stage procedure. First, an expander is placed behind the pectoralis muscle (see Figure 10-1). The expander is used to stretch the skin and is ultimately replaced by a permanent breast implant (saline or silicone) during a separate procedure several months later.

TABLE 10-2: PATIENT EDUCATION POINTS FOR A PROSTHETIC FITTING

- In most cases there is insurance coverage for the prosthetics at designated intervals as well as coverage for bras.

- Fitting a permanent prosthesis usually takes at least 1 to 2 hours. First the bra is fit, followed by a variety of types of prosthetics.

- As a woman's body changes because of treatment or the normal effects of aging, different prostheses or bras might be needed. The fit of the prosthesis should be assessed on a regular (usually annual) basis.

- There are many different types of prosthetics and women should be open to trying different options.

- It might be helpful to bring a supportive person with her to the fitting.

- The woman should wear a tightly fitting solid top to the fitting. She may also want to bring articles of clothing she likes to wear and is concerned that she may not be able to wear. Often, adjustments can be made so women can continue to wear favorite items of clothing.

- In some cases a woman may be able to continue to wear the same bras she wore preoperatively. She should bring these bras to the fitting.

(Mahon & Casey, 2003)

FIGURE 10-1: BREAST RECONSTRUCTION TISSUE EXPANDER

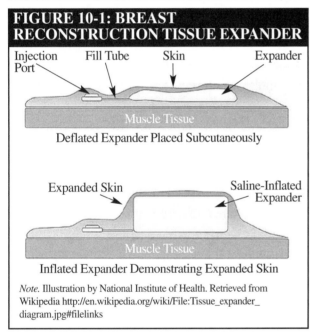

Deflated Expander Placed Subcutaneously

Inflated Expander Demonstrating Expanded Skin

Note. Illustration by National Institute of Health. Retrieved from Wikipedia http://en.wikipedia.org/wiki/File:Tissue_expander_diagram.jpg#filelinks

Implant reconstruction can be the best option for some patients. Potential long-term complications include capsular contracture, deformity, and pain, particularly if the patient has had or is going to have radiation therapy as part of the cancer treatment. There is a risk of requiring further surgery due to these complications. Most implants will last about 10 to 15 years, so over time, a younger woman will need to have an implant replaced (Spittler, 2008).

The latissimus procedure uses muscle from the back of the shoulder blade, which is brought around to the breast mound to help create a new breast. During the procedure, a section of skin, fat, and muscle is detached from the back and brought to the breast area (see Figure 10-2). Patients will have a scar on their back shoulder region that can sometimes be seen through a tank-top, swimsuit, or sundress (Resnick & Belcher, 2002). Women who are very active in sports should know that this procedure can reduce the ability to participate in such activities as golf, climbing, swimming, or tennis.

Transverse rectus abdominus myocutaneous flap, often called the TRAM flap surgery, is a common breast reconstruction technique that utilizes skin, fat, and rectus abdominus muscle from the lower abdomen (see Figure 10-3). The tissue (or flap) is then relocated to the chest to create the new breast (Resnick & Belcher, 2002). This procedure also results in a tightening of the lower abdomen, or a "tummy tuck."

There are several ways to make a TRAM flap. A pedicled flap is transferred to the chest by tunneling the tissue under the skin up to the chest to create a new breast. The free TRAM flap involves disconnecting the flap from the patient's body,

FIGURE 10-2: BREAST RECONSTRUCTION USING A LATISSIMUS DORSI FLAP

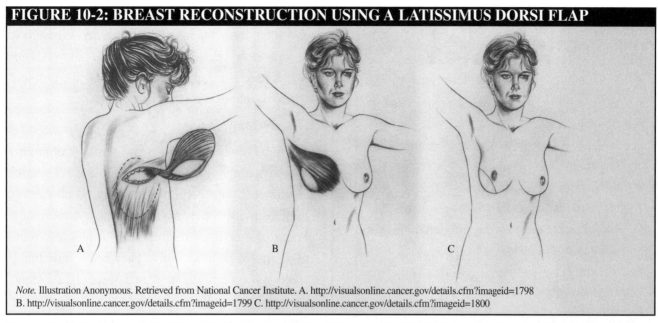

Note. Illustration Anonymous. Retrieved from National Cancer Institute. A. http://visualsonline.cancer.gov/details.cfm?imageid=1798
B. http://visualsonline.cancer.gov/details.cfm?imageid=1799 C. http://visualsonline.cancer.gov/details.cfm?imageid=1800

FIGURE 10-3: BREAST RECONSTRUCTION USING A TRAM FLAP

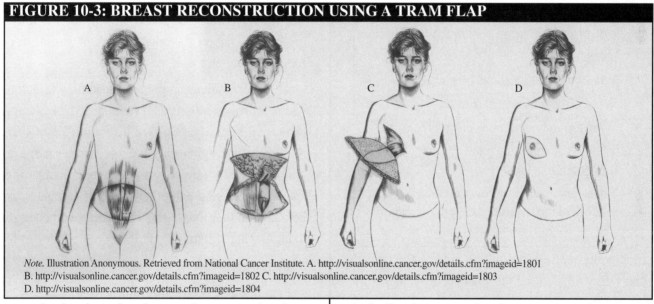

Note. Illustration Anonymous. Retrieved from National Cancer Institute. A. http://visualsonline.cancer.gov/details.cfm?imageid=1801
B. http://visualsonline.cancer.gov/details.cfm?imageid=1802 C. http://visualsonline.cancer.gov/details.cfm?imageid=1803
D. http://visualsonline.cancer.gov/details.cfm?imageid=1804

transplanting it to the chest, and reconnecting it to the body using microsurgery. The muscle-sparing TRAM flap is similar to the free TRAM except the amount of muscle taken is typically very minimal.

The decision to undergo breast reconstruction is a major one. Women should be instructed to get at least two opinions and to ask many questions. A list of sample questions is included in Table 10-3.

Adjusting to Changes Following Breast Surgery

Sexual problems have been linked to mastectomy and lumpectomy (Bakewell & Volker, 2005). Losing a breast can be very distressing. The most common sexual side effect from these procedures

is feeling less attractive. In our culture, breasts are often viewed as a basic part of beauty and womanhood. If a breast is removed, a woman may feel less secure about whether her partner will accept her and still find her sexually pleasing. The breasts and nipples are also sources of sexual pleasure for many women and their partners. Touching the breasts is a common part of foreplay. Some women can reach orgasm just from having their breasts stroked. For many others, breast stroking adds to sexual excitement.

Surgery for breast cancer can interfere with pleasure from breast caressing. Some women still

TABLE 10-3: QUESTIONS TO ASK WHEN CONSIDERING RECONSTRUCTIVE SURGERY

- What are the possible surgical options?
- What are the benefits of the recommended procedure?
- What are the risks of the recommended procedure?
- What are the limitations of the recommended procedure?
- How many times has the surgeon done this particular procedure?
- Do you have pictures of women you have done this procedure on?
- What type of anesthesia will be used?
- How long with the surgery take?
- What follow-up procedures will be needed?
- Where will the incisions be placed?
- What is the anticipated recovery?
- What are the restrictions during recovery?
- When is it recommended that reconstruction begin?
- What are the estimated costs and how much will the insurance cover?

(Resnick & Belcher, 2002; Spittler, 2008).

enjoy being stroked around the area of the healed scar. Others dislike being touched there and may no longer enjoy having the remaining breast and nipple touched. Communication about what is and is not pleasurable may help women to adjust to surgical changes.

Some women who have had a mastectomy feel self-conscious being the partner on top during sex. This position makes it easy to notice that the breast is missing. Some women who have had mastectomies wear a short nightgown or camisole, or even just a bra, with the prosthesis inside during sexual activity. Other women find the breast prosthesis awkward or in the way during intercourse. Women should be encouraged to communicate with their partner about preferences (Katz, 2007).

A few women have long-term pain in their chests and shoulders after radical mastectomy. It may help to support the chest and shoulder with pillows during sex. It may also help if the woman avoids positions where weight rests on the chest or arm.

Hysterectomy

A hysterectomy does not usually change a woman's ability to feel sexual pleasure. The vagina is shortened but there are generally no changes in the sensitivity in the area around the clitoris and the lining of the vagina. Some women feel less feminine after a hysterectomy. They may view themselves as "an empty shell" or not feel like a "real" woman. Such negative thoughts can keep women from thinking about the sexual function that they still have (Rannestad, 2005). For women who do not have radiation therapy, the risk of sexual dysfunction is much lower.

If cancer is causing pain or bleeding with intercourse, a hysterectomy can help stop those symptoms and actually improve a woman's sex life. Although the vagina may be shorter after surgery, couples usually adjust to this change. Extra time spent on caressing and other forms of foreplay can help ensure that the vagina has lengthened enough to allow intercourse.

Abdominoperineal Resection

An abdominoperineal (AP) resection for colon cancer includes removal of the lower colon and rectum. It also creates a colostomy so that stool can pass out of the body. An AP resection does not damage the nerves that control the feeling in a woman's genitals and allow orgasm. Some women may notice vaginal dryness, especially if their ovaries were removed. If so, a water-based gel can help make intercourse more comfortable.

Intercourse in some positions may be uncomfortable or even painful. Without a rectum to cushion the vagina, the vagina may move more during intercourse. When this happens, it may pull on the tissues that hold the vagina and uterus in place inside the pelvis. A couple may need to try different positions to find one that works for them (Wilmoth, 2006b).

A colostomy requires much communication between couples and often some changes, but sexual satisfaction can be achieved (Katz, 2007). The appliance needs to fit correctly. It is best to empty the ostomy appliance before sexual intercourse. This will reduce the chance of a major leak. If it does leak, be ready to jump into the shower with your partner and then try again. Some women like to use a pouch to cover the stoma and to make the pouch appear less "medical." Depending on the ostomy it may be possible to wear a special small-sized ostomy pouch during sexual activity. Some women wear a wide sash around the waist to keep the pouch out of the way. Others tape the pouch to the body to keep it from moving around. Still others wear a T-shirt to cover the appliance.

To reduce rubbing against the appliance, choose positions for sexual activity that keep the partner's weight off the ostomy (Katz, 2007). Some women like to be on the bottom during intercourse and find it helps to put a small pillow above the ostomy faceplate. With this approach the partner can lie on the pillow rather than on the appliance.

Since a colostomy is not active all the time, it is sometimes possible to plan sexual activity for a time of day when the ostomy is usually not active. Women who irrigate the colostomy, may be able to wear just a stoma cover or a small safety pouch during intercourse. They should be advised to also avoid eating foods that produce gas on days when they are likely to have intercourse.

FERTILITY

Both radiation therapy and chemotherapy are associated with increased risks of infertility. Sterility from these therapies may be temporary or permanent. The occurrence of this toxicity is related to a number of factors, including the individual's gender, age at the time of treatment, type of therapeutic agent, radiation field, total dose, single versus multiple agents, and length of time since treatment (Katz, 2007).

When treatment-related or disease-related dysfunction is a possibility, every effort should be made to provide adequate information and education on reproduction and fertility. Conveying such information can be complicated, especially in younger women. Current estimates suggest that only about one-half of women of child-bearing age receive the information they need from their health care providers about cancer-related infertility at the time of diagnosis and treatment planning (Canada & Schover, 2005).

With chemotherapy, the extent of damage to a patient's fertility depends on the agent administered, the doses received, and the patient's age at the time of treatment. Age is an important factor as well as the agents utilized and length of treatment. Evidence suggests that patients older than 35 to 40 years of age are most susceptible to the ovarian effects of chemotherapy (Simon, Lee, Partridge, & Runowicz, 2005). Predicting the outcome for any individual patient is difficult, as the course of ovarian functioning following chemotherapy is variable. Older age, higher doses, and longer duration all increase the toxic effects of chemotherapy on the ovary. With the same chemotherapeutic regimen (cyclophoshamide, methotrexate, and fluorouracil), rates of amenorrhea are 35% to 40% in women less than 40 years of age compared with 80% to 95% in women older than 40 years of age (Simon et al., 2005).

The alkylating agents have been shown to be damaging to fertility. The following agents have also been associated with infertility: cyclophosphamide, cisplatin, and ifosfamide. Although chemotherapy causes ovarian damage, there appears to be no risk of toxicity to future offspring of women treated with these agents before pregnancy (Katz, 2007).

Women over 40 years of age have a smaller pool of remaining oocytes. When radiation therapy is given it takes only 5 to 6 Gy to produce permanent ovarian failure, whereas 20 Gy are needed to produce permanent ovarian failure in women younger than 40 years of age (Simon et al., 2005).

At present, there are few means to protect fertility in women undergoing therapy for malignancy. Movement of the ovaries out of the field of radiation (ovariopexy), either laterally, toward the iliac crest, or behind the uterus, may help preserve fertility when high doses of radiation therapy are being applied. In some women ovarian failure will still occur (Simon et al., 2005).

As part of the informed consent process, oncology professionals should discuss reproductive cell and tissue banking with patients at risk for gonadal failure. If the patient is concerned about fertility it is necessary to refer to a reproductive endocrinologist before chemotherapy or radiation.

Freezing oocytes has had some success, but with significant limitations and only a small number of reported pregnancies (Simon et al., 2005). In oocyte cryopreservation, which is still considered experimental, reproductive cells/tissue are cryopreserved for future use in artificial insemination for patients who wish to protect their reproductive capacity. Removal of the entire ovary for freezing is also a technique with a promising future for preserving fertility (Bedaiwy & Falcone, 2004). Following treatment, the embryos may be implanted into the woman who may be able to carry a pregnancy to term. Overall current survival rates for the freeze-thaw process range from 15% to 43%, with approximately 45% fertilization rates but only 1% to 2% clinical pregnancy rates (Simon et al., 2005).

These options may not be appropriate for all patients. Counseling is an important part of the decision-making process for patients. Thinking through these decisions at a time when women are struggling with issues of a potentially deadly disease and toxic therapy is very difficult. Patients need to consider costs, stress, time, emotions, and potential inclusion of another individual in the pregnancy process (such as a surrogate). For many patients, the financial costs associated with in vitro fertilization and subsequent embryo cryopreservation is cost prohibitive. Consideration also needs to be given to the current rate of failure for in vitro fertilization procedures.

Younger women with cancer must cope with having cancer at a young age as well as infertility, most likely caused by treatment for the malignancy. Women who must undergo a hysterectomy for gynecologic cancer must also cope with issues related to being unable to carry a pregnancy.

ASSESSMENT

Practice standards address the need to assess patients' sexuality as well as the outcomes that nurses can help patients and their partners achieve. Thus, the standards of practice put discussions of sexuality as an area of nursing responsibility. Healthcare providers often feel ill prepared for such discussions and fear opening up a "Pandora's box" when they do not have enough time to devote to such sensitive issues. They may be uncertain about how to deal with the complex and multifaceted problems of intimacy and relationships in the face of cancer.

A comprehensive sexual assessment includes a complete medical and psychosexual history with a physical examination, including a pelvic exam (Wilmoth, 2006a; Wilmoth, 2006b). This may be obtained by a single provider or several, as part of a multidisciplinary approach.

One of the most important factors in adjustment after being diagnosed with cancer is the person's feelings about his or her sexuality prior to cancer (Katz, 2007). Whatever the past experience, exploring sexuality issues during diagnosis and treatment provides a prime opportunity to help women deal with their sexuality during and after treatment.

An evaluation of an individual's sexual function should include clarification of the nature of the woman's problem, concern, or complaint. Assessment should include a variety of aspects of current sexual function, including:

- frequency of experiencing spontaneous desire for sex

- ease of feeling subjective pleasure with sexual stimulation

- signs of physiological arousal, including vaginal expansion

- amount of vaginal lubrication

- ability to reach an orgasm

- types of sexual stimulation that can trigger an orgasm

- pain in the genital area.

An individual's pre-illness sexual development and function are another important aspect to assess. The level of sexual functioning before diagnosis and treatment, interest, satisfaction, and importance of sexual functioning in the relationship all influence the patient's potential distress related to current sexual status. Women who are already experiencing sexual difficulties may be especially vulnerable to the effects of treatment (Katz, 2007).

The patient may or may not have an available partner at the time of diagnosis. Sexuality should be taken no less seriously if there is no partner. Treatment still has an impact on self-perception and sexuality. This should be assessed by the health care professional (Katz, 2007).

For patients with a partner, the clinician should consider and discuss the duration, quality, and stability of the relationship before diagnosis. This includes a nonjudgmental approach to both heterosexual and homosexual lifestyles.

Many women fear rejection and abandonment with the cancer diagnosis. The nurse should inquire about the partner's response to the illness and the patient's concerns about the impact of treatment on the partner and relationship. Partners share many of the same reactions as patients in that their most significant concerns typically relate to loss and fear of death (Hawkins et al., 2008). Moreover, the partner's physical, sexual, and emotional health should be considered before the diagnosis and at the time of the assessment.

Anxiety and depression are two common reactions to a diagnosis of cancer and can have a negative effect on sexual function. Assessment should consider present psychosocial functioning as well as past functioning, including psychological treatment. Current use of psychotropic medications should also be reviewed with respect to impact on sexual function.

Comorbid conditions that increase the risk of sexual dysfunction include diabetes, hypertension, and vascular disease. Smoking and substantial alcohol consumption also have a negative impact on sexual functioning (Katz, 2007). Some medications have a negative effect on sexual function, especially antihypertensives and some antidepressants.

After all of the assessment data is collected, it must be organized. An acronym for organizing an assessment is B-E-T-T-E-R.

- **B**ring up topics so the patient knows sexuality can be discussed

- **E**xplain concern about all aspects of the patient's life

- **T**ell the patient that sexual dysfunction can occur and that resources are available

- **T**iming of sexual issue discussions during a visit or over many visits

- **E**ducate patients about adverse effects of treatment

- **R**ecord assessments and interventions
(Mick, Hughes, & Cohen, 2004).

A common strategy of assessment is to move from less sensitive to more sensitive issues. The following questions show one example:

1. Has your role as a parent, spouse, or intimate friend changed since you were diagnosed with or treated for cancer?

2. Do you feel differently about yourself or your body since you were diagnosed with or treated for cancer?

3. Has your sexual functioning changed (or do you think it will change) due to your diagnosis or cancer treatment? [If yes] How has it or will it change?

One of the acronyms used to organize a sexual assessment and plan for intervention is the P-LI-SS-IT model, which represents the levels of permission, limited information, specific suggestion, and intensive therapy (Annon, 1976). The tone and setting of assessment can be as important as the questions asked. The goal is to build trust in the patient and protect confidentiality. The nurse should also be aware of verbal and nonverbal communication that can influence data gathered on sexual health, such as self-esteem and body image (Katz, 2007).

The PLISSIT model was first proposed by Jack Annon in 1976. It provides a hierarchy for intervention for persons experiencing sexual dysfunction. The assumption underlying the PLISSIT model is that there are varying degrees of need for intervention; most people who are dissatisfied with their sex function do not need intensive sexual therapy. The model is primarily intended for use by healthcare professionals who are not trained as sexual therapists, such as nurses.

By assessing patients' sexuality, nurses give patients *permission* to voice their concerns and ask questions about sexual function. Nurses can provide *limited information* by educating patients about medication and treatment effects on sexuality. Similarly, nurses can offer *specific suggestions*

such as positions for intercourse that may reduce dyspareunia. When *intensive therapy* is indicated for those with serious sexual issues, it is conducted by certified sexual therapists (Wilmoth, 2006a).

Sexual assessment ensures that patients receive the care to which they are entitled, provides a baseline of their knowledge and understanding of their disease and treatment side effects and, most importantly, serves as a way for nurses to "give permission" to patients to discuss their concerns about sexuality.

Two other communication techniques commonly used when talking about sexuality are "unloading" and "bridge" statements. Unloading lets patients know that others have similar concerns and that any questions they might have are within the "norm." Examples of unloading questions are:

•   Many women have concerns about their sexual functioning after being treated for cancer. What are some of your concerns?

•   Some women find they have vaginal dryness when they try to have intercourse after finishing chemotherapy. What has your experience been with vaginal dryness since finishing chemotherapy?

Bridge statements facilitate the transition from easy to more uncomfortable topics, assist in incorporating sensitive topics into interviews, help interviewers gain valuable information, and legitimize inquiries. Examples of bridge statements include:

•   Many active people like yourself want to continue having a close sexual relationship but don't feel that it's a perfectly normal thing or safe thing to do. How do you feel?

•   What has your oncologist told you about the effects of your treatment on having sex?

INTERVENTIONS

Interventions to address sexual dysfunction are based on correcting the underlying cause whenever possible, such as fatigue or pain. In many cases, when sexual dysfunction is related to treatment, the underlying cause cannot be treated. In this case, healthcare professionals need to implement interventions to enhance sexual health. Examples of such interventions are shown in Table 10-4. Healthcare providers can help educate couples by offering practical suggestions to overcome changes in responsiveness to sexual stimulation. Couples should allow plenty of time for sexual expression, with sufficient foreplay, to develop the fullest possible sexual arousal.

Healthcare providers need to reassure patients and their significant others that even when intercourse is difficult or impossible, their sex lives are not over. Couples can give and receive pleasure and satisfaction by expressing their love and intimacy with their hands, mouths, tongues, and lips. Healthcare providers should encourage couples to express affection in alternative ways (hugging, kissing, nongenital touching) until they feel ready to resume sexual activity. Couples should be encouraged to communicate honest feelings, concerns, and preferences (Katz, 2007). For some couples, early morning may be a good restful time for sexual expression. Conditions that facilitate sexual pleasure should be explored and may include relaxation, dreams, fantasy, deep breathing, and recalling positive experiences with the partner.

More specific information for the evaluation and treatment of female sexual dysfunction, including painful intercourse (dyspareunia), vaginismus, inhibited orgasm, sexual arousal, and desire disorders, may require a referral to a specialist.

TABLE 10-4: STRATEGIES TO COPE WITH CHANGES IN SEXUALITY

- Learn as much as you can about the effects your cancer treatment may have on sexuality. Talk with your doctor, nurse, or any other member of your healthcare team. When you know what to expect, you can plan how you might handle those issues.
- Focus on physical recovery, including diet and physical activities.
- Ask your physician or nurse about maintaining or resuming sexual activity. Include your partner in discussions.
- Discuss fertility and birth control with your physician.
- Report vaginal discharge or bleeding, fever, or pain to your physician or nurse.
- Choose a time for intimacy when you and your partner are rested and free from distractions.
- Create a romantic mood.
- In times of increased fatigue, communicate to your partner to take a more active role in touching.
- If some part of your body is tender or sore, you can guide your partner's touches to create the most pleasure and avoid pain.
- Try different positions until you find one that is more comfortable and less tiring for you.
- Use a water-soluble lubricant if needed.
- Use pain medications, if needed.
- Remember that cancer is not contagious.
- Remember that being intimate will not make the cancer come back or grow.
- Remember that your partner is also affected by your cancer, so talk about both of your feelings and fears.
- Explore different ways of showing love (hugging and holding, stroking and caressing, talking).
- If needed, find humor where you can.

(Frumovitz et al., 2005; Katz, 2007; Wilmoth, 2006a)

SUMMARY

Sexuality in a woman's life is important no matter what her age, experience, or status in life. Women with a cancer diagnosis need information about how their cancer and its treatment phases will affect sexuality. Any effort to support the woman with information or tools to optimize functioning should be preceded by a thorough, sensitive assessment. Above all, support about these issues helps her and her partner cope with changes in her sexuality, sexual functioning, and the impact of cancer on her fertility. When practitioners normalize discussion about sexual health and intimacy as part of overall quality-of-life concerns, it becomes easier for patients and physicians to communicate. Additionally, healthcare providers can support patients and their partners by personalizing treatment plans, by referring when appropriate, and by engendering hope.

EXAM QUESTIONS

CHAPTER 10
Questions 83-88

Note: Choose the one option that BEST answers each question.

83. When a woman is diagnosed with cancer, factors that can affect her sexuality are

    a. uncertainty, grief, depression and fatigue.

    b. changes in relationships and changes in roles.

    c. support and education.

    d. time and distance.

84. To help a woman with vaginal dryness, recommend

    a. oil-based lubrication.

    b. water-based gel lubrication.

    c. rest.

    d. heat.

85. A physiologic sexual dysfunction that occurs after pelvic radiation is

    a. increased vaginal lubrication.

    b. radioactivity of the vagina.

    c. decreased elasticity of the vagina.

    d. decreased risk of vaginal infections.

86. Mrs. G. returns for follow-up after formation of a colostomy for rectal cancer. She asks questions about resuming intercourse. An appropriate suggestion would be

    a. to avoid anal intercourse.

    b. to avoid vaginal intercourse.

    c. to secure the ostomy bag during intercourse.

    d. to avoid face to face positions.

87. The first level of assessment ("P") in the PLISSIT model conveys the message that

    a. any sexual activity is appropriate.

    b. discussing sexual issues is appropriate.

    c. all women should remain sexually active.

    d. information about sexual function should be referred to a counselor.

88. Interventions with cancer patients to correct sexual dysfunction and restore sexual integrity are based on

    a. correcting the underlying cause.

    b. the patient's prognosis.

    c. the marital status and sexual preference.

    d. the comfort level of the nurse.

REFERENCES

American Cancer Society. (2010). *Cancer facts & figures 2010*. Atlanta, GA: American Cancer Society.

Annon, J.S. (1976). *The behavioral treatment of sexual problems: Brief therapy* (Volume 1). New York: Harper & Row.

Bakewell, R.T. & Volker, D.L. (2005). Sexual dysfunction related to the treatment of young women with breast cancer. *Clinical Journal of Oncology Nursing, 9*(6), 697-702, 722-724.

Bedaiwy, M. & Falcone, T. (2004). Ovarian tissue banking for cancer patients: Reduction of post-transplantation ischaemic injury: Intact ovary freezing and transplantation. *Human Reproduction, 19*(6), 1242-1244.

Boehmke, M.M. & Dickerson, S.S. (2005). Symptom, symptom experiences, and symptom distress encountered by women with breast cancer undergoing current treatment modalities. *Cancer Nursing, 28*(5), 382-389.

Camporeale, J. (2008). Basics of radiation treatment. *Clinical Journal of Oncology Nursing, 12*(2), 193-195.

Canada, A.L. & Schover, L.R. (2005). Research promoting better patient education on reproductive health after cancer. *Journal of the National Cancer Institute: Monographs,* (34), 98-100.

Frumovitz, M., Sun, C.C., Schover, L.R., Munsell, M.F., Jhingran, A., Wharton, J.T., et al. (2005). Quality of life and sexual functioning in cervical cancer survivors. *Journal of Clinical Oncology, 23*(30), 7428-7436.

Graziottin, A. & Basson, R. (2004). Sexual dysfunction in women with premature menopause. *Menopause, 11*(6, Part 2), 766-777.

Hawkins, J.W., Roberto-Nichols, D.M., & Stanley-Haney, J.L. (2008). *Guidelines for nurse practitioners in gynecologic settings* (9th ed.). New York: Springer.

Hogle, W.P. (2003). Radiation therapy 101: The basics every nurse needs to know. *Clinical Journal of Oncology Nursing, 7*(2), 230-232.

Katz, A. (2007). *Breaking the silence on cancer and sexuality: A handbook for healthcare providers.* Pittsburgh, PA: Oncology Nursing Society.

Levine, K.B., Williams, R.E., & Hartmann, K.E. (2008). Vulvovaginal atrophy is strongly associated with female sexual dysfunction among sexually active postmenopausal women. *Menopause, 15*(4, Part 1), 661-666.

Mahon, S.M. & Casey, M. (2003). Patient education for women being fitted for breast prostheses. *Clinical Journal of Oncology Nursing, 7*(2), 194-199.

Mick, J., Hughes, M., & Cohen, M.Z. (2004). Using the BETTER model to assess sexuality. *Clinical Journal of Oncology Nursing, 8*(1), 84-86.

Poirier, P. (2007). Factors affecting performance of usual activities during radiation therapy. *Oncology Nursing Forum, 34*(4), 827-834.

Rannestad, T. (2005). Hysterectomy: Effects on quality of life and psychological aspects. Best practice & research: *Clinical Obstetrics & Gynaecology, 19*(3), 419-30.

Resnick, B. & Belcher, A.E. (2002). Breast reconstruction: Options, answers, and support for patients making a difficult personal decision. *American Journal of Nursing, 102*(4), 26-33.

Roberts, S., Livingston, P. White, V. & Gibbs, A. (2003). External breast prosthesis use: experiences and views of women with breast cancer, breast care nurses, and prosthesis fitters. *Cancer Nursing 2003; 26*(3):179-186.

Rogers, M. & Kristjanson, L.J. (2002). The impact on sexual functioning of chemotherapy-induced menopause in women with breast cancer. *Cancer Nursing, 25*(1), 57-65.

Schultz, P.N., Klein, M.J., Beck, M.L., Stava, C., & Sellin, R.V. (2005). Breast cancer: Relationship between menopausal symptoms, physiologic health effects of cancer treatment and physical constraints on quality of life in long-term survivors. *Journal of Clinical Nursing, 14*(2), 204-211.

Simon, B., Lee, S.J., Partridge, A., & Runowicz, C.D. (2005). Preserving fertility after cancer. *CA: A Cancer Journal for Clinicians, 55*(4), 211-228.

Spittler, C.A. (2008). Breast reconstruction using tissue expanders: Assessing patients' needs utilizing a holistic approach. *Plastic Surgical Nursing, 28*(1), 27-32.

Stead, M.L. (2003). Sexual dysfunction after treatment for gynaecologic and breast malignancies. *Current Opinion in Obstetrics & Gynecology, 15*(1), 57-61.

Watkins-Bruner, D., Haas, M.L., & Gosselin-Acomb, T.K. (2005). *Manual for radiation oncology nursing practice and education* (3rd ed.). Pittsburgh, PA: Oncology Nursing Society.

Wedding, U., Koch, A., Röhrig, B., Pientka, L., Sauer, H., Höffken, K., et al. (2007). Requestioning depression in patients with cancer: Contribution of somatic and affective symptoms to Beck's Depression Inventory. *Annals of Oncology, 18*(11), 1875-1881.

Wilmoth, M.C., Coleman, E.A., Smith, S.C., & Davis, C., (2004). Fatigue, weight gain, and altered sexuality in patients with breast cancer: Exploration of a symptom cluster. *Oncology Nursing Forum, 31*(6), 1069-1075.

Wilmoth, M.C. (2006a). Sexuality. In I.M. Lubkin & P.D. Larsen (Eds.), *Chronic illness: Impact and interventions* (6th ed., pp. 285-304). Sudbury, MA: Jones and Bartlett.

Wilmoth, M.C. (2006b). Life after cancer – What does sexuality have to do with it? *Oncology Nursing Forum, 33*(5), 905-910.

CHAPTER 11

COMPLEMENTARY AND ALTERNATIVE MEDICINE

CHAPTER OBJECTIVE

After completing this chapter on complementary and alternative medicine (CAM), the reader will be able to discuss why cancer patients seek out CAM options, list some common CAMs, and identify ways to evaluate their merit and usefulness.

LEARNING OBJECTIVES

After studying this chapter, the reader will be able to

1. recognize motivations for cancer patients to try CAMs.

2. identify established CAMs.

3. identify reputable resources to learn more about CAMS.

4. discuss the benefits and risks of using CAMs.

INTRODUCTION

No discussion of cancer in women is complete without addressing the attraction and use of CAMs for treatment of side effects associated with cancer and its treatment. This is a rapidly emerging field and CAM can have a direct affect on cancer treatment – some of these effects can be positive and some can be negative. For this reason, nurses need to be aware of CAMs, and take direct steps to accurately assess if women are incorporating these strategies into their cancer care.

CAM DEFINED

Complementary medicine is used along with standard medical treatments. One example is using acupuncture to help with side effects of cancer treatment. Alternative medicine is used in place of standard medical treatments. An example is using a special diet to treat cancer instead of a method that an oncologist suggests. Integrative medicine is a total approach to care that involves the patient's mind, body, and spirit. It combines standard medicine with the CAM practices that have shown the most promise. For example, some women use relaxation as a way to reduce stress during chemotherapy. To date, no CAM has been proven universally effective in the treatment of cancer, but there is promising research that they may be a valuable adjunct to treatment (Chong, 2006). CAMs can be categorized into five areas which are shown in Table 11-1.

The challenge for nurses and other healthcare providers is to be supportive of patients who use CAMs, while also being appropriate advocates. CAMs can be promoted by charlatans who seek out the vulnerable (Smith, 2005). The obligation of health care providers is to help patients sort through information, support studies that generate documented effectiveness data, and focus on those promising and effective, safe options.

TABLE 11-1: CATEGORIES OF CAM THERAPIES

Mind-Body Medicines: CAM practices based on the belief that your mind is able to affect your body. Some examples include:

- Meditation
- Biofeedback
- Hypnosis
- Yoga
- Imagery
- Art, music, or dance therapy

Biologically Based Practices: CAM uses natural products, such dietary supplements and herbal products. Some examples are:

- Vitamins
- Herbs
- Foods
- Special diets

Manipulative and Body-Based Practices: CAM practices based on working or moving one or more body parts. Some examples include:

- Massage
- Chiropractic care
- Reflexology

Energy Medicine: CAM practice based on the belief that the body has energy fields that can be used for healing and wellness. Some examples are:

- Tai Chi
- Reiki
- Therapeutic touch

Whole Medical Systems: CAM practices that consider the mind, body, and spirit. Some examples are:

- Ayurvedic medicine
- Chinese medicine
- Acupuncture
- Homeopathy
- Naturopathic medicine

(Astin, Shapiro, Eisenberg, & Forys, 2003; Smith, 2005)

Some women with cancer are concerned that their healthcare providers will not approve of the use of CAM. Communication with a healthcare provider is important to ensure that there are no dangerous interactions between traditional cancer therapies and CAM. For this reason, nurses need to continually assess whether patients are using CAM. An environment of open communication will help prevent complications. CAM may help women to:

- cope with the diagnosis
- reduce stress
- reduce fatigue
- provide a sense of control
- manage side effects of cancer and treatment, such as pain or nausea.

    Any discussion of CAM should include:

- potential interactions with treatment or medications
- explanations of the physiologic basis of how CAM might work
- referrals to reputable CAM providers and practitioners.

PREVALENCE

The prevalence of CAM use in the general population has substantially increased from 1990 to 2005. In December 2008, the National Center for Complementary and Alternative Medicine (NCCAM) released new findings on Americans' use of CAM. In the United States, approximately 38% of adults with cancer are using some form of CAM (NCCAM, 2008). People of all backgrounds use CAM. However, CAM use among adults is greater among women and those with higher levels of education and higher incomes.

    CAM users are more likely to use more than one CAM therapy in conjunction with conventional medicine. Commonly cited reasons for CAM use include the beliefs that these therapies can

- boost immune function

- prevent cancer and/or improve quality of life

- increase the feeling that patients are more in control and play an active role in their own care

- palliate symptoms of cancer treatment

(Chong, 2006).

Preferences for CAM therapies vary. Several studies report a high prevalence of the use of prayer, dietary supplements, massage, and relaxation techniques. The use of dietary supplements is estimated to be particularly popular in patients with breast, gynecologic, and prostate cancers (Smith, 2005).

Nondisclosure of CAM use by patients with cancer has been well documented, with studies reporting rates from 40% to 70% (Chong, 2006). Reasons given for nondisclosure on the part of patients were, "it wasn't important for the doctor to know" and "the doctor never asked." It is also speculated that patients do not see CAM's potential to affect their standard cancer treatment, and patients did not perceive the therapy they were using as CAM (especially if it is marketed as a natural supplement, vitamin, or food product). Other possible reasons are feared disinterest or negative response by the provider or the view that the discussion of CAM is a poor use of time or inappropriate (Smith, 2005). The reality that patients do not reveal CAM use to the healthcare team is of particular concern because the safety and efficacy of some CAM therapies are not yet fully known.

NATIONAL CENTER FOR COMPLEMENTARY AND ALTERNATIVE MEDICINE

In 1998, the National Institutes of Health (NIH) established NCCAM. It was established to conduct basic and clinical research, train researchers, and educate and communicate findings concerning

therapeutic and preventive CAMs. NCCAM is the lead agency in the U.S. for scientific research on CAM. Nurses should learn to access the many resources available at the CAM website if they have specific questions about a treatment (http://nccam.nih.gov). The mission of NCCAM is to:

- explore CAM healing practices in the context of rigorous science

- train CAM researchers

- disseminate sound information to the public and professionals.

The mission of NCCAM is accomplished through several strategies. NCCAM sponsors and conducts research using scientific methods and advanced technologies to study CAM. Currently there are four primary areas of focus:

- advancing scientific research

- training CAM researchers

- disseminating news and information

- supporting integration of proven CAM therapies.

Nurses need to become familiar with the many resources that are available at the NCCAM website. There is a comprehensive list of CAM therapies that includes a description of the therapy, pictures, the scientific basis of the therapy, and safety considerations. Patients can also be referred to this website if they have additional questions.

HELPFUL CAMS IN CANCER PATIENT CARE

CAM use is subjective and the benefits of CAM are of unique benefit to each individual. Each individual usually has a unique experience with CAM. Although the positive track record of many CAMs is reported, few reports document the benefits of certain CAMs related to cancer and cancer treatment. The following section is not exhaustive and only highlights some common CAMs, which cancer patients and clinicians report to be reasonably safe and sometimes helpful.

Acupuncture

Acupuncture is a technique in which very thin needles of varying lengths are inserted through the skin to treat a variety of conditions. It may help treat nausea caused by chemotherapy drugs and surgical anesthesia (Sherman et al., 2005). A recent analysis of 11 studies looked at the effect of acupuncture in reducing nausea and vomiting related to chemotherapy (Ezzo et al., 2006). The report suggested that acupuncture may reduce the vomiting that occurs shortly after chemotherapy is given, even though it had little effect on nausea. It does not seem to help with delayed vomiting. Acupuncture has been utilized as an adjunct with some success in comprehensive smoking cessation programs (Mayo Clinic, 2007).

When done by a trained professional, acupuncture is generally considered safe. The number of complications reported that are related to acupuncture have been relatively few; however, there is a risk that a patient may be harmed if the acupuncturist is not well trained (Ernst, Strzyz, & Hagmeister, 2003). Although the needles used in traditional needle acupuncture are very fine, they can cause dizziness, fainting, local internal bleeding, nerve damage, and increased pain (see Figure 11-1). The risk of infection is low because acupuncturists in the United States use sterile needles that are discarded after a single use.

Aroma Therapy

Aromatherapy is the use of fragrant substances, called essential oils, distilled from plants to alter mood or improve health. These highly concentrated aromatic substances are either inhaled or applied during massage. Approximately 40 essential oils are commonly used in aromatherapy; among the most commonly used are lavender, rosemary, eucalyptus, chamomile, marjoram, jasmine, peppermint, lemon, and geranium.

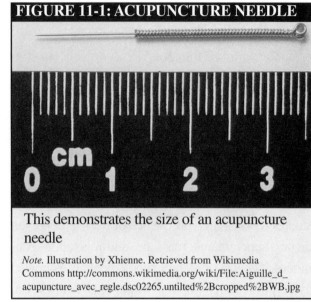

FIGURE 11-1: ACUPUNCTURE NEEDLE

This demonstrates the size of an acupuncture needle

Note. Illustration by Xhienne. Retrieved from Wikimedia Commons http://commons.wikimedia.org/wiki/File:Aiguille_d_ acupuncture_avec_regle.dsc02265.untilted%2Bcropped%2BWB.jpg

There are different ideas as to how aromatherapy may work. Scent receptors in the nose are known to send chemical messages through the olfactory nerve to the brain's limbic region, which influences emotional responses, heart rate, blood pressure, and respiration. These connections explain the effects of essential oils' pleasant smells. The effects may partly depend on previous associations of the person with a particular scent. Laboratory studies suggest that the oils can affect organ function, although whether this can be useful is not yet clear (Campenni, Crawley, & Meier, 2004). Many aromatherapists are trained as massage therapists, psychologists, social workers, or chiropractors and use the oils as part of their practices. The essential oils can be used one at a time or in combination and may be inhaled or applied to the skin (see Figure 11-2).

Early clinical trials suggest aromatherapy may have some benefit as a complementary treatment in reducing stress, pain, nausea, and depression. Some studies show no difference in outcome between massage with aromatherapy oils and massage without them (Soden, Vincent, Craske, Lucas, & Ashley, 2004). There are also reports that inhaled peppermint, ginger, and cardamom oil seem to relieve the nausea caused by chemotherapy and radiation.

FIGURE 11-2: AROMATHERAPY

Aromatherapy oils are heated for inhalation

Note. Illustration Anonymous. Retrieved from Wikimedia Commons http://commons.wikimedia.org/wiki/File:Aromatas.JPG

Aromatherapy is generally safe. However, essential oils usually should not be taken internally as many of them are poisonous. Some oils can cause sensitization (allergy to the oil) and may cause irritation if applied undiluted to the skin.

Art Therapy

Art therapy is used to help people manage physical and emotional problems by using creative activities to express emotions. It provides a way for people to come to terms with emotional conflicts, increase self-awareness, and express unspoken and often unconscious concerns about their illness and their lives. It may include dance and movement, drama, poetry, and photography as well as the more traditional art methods.

In art therapy patients are given the tools they need to produce paintings, drawings, sculptures, and many other types of artwork. Art therapists work with patients individually or in groups. The role of the art therapist is to help patients express themselves through their creations and to talk to patients about their emotions and concerns as they relate to their art.

Case studies have reported that art therapy benefits patients with both emotional and physical ill-nesses (Walsh, Martin, & Schmidt, 2004). Some of the potential uses of art therapy include use in reducing anxiety levels, improving recovery times, decreasing hospital stays, improving communication and social function, and pain control.

Art therapy is considered safe when conducted by a skilled therapist. It may be useful as a complementary therapy to help people with cancer deal with their emotions. Although uncomfortable feelings may be stirred up at times, this is considered part of the healing process. More information about art therapy is available through the American Art Therapy Association, including how to locate a licensed art therapist (http://www.arttherapy.org/index.htm).

Biofeedback

Biofeedback is a treatment method that uses monitoring devices to help people consciously control physical processes such as heart rate, blood pressure, temperature, sweating, and muscle tension that are usually controlled automatically. By helping a patient change heart rate, skin temperature, breathing rate, muscle control, and other such activities in the body, biofeedback can reduce stress and muscle tension from a number of causes. It can promote relaxation and, through a greater awareness of bodily functions, it can help a person regulate or alter other physical functions. Biofeedback is often a matter of trial and error as patients learn to adjust their thinking and connect changes in thought, breathing, posture, and muscle tension with changes in physical functions that are usually controlled unconsciously.

Although biofeedback has no direct effect on the development or progress of cancer, it can improve the quality of life for some people with cancer (Astin et al., 2003). Research has found that biofeedback can be helpful for patients in regaining urinary and bowel continence after surgery. In another clinical trial, relaxation therapy was more effective than biofeedback in reducing some side effects of chemotherapy. Biofeedback is often used along with relaxation for the best results.

Biofeedback is thought to be a safe technique. It is noninvasive. Biofeedback requires a trained and certified professional to manage equipment, interpret changes, and monitor the patient. Physical therapists often provide this therapy. A typical session takes 30 to 60 minutes (Mayo Clinic, 2007).

Guided Imagery

Guided imagery involves the use of the imagination to create sights, sounds, smells, tastes, or other sensations to create a kind of purposeful daydream. The techniques used in guided imagery can help to reduce stress, anxiety, and depression; manage pain; lower blood pressure; ease some of the side effects of chemotherapy; and create feelings of being in control (Astin et al., 2003).

For people with cancer, guided imagery can relieve nausea and vomiting from chemotherapy, relieve stress associated with having cancer, enhance the immune system, improve weight gain, combat depression, and lessen pain (Astin et al., 2003).

Imagery techniques are considered safe, especially under the guidance of a trained health professional. They are best used as complementary therapy; that is, along with conventional medical treatment.

Massage

Massage involves manipulation, rubbing, and kneading of the body's muscle and soft tissue to enhance function of those tissues and promote relaxation (Mayo Clinic, 2007). In all forms of massage, therapists use their hands (and sometimes forearms, elbows, and massage tools) to manipulate the body's soft tissue. Massage strokes can vary from light and shallow to firm and deep and from slow steady pressure to quick tapping (Figure 11-3). The choice will depend on the health and needs of the individual and the training and style of the massage therapist.

FIGURE 11-3: MASSAGE THERAPY

Note. Illustration by U.S. Air Force Tech. Sgt. Christopher A. Campbell. Retrieved from Wikimedia Commons http://commons.wikimedia.org/wiki/File:Massage_Lakenheath.jpg

In a research review, Deng & Cassileth (2005) reported that massage therapy has been shown to reduce pain and anxiety in randomized controlled trials. It can decrease stress, anxiety, depression, pain, and fatigue in some patients.

Massage or manipulation of a bone in an area of cancer metastasis could result in a bone fracture (Mayo Clinic, 2007). Also, people who have had radiation may find even light touch on the treatment area to be uncomfortable. Women with cancer should consult their physicians before undergoing any type of therapy that involves manipulation of joints and muscles. It is contraindicated in persons with signicant risk for a deep vein thrombosis (Mayo Clinic, 2007). Women receiving radiation treatment should not have lotion or oil used on the areas on which radiation is delivered.

Meditation

Meditation is a mind-body process that uses concentration or reflection to relax the body and calm the mind. Meditation may be done by choosing a quiet place free from distraction, sitting or resting quietly with eyes closed, noticing breathing and physical sensations, and noticing and then letting go of all intruding thoughts. The person may also achieve a relaxed, yet alert, state by focusing on a pleasant idea or thought or by chanting a phrase or special sound silently or aloud. The ultimate goal of meditation is to separate oneself mentally from the outside world by suspending the usual stream of consciousness. Some practitioners recommend two 15 to 20 minute sessions a day (Figure 11-4).

FIGURE 11-4: MEDITATION

Note. Illustration by Sarvodaya Shramadana. Retrieved from Wikimedia Commons http://commons.wikimedia.org/wiki/File:Early_Morning_Meditation.jpg

Meditation has been studied in clinical trials as a way of reducing stress on both the mind and body. Research shows that meditation can help reduce anxiety, stress, blood pressure, chronic pain, and insomnia. Meditation may help with symptoms of anxiety and mood disturbance. (Smith, Richardson, Hoffman, & Pilkington, 2005).

There are a number of different types of meditation. Although there are step by step guides available, most benefit from an initial session with a therapist skilled in teaching meditation skills (Mayo Clinic, 2007).

Music Therapy

Music therapy is offered by licensed healthcare professionals who use music in order to promote healing and enhance quality of life. Music therapy may be used to encourage emotional expression, promote social interaction, relieve symptoms, and for other purposes (Clark et al., 2006). Music therapists may use active (such as engaging the patient in singing or playing instruments) or passive (such as playing or singing for the patient) methods, depending on the patient's needs and abilities. Music therapy can help to reduce pain and relieve chemotherapy-induced nausea and vomiting. It may also relieve stress and provide an overall sense of well-being. Music therapy can lower heart rate, blood pressure, and breathing rate and can improve comfort, relaxation, and pain control (Pelletier, 2004). Sometimes, it is also used for distraction.

Music therapists design music sessions for individuals and groups based on their needs and tastes. Some aspects of music therapy include making music, listening to music, writing songs, and talking about lyrics. It may also involve imagery and learning through music. Music therapy can be provided in different places, such as hospitals, cancer centers, hospices, at home, or anywhere people can benefit from its calming or stimulating effects. The patient does not need to have any musical ability to benefit from music therapy.

In general, music therapy provided under the care of a professionally trained therapist has a helpful effect and is considered safe when used along with standard treatment. Musical intervention by untrained people can be ineffective, or even cause increased stress and discomfort. More information about professional licensed musical therapists is available through the American Music Therapy Association (http://www.musictherapy.org).

Psychotherapy

Psychotherapy covers a wide range of approaches designed to help people change their ways of thinking, feeling, or behaving. Psychotherapy can help people, including those with cancer, find the inner strength they need to improve their coping skills, allowing them to more fully enjoy their lives. Psychotherapy can be used to help people deal with the diagnosis and treatment of cancer. It can also be useful in overcoming depression and anxiety, which are common in people with cancer (Chow, Tsao, & Harth, 2004).

Psychotherapy is available in many forms. People may seek individual therapy, where there is a one-on-one relationship with a therapist. There are also therapists who work with couples or entire families, in order to deal with the impact of the cancer and its diagnosis on those most closely affected. Psychotherapy may also be practiced with groups, in which a number of people meet together to discuss common experiences and issues and to learn specific coping techniques.

Psychotherapists vary in the amount of their training and experience in dealing with issues that are important for people with cancer. Psychotherapy may be performed by practitioners with a number of different qualifications, including psychologists, marriage and family therapists, licensed clinical social workers, counselors, psychiatric nurses, and psychiatrists (Smith, 2005). Difficult personal issues that arise from psychotherapy can also be emotionally upsetting or uncomfortable.

Spirituality

Spirituality is generally described as an awareness of something greater than the individual self. It is often expressed through religion or prayer, although there are many other paths of spiritual pursuit and expression. Studies have found spirituality and religion are very important to the quality of life for some people with cancer. The psychological benefits of praying may include reduction of stress and anxiety, promotion of a more positive outlook, and the strengthening of the will to live (Lin & Bauer-Wu, 2003).

Spirituality has many forms and can be practiced in many ways. Prayer, for example, may be silent or spoken out loud and can be done alone in any setting or in groups. Spirituality has been shown to improve quality of life in persons with cancer (Mayo Clinic, 2007).

Spirituality can also be practiced without a formal religion. Meditation, 12-step work (as practiced in Alcoholics Anonymous and similar groups), and seeking meaning in life all involve spirituality (Smith, 2005). Many medical institutions and practitioners include spirituality and prayer as important components of healing. In addition, hospitals have chapels and contracts with ministers, rabbis, clerics, and voluntary organizations to serve their patients' spiritual needs.

Support Groups

Support groups present information, provide comfort, teach coping skills, help reduce anxiety, and provide a place for people to share common concerns and emotional support and, for many patients, can improve quality of life (Goodwin, 2005).

Many different kinds of support groups are available and they vary in their structure and activities (Mayo Clinic, 2007). A self-help support group is fully organized and managed by its members, usually volunteers. It is typically facilitated by members who are affected by the same type of cancer. Professionally operated support groups are facilitated by professionals who do not share the problem of the members, such as social workers, psychologists, or members of the clergy. The facilitator controls discussions and provides other managerial service. Such professionally operated groups are often found in institutional settings, such as a hospital or outpatient clinic.

Some support groups are time-limited, whereas others are ongoing. There are also support groups made up of people with the same type of cancer and others that include people who are having the same kind of treatment. Support groups are available for patients, family members, and other caregivers of people with cancer. The format of different groups varies from lectures and discussions to exploration and expression of feelings. Topics discussed by support groups are those of concern to the members and those the group leader thinks are important. They may be led by survivors, group members, or trained professionals. Benefits include that most support groups involve little or no cost to the participants.

Support groups can enhance the quality of life for people with cancer by providing information and support to overcome the feelings of aloneness and helplessness that sometimes result from a diagnosis of cancer. Some people with cancer are better able to deal with their disease when supported by others in similar situations (Penson, Talsania, Chabner, & Lynch, 2004).

Support groups vary in quality and focus. People with cancer may find the support group they have joined does not discuss topics of interest to them. Some people may find a support group upsetting because it stirs up too many uncomfortable feelings or because the leader is not skilled enough. Information that is shared in some groups may not always be reliable (Zabalegui, Sanchez, Sanchez, & Juando, 2005). Support groups that are on the Internet should be used with caution. This method cannot always assure privacy or confidentiality, and the people involved may have no special training or qualifications, especially if found in unmonitored chat rooms.

Tai Chi

Tai chi is an ancient Chinese martial art. It is a mind-body, self-healing system that uses movement, meditation, and breathing to improve health and well-being. Tai chi is useful as a form of exercise that may improve posture, balance, muscle

mass and tone, flexibility, stamina, and strength in older adults. Tai chi is also recognized as a method to reduce stress that can provide the same cardiovascular benefits as moderate exercise, such as lowered heart rate and blood pressure (Li et al., 2004).

The slow, graceful movements of tai chi, accompanied by rhythmic breathing, relax the body as well as the mind. Each form contains between 20 to 100 moves and can require up to 20 minutes to complete the movements, which are practiced in pairs of opposites; for example, a turn to the left follows a turn to the right (Figure 11-5). While doing these exercises, the person is urged to pay close attention to her breathing, which is centered in the diaphragm. Tai chi emphasizes technique rather than strength or power, although the slow, precise movements require good muscle control.

FIGURE 11-5: TAI CHI

Note. Illustration by World Tai Chi & Qigong Day. Retrieved from Wikimedia Commons http://commons.wikimedia.org/wiki/File:Ireland Killarney2WIKI.jpg

Tai chi has been associated with a sense of improved well-being and increased motivation to continue exercising. Many like tai chi because it is self-paced, noncompetitive, and does not require large amounts of space, special equipment, or clothing (Mayo Clinic, 2007). For some, it can reduce stress and provide the same cardiovascular benefits as moderate exercise, such as reduced heart rate and blood pressure (Mustian, Katula, & Zhao, 2006). Tai chi is considered to be a relatively safe, moderate physical activity. As with any form of exercise, it is important to be aware of physical limitations and patients should talk with their doctors before starting any type of therapy that involves movement of joints and muscles.

Yoga

Yoga is a form of non-aerobic exercise that involves a program of precise posture, breathing exercises, and meditation (see Figure 11-6). It is a way of life that combines ethical standards, dietary guidelines, physical movements, and meditation to create a union of mind, body, and spirit.

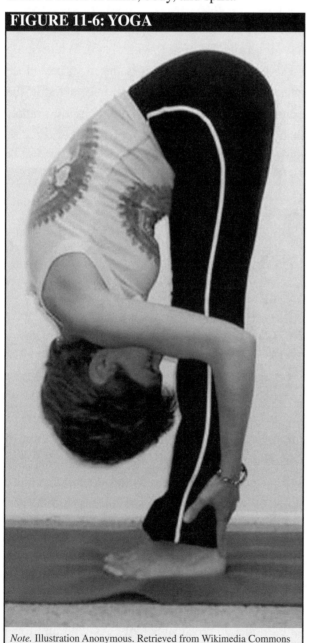

FIGURE 11-6: YOGA

Note. Illustration Anonymous. Retrieved from Wikimedia Commons http://commons.wikimedia.org/wiki/File:Yoga_posture_forward_bend _variation.jpg

A typical yoga session can last between 20 minutes and 1 hour. A yoga session starts with the person sitting in an upright position and performing gentle movements, all of which are done very slowly, while taking slow, deep breaths from the abdomen. Yoga requires several sessions a week in order for a person to become proficient. Yoga can be practiced at home without a teacher or in group classes. There are also many books and DVDs available on yoga. It is often offered through groups such as the Wellness Community (http://www.thewellnesscommunity.org).

Yoga can be used to control physical functions, such as blood pressure, heart rate, breathing, metabolism, body temperature, brain waves, and skin resistance (Cohen, Warneke, Fouladi, Rodriguez, & Chaoul-Reich, 2004). This can result in improved physical fitness, lower levels of stress, and increased feelings of relaxation and well-being. Some yoga postures are hard to achieve, and damage can occur from overstretching joints and ligaments. Persons should check with their physicians before initiating a program of yoga.

DIETARY SUPPLEMENTS

Many patients consider using dietary supplements, such as vitamins, herbs, or any product made from plants, as part of their cancer treatment. Currently, there are few governmental standards in place to control the production and ensure the safety, effectiveness, and quality of dietary supplements. Although the U.S. Food and Drug Administration (FDA) put out new regulations in 2007 to help improve the safety and consistency of supplements, some of these rules will not be fully in effect until 2010 (Mayo Clinic, 2007).

Patients must understand that dietary supplements, like medications, have potential risks and side effects. They can usually be used safely within certain dosage guidelines (Smith, 2005). However, unlike drugs, dietary supplements are primarily "self-prescribed," with little or no input from an informed healthcare provider. Often, there is not enough reliable information about the safe use and potential risks of dietary supplements.

Interestingly, dietary supplements, such as vitamins, herbals, and botanicals, are sold over the counter without a prescription, whereas medications are more closely regulated and controlled. Both have the potential for significant side effects and interactions with other supplements and medications. Patients often make the mistake of assuming that because supplements are sold over the counter, sometimes with little or no direction on the label, they are completely safe to take, even in high doses. In fact, large doses of some vitamins or minerals can be dangerous and toxic. Another common misconception is that if the substance is natural it is safe (Mayo Clinic, 2007).

Many people also assume that dietary supplements can safely be taken along with any prescription drugs. This is also not true. Most drug companies and producers of herbal supplements do not do research on possible drug interactions, so the risks of taking supplements with many medications are unknown.

All over-the-counter and prescription drugs are regulated in the United States by the FDA. Because dietary supplements (including all forms of botanicals and vitamins) are not considered drugs, they are not put through the same strict safety and effectiveness requirements that are applied to other drugs (Smith, 2005). Guidelines for selecting dietary supplements are included in Table 11-2.

PATIENT EVALUATION OF CAMS

With CAM availability and use ever increasing, patients should not be left to navigate the territory alone. Thus, advocacy for the patient – in the form of helping her evaluate CAMs – becomes the appropriate focus of nurses and other healthcare providers. Assessment of medical and lifestyle history should include direct questions about CAM. If a patient uses CAM it should be explored in more detail to determine if it is safe for an individual patient. Patients should be informed that CAM can be a useful adjunct to therapy, but only after discussing the safety in each individual situation. Patients should also be given guidance on selecting an appropriate CAM therapy and practitioner.

Table 11-3 provides a list of questions that patients can ask when considering CAMs. With the amount of CAM information and publicity on the Internet, no coaching of patients about CAMs is complete without guidance in reviewing potential treatments.

TABLE 11-2: PATIENT EDUCATION AND GUIDELINES FOR CHOOSING SAFE DIETARY SUPPLEMENT PRODUCTS (1 OF 2)

- Speak with a healthcare provider about any supplement under consideration. They should evaluate the supplement at reputable sources such as NCCAM or the NIH Office of Dietary Supplements (http://dietary-supplements.info.nih.gov).

- When shopping for supplements, the patient should look for USP or NF on the package label. The United States Pharmacopeia – National Formulary (USP-NF) is a book of public pharmacology standards. It contains standards for medicines, dosage forms, drug substances, medical devices, and dietary supplements.

- When shopping for a botanical, be sure to find a product that uses only the effective part of the plant. Avoid botanicals that have been made using the entire plant, unless the entire plant is recommended.

- The patient should be taught to consider the name and reputation of the manufacturer or distributor. Is it a nationally known name? Large companies with a reputation to uphold are more likely to manufacture their products under strict, quality-controlled conditions.

TABLE 11-2: PATIENT EDUCATION AND GUIDELINES FOR CHOOSING SAFE DIETARY SUPPLEMENT PRODUCTS (2 OF 2)

- The label should provide a way to contact the company if there are questions or concerns about the product. Reputable manufacturers will provide contact information on the label or packaging of their products.

- Patients should try to avoid mixtures of many different supplements. The more ingredients, the greater the chances of harmful effects.

- Patients should try to avoid supplements priced significantly lower than similar products; they are likely to be of lower quality.

- In particular, patients should be taught to avoid products that claim to be "miracle cures," "breakthroughs," or "new discoveries"; to have benefits but no side effects; or to be based on a "secret ingredient" or method. Such claims are almost always fraudulent, and the product may contain potentially harmful substances or contaminants.

- Patients should be taught to avoid products that claim to be effective treatment for a wide variety of unrelated illnesses. If a supplement claims that it can diagnose, treat, cure, or prevent disease, such as "cures cancer," the product is being sold illegally as a drug.

(Smith, 2005; Chong, 2006)

TABLE 11-3: SELECTING A CAM PRACTITIONER

Issues to consider when selecting a CAM Practitioner

- Choosing a CAM provider should be done with the same care as choosing any other member of the healthcare team. Patients seeking a CAM practitioner should speak with their healthcare provider(s) or someone knowledgeable about CAM, regarding the therapy under consideration. The provider may be able to make a recommendation for the type of CAM practitioner the patient is seeking.

- Before engaging a CAM practitioner the patient should ask basic questions about his or her credentials and practice. Where did the practitioner receive training? What licenses or certifications does he or she have? How much will the treatment cost? Patients should contact CAM professional organizations to get the names of practitioners who are certified. This means that they have proper training in their fields.

- CAM can be expensive. Patients should check with their insurers to see if the cost of therapy will be covered.

- After selecting a practitioner, the patient should make a list of questions to ask at the first visit. Ideally, she should bring a friend or family member who can help ask questions and note answers.

- On the first visit, the patient should be prepared to answer questions about her health history, including injuries, surgeries, and major illnesses as well as prescription medicines, vitamins, and other supplements.

- The patient should assess the first visit and decide if the practitioner is a good fit. Things to consider include level of comfort, willingness to answer questions, and reasonableness of the treatment plan.

SUMMARY

The use of CAMs is widespread, especially with women. Although no CAM has been shown to be effective in replacing conventional cancer treatment, CAMs have been shown to boost the perceived effectiveness of treatment and help patients better deal with treatment adverse effects. CAMs provide physical, emotional, and spiritual methods for mind-body interventions, biologically-based treatments, manipulative and body-based treatments, and energy therapies. CAM programs in practice are in their infancy. Clinicians are still educating themselves about what is needed to provide CAM options to patients. When integrating CAMs into practice, clinicians should help patients assess their reliability, their ability to blend with standard treatment protocols, and their real and perceived benefits to quality of life.

EXAM QUESTIONS

CHAPTER 11
Questions 89-94

Note: Choose the one option that BEST answers each question.

89. Women diagnosed with cancer choose to use CAM cancer treatments because they

    a. offer a sense of control.
    b. are inexpensive.
    c. are harmless.
    d. are pure.

90. Part of the mission of NCCAM is to

    a. train CAM researchers.
    b. promote the use of CAM.
    c. discourage the use of CAM.
    d. review all CAM research protocols.

91. A reliable source of information about CAM is

    a. patient testimonials.
    b. support groups.
    c. NCCAM.
    d. books on CAM,

92. An established form of complementary therapy is

    a. antidepressants.
    b. massage.
    c. antiemetics.
    d. pain medications.

93. An example of CAM includes

    a. paxitaxel.
    b. gamma knife radiation.
    c. sentinel node biopsy.
    d. music therapy.

94. A common misconception about the use of dietary supplements is

    a. they cannot ever be used by cancer patients.
    b. if the substance is natural it is safe.
    c. they are rarely used by cancer patients.
    d. vitamins and minerals are most helpful in very large doses.

REFERENCES

American Cancer Society. (2009). *American Cancer Society's complementary and alternative cancer methods handbook* (2nd ed.). Atlanta, GA: American Cancer Society.

Astin, J.A., Shapiro, S.L., Eisenberg, D.M., & Forys, K.L. (2003). Mind-body medicine: State of the science, implications for practice. *Journal of the American Board of Family Practice, 16*(2), 131-147.

Campenni, C.E., Crawley, E.J., & Meier, M.E. (2004). Role of suggestion in odor-induced mood change. *Psychological Reports, 94*(3, Part 2), 1127-1136.

Chong, O. (2006). An integrative approach to addressing clinical issues in complementary and alternative medicine in an outpatient oncology center. *Clinical Journal of Oncology Nursing, 10*(1), 83-88.

Chow, E., Tsao, M.N., & Harth, T. (2004). Does psychosocial intervention improve survival in cancer? A meta-analysis. *Palliative Medicine, 18*(1), 25-31.

Clark, M., Isaacks-Downton, G., Wells, N. Redlin-Frazier, S., Eck, C., Hepworth, J.T., et al. (2006). Use of preferred music to reduce emotional distress and symptom activity during radiation therapy. *Journal of Music Therapy, 43*(3), 247-265.

Cohen, L., Warneke, C., Fouladi, R.T., Rodriguez, M.A., & Chaoul-Reich, A. (2004). Psychological adjustment and sleep quality in a randomized trial of the effects of a Tibetan yoga intervention in patients with lymphoma. *Cancer, 100*(10), 2253-2260.

Deng, G. & Cassileth, B.R. (2005). Integrative oncology: Complementary therapies for pain, anxiety, and mood disturbance. *CA: A Cancer Journal for Clinicians, 55*(2), 109-116.

Ernst, G., Strzyz, H., & Hagmeister, H. (2003). Incidence of adverse effects during acupuncture therapy – A multicentre survey. *Complementary Therapies in Medicine, 11*(2), 93-97.

Ezzo, J.M., Richardson, M.A., Vickers, A., Allen, C., Dibble, S.L., Issell, B.F., et al. (2006). Acupuncture-point stimulation for chemotherapy-induced nausea or vomiting. *Cochrane Database of Systematic Reviews,* (2), CD002285.

Goodwin, P.J. (2005). Support groups in advanced breast cancer. *Cancer, 104*(11 Suppl), 2596-2601.

Li, F., Fisher, K.J., Harmer, P., Irbe, D., Tearse, R.G., & Weimer, C. (2004). Tai chi and self-rated quality of sleep and daytime sleepiness in older adults: A randomized controlled trial. *Journal of the American Geriatrics Society, 52*(6), 892-900.

Lin, H.R. & Bauer-Wu, S.M. (2003). Psycho-spiritual well-being in patients with advanced cancer: An integrative review of the literature. *Journal of Advanced Nursing, 44*(1), 69-80.

Mayo Clinic. (2007). *Mayo Clinic book of alternative medicine: The new approach to using the best of natural therapies and conventional medicine.* New York: Time Incorporated.

Mustian, K.M., Katula, J.A., & Zhao, H. (2006). A pilot study to assess the influence of tai chi chuan on functional capacity among breast cancer survivors. *Journal of Supportive Oncology, 4*(3), 139-145.

National Center for Complementary and Alternative Medicine. (2008). *The use of complementary and alternative medicine in the United States.* Retrieved February 28, 2010, from http://nccam.nih.gov/news/camstats/2007/camuse.pdf

Pelletier, C.L. (2004). The effect of music on decreasing arousal due to stress: A meta-analysis. *Journal of Music Therapy, 41*(3), 192-214.

Penson, R.T., Talsania, S.H., Chabner, B.A., & Lynch, T.J., Jr. (2004). Help me help you: Support groups in cancer therapy. *Oncologist, 9*(2), 217-225.

Sherman, K.J., Cherkin, D.C., Eisenberg, D.M., Erro, J., Hrbek, A., & Deyo, R.A. (2005). The practice of acupuncture: Who are the providers and what do they do? *Annals of Family Medicine, 3*(2), 151-158.

Smith, J.E., Richardson, J., Hoffman, C., & Pilkington, K. (2005). Mindfulness-based stress reduction as supportive therapy in cancer care: Systematic review. *Journal of Advanced Nursing, 52*(3), 315-327.

Soden, K., Vincent, K., Craske, S., Lucas, C., & Ashley, S. (2004). A randomized controlled trial of aromatherapy massage in a hospice setting. *Palliative Medicine, 18*(2), 87-92.

Walsh, S.M., Martin, S.C., & Schmidt, L.A. (2004). Testing the efficacy of a creative-arts intervention with family caregivers of patients with cancer. *Journal of Nursing Scholarship, 36*(3), 214-219.

Zabalegui, A., Sanchez, S., Sanchez, P.D., & Juando, C. (2005). Nursing and cancer support groups. *Journal of Advanced Nursing, 51*(4), 369-381.

CHAPTER 12

PATIENT EDUCATION CONSIDERATIONS

CHAPTER OBJECTIVE

After completing this chapter, the reader can discuss ways for the clinician and patient to evaluate and access a variety of educational resources.

LEARNING OBJECTIVES

After studying this chapter, the reader will be able to

1. discuss the nurse's role in patient education.

2. identify at least two benefits and two limitations of written educational resources.

3. describe the role of support groups in patient education.

4. list criteria to evaluate Web sites that present healthcare and patient information.

5. identify at least three Web sites that provide accurate and timely cancer-related information.

INTRODUCTION

The amount of information available regarding a diagnosis of cancer can be very overwhelming. Web sites, books, pamphlets, and help lines are available to provide information regarding diagnosis and treatment options and the use of complementary and alternative treatments. While many of the resources available provide quality information there are numerous warnings in both the academic and popular press regarding a wide range of medical misinformation and misrepresentation.

IMPORTANCE OF PATIENT EDUCATION

Helping patients to identify appropriate sources of information regarding cancer should be a priority for nurses throughout the cancer trajectory. During the initial assessment, the nurse should determine if the patient wants a large amount of information or if only the essential information should be provided over time.

Patient education is one of the most important and challenging services that nurses provide to patients. The nurse-patient relationship has shifted away from a paternalistic approach to one incorporating patients in decision making (Dickerson, Boehmke, Ogle, & Brown, 2005). In order to make good decisions, patients depend on timely and accurate information. Information on cancer can be delivered with written materials, through support groups, via the Internet, through cancer information centers, and other novel approaches.

Newly diagnosed patients with cancer often have complex educational and informational needs and are often challenged and expected to choose from a variety of diagnostic, treatment, and symptom management options that were not available previously (Balmer, 2005). Diagnostic procedures may include genetic testing, the use of tumor markers, or high-tech imaging to help guide treatment decisions. Complex surgical techniques, novel chemotherapy regimens, targeted therapies, and genetic approaches to treatment are available to patients with cancer. New antiemetics and biologic response modifiers allow for the administration of complicated chemotherapy regimens. Patients may choose to participate in clinical trials or undergo complex treatment regimens that might require innovative nursing interventions and comprehensive education to keep patients on track. Making informed treatment decisions becomes a high priority when so many choices are available (Dickerson et al., 2006).

Information related to treatment options that are provided to patients, family members, and caregivers may be extremely complex and confusing. In a busy unit, nurses often have little time to teach patients (Balmer, 2005). Work-related constraints and inadequate reimbursement can interfere with setting time aside for patient education. The Oncology Nursing Society's position statement on oncology services in the ambulatory practice setting acknowledges the challenges that oncology nurses face in providing complex cancer care in an environment of cost-cutting and downsizing (Oncology Nursing Society, 2006). Despite these constraints, nurses need to make patient education a priority to assure fewer complications with care and improved quality of life.

Teaching is often less effective in patients who experience high anxiety levels secondary to a cancer diagnosis (Williams & Schreier, 2005). If a patient is experiencing significant anxiety or pain, that must first be addressed prior to delivering an educational message, because the pain or anxiety can greatly limit a patient's ability to participate in and understand educational messages and materials. However, patient safety may depend on adequate understanding of the side effects of treatment and managing them at home. Optimal teaching plans ensure that the extent, content, and timing of information given to patients are tailored to meet their needs (Balmer, 2005). Patients who have difficulty using standard written materials or those who learn best from auditory or visual information may require innovative and nontraditional teaching methods.

WRITTEN MATERIALS

Traditional oncology teaching tools include written booklets and teaching sheets that can be expensive to print, require significant storage space, and need periodic updates. Because of those constraints, educational materials housed in healthcare facilities may be limited and information about rare cancers or unusual procedures may be difficult to find. Despite these limitations, there is still a place for printed literature in patient education. Most importantly, it can serve as a reinforcement of information after the patient leaves the medical setting.

Complex as well as easy-to-read booklets are intended to help patients and caregivers communicate with healthcare providers about their treatment and support needs. The easy-to-read booklets are often developed for newly diagnosed patients and individuals with lower reading levels. In order for such publications to be a useful adjunct to public education, patients must be able to comprehend the material, which requires varying degrees of health literacy.

Approximately one in five Americans is functionally illiterate. It is estimated that one in five Americans reads at a fifth grade level or lower. This is not necessarily due to learning disorders or low IQ. It is often linked to poverty, unemployment, being part of a minority group, or advancing age. Persons who are illiterate may be very functional as they have learned to compensate in other ways for their lack of reading skills (Balmer, 2005). These statistics need to be considered in the development of patient education materials.

An Institute of Medicine (Nielsen-Bohlman, Panzer, & Kindig, 2004) report defined health literacy as "the degree to which individuals can obtain, process, and understand basic health information and services they need to make appropriate health decisions" (p. 1). Readers of easy-to-read materials are not limited to those with little education, those who speak English as a second language, and children. Individuals who need easy-to-read materials are found in every race, ethnicity, age, and income group.

Another issue with literacy in oncology patients relates to an increased risk of cognitive dysfunction compared with those who have never had cancer or cancer treatment (Heflin et al., 2005). Cognitive dysfunction is a frequent finding in people with cancer, but it may go unnoticed. Cognitive problems result from many causes, including the direct effects of cancer on the central nervous system, indirect effects of certain cancers, and effects of cancer treatment on the brain. Cognitive dysfunction is often compounded by the mental and emotional aspects of dealing with a cancer diagnosis, including information overload, the stress of living with uncertainty and making treatment decisions, changes in schedule, anxiety, fear, and financial pressures. Ultimately, cognitive dysfunction also impacts literacy.

Some patients desire more complex and detailed information. This information is available from many agencies including the NIH, the American Cancer Society (ACS) and the National Comprehensive Cancer Network (NCCN). Many of these detailed guides can be accessed and downloaded from the agencies websites.

The following issues should be considered when determining if a brochure is acceptable for persons with lower health literacy. These concepts also apply when designing print pieces.

- There should be only one main objective or focus – not multiple concepts.

- Sometimes material is easier to understand if it is organized more as a conversation.

- Each page should flow into the next and mutually supporting concepts should be on the same page spread.

- The author should avoid using words with more than one meaning.

- The piece should be culturally sensitive (See Figure 12-1).

- The font should not be small and there should be a balance of white space and pictures with text. Too much text is overwhelming to persons with lower literacy (Karten, 2007).

FIGURE 12-1: CULTURALLY SENSITIVE INFORMATION

Cancer in Women of Color

NATIONAL INSTITUTES OF HEALTH
NATIONAL CANCER INSTITUTE

Note. Illustration Anonymous. Retrieved from National Cancer Institute http://visualsonline.cancer.gov/details.cfm?imageid=3498

Some patients are searching for more detailed and complex information. They may desire to access books and materials typically utilized by healthcare providers. In some cases, medical librarians may be able to assist with more intensive searches. This is an often overlooked resource in oncology.

SUPPORT GROUPS AS AN EDUCATIONAL RESOURCE

Support groups may include education, behavioral training, and group interaction. Behavioral training can involve muscle relaxation or meditation to reduce stress or the effects of chemotherapy or radiation therapy. Other groups function as an educational forum for group education. Still others provide a place for persons to share their feelings, concerns, and fears. Many support groups combine multiple approaches. People with cancer are often encouraged by healthcare professionals to seek support from groups of people who have direct or indirect experiences with the same type of cancer. Whether it is the direct purpose of the group or not, education about cancer and how to manage issues related to cancer occurs in support groups. For this reason, nurses need to understand what goes on in various groups their patients might participate in and provide patients with information on how to select a group that will provide reputable information.

Some support groups take place on the Internet (Chernecky, Macklin, & Walter, 2006). There are strengths and weaknesses associated with this support and education approach (see Table 12-1). They usually involve interacting with people by sending and receiving messages via computer. These groups vary widely in quality. Some are led by moderators in chat-rooms or on e-mail lists, and others are not moderated.

Some people may find online support groups helpful. For some, it may be comforting to share experiences with other people who are facing the same experiences. Online support groups are groups of people who share information and support over the Internet through chat rooms, discussion boards, or mailing lists. These Web sites allow people to connect with others who might otherwise be difficult to reach because of rarity of diagnosis, situation, or

TABLE 12-1: ADVANTAGES AND DISADVANTAGES OF INTERNET-BASED SUPPORT GROUPS

Advantages
- Eliminate prejudices that sometimes rise from face-to-face support groups (such as age, gender, dress, or social status)
- Around-the-clock availability
- Reasonable cost
- Ability to read others' comments without responding, until the user is comfortable with the group
- Ability to avoid being seen while affected by chemotherapy or the disease
- Geography is not a limitation

Disadvantages
- Typically no professional facilitator
- Inability to include (assess) nonverbal behavior
- Potential for non-cancer-related patients to present themselves falsely
- Language may be offensive
- Lag time between comments (postings)
- For some, delay in developing relationships and trust because of online communication only

geographic locations. They also allow a person to keep her real identity private if she chooses.

Still, these places may not be the best sources of health information, especially if they are not monitored by trained professionals or experts. Any information obtained in an online group should be discussed with a healthcare provider to determine if it is accurate or appropriate to apply in an individual situation.

Some support groups are organized according to the cancer type (Penson, Talsania, Chabner, & Lynch, 2004). For example, women with breast cancer may not be as comfortable in a mixed diagnosis group with men who have lung cancer or other types of cancer. In some circumstances, this type of grouping seems more natural and enables people to address common issues more effectively. Many women prefer to be in same sex and same tumor type groups (Goodwin, 2005).

The stage of the cancer experience is another way to organize a support group (Goodwin, 2005). The issues that arise for a person with a new diagnosis are different than for those who have recurrent cancer. For some, this is a very important distinction in choosing a support group.

Open membership in a group means that members may come and go within the group freely. There is often no requirement to sign up for the group ahead of time and no expectation that a patient will stay in a group over the group's time course. If an individual chooses to attend three meetings and is then unable to attend the next four, but wants to return again later, it is appropriate. In an open membership group, the membership will change with each group meeting. It is a poor choice for persons who are interested in consistent or intimate relationships or friendships. It is a good choice for persons who are not sure of a group or able to commit regularly to a group.

In a closed group, the group members usually pre-register for the group. The group achieves a certain number or mix and is then closed to new members. In a closed group, the members are usually expected to commit to a certain number of sessions in attendance. The advantage of this type of group is the consistency of the group members and the ability to get to know one another well and therefore support each other more fully. Sometimes this is just not feasible for cancer patients or their families given the demands of the illness. Closed groups often have a specific plan of education or topics to be discussed.

Most cancer support groups are peer support groups (Goodwin, 2005). This type of group typically consists of those who have similar experiences. The group may be led by a lay person or health professional. Shared experiences and information is why these groups are often cohesive. It can provide comfort, companionship, and a safe place to go with fear, guilt, pain, and depression. Not only is the peer network supportive, but it can also be empowering. Laughing about the unique experiences one has as a cancer survivor is best done with others who have similar experiences. Similarity of experiences can be very supportive. Education may be the framework for such a groups followed by a discussion.

An educational intervention group is a group that meets to share information on topics related to cancer. This type of group might include having a medical expert speak on a specific topic, such as infertility, genetics, a specific treatment, or side effect. Following the presentation, the group has a question and answer discussion with the expert. This type of group focuses more on medical information, but often provides some emotional support in the process of sharing. Sometimes, having a concrete topic makes it easier to move into personal discussion with people who find it hard to talk about their feelings otherwise (Zabalegui, Sanchez, Sanchez, & Juando, 2005). Also, having more information about the disease or treatment helps patients feel more in control.

Telephone support groups communicate by telephone, often by conference call (Marcus et al., 2002). This is helpful for people who are unable or unwilling to participate face-to-face. These groups can take any form. Some may be educational, whereas others may be focused on stress management. Some may have open membership, and others may be closed to new members. They can be time limited or ongoing. Sometimes, participants contact each other in-between group sessions and provide individual support. This type of group can be challenging because members are not able to see each other's facial expressions. Careful listening and concentration are required. This may be a good option for someone who is physically immobile yet desires more contact with people. It is important that these groups are affiliated with a reputable organization and hosted by a trained professional (Coleman et al., 2005).

Support groups can be traditional discussions, classes to learn new skills, or exercise/lifestyle classes. All of these formats enable people to share with others and learn new ways to manage their cancer diagnoses and treatments (see Figure 12-2).

FIGURE 12-2: SUPPORT GROUPS

Note. Illustration by Rhoda Baer. Retrieved from National Cancer Institute http://visualsonline.cancer.gov/details.cfm?imageid=7501

There are also support groups for children who have parents with a diagnosis of cancer. A support group for children gives them a safe place to verbalize their frustrations and ask questions. It can provide much education for children that is delivered at an age-appropriate level. It is often very therapeutic for children to meet other children whose parents have cancer. Children can feel very isolated if a parent is sick and think that no one else has the same feelings and worries. Support groups for children should be lead by professionals. People like school-teachers or guidance counselors, art therapists, music therapists, oncology social workers, or nurses who have experience with children are examples of possible group leaders (Kennedy, McIntyre, Worth, & Hogg, 2008). The professional should be knowledgeable about cancer and the issues it raises for families. Parents can check with resources in their community to find support groups for children whose parents have cancer.

INTERNET – A COMMUNICATION TOOL

The Internet has become an integral part of the way our world communicates. For healthcare providers and their patients, the Internet offers an unprecedented tool of contact, convenience, and personal control. Information is abundant, available anytime, and provides disease reviews, treatment information, clinical trials, latest research news, decision-making tools, and discussion groups. Patients utilize the Internet in similar ways.

Nurses must understand how the Internet has influenced the ways in which patients learn about and cope with their diseases. Nurses encounter a number of challenges in integrating online information into patient teaching. These challenges include time constraints, new diagnostic procedures, complex treatment protocols, lack of training, and insufficient access to hardware and software. Advantages associated with the use of the Internet include access 24 hours a day, seven days a week to current information in a variety of patient-friendly formats. Although the Internet may be a source of empowerment for patients, it can overwhelm users because of the sheer amount of information that is available. Others may be unable to access Internet resources based on income, education, physical limitations, or ethnic background. Issues of trustworthiness and security are concerns in all cases where online sources are used for health-related information. Nurses are uniquely suited to use online resources to aid in patient education and support. Computer skills previously gained in other aspects of nursing practice can provide a basis for integrating online resources into patient care.

For many patients, the Internet has become one of the first places to go for important information, including health information that ultimately guides treatment decisions. The Internet provides instant access to almost any topic. Many households have at least one computer and access to the Internet.

Others access the Internet at work or other public places such as libraries that provide access (see Figure 12-3).

FIGURE 12-3: INTERNET INFORMATION SEARCHES

Note. Illllustration by Bill Branson. Retrieved from National Cancer Institute http://visualsonline.cancer.gov/details.cfm?imageid=3758

There is an enormous amount of cancer information on the Internet. This information can help people facing cancer make decisions about their illnesses and treatment. It is important for patients and families to understand that just because there is a lot of information available, it does not provide any guarantee that the information is current or accurate. Websites can provide basic facts about certain types of cancer, assist in locating the most current clinical trials, and provide information and support in dealing with cancer. It is possible to access information on research articles, doctors and hospitals, cancer treatment guidelines, drug information, and information on complementary and alternative therapies.

Unfortunately, there is a great deal of inaccurate information out there too. The Internet is not a peer-reviewed journal and anyone can post almost anything. Just because it is posted, does not mean it is accurate. Some inaccurate information comes from well-meaning, but misinformed, people. There are also those who purposely try to deceive people, either to sell their ideas or their products. Because of this, it is important to teach patients to consider the credentials and reputation of the person or organization providing the information.

Always remember, not all information is good information.

There are millions of Web sites on the Internet. Finding sites that are responsible, accurate, and address an individual's specific concern or question can be more challenging than it appears.

There are definite advantages to the Internet in some cases for patient education. The Internet can offer patients more flexible and user-friendly formats than traditional written teaching materials. Online sources also provide a variety of teaching tools that use audio and video formats, which may be beneficial to people who have limited visual or language skills. Patients often feel empowered when they have access to information and have been reported to cope better and experience less uncertainty when using the Internet as a resource for obtaining health-related material (LaCoursiere, Knobf, & McCorkle, 2005). Online information can reinforce teaching provided in the healthcare setting, at a time of patients' choosing.

There are clearly disadvantages to the Internet for patient education. For some patients, the volume of information is excessive and can be overwhelming. Internet searches may not provide information that is personally relevant. The Internet is a potentially powerful tool for the education of patients, but its usefulness is limited by accessibility factors. Those who are most likely to have a computer from which to access the Internet, generally have higher incomes and levels of education, whereas those lacking access are more likely to have low income, have less education, and be from a minority group or disabled (Eysenbach, 2003). Although older adults in the United States are using technology in increasing numbers, they typically report more difficulty than younger people in learning to operate computers and use the Internet effectively. Many adults may also experience frustration when using the Internet to obtain health information because many online sites require at least a high-school proficiency in reading (Eysenbach, 2003).

One approach to help patients access safe information is to provide them with a list of Web addresses to sites that are reputable. Patients can type the Web address (also known as the uniform resource locator, or URL) of the exact Web site and be taken there. This approach ensures patients' access to safe information. If the site does not have the information the patient is searching for, this method can be a source of frustration with patients. Other considerations when evaluating Internet sites are shown in Table 12-2.

Nurses can integrate Internet resources into practice first, by reviewing reputable sites, and then incorporating the information into teaching sessions with patients. Computers with Internet access and appropriate links to patient-related material could be provided in clinic waiting rooms. If clinics provide their own Web sites for patient information, those Web sites should be user friendly and easy to navigate (Chernecky et al., 2006; Friedman, Hoffman-Goetz, & Arocha, 2006). Volunteers with technological savvy could assist patients who wish to access information on clinic computers. Patient education materials, offered on CDs and DVDs, may be alternatives to online resources. Handouts should be available for those who prefer hard copies of educational material or links to online

TABLE 12-2: TIPS FOR FINDING HEALTH INFORMATION RESOURCES ON-LINE

- Choosing an on-line health information resource is like choosing a healthcare provider. In most cases an individual is encouraged to get opinions from several providers. Therefore, individuals shouldn't rely on just one Internet site for all health information. A good rule of thumb is to find a Web site that has a person, institution, or organization in which the user already has confidence. If possible, the user should seek information from several sources and not rely on a single source of information.

- The user should trust what is seen or read on the Internet only if the user can validate the source of the information. Authors and contributors should always be identified, along with their affiliations and financial interests, if any, in the content. Phone numbers, e-mail addresses, or other contact information should also be provided.

- Question Web sites that credit themselves as the sole source of information on a topic as well as sites that disrespect other sources of knowledge.

- The user should not be fooled by a comprehensive list of links. Any Web site can link to another and this in no way implies endorsement from either site.

- Find out if the site is professionally managed and reviewed by an editorial board of experts to ensure that the material is both credible and reliable. Sources used to create the content should be clearly referenced and acknowledged.

- Medical knowledge is continually evolving. Make sure that all clinical content includes the date of publication or modification.

- Any and all sponsorship, advertising, underwriting, commercial funding arrangements, or potential conflicts should be clearly stated and separated from the editorial content. A good question to ask is: Does the author or authors have anything to gain from proposing one particular point of view over another?

- Avoid any on-line physician who proposes to diagnose or treat without a proper physical examination and consultation regarding medical history.

- Read the Web site's privacy statement and make certain that any personal medical or other information supplied will be kept absolutely confidential.

- Most importantly, users should be warned to utilize common sense. This includes to shop around, always get more than one opinion, be suspicious of miracle cures, and always read the fine print.

(Chernecky et al., 2006; Dickerson et al., 2006; Eysenbach, 2003) resources. Audio tapes or videos could be offered to those who are unable or unwilling to use computer resources.

More commonly, patients are searching for information on a certain topic and do not exactly know where to look for it. In this case the patient typically accesses a search engine. The patient enters a keyword or phrase into a search engine, and the engine looks through the World Wide Web for the desired information and provides a list of links to Web pages related to the word or phrase entered. Most search engines are free to the user. Examples of search engines include:

- Google (www.google.com)

- Yahoo (www.yahoo.com)

- MSN (www.msn.com)

- AltaVista (www.altavista.com)

- Hotbot (www.hotbot.com)

- About.com (www.about.com)

- Good Search (www.goodsearch.com)

Some of the sites, such as Google, are designed mainly for searching, whereas others, such as Yahoo, have a search engine as part of a larger Web site that also has other functions. Patients need education and reminders that all of these search engines return "sponsored" findings with their search results. Often, these links are at the top of the result list. Sometimes, patients find helpful information links there, but many of the sponsors are trying to sell a product to make money. Although seller information can be helpful for many products, it is not likely to be the kind of information patients should use in choosing a cancer treatment.

Most Web sites also have lists of Web links or a place that one can click on to go to similar types of sites. A link will usually be underlined, or in a special color, or have some other sort of sign to let the user know that if they click on it, they will be taken to another place on the Internet. Patients need to

understand that a link could lead them to a less than reputable site.

Cancer information on the Internet comes from many different sources. Many of these sources are people or groups that really want to help others learn more. Many reputable professional organizations provide a wealth of useful and accurate information at no cost via the Internet. A sample of such organizations is shown in Table 12-3. However, because anyone can post information on the Internet, some people may be passing along information that is wrong.

TABLE 12-3: REPUTABLE INTERNET SITES FOR CANCER INFORMATION
American Cancer Society   www.cancer.org
Cancer.Net   www.cancer.net/portal/site/patient
CancerWise (an online newsletter from The University of Texas, MD Anderson Cancer Center)   www.cancerwise.org
Medline Plus   www.nlm.nih.gov/medlineplus/cancers.html
National Cancer Institute (NCI)   www.cancer.gov
National Comprehensive Cancer Network   www.nccn.org
Centers for Disease Control and Prevention (CDC)   www.cdc.gov
Federal Trade Commission (FTC)   www.ftc.gov
National Institutes of Health (NIH)   www.nih.gov
National Center for Complementary and Alternative Medicine (part of NIH)   http://nccam.nih.gov
U.S. Food & Drug Administration (FDA)   www.fda.gov

Unfortunately, some Internet sites are set up to deceive patients. Scam artists and other dishonest people use the Internet for two important reasons, including the low cost and relative anonymity when posting information. Selling a product (bogus or not) over the Internet generally costs much less money than opening and running an actual store. The Internet also allows the author of the web page to get information, messages, or products out to people all over the world. All it takes is some computer programming experience and a computer to host the Web site.

The impersonal nature of the Web makes it easier to mislead people. A patient might be reluctant to purchase a dietary supplement from a small run-down building in an undesirable neighborhood, but could easily be misled and tricked into purchasing the same supplement from the same retailer if it was offered through an Internet site that was well-constructed. The product could be bogus in either case, but the anonymity of the Internet makes it more difficult to discern if the item, business, or information is legitimate. This is why patients should be instructed to exercise caution when obtaining information from the Internet and especially before purchasing medications, supplements, or other medical devices online.

Patients should be instructed that the information found on the Internet should not take the place of medical advice. Any health-related problem should be discussed with a healthcare provider. This is true for making a diagnosis as well as with many of the risk assessment models available online. Even if a risk calculation is made, the risk needs to be interpreted by a medical professional and used to guide screening or prevention decisions. There is no other way to get the same experience and care as sitting down with a healthcare provider who can examine a health history, an individual's unique medical situation, and symptoms. Considerations for evaluating a website are shown in Table 12-4.

The most reliable sources of health information tend to be government agencies, hospitals, universities, and major public health and health advocacy

TABLE 12-4: EVALUATING MEDICAL RESOURCES ON THE WEB
• Who runs this site?
• Who pays for the site?
• What is the purpose of the site?
• Where does the information come from?
• What is the basis of the information?
• How is the information selected?
• How current is the information?
• How does the site choose links to other sites?
• What information about the user does the site collect, and why?
• How does the site manage interactions with visitors?

organizations, such as the American Cancer Society, whose information is reviewed by noted experts and updated often.

The source of funding for the site should also be easy to figure out, as it can affect what is presented on the site and how it is presented. Government sites end in gov. Many universities provide reputable information for their patients; the site frequently ends in edu. If the source is a commercial business, such as an advertiser or provider of a service or product, there may be some bias or prejudice in the information. These sites frequently end in com. Not for profit sites and organizations typically end in org. Even on non-profit Web sites, if the site is full of ads or is supported or funded by an outside company, it's important for the patient to ask whether the information there might be slanted in some way. This is not always the case, but it should make the user more cautious.

The U.S. Federal Trade Commission (FTC) has developed a list of claims that should make an individual suspicious of a Web site:

• Claims of a "scientific breakthrough," "miraculous cure," "secret ingredient," or "ancient remedy."

- Claims that a product can cure a wide range of illnesses. (No single product can do this.)

- Case histories of people who have had amazing results (but no clear scientific data).

- Claims that a product is available only from one source (especially if you must pay in advance).

- Claims of a "money-back" guarantee. (Although this may make the product seem risk-free, it is often impossible to actually get your money back.)

- Web sites that fail to list the company's name, street address, phone number, and other contact information (FTC, 2001).

Problems in any of these areas should raise a red flag – a warning – to the user that the site may contain information that is not based on careful science and cannot be trusted. This may be especially important when looking at sites promoting complementary or alternative cancer treatments.

Another tool to assess the quality of a Web site is the Health On the Net Foundation (HON). HON is an organization based in Switzerland whose mission is to guide people to useful and reliable online medical and health information. To be allowed to display the HON logo, participating Web sites must agree to abide by an ethical code of conduct. The HON code tries to improve the quality of medical information on the Internet through some basic principles, which cover things like authorship, documentation of materials, and sponsorship of the site.

The organization also tries to actively promote effective Internet use with specific medical search engines that provide reliable and scientifically sound information. For more information, visit the HON Web site (www.hon.ch).

CANCER INFORMATION CENTERS

Many institutions as well as the government provide patient education through cancer information centers. Many patients benefit from this coordinated approach to patient education.

The American Cancer Society's National Cancer Information Center (NCIC) is a nationwide help line that is open 24 hours a day, 7 days a week. It answers calls and emails from cancer patients, family members, and friends of cancer patients, and others who have questions about cancer-related issues. The database includes information about various types of cancer, cancer treatments, how to manage symptoms, prevention and detection guidelines, and many other topics. Each document in the database has been written and reviewed by a team of medical experts and further reviewed by editorial professional staff to translate any difficult medical terminology. This comprehensive information helps cancer patients better understand their disease and make informed decisions about their care.

Individuals who contact the ACS with more specific medical and cancer-related questions may be referred to Oncology Nurse Information Specialists. They provide clinical information, such as information on treatments, side effects of treatments, testing, and disease-related questions. The Cancer Information Specialists answer more than 1.4 million calls yearly (ACS, 2010).

The National Cancer Institute's Cancer Information Service (CIS) provides current and accurate cancer information to patients, their families, the public, and health professionals. It serves the United States, Puerto Rico, the U.S. Virgin Islands, and the Pacific Islands. The Cancer Information Service provides personalized, confidential responses to specific questions about cancer. There are two ways that patients can access this service.

- By telephone: U.S. residents may call the CIS toll free at 1-800-4-CANCER (1-800-422-6237). Information specialists answer calls Monday through Friday from 9:00 a.m. to 4:30 p.m. local time, in English or Spanish. Callers with TTY equipment may call 1-800-332-8615. Callers also have the option of listening to recorded information about cancer 24 hours a day, 7 days a week.

- Online: Information specialists also offer online assistance in English, Monday through Friday from 9:00 a.m. to 11:00 p.m. Eastern Time at www.cancer.gov.

Many institutions offer cancer information centers, which often operate on a walk-in basis to assist anyone whose life has been affected by cancer. Such centers might serve patients, their families, medical professionals, and others who need current information on cancer prevention; early detection, diagnosis and treatment; coping; and community resources (see Figure 12-4). Cancer information centers might typically provide:

- Internet searches
- Educational programs
- Literature, videotapes, and audio tapes
- Lending library of books
- Smoking cessation programs
- Support groups
- Classes on chemotherapy and other treatments
- Wigs and turbans
- Breast prostheses
- Nutritional supplements
- Personalized one on one education and support

FIGURE 12-4: CANCER INFORMATION CENTERS

Note. Illustration by Bill Branson. Retrieved from National Cancer Institute http://visualsonline.cancer.gov/details.cfm?imageid=3749

NONTRADITIONAL APPROACHES TO PATIENT EDUCATION

Nurses should not forget that there are other ways to approach and incorporate patient education into their practices. These approaches vary from one institution to another. Nurses need to think about ways to creatively increase patient education opportunities in their institution.

Posters can be effective and inexpensive teaching tools. They can be purchased from commercial agencies and often are available free of charge from organizations such as the ACS. Such posters provide a way to provide a quick message.

Bulletin boards are another effective way to deliver information. They can be placed in waiting rooms and examination rooms. The information can be updated or changed on a regular basis. Bulletin boards are relatively inexpensive and can provide a means to tailor education to a specific population, geographic region, or type of cancer. If a nurse provides the educational material, often a volunteer can creatively construct the bulletin board in a visually appealing way.

Sometimes the nurse can distribute an item to promote a healthy lifestyle. Examples include sunscreen samples, hats to block ultraviolet light exposure, or a recipe with a healthy food item. Pedometers are often relatively inexpensive and can be used to promote participation in a walking program. When such items are distributed, there needs to be an educational message to promote the proper use of such an item.

SUMMARY

Patient education is a continual challenge for nurses. There are traditional forms of patient education, including individual sessions and brochures. These can be an effective form of patient education in many cases. The Internet is rapidly becoming a source of cancer information. Patients need to be instructed on how to access reliable information on the Internet. Support groups also provide a source of education and patients need to be referred to reputable groups. Nurses also need to consider the individual environments in which they practice and select educational approaches that meet the needs of the particular populations they serve.

CHAPTER 12
Questions 95-100

Note: Choose the one option that BEST answers each question.

95. The purpose of the educational component of nursing is to help patients acquire the knowledge they need to

    a. comply with physician's orders.

    b. learn what health professionals believe they need to know.

    c. understand the particular diagnosis.

    d. participate in treatment decisions and self-care.

96. Mrs. A. is recovering from a hemicolectomy she had 3 days ago. The nurse is ready to begin a 15-minute teaching session on ostomy care. A major barrier that needs to be addressed prior to beginning this patient education is

    a. her socioeconomic status.

    b. her pain, rated a 7 out of 10.

    c. the type of college degree she has completed.

    d. her ability to walk.

97. When developing health-related materials, they should be targeted at individuals with a

    a. 3rd grade reading level.

    b. 5th grade reading level.

    c. 7th grade reading level.

    d. 9th grade reading level.

98. The World Wide Web can provide patients with cancer with

    a. a physical assessment.

    b. private and confidential information.

    c. always accurate information.

    d. access to national and worldwide support groups.

99. When accessing an Internet healthcare Web site, be cautious if

    a. respected physicians and nurses are on its editorial review board.

    b. the Web site credits itself as the sole source of information on a topic.

    c. it was updated in the past 3 days.

    d. the affiliations of the editorial review board are posted.

100. A Web site that provides accurate health-related information is

    a. www.cancer.org (American Cancer Society).

    b. www.Laetrile.org (Laitrile interest group).

    c. www.foxnews.com (Fox News Service).

    d. www.docinabox.com (Private MD).

This concludes the final examination.

Please answer the evaluation questions found on page v of this workbook.

REFERENCES

American Cancer Society. (2010). *Cancer facts & figures 2010.* Atlanta, GA: American Cancer Society.

Balmer, C. (2005). The information requirements of people with cancer: Where to go after the "patient information leaflet"? *Cancer Nursing, 28*(1), 36-44.

Chernecky, C., Macklin, D., & Walter, J. (2006). Internet design preferences of patients with cancer. *Oncology Nursing Forum, 33*(4), 787-792.

Coleman, E.A., Tulman, L., Samarel, N., Wilmoth, M.C., Rickel, L., Rickel, M., et al. (2005). The effect of telephone social support and education on adaptation to breast cancer during the year following diagnosis. *Oncology Nursing Forum, 32*(4), 822-829.

Dickerson, S.S., Boehmke, M., Ogle, C., & Brown, J.K. (2006). Seeking and managing hope: Patients' experiences using the Internet for cancer care. *Oncology Nursing Forum, 33*(1), E8-E17. Retrieved January 2, 2008, from http://ons.metapress.com/content/c213l8332p0 85456/fulltext.pdf

Eysenbach, G. (2003). The impact of the Internet on cancer outcomes. *CA: A Cancer Journal for Clinicians, 53*(6), 356-371.

Federal Trade Commission. (2001). *FTC facts for consumers: 'Miracle' health claims add a dose of skepticism.* Retrieved February 28, 2010, from http://www.ftc.gov/bcp/edu/pubs/consumer/ health/hea07.pdf

Friedman, D.B., Hoffman-Goetz, L., & Arocha, J.F. (2006). Health literacy and the World Wide Web: Comparing the readability of leading incident cancers on the Internet. *Medical Informatics and the Internet in Medicine, 31*(1), 67-87.

Goodwin, P.J. (2005). Support groups in advanced breast cancer. *Cancer, 104*(11 Suppl), 2596-2601.

Heflin, L.H., Meyerowitz, B.E., Hall, P., Lichtenstein, P., Johansson, B., Pedersen, N.L., et al. (2005). Cancer as a risk factor for long-term cognitive deficits and dementia. *J Natl Cancer Inst. 2005 Jun 1;97*(11):854-6.

Karten, C. (2007). Easy to write? Creating easy-to-read patient education materials. *Clinical Journal of Oncology Nursing, 11*(4), 506-510.

Kennedy, C., McIntyre, R., Worth, A., & Hogg, R. (2008). Supporting children and families facing the death of a parent: Part 2. *International Journal of Palliative Nursing, 14*(5), 230-237.

LaCoursiere, S.P., Knobf, M.T., & McCorkle, R. (2005). Cancer patients' self-reported attitudes about the Internet. *Journal of Medical Internet Research, 7*(3), e22. Retrieved February 2, 2009, from http://www.jmir.org/2005/3/e22

Marcus, A.C., Garrett, K.M., Kulchak-Rahm, A., Barnes, D., Dortch, W., & Juno, S. (2002). Telephone counseling in psychosocial oncology: A report from the Cancer Information and Counseling Line. *Patient Education and Counseling, 46*(4), 267-275.

Nielsen-Bohlman, L., Panzer, A.M., & Kindig, D.A. (Eds.). (2004). *Health literacy: A prescription to end confusion.* Washington, DC: National Academies Press.

Oncology Nursing Society. (2006). Oncology Nursing Society Position: Oncology services in the ambulatory practice setting. *Oncology Nursing Forum, 33*(4), 687-688.

Penson, R.T., Talsania, S.H., Chabner, B.A., & Lynch, T.J., Jr. (2004). Help me help you: Support groups in cancer therapy. *Oncologist, 9*(2), 217-225.

Williams, S.A. & Schreier, A.M. (2005). The role of education in managing fatigue, anxiety, and sleep disorders in women undergoing chemotherapy for breast cancer. *Applied Nursing Research, 18*(3), 138-147.

Zabalegui, A., Sanchez, S., Sanchez, P.D., & Juando, C. (2005). Nursing and cancer support groups. *Journal of Advanced Nursing, 51*(4), 369-381.

APPENDIX A

SELECTED NURSING INTERVENTIONS FOLLOWING SURGERY

Nursing Diagnosis	Possible Nursing Interventions
Impaired skin integrity	1. Assess skin reactions. 2. Instruct patient and family to keep skin clean. 3. Instruct patient to avoid shaving within area of treatment. 4. Apply moisturizing lotion as directed for skin dryness. 5. Change dressings as instructed.
Activity intolerance	1. Assess level of fatigue. 2. Advise patient to plan rest periods throughout the day. 3. Maintain nutritional intake. 4. Utilize resources to conserve energy. 5. Obtain assistance for chores and transportation as needed.
Anorexia	1. Assess appetite. 2. Monitor weight. 3. Recommend frequent, small meals. 4. Advise on use of nutrient-dense foods such as nutritional supplements. 5. Refer to a dietician.
Pain	Pain typically is located in lower pelvis, radiating down the back of the leg (sciatic nerve or pain occurs because of metastasis to bone or other organs). 1. Assess level of pain using appropriate tools (1 to 10 scale). 2. Assess level of insomnia using appropriate tools. 3. Assess level of anxiety using appropriate tools. 4. Teach patient and family about principles of pain management) – addiction versus tolerance, medication (dose, route, steady state of medication), synergy of adjunct medications, cognitive/behavioral techniques to decrease pain, tolerance and addiction, and adverse effects (constipation). 5. Administer narcotics to cover pain, including breakthrough pain.
Preoperative: Bowel	1. Bowel rest before surgery; enemas and nothing by mouth, as ordered.
Ascites	1. Assess for signs and symptoms – weight gain, trouble breathing, shortness of breath, nausea/vomiting, increased pain over 2 to 4 days. 2. Encourage proper diet, pain control, and activity. 3. Report symptoms to physician. 4. Support postoperative paracentesis or pleurocentesis.

275

continued on next page

5. Administer oral diuretics, as prescribed.

6. Support the patient pre- and post-sclerosing procedures.

Pericardial effusion	1. Assess for signs and symptoms – nausea/vomiting, chest pain, dizziness, swollen hands/feet, feeling restless, change in memory or being confused.
	2. Report symptoms to physician.
Pulmonary Embolism and Deep Vein Thrombosis (DVT)	(Bedrest and immobility after pelvic surgery increases the risk.)
	1. Assess for pulmonary embolism and DVT.
	2. Administer anticoagulation therapy as ordered.
	3. Administer pneumatic calf compression as ordered.
	4. Support non-weight bearing leg movement as ordered.
Impaired Wound Healing	1. Assess wound areas for infection – genitourinary and GI tracts near surgical incisions.
	2. Prevent infection and contamination with monitoring, hygiene, and frequent dressing changes and as needed debridement.
Bleeding	(Bleeding may be associated with all post-surgical courses and also with cramping, which may be a sign of bowel obstruction – especially in ovarian cancer.)
	1. Monitor sites of bleeding for signs and symptoms – mouth, skin, urine, vomit, and vaginal bleeding.
	2. Support prevention through skin care (avoiding falls, protecting skin from cuts and scrapes), mouth care, and digestive support (stool softeners, diet, exercise).
	3. Manage bleeding: Apply pressure and ice to bleeding areas.
	4. Note color and amount of bleeding.
	5. Report bleeding occurrences, as needed, to physician.

APPENDIX B

SELECTED NURSING DIAGNOSES FOR RADIATION THERAPY

Nursing Diagnoses	Possible Nursing Interventions
Impaired skin integrity	1. Assess skin reactions. 2. Instruct patient and family to keep skin clean. 3. Instruct patient to avoid shaving within area of treatment. 4. Apply moisturizing lotion as directed for skin dryness as ordered. 5. If pruritus occurs, apply a thin layer of hydrocortisone cream as ordered.
Enteritis and Proctitis	(Bladder and bowel hypercontractility can occur 2 to 3 weeks postradiation) 1. Educate patient before surgery (changes in sense to urge, bladder and bowel incontinence – may need catheter, changed innervation to appliances). 2. Monitor for signs and symptoms. *Voiding:* 3. Restrict fluid intake to 2L/daily. 4. Promote regular scheduled for voiding. 5. Provide analgesics and antispasmotics. *Bowel:* 6. Manage with antidiarrheals, as needed. 7. Support low residue diets; avoid fruits and vegetables that promote diarrhea.
Chronic Cystitis	1. Monitor and assess for signs and symptoms – pain, infection, urgency, frequency, and inability to empty bladder. 2. Promote fluid intake. 3. Use good hygiene. 4. Instruct patient to avoid caffeine. 5. Administer medication, as ordered.
Constipation, Small Bowel Obstruction	1. Monitor for signs and symptoms – pain, consistency of stools, and bloody stools. 2. Administer nasogastric (NG) suction and I.V. fluids, as needed. 3. Support patient while on nothing by mouth status and while NG tube is in place; manage nausea and vomiting. 4. Promote fluid intake, as appropriate. 5. Perform mouth care. 6. Report symptoms to physician, as needed.

continued on next page

Diarrhea	1. Monitor for signs and symptoms – pain, infection, and reduced bowel pattern. 2. Promote fluid intake, as appropriate. 3. Promote low-residue diet. 4. Monitor for signs of infection. 5. Administer antidiarrheal medication, as ordered. 6. Avoid fatty foods and rich desserts. 7. Administer medication, as ordered. 8. Report symptoms to physician, as needed.
Vaginitis	1. Monitor for signs and symptoms – pain, drainage, and infection. 2. Promote fluid intake. 3. Use good hygiene. 4. Instruct patient to avoid caffeine.
Leg Edema *Thrombophlebitis*	1. Monitor for signs and symptoms – pain, redness, inflammation, and swelling.
Fistula *Formation*	(Vaginal or cervical radiation can form vaginal fistulas – vesicovaginal (bladder) and rectovaginal (bowel) – because radiation thins the vaginal wall). 1. Monitor for signs of fistula. 2. Advocate for surgical closure. 3. Manage temporary urinary or fecal diversions. 4. Promote wound healing of fistula and manage necrosis of tissue. 5. Support cleanliness with sitz baths and pad changes, protect skin, and prevent dryness. 6. Administer antibiotics, as prescribed.
Fatigue	1. Assess level of fatigue. 2. Advise patient to plan rest periods throughout the day. 3. Maintain nutritional intake. 4. Utilize resources to conserve energy. 5. Obtain assistance for chores and transportation, as needed.
Anorexia	(May be especially pronounced in ovarian cancer, due to ascites and early satiation [from increased girth and protein loss]). 1. Assess appetite. 2. Monitor weight. 3. Recommend frequent, small meals, and cold foods. 4. Advise on use of nutrient-dense foods such as nutritional supplements. 5. Administer appetite stimulants, as prescribed (Megace, corticosteroids and metoclopramide).

APPENDIX C

NURSING INTERVENTIONS FOR PERSONS RECEIVING CHEMOTHERAPY

Nursing Diagnosis	Possible Nursing Interventions
Fluid volume deficit related to nausea and vomiting	1. Assess for nausea and vomiting. 2. Instruct patient to use antiemetics before chemotherapy and as needed. 3. Monitor hydration status. 4. Encourage fluids. 5. Utilize nonpharmacologic measures to manage nausea and vomiting: relaxation exercises or distraction. 6. Encourage small frequent meals. 7. Provide diet that is low in fat and nonsweet; encourage fluids. 8. Provide mouth care frequently during the day.
Nephrotoxicity	(Many gynecologic malignancies include cisplatin-based chemotherapy protocols.) 1. Monitor laboratory values: electrolytes and especially creatinine and blood urea nitrogen levels. 2. Provide hydrating I.V. fluids and medications, as ordered. 3. Monitor intake and output. 4. Encourage fluids. 5. Control nausea and vomiting. 6. Observe and monitor "glove and stocking" anesthesia after chemotherapy treatments end and gait changes – encourage patient to prevent falls and promote safety.

Altered oral mucous membrane	1. Assess oral cavity: tenderness, ulceration, bleeding, and infections.
	2. Instruct patient about mouth care:
	  • Brush teeth after each meal.
	  • Floss teeth at bedtime, if patient normally practices flossing.
	  • Perform frequent oral rinses with warm normal saline solution.
	3. Advise on diet consisting of non-spicy, non-acidic, room-temperature, or cool foods.
	4. Maintain hydration.

Risk for infection related to neutropenia	1. Monitor blood counts: white blood count, neutrophils; assess for neutropenia. 2. Institute neutropenia precautions when white blood cell count is decreased. 3. Instruct patient about risk for infection:

279

continued on next page

- Monitor temperature: be alert for fever, chills, sweats, myalgias; report these occurrences.
- Avoid crowds.
- Avoid persons with colds or other respiratory infections.
- Avoid sharing eating utensils or beverage containers.
- Avoid handling animal excreta (for example, cat litter box or bird cage).
- Preserve and protect skin integrity.

Thrombocytopenia	1. Monitor platelet count. 2. Institute bleeding precautions when platelet count is decreased. 3. Assess skin, mucous membranes, bowel movements, urine, emesis, and secretions for signs of bleeding. 4. Assess signs of hemorrhage: hypotension, changes in consciousness, headache, vomiting, and tachycardia. 5. Protect skin integrity: avoid venipuncture and intramuscular injections. 6. Perform mouth care and avoid traumatizing oral mucosa. 7. Institute bowel program to prevent constipation. 8. Avoid trauma to rectal tissues: avoid rectal medication, rectal thermometer, and enemas. 9. Use electric razor. 10. Provide safe environment that eliminates hazards for injury.

Activity intolerance related to anemia	1. Assess for fatigue.
	2. Monitor blood counts: red blood cells and hematocrit.
	3. Recommend measures to minimize fatigue:
	  • Pace activities.
	  • Plan rest periods during the day.
	4. Administer blood products, as ordered.
	5. Ensure adequate nutritional intake.

Knowledge deficit related to chemotherapy and self-care measures	1. Assess level of understanding about chemotherapy. 2. Provide information about chemotherapy: effects, adverse effects, and symptoms to report. 3. Provide educational booklets, videotapes, and audiotapes as they are available. 4. Evaluate comprehension of patient education.

APPENDIX D

NURSING INTERVENTIONS FOR COMPLICATIONS FROM TREATMENT

Nursing Diagnoses	Possible Nursing Interventions
Insomnia	1. Assess sleep patterns through a sleep log.
	2. Instruct patient and family about optimal sleep preparation – relaxation, no alcohol, avoid heavy or spicy foods, avoid nicotine, and exercise.
	3. Medicate, as directed, by physician.
	4. Develop a routine for sleep – schedule and place.
	5. Avoid day-time napping.
Lymphedema	1. Focus on prevention – exercise, skin care, and prevent injury.
	2. Report signs of infection (redness, warmth, red streaks, inflamed areas).
	3. Reports signs of swelling – tightness of clothing or rings; numbness or pain.
	4. Support massage and stretching, as appropriate.
	5. Elevate extremity, as needed.
	6. Use compression sleeve or stocking to limit swelling; promote drainage.

APPENDIX E

NURSING INTERVENTIONS FOR PSYCHOSOCIAL ISSUES

Nursing Diagnosis	Possible Nursing Interventions
Anxiety	1. Assess level of anxiety (see Chapter 9). 2. Allow patient and family to verbalize issues and concerns. 3. Provide education about illness and treatment.
Body image disturbance	1. Assess patient understanding about body image changes. 2. Provide education about changes and rehabilitative measures available. 3. Allow patient and family to discuss issues and concerns about body image changes.
Knowledge deficit related to surgery and self-care measures	1. Assess patient's and family's understanding about surgery and self-care measures. 2. Provide education about surgery and self-care measures; utilize available multimedia patient education tools: booklets, videos, and audiotapes. 3. Evaluate patient's comprehension of educational materials.
Depression	1. Monitor signs and symptoms (see Chapter 9). 2. Administer medications, as prescribed. 3. Provide support for improved sleep, diet, and exercise. 4. Provide support for patient and family to move through short- and long-term grieving process.

GLOSSARY

absolute risk: Measure of the occurrence of cancer, either incidence (new cases) or mortality (deaths), in the general population.

acupressure: The application of pressure or localized massage to specific sites on the body to control symptoms, such as pain or nausea. Also used to stop bleeding.

acupuncture: The technique of inserting thin needles through the skin at specific points on the body to control pain and other symptoms.

adenocarcinoma: Cancer that begins in cells that line certain internal organs and that have glandular (secretory) properties.

adenoma: A noncancerous tumor.

adjuvant therapy: Treatment given after the primary treatment to increase the chances of a cure. Adjuvant therapy may include chemotherapy, radiation therapy, hormone therapy, or biological therapy.

AJCC staging system: A system developed by the American Joint Committee on Cancer for describing the extent of cancer in a patient's body. The descriptions include TNM: T describes the size of the tumor and if it has invaded nearby tissue, N describes any lymph nodes that are involved, and M describes metastasis (spread of cancer from one body part to another).

alkylating agents: A family of anticancer drugs that interfere with the cell's deoxyribonucleic acid and inhibit cancer cell growth.

alopecia: The lack or loss of hair from areas of the body where hair is usually found. Alopecia can be an adverse effect of some cancer treatments.

alternative medicine: Practices not generally recognized by the medical community as standard or conventional medical approaches and used instead of standard treatments. Alternative medicine includes the taking of dietary supplements, megadose vitamins, and herbal preparations; the drinking of special teas; and practices such as massage therapy, magnet therapy, spiritual healing, and meditation.

antidepressant: A drug used to treat depression.

antiestrogen: A substance that blocks the activity of estrogens, the family of hormones that promote the development and maintenance of female sex characteristics.

aromatase inhibition: Prevention of the formation of estradiol, a female hormone, by interfering with an aromatase enzyme. Aromatase inhibition is a type of hormone therapy used in postmenopausal women who have hormone-dependent breast cancer.

attributable risk: Amount of disease within the population that could be prevented by alteration of a risk factor.

axillary dissection: Surgery to remove lymph nodes found in the armpit region. Also called axillary lymph node dissection.

axillary lymph node dissection: Surgery to remove lymph nodes found in the armpit region. Also called axillary dissection.

axillary lymph nodes: Lymph nodes found in the armpit that drain the lymph channels from the breast.

benign proliferative breast disease: A group of noncancerous conditions that may increase the risk of developing breast cancer. Examples include ductal hyperplasia, lobular hyperplasia, and papillomas. Sometimes referred to as fibrocystic change.

biofeedback: A method of learning to voluntarily control certain body functions such as heartbeat, blood pressure, and muscle tension with the help of a special machine. This method can help control pain.

biopsy: The removal of cells or tissues for examination under a microscope. When only a sample of tissue is removed, the procedure is called an incisional biopsy or core biopsy. When an entire lump or suspicious area is removed, the procedure is called an excisional biopsy. When a sample of tissue or fluid is removed with a needle, the procedure is called a needle biopsy or fine needle aspiration.

brachytherapy: A treatment which allows radioactive material – sealed in needles, seeds, wires or catheters – to be placed in or near a tumor. The treatment is also called internal radiation, implant radiation, or interstitial radiation.

BRCA1: A gene on chromosome 17 that normally helps to suppress cell growth. A person who inherits an altered version of the BRCA1 gene has a higher risk of getting breast, ovarian, or prostate cancer.

BRCA2: A gene on chromosome 13 that normally helps to suppress cell growth. A person who inherits an altered version of the BRCA2 gene has a higher risk of getting breast, ovarian, or prostate cancer.

breast cancer in situ: Abnormal cells that are confined to the ducts or lobules in the breast. There are two forms, called ductal carcinoma in situ (DCIS) and lobular carcinoma in situ (LCIS).

breast implant: A silicone gel-filled or saline-filled sac placed under the chest muscle to restore breast shape.

breast reconstruction: Surgery to rebuild a breast's shape after a mastectomy.

breast-conserving surgery: An operation to remove the breast cancer but not the breast itself. Types of breast-conserving surgery include lumpectomy (removal of the lump), quadrantectomy (removal of one quarter of the breast), and segmental mastectomy (removal of the cancer as well as some of the breast tissue around the tumor and the lining over the chest muscles below the tumor).

c-erbB-2: The gene that controls cell growth by making the human epidermal growth factor receptor 2; also called HER-2/neu.

cervical intraepithelial neoplasia (CIN): A general term for the growth of abnormal cells on the surface of the cervix. Numbers from 1 to 3 may be used to describe how much of the cervix contains abnormal cells.

cervix: The lower, narrow end of the uterus that forms a canal between the uterus and vagina.

colon: The long, tube-like organ that is connected to the small intestine and rectum. The colon removes water and some nutrients and electrolytes from digested food. The remaining material, solid waste called stool, moves through the colon to the rectum and leaves the body through the anus. Also called the large intestine.

colon cancer: A disease in which malignant (cancer) cells are found in the tissues of the colon.

colon polyps: Abnormal growths of tissue in the lining of the bowel. Polyps are a risk factor for colon cancer.

colonoscope: A thin, lighted tube used to examine the inside of the colon.

colonoscopy: An examination of the inside of the colon using a thin, lighted tube (called a colonoscope) inserted into the rectum. If abnormal areas are seen, tissue can be removed and examined under a microscope to determine whether disease is present.

colostomy: An opening into the colon from the outside of the body. A colostomy provides a new path for waste material to leave the body after part of the colon has been removed.

complementary and alternative medicine (CAM): Forms of treatment that are used in addition to (complementary) or instead of (alternative) standard treatments. These practices are not considered standard medical approaches. CAM includes dietary supplements, megadose vitamins, herbal preparations, special teas, acupuncture, massage therapy, magnet therapy, spiritual healing, and meditation.

complementary medicine: Practices not generally recognized by the medical community as standard or conventional medical approaches. They are typically used to enhance or complement standard treatments. Complementary medicine includes dietary supplements, megadose vitamins, herbal preparations, special teas, acupuncture, massage therapy, magnet therapy, spiritual healing, and meditation.

complete hysterectomy: Surgery to remove the entire uterus, including the cervix. Sometimes, not all of the cervix is removed. Also called total hysterectomy.

computed tomography (CT) scan: A series of detailed pictures of areas inside the body taken from different angles; the pictures are created by a computer linked to an X-ray machine. Also called computerized tomography and computerized axial tomography (CAT) scan.

cone biopsy: Surgery to remove a cone-shaped piece of tissue from the cervix and cervical canal. Cone biopsy may be used to diagnose or treat a cervical condition. Also called conization.

corpus: The body of the uterus.

curettage: Removal of tissue with a curette, a spoon-shaped instrument with a sharp edge.

cutaneous breast cancer: Cancer that has spread from the breast to the skin.

cyst: A sac or capsule filled with fluid.

DCIS: Ductal carcinoma in situ. Abnormal cells that involve only the lining of a duct. The cells have not spread outside the duct to other tissues in the breast. Also called intraductal carcinoma.

Diethylstilbestrol (DES): A synthetic hormone that was prescribed from the early 1940s until 1971 to help women with complications of pregnancy. DES has been linked to an increased risk of clear cell carcinoma of the vagina in daughters of women who used DES. DES may also increase the risk of breast cancer in women who used DES.

digital rectal examination (DRE): An examination in which a doctor inserts a lubricated, gloved finger into the rectum to feel for abnormalities.

dilation and curettage (D&C): A minor operation in which the cervix is expanded enough (dilation) to permit the cervical canal and uterine lining to be scraped with a spoon-shaped instrument called a curette (curettage).

ductal carcinoma: The most common type of breast cancer. It begins in the cells that line the milk ducts in the breast.

ductal carcinoma in situ (DCIS): Abnormal cells that involve only the lining of a duct. The cells have not spread outside the duct to other tissues in the breast. Also called intraductal carcinoma.

endocervical curettage: The scraping of the mucous membrane of the cervical canal using a spoon-shaped instrument called a curette.

endometrial: Having to do with the endometrium (the layer of tissue that lines the uterus).

endometrial disorder: Abnormal cell growth in the endometrium (the lining of the uterus).

endometriosis: A benign condition in which tissue that looks like endometrial tissue grows in abnormal places in the abdomen.

endometrium: The layer of tissue that lines the uterus.

endoscope: A thin, lighted tube used to look at tissues inside the body.

epithelial ovarian cancer: Cancer that occurs in the cells lining the ovaries.

epithelium: A thin layer of tissue that covers organs, glands, and other structures within the body.

estrogen receptor (ER): Protein found on some cancer cells to which estrogen will attach.

estrogen receptor positive (ER+): Breast cancer cells that have a protein (receptor molecule) to which estrogen will attach. Breast cancer cells that are ER+ need the hormone estrogen to grow and will usually respond to hormone (antiestrogen) therapy that blocks these receptor sites.

estrogen receptor negative (ER-): Breast cancer cells that do not have a protein (receptor molecule) to which estrogen will attach. Breast cancer cells that are ER- do not need the hormone estrogen to grow and usually do not respond to hormone (antiestrogen) therapy that blocks these receptor sites.

estrogens: A family of hormones that promote the development and maintenance of female sex characteristics.

estrogen replacement therapy (ERT): Hormones (estrogen, progesterone, or both) given to postmenopausal women or to women who have had their ovaries surgically removed. Hormones are given to replace the estrogen no longer produced by the ovaries.

external-beam radiation: Radiation therapy that uses a machine to aim high-energy rays at the cancer. Also called external radiation.

fallopian tubes: Part of the female reproductive tract. The long slender tubes through which eggs pass from the ovaries to the uterus.

familial adenomatous polyposis (FAP): An inherited condition in which numerous polyps (growths that protrude from mucous membranes) form on the inside walls of the colon and rectum. It increases the risk for colon cancer. Also called familial polyposis.

familial polyposis: An inherited condition in which numerous polyps (growths that protrude from mucous membranes) form on the inside walls of the colon and rectum. It increases the risk for colon cancer. Also called familial adenomatous polyposis or FAP.

fibroid: A benign smooth-muscle tumor, usually in the uterus or gastrointestinal tract. Also called leiomyoma.

genetic counseling: A communication process between a specially trained health professional and a person concerned about the genetic risk of disease. The person's family and personal medical history may be discussed, and counseling may lead to genetic testing.

genetic testing: Analyzing DNA to look for a genetic alteration that may indicate an increased risk for developing a specific disease or disorder.

gonads: The part of the reproductive system that produces and releases eggs (ovaries) or sperm (testicles/testes).

gynecologic: Having to do with the female reproductive tract (including the cervix, endometrium, fallopian tubes, ovaries, uterus, and vagina).

gynecologic cancer: Cancer of the female reproductive tract, including the cervix, endometrium, fallopian tubes, ovaries, uterus, and vagina.

gynecologic oncologist: A physician who specializes in treating cancers of the female reproductive organs.

gynecologist: A physician who specializes in treating diseases of the female reproductive organs.

HER-2/neu: Human epidermal growth factor receptor 2. The HER-2/neu protein is involved in growth of some cancer cells. Also called c-erbB-2.

hereditary nonpolyposis colon cancer (HNPCC): An inherited disorder in which affected individuals have a higher-than-normal chance of developing colon cancer and certain other types of cancer, usually before 60 years of age. Also called Lynch syndrome.

high-grade squamous intraepithelial lesion (HSIL): A precancerous condition in which the cells of the uterine cervix are moderately or severely abnormal.

hormone receptor: A protein on the surface of a cell that binds to a specific hormone. The hormone causes many changes to take place in the cell.

hormone receptor test: A test to measure the amount of certain proteins, called hormone receptors, in cancer tissue. Hormones can attach to these proteins. A high level of hormone receptors may mean that hormones help the cancer grow.

hormone replacement therapy (HRT): Hormones (estrogen, progesterone, or both) given to postmenopausal women or women who have had their ovaries surgically removed, to replace the estrogen no longer produced by the ovaries.

hormone responsive: In oncology, describes cancer that responds to hormone treatment.

hormone therapy: Treatment that adds, blocks, or removes hormones. For certain conditions (such as diabetes or menopause), hormones are given to adjust low hormone levels. To slow or stop the growth of certain cancers (such as prostate and breast cancer), hormones may be given to block the body's natural hormones. Sometimes surgery is needed to remove the source of hormones. Also called hormonal therapy, hormone treatment, or endocrine therapy.

hormones: Chemicals produced by glands in the body and circulated in the bloodstream. Hormones control the actions of certain cells or organs.

hysterectomy: An operation in which the uterus is removed.

incidence: Number of new cancers in a given time period in a specific population.

in situ cancer: Early cancer that has not spread to neighboring tissue.

in vitro: In the laboratory (outside the body). The opposite of in vivo (in the body).

in vivo: In the body. The opposite of in vitro (outside the body or in the laboratory).

incidence: The number of new cases of a disease diagnosed each year.

incision: A cut made in the body to perform surgery.

incisional biopsy: A surgical procedure in which a portion of a lump or suspicious area is removed for diagnosis. The tissue is then examined under a microscope.

infiltrating ductal carcinoma: The most common type of invasive breast cancer. It starts in the cells that line the milk ducts in the breast, grows outside the ducts, and often spreads to the lymph nodes.

inflammatory breast cancer: A type of breast cancer in which the breast looks red and swollen and feels warm. The skin of the breast may also show the pitted appearance called peau d'orange (like the skin of an orange). The redness and warmth occur because the cancer cells block the lymph vessels in the skin.

internal radiation: A procedure in which radioactive material sealed in needles, seeds, wires, or catheters is placed directly into or near a tumor. Also called brachytherapy, implant radiation, or interstitial radiation therapy.

interstitial radiation therapy: A procedure in which radioactive material sealed in needles, seeds, wires, or catheters is placed directly into or near a tumor. Also called brachytherapy, internal radiation, or implant radiation.

intraductal carcinoma: Abnormal cells that involve only the lining of a duct. The cells have not spread outside the duct to other tissues in the breast. Also called ductal carcinoma in situ.

invasive cervical cancer: Cancer that has spread from the surface of the cervix to tissue deeper in the cervix or to other parts of the body.

jaundice: A condition in which the skin and the whites of the eyes become yellow, urine darkens, and the color of stool becomes lighter than normal. Jaundice occurs when the liver is not working properly or when a bile duct is blocked.

laparoscopy: The insertion of a thin, lighted tube (called a laparoscope) through the abdominal wall to inspect the inside of the abdomen and remove tissue.

lobular carcinoma in situ (LCIS): Abnormal cells found in the lobules of the breast. This condition seldom becomes invasive cancer; however, having lobular carcinoma in situ increases one's risk of developing breast cancer in either breast.

lumpectomy: Surgery to remove the tumor and a small amount of normal tissue around it.

magnetic resonance imaging (MRI): A procedure in which a magnet linked to a computer is used to create detailed pictures of areas inside the body. Also called nuclear magnetic resonance imaging.

mammogram: An X-ray of the breast.

mammography: The use of X-rays to create a picture of the breast.

medullary breast carcinoma: A rare type of breast cancer that often can be treated successfully. It is marked by lymphocytes (a type of white blood cell) in and around the tumor that can be seen when viewed under a microscope.

microcalcifications: Tiny deposits of calcium in the breast that cannot be felt but can be detected on a mammogram. A cluster of these very small specks of calcium may indicate that cancer is present.

modified radical mastectomy: Surgery for breast cancer in which the breast, some of the lymph nodes under the arm, the lining over the chest muscles, and sometimes part of the chest wall muscles are removed.

mortality: Number of people who die from a specific cancer during a defined time period.

needle biopsy: The removal of tissue or fluid with a needle for examination under a microscope. Also called fine needle aspiration.

negative axillary lymph nodes: Lymph nodes in the armpit that are free of cancer.

neoadjuvant therapy: Treatment given before the surgical treatment. Examples of neoadjuvant therapy include chemotherapy, radiation therapy, and hormone therapy. The goal is to shrink the tumor so it can be surgically excised.

node-negative: Cancer that has not spread to the lymph nodes.

node-positive: Cancer that has spread to the lymph nodes.

nodule: A growth or lump that may be cancerous or noncancerous.

oophorectomy: Surgery to remove one or both ovaries. It is often done with a laparoscope.

ovarian: Having to do with the ovaries, the female reproductive glands in which the ova (eggs) are formed. The ovaries are located in the pelvis, one on each side of the uterus.

ovarian ablation: Surgery, radiation therapy, or a drug treatment to stop the functioning of the ovaries. Also called ovarian suppression.

ovarian epithelial cancer: Cancer that occurs in the cells lining the ovaries.

ovarian suppression: Surgery, radiation therapy, or a drug treatment to stop the functioning of the ovaries. Also called ovarian ablation.

ovaries: The pair of female reproductive glands in which the ova, or eggs, are formed. The ovaries are located in the pelvis, one on each side of the uterus.

Paget's disease of the nipple: A form of breast cancer in which the tumor grows from ducts beneath the nipple onto the surface of the nipple. Symptoms commonly include itching and burning and an eczema-like condition around the nipple, sometimes accompanied by oozing or bleeding.

Papanicolaou (Pap) test: The collection of cells from the cervix for examination under a microscope. It is used to detect changes that may be cancer or may lead to cancer, and can show noncancerous conditions, such as infection or inflammation. Also called a Pap smear.

peau d'orange: A dimpled condition of the skin of the breast, resembling the skin of an orange, sometimes found in inflammatory breast cancer.

positive axillary lymph nodes: Lymph nodes in the area of the armpit (axilla) to which cancer has spread. This spread is determined by surgically removing some of the lymph nodes and examining them under a microscope to see whether cancer cells are present.

progesterone: A female sex hormone released by the ovaries during every menstrual cycle to prepare the uterus for pregnancy and the breasts for milk production (lactation). In breast cancer, tumor growth may depened on progesterone. If the woman's tumor does rely on progesterone for growth, she is progesterone receptor positive (PR+). If it does not, she is progesterone receptor negative (PR-).

progesterone receptor positive (PR+): In breast cancer, if the woman's tumor growth is affected by progesterone.

progesterone receptor negative (PR-): In breast cancer, if the woman's tumor growth is not affected by progesterone.

preventive mastectomy: Surgery to remove one or both breasts in order to decrease the risk of developing breast cancer. Also called prophylactic mastectomy.

prophylactic mastectomy: Surgery to remove one or both breasts in order to decrease the risk of developing breast cancer. Also called preventive mastectomy.

prophylactic oophorectomy: Surgery intended to reduce the risk of ovarian cancer by removing the ovaries before disease develops.

radiation therapy: The use of high-energy radiation from X-rays, gamma rays, neutrons, and other sources to kill cancer cells and shrink tumors. Radiation may come from a machine outside the body (external-beam radiation therapy), or from materials called radioisotopes. Radioisotopes produce radiation and can be placed in or near the tumor or in the area near cancer cells. This type of radiation treatment is called internal radiation therapy, implant radiation, interstitial radiation, or brachytherapy. Systemic radiation therapy uses a radioactive substance, such as a radiolabeled monoclonal antibody, that circulates throughout the body. Also called radiotherapy, irradiation, and X-ray therapy.

radical mastectomy: Surgery for breast cancer in which the breast, chest muscles, and all of the lymph nodes under the arm are removed. For many years, this was the operation most used, but it is used now only when the tumor has spread to the chest muscles. Also called the Halsted radical mastectomy.

raloxifene: A drug that belongs to the family of drugs called selective estrogen receptor modulators (SERMs) and is used in the prevention of osteoporosis in postmenopausal women. Raloxifene is also being studied as a cancer prevention drug.

reconstructive surgery: Surgery that is done to reshape or rebuild (reconstruct) a part of the body changed by previous surgery.

regional lymph node dissection: A surgical procedure to remove some of the lymph nodes that drain lymph from the area around a tumor. The lymph nodes are then examined under a microscope to see if cancer cells have spread to them.

relative risk: Comparison of the incidence or deaths among those with a particular risk factor compared to those without the risk factor.

resection: Removal of tissue or part or all of an organ by surgery.

risk factor: Trait or characteristic that is associated with a statistically significant and an increased likelihood of developing a disease.

salpingo-oophorectomy: Surgical removal of the fallopian tubes and ovaries.

Schiller test: A test in which iodine is applied to the cervix. The iodine colors healthy cells brown; abnormal cells remain unstained, usually appearing white or yellow.

selective estrogen receptor modulator (SERM): A drug that acts like estrogen on some tissues but blocks the effect of estrogen on other tissues. Tamoxifen and raloxifene are SERMs.

sentinel lymph node: The first lymph node to which cancer is likely to spread from the primary tumor. Cancer cells may appear first in the sentinel node before spreading to other lymph nodes.

sentinel lymph node biopsy: Removal and examination of the sentinel node(s) (the first lymph node(s) to which cancer cells are likely to spread from a primary tumor). To identify the sentinel lymph node(s), the surgeon injects a radioactive substance, blue dye, or both near the tumor. The surgeon then uses a scanner to find the sentinel lymph node(s) containing the radioactive substance or looks for the lymph node(s) stained with dye. The surgeon then removes the sentinel node(s) to check for the presence of cancer cells.

sentinel lymph node mapping: The use of dyes and radioactive substances to identify the first lymph node to which cancer is likely to spread from the primary tumor. Cancer cells may appear first in the sentinel node before spreading to other lymph nodes and other places in the body.

staging: Performing examinations and tests to learn the extent of the cancer within the body, especially whether the disease has spread from the original site to other parts of the body. It is important to know the stage of the disease in order to plan the best treatment.

tamoxifen: An anticancer drug that belongs to the family of drugs called antiestrogens. Tamoxifen blocks the effects of the hormone estrogen in the body. It is used to prevent or delay the return of breast cancer or to control its spread.

total estrogen blockade: Therapy used to eliminate estrogen in the body. This may be done with surgery, radiation therapy, chemotherapy, or a combination of these procedures.

total hysterectomy: Surgery to remove the entire uterus, including the cervix. Sometimes, not all of the cervix is removed. Also called complete hysterectomy.

total mastectomy: Removal of the breast. Also called simple mastectomy.

transvaginal ultrasound: A procedure used to examine the vagina, uterus, fallopian tubes, and bladder. An instrument is inserted into the vagina, and sound waves bounce off organs inside the pelvic area. These sound waves create echoes, which a computer uses to create a picture called a sonogram. Also called TVS.

ultrasound: A procedure in which high-energy sound waves (ultrasound) are bounced off internal tissues or organs and make echoes. The echoes form a picture of body tissues called a sonogram. Also called ultrasonography.

INDEX

Page references followed by *fig* indicate an illustrated figure; followed by *t* indicate a table; followed by a *b* indicate a box.

Western Schools® offers over 2,000 hours to suit all your interests – and requirements!